DATE DUE

MAR 1 5 1998			

DEMCO 38-297

DEMCO

ENERGY CONSERVATION THROUGH BUILDING DESIGN

AN ARCHITECTURAL RECORD BOOK

McGraw Hill Book Company

New York   St. Louis   San Francisco   Auckland
Bogotá   Düsseldorf   Johannesburg   London
Madrid   Mexico   Montreal   New Delhi
Panama   Paris   São Paulo   Singapore
Sydney   Tokyo   Toronto

CONSERVATION THROUGH BUILDING DESIGN

EDITED BY DONALD WATSON

Library of Congress Cataloging in Publication Data

Main entry under title:

Energy conservation through building design.

"An Architectural record book."
Includes bibliographical references and index.
1. Buildings—Energy conservation. 2. Architecture and energy
conservation. I. Watson, Donald, 1937–
TJ163.5.B84E54   721   78-17498
ISBN 0-07-068460-X

1234567890HDHD7865432109

The editor for this book was Sue Cymes, the production editor was
Patricia Barnes Werner, and the designer was Andrew Steigmeier.

It was set in Optima by Monotype Composition Company. It was
printed and bound by Halliday Lithographic Corporation.

TABLE OF CONTENTS

ACKNOWLEDGMENTS

The effort represented by the contributions in this volume began many years ago and involve the talents of an extraordinary group of people. In December 1975, the Association of Collegiate Schools of Architecture (ACSA) held its annual Teachers Seminar in Washington, DC, with "energy and architecture" as its subject, under joint sponsorship with the American Institute of Architecture Research Corporation (AIA/RC) and with John Eberhard and Sanford Greenfield providing major roles in organizing the seminar. It was attended by faculty representatives from most of the architectural schools, and they there discussed the special needs and problems of incorporating energy concerns into architectural design.

A special issue of the *Journal of Architectural Education* (February 1977) on "Energy and Architecture" followed, which I had the privilege of editing with an editorial board that included Ralph Knowles, Charles Moore, Troy McQueen, and Jeff Cook. In the year-long preparation for the Journal issue, many articles were invited, reviewed, rewritten, and ultimately published, with the aid of grants from the National Science Foundation (RANN/ NSF) and the National Bureau of Standards (NBS), and with the outstanding effort of Dave Clarke and Ila Deshler of the ACSA Publications Committee Staff. The focus of the *JAE* issue was the teaching of energy in architecture. The response to its publication was so favorable that the effort was begun that resulted in this book. With the enthusiastic support of Walter Wagner, editor of *Architectural Record,* it was possible to conceive of a hard-bound volume, to reprint some of the articles from the *JAE* issue which itself was soon out of print, and to expand the contributions, particularly to reach a group that was larger than the academic audience and more closely involved in the professional practice of design.

I recall a discussion I then had with Ralph Knowles in Washington one evening in front of Blair House, where a new president-elect had set up office and had already talked about the importance with which the new administration would view the energy crisis. It was in that conversation that the emphasis of this book was defined—on environmental quality rather than "minimum energy," on appropriate climate and energy design as integral with architecture rather than as an "HVAC problem." These premises and others that are stated in the introductory chapter are the result of conversations with Ralph Knowles, Murray Milne, and Larry

Spielvogel who joined me as the editorial advisory group for the present effort. Larry had been a reader for the *JAE* endeavor and had offered an insight which remains a key to the challenge before the design professions: how are architects and engineers being educated to work together to overcome the gaps that in professional practice lead to lack of coordination and, worse, a loss of opportunities for creative collaboration. Thus, the intent of this book is to bridge gaps: between architect and engineer, between research and practice, between technical means and ethical and aesthetic values.

Each of the contributors to this book has had to put up with an editor who has asked for continual rewrites and clarifications throughout, and the editor is fortunate that they have agreed. In addition to the editorial board members, technical readers for individual chapters include Everett Barber, Jr., Jeffrey Cook, Ezra Ehrenkrantz, William Meyer, William Mitchell, Richard Rittleman, and John Yellott, and their expert assistance is gratefully acknowledged. Responsibility for remaining errors rests with me. The help of Paul Edmeades and Nancy Locke in preparing the illustrations and final manuscript was responsible for seeing this book off to the publisher reasonably within its deadline. To the many other individuals who have helped with their comments, their interest, and enthusiasm and to those whose efforts will be increasingly important to continue the impetus of the conservation initiative, this book is respectfully dedicated.

Donald Watson, Editor

Guilford, Connecticut
December 21, 1977

PREFACE

Changes in energy supply and energy sources will have the most profound effect on building design and urban form since the beginning of the Industrial Revolution. Chances are that buildings now on the drawing boards or in construction will still be standing in the year 2028—50 years from now. If the figures quoted by several of the contributors to this book are realistic (and I think they are), we will not have the fossil fuel energy to economically heat, cool, or light today's buildings 50 years from now.

This book gathers together some of the most significant information available on how architects, engineers, building owners, and managers can plan and operate buildings today that will have a future in tomorrow's world.

Some people view the predicted disappearance of cheap fossil fuels with horror or disbelief. I, for one, welcome the new possibilities which will emerge out of new limitations. During most of this century, architects and engineers have designed buildings free of the natural constraints out of which all great architecture springs. Cheap energy and the worldwide availability of modern industrial materials have permitted designers to ignore the specifics of place and the unique qualities of regional climate and customs. Oppressive and bland technological solutions have replaced the natural wisdom and beauty growing out of centuries of experimentation and adaptation.

The early essays in this book show how the availability of plentiful, high-grade fuels short-circuited traditional architectural concerns for building and urban form appropriate to local climate, available materials, and indigenous needs. One result is that buildings have become ever more wasteful of energy. The contributors to this volume present various strategies for more responsible design of the built environment. Simple modifications to the mechanical systems of existing buildings together with greater awareness on the part of building occupants can easily cut energy use in half. New buildings can be designed for comfort, beauty, and utility, using only a fraction of the fossil fuel budget of today's buildings.

Our experience in California is instructive. In 1975, Governor Brown announced a program to construct new state office buildings in many major cities in the State. Our aim was to show that new buildings could be designed to current standards of comfort, use, and economy and make full use of the potential of renewable resources such as solar energy, as well as conserving existing fossil fuels. The first several buildings are being designed by the Office of the State Architect. Another major building was the subject of a state-wide competition to design an energy-efficient office building. Other buildings are being designed by private architects. In each case, we are discovering that through a careful orchestration of techniques—including reduction of unnecessary lighting levels, careful attention to orientation, heat transfer in walls and windows, the use of building mass for thermal storage, and other techniques compatible with the specific microclimate—we are able to design buildings whose energy budget averages 20,000 Btu/ft²/year, less than 20% of the energy used by buildings built a few years ago.

Such gains have not been won easily. What is required is a new kind of cooperation between architects and the engineering disciplines. Architects have to learn more about such basics as heat transfer and thermodynamics; engineers have to see the building as a dynamic whole environment, changing through the seasons and cycles of use. A great deal of basic research is required to learn more about microclimates, daylighting, natural ventilation, the thermal properties of materials, and heat flow. Out of this research and rethinking of basics will come a more mature and richer architectural expression. To create such change will require commitment on the part of professionals and clients, incentives and support from government, and a renewed awareness of the importance of architecture by all Americans.

As Don Watson suggests in his introductory essay, tomorrow's architectural lessons will be learned from the temple of Nature, rather than through a study of classic forms that guided architecture in the past or through the mere mastery of material technology that makes possible today's massive and alienating structures, too often devoid of any visible connection to the resource base and natural systems that make life possible. An appreciation of the complexity and possibilities of natural systems will be the underpinning for a new architecture and a new society. The most sophisticated modern technology does not compare in complexity, simplicity, or efficiency to natural processes that have taken millenia to evolve. For example, the explosions within a nuclear reactor capture energy by simulating primitive atomic reactions that predate the birth of our planet. By contrast, the capturing of solar energy that takes place in a green leaf through photosynthesis has taken eons to evolve in a benign and beneficial way.

A truly evolutionary post-industrial architecture will reject dependence on energy sources that threaten our own health and the stability of the ecosystems on which our lives depend. This book—written by a group of distinguished experts—is an important contribution towards the evolution of a new and vital architecture for our planet.

Sim Van der Ryn   Sacramento, CA

1

INTRODUCTION:

ENERGY CONSERVATION THROUGH BUILDING DESIGN

Donald Watson

Energy adds a new standpoint from which to better understand building design. But the subject of study—architecture and its environmental and social context—is not new. The objective of design is to improve the quality of buildings and the environment.

This book brings together key articles and references that offer the design professional the basic concepts and directions necessary for a reasoned approach to energy conservation through building design. Part of the current need is to bridge information gaps between research and practice and to communicate with individuals with different interests and backgrounds, including architects, mechanical engineers, land planners, building financiers and developers, government officials and building owners, as well as with anyone interested and involved—as we all should be—in the still undetermined impact of energy resource constraints on the quality of life.

To place the subject of energy and building design in historical, economic, and cultural perspective, consider the following points:

1. Throughout history, climatic, energy, and resource requirements have been fundamental to the art and craft of architecture.

2. While "minimum energy cost" is a measure of economic and social choices—the more so if real energy costs and benefits could be so represented—the purpose of design is to preserve and enhance the quality of environments we design and build.

3. Just as building design can be seen to have global impact in terms of energy and resources, an equally compelling role of architecture is to give form to our cultural aspirations and the ethical and aesthetic values by which we measure the quality of life.

Rather than limiting design choices and thus disinheriting architects and engineers of their prerogatives, the urgency of energy questions imparts special relevance and responsibility to the role of design. Energy is limited only because of limits in the way it is viewed, a "crisis" only because its implications have been too long overlooked. In this view, the best "energy saver" is the creative design imagination and, to its inspiration, the chapters that follow are committed.

1. This section was written with the collaboration of Jeffrey Cook, to whom I am indebted for insights and examples and who allowed me to borrow freely from his manuscript, "History of Energy in Building."

An Historical Perspective[1]

Energy efficiency is not a new criterion of design. The context of building has always been defined by climatic and material limitations. Even when these are severe, they have not prevented

(a)

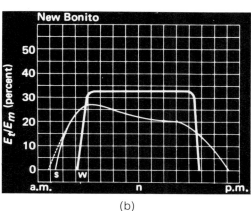

(b)

Fig. 1 (a) Pueblo Bonito: A nineteenth-century etching (*Contributions to North American Ethnology*, 1881); (b) an analysis of the structure shows winter irradiation in winter (w) to be constant from 8:00 am to 4:00 pm and greater than in summer (s), during which it decreases during the afternoon when the sol-air temperature is greatest. (From Ralph Knowles, *Energy and Form*.)

building designers from evolving solutions of great craft and elegance.

Indigenous and vernacular building at its best is a direct expression of adaption to climate and resource constraints. Ralph Knowles has shown that the pueblo structures in the American Southwest could not be improved upon for natural control of seasonal climatic impacts, given the then available adobe construction technology[2] (*Figure 1*). Several architectural historians, including James Marston Fitch, have traced Early American colonial building styles to the exigencies imposed by environment and building methods. Building forms evolved with successive generations of colonists and were adapted to their changing context and climates as the settlers moved west and south.[3] Fitch's scholarly orientation did not prevent him from seeing in primitive dwelling design notable responses to climate and craft, as stated in an article co-authored with Daniel Branch in 1960:

Western man, for all his impressive knowledge and technological apparatus, often builds less well than did his primitive predecessor. A central reason for his failure lies in consistent

2. Ralph Knowles: *Energy and Form: An Ecological Approach to Urban Growth*, MIT Press, Cambridge, MA, 1974.

3. James Marston Fitch: *American Building I: Historical Forces that Shaped It*, Houghton Mifflin Company, Boston, 1966; R. Philsbury and A. Kardos: *A Field Guide to the Folk Architecture of the Northeastern U.S.*, Geographical Publications at Dartmouth, Hanover, NH, 1970.

ENERGY
CONSERVATION
THROUGH
BUILDING
DESIGN

underestimation of the environmental forces that play upon his buildings and cities, and consistent overestimation of his own technological capacities. Still, the worst he faces is a dissatisfied client. When the primitive architect errs, he faces a harsh and unforgiving nature.[4]

Most recently, a renewed appreciation of the indigenous tradition in architecture has resulted in a literature devoted quite expressly to its analysis, not only from an interest in cultural preservation, but for the lessons offered to modern designers working within similar climates and cultures.[5] One of many elegant examples is offered by the vernacular, "oriental" house of Baghdad, Iraq (*Figure 2*). Its strategies of adaption to impressive climatic extremes include zoning of the internal plan: family activities move between lower rooms (heavy masonry) on summer days and courtyard and roof terraces on summer nights, and to the second floor (light wood and glass) during the winter, thus taking advantage of distinct building solutions for different seasons, all within the courtyard plan, itself an appropriate climatic and cultural prototype.[6]

An example from Roman antiquity, the Forum Baths in Ostia near Rome (circa 250 AD), combined direct solar heating and "hypocaust" (underfloor) warm-air heating. The Forum Baths is a large public building with a series of rooms used in sequence, each with a distinct temperature and humidity requirement. Among the questions presented to archaeologists was whether the principal rooms with large apertures exposed to the winter sun were glazed (*Figure 3*). Although there was no evidence of glazing on the jambs of window openings, it was considered unlikely that these large spaces could perform thermally without some sort of protection from the outdoors. However, studies of the Ostia design and construction by architect Edwin D. Thatcher show that the baths would indeed work because of the combination of underfloor and wall-channel heating flues around the rooms, and the orientation of openings to winter solar heat gain (suntanning and drying being part of the bathing regime).[7]

The fireplace-flue heating system used in the Forum Baths is integral with the wall and floor structure, an early and exemplary application of radiant heating. After the fall of the Roman Empire and the emergence of the European countries from the Dark Ages, the lessons had to be relearned. The history of the fireplace during this time characterizes the evolution of building technology and design. First, there was the open fire in the center of the room with smoke exiting through doors and roof openings. Then, in the multistoried feudal castle, flues were incorporated into the wall construction—an early example at Colchester, England, dating around 1090 AD. The stove appeared in Europe at Alsace, France in 1490, made of brick and tile. Subsequently, wood or coal fires were enclosed in special metal and masonry ovens, often with

4. James Marston Fitch and Daniel P. Branch: "Primitive Architecture and Climate," *Scientific American*, vol. 203, no. 6 (December 1960).

5. Paul Oliver, ed.: *Shelter and Society*, Barrie & Rockliff, The Cresset Press, London, 1969; Donald Watson and Alain Bertaud: "Indigenous Architecture as the Basis of House Design in Developing Countries," *Habitat*, vol. 1, no. 3/4 (1976).

6. Muthana El Bayatay: "New Housing for Iraq Based on Traditional Precedents," School of Architecture, Yale University, Master of Environmental Design Program, unpublished thesis, 1977.

7. Edwin D. Thatcher: "The Open Rooms of the Terme del Foro at Ostia," *Memoirs of the Acadamy in Rome*, vol. 24, 1956.

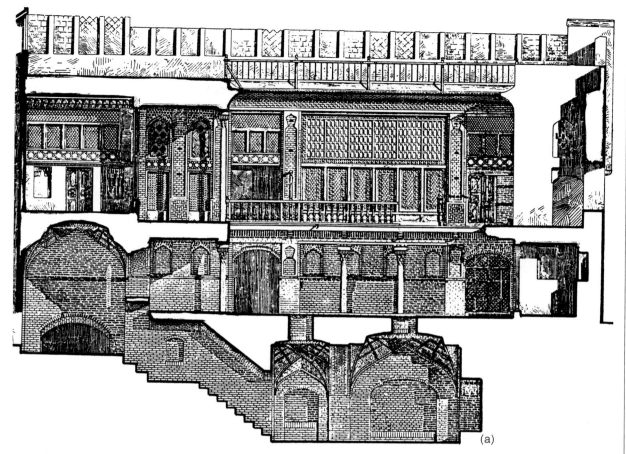

Fig. 2 (a) Traditional House, Bagdad, Iraq (After D. Reuther: *wohn-haus in Bagdad and Anderen Stadem des Trak, 1910*); (b) comfort-zone analysis shows the hourly outside temperature (°C) throughout the year. Clustered courtyard building types provide mutual summer shading and permit sufficient winter irradiation on the second-story structures to provide direct solar heating.

		J	F	M	A	M	J	J	A	S	O	N	D	
AM	6	4.3	5.9	9.6	14.6	20.6	23.4	25.5	24.6	21.0	16.2	10.3	5.7	
	8	5.6	7.2	10.9	16.0	22.1	25.1	27.1	26.4	22.9	18.1	11.8	6.9	SUNRISE
	10	11.2	13.4	17.2	22.9	29.3	33.7	35.9	35.5	31.9	26.3	18.7	12.7	
	12	14.3	15.9	20.8	26.7	33.6	38.3	40.9	40.7	36.9	31.0	22.6	15.9	
PM	2	16.0	18.7	22.7	28.7	35.8	41.0	43.4	43.3	39.8	33.4	24.6	17.6	
	4	15.1	17.7	21.6	27.5	34.5	39.5	42.0	41.9	38.2	32.0	23.4	16.7	SUNSET
	6	12.4	14.8	18.8	24.2	31.0	35.5	39.9	37.5	34.0	28.0	20.1	12.8	
	8	9.4	11.5	15.2	20.8	27.2	30.9	33.2	32.8	29.1	23.9	16.5	10.9	
	10	8.1	9.9	13.8	19.1	25.3	28.9	31.0	30.4	26.9	21.8	14.9	9.3	
	12	7.0	8.7	12.3	17.7	23.8	27.1	29.3	28.5	25.0	20.1	13.4	8.2	
AM	2	6.0	7.7	11.3	16.7	22.8	25.8	27.8	27.1	23.7	18.8	12.3	7.3	
	4	5.0	6.7	10.3	15.4	21.3	24.4	26.4	25.7	22.1	17.2	11.1	6.3	(b)

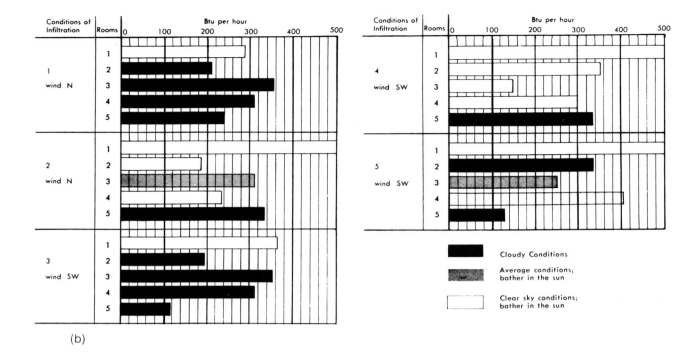

Conditions of Infiltration	Rooms	Btu per hour

(b)

Fig. 3 (a) Winter sun penetration; (b) heat-gain and heat-loss analysis of the Forum Baths at Ostia. (By permission, Edwin D. Thatcher.)

(a)

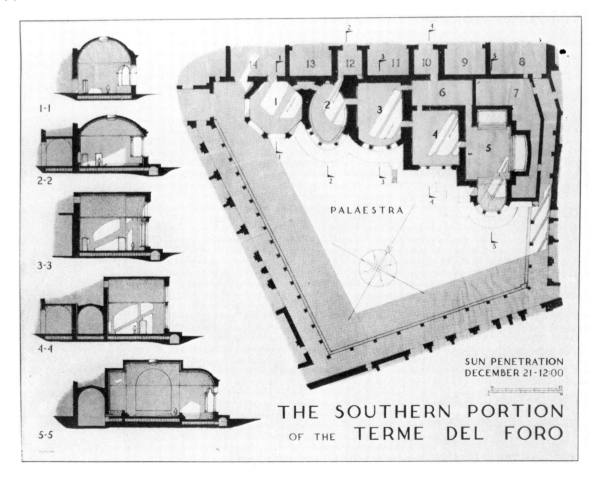

PALAESTRA

SUN PENETRATION
DECEMBER 21·12:00

THE SOUTHERN PORTION
OF THE TERME DEL FORO

extended flues built in a labyrinthine pattern within the fireplace wall so that its mass was heated from the combustion flue and became a radiant heating element. The dimensioning of such a flue design, developed from German and Russian precedents, was the subject of an engineering treatise by architect Carl John Cronstedt and General Fabian Wrede of Sweden in 1775[8] (*Figure 4*). Thereafter, the fireplace or stove element was developed as a piece of equipment, engineered not only for heating, but also for ventilation.[9] Iron stoves could also be mass-produced, the first manufactured cast-iron stove reputedly dating from 1642, built in Lynn, Massachusetts. The science was further developed by Benjamin Franklin, who had introduced the "Pennsylvania Stove"

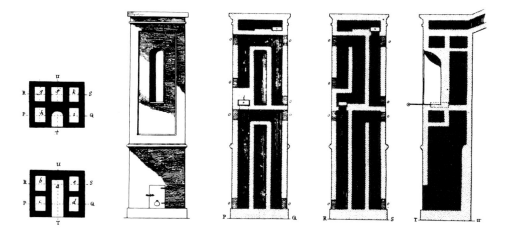

Fig. 4 Cross sections of eighteenth-century Swedish fireplace design. (From Britt Tunander and Ingemar Tunander, *Kakelugnar.*)

in 1744.[10] Franklin's royalist counterpart and contemporary, Benjamin Thompson, Count of Rumford, practiced and wrote about improved fireplace design in London and the colonies.[11]

The efforts of Franklin and Count Rumford to reduce the smoke in rooms indicate that an effective tradition of designing satisfactory fuel-burning devices for buildings had not evolved with any great consistency for over 500 years. The chimney doctors popularized their art too late. By 1784, James Watt had already heated his office by steam, fulfilling Renaissance proposals to use piped hot water for space heating. Pipes allowed designers to remove the fires to a remote location.

As detailed in the next chapter, succeeding generations of architects and the new profession of mechanical engineering then began to develop and use central heating and ventilation systems. Coal, the primary fuel for the nineteenth century and the emerging industrial economy, determined not only the relationship between heating technology and design within buildings, but patterns of

8. Britt Tunander and Ingemar Tunander: *Kakelugnar*, ICA-Forlaget Vasteras, Sweden, 1973.
9. J. Pickering Putnam: *The Open Fireplace in all Ages*, J. R. Osgood, Boston, 1881, and *Smithsonian Reports*, 1873.
10. Franklin's best-known publication on the subject, "Observations on the Causes and Cure of Smoky Chimneys," was completed in 1785 while Franklin was en route from Europe to America. *Transactions of the American Philosophical Society*. Philadelphia, 1786. It discusses coal burning, chimney design and maintenance, and designs for a new stove.
11. G. Curtis Gillespie: *Rumford Fireplaces*, Comstock, New York, 1906.

| ENERGY
CONSERVATION
THROUGH
BUILDING
DESIGN

human settlement. Agreeable living conditions could not be found next to coal-burning factories, railroads, or even commercial districts. Decentralization and separation of work from residence and play then resulted in urban segregation by zone and by class.

Oil and natural gas, cleaner to burn and easier to transport and to store, simply cleaned up the coal act. Their uniform quality enabled much finer control of energy conversion and transport. Accordingly, as heat energy could be moved more easily from the point of production to the point of use, the energy performance of the building envelope could be disregarded. Fossil fuels became the energy substitute for climate-responsive building design.

The impact of the climatic context was not ignored by the early-twentieth-century architects who contributed to the modern movement, which, for the Bauhaus designers, was to be the result of rational analysis and its formal expression in new construction materials and processes.

Gropius designed his own house in Lincoln, Massachusetts as a "sun-tempered" structure[12] (*Figure 5*). The Keck brothers in Chicago built the Crystal House for the Chicago Worlds Fair in 1933–1934 as an exploration of the aesthetics of glass and steel and discovered it was so well heated by direct solar gain that they then embarked upon a decade-long investigation of solar-oriented dwellings that gave occasion for the first popular use of the term "solar house" in local newspapers at the time. In 1927, Buckminster Fuller, an iconoclast in his own tradition, proposed the Dymaxion house, based upon concepts of energy efficiency and industrial production.[13] Le Corbusier, too, was inspired by the industrial aesthetic of oceanliners and airplanes, and in *Precisions*, published in 1930, proposed his own vision of the modern house in which the walls are plenums—or "neutral walls" as he called them—for artificial control of heating or cooling needs. But at heart, Corbusier was a Mediterranean and became better known for a design vocabulary based on celebrating the natural elements of sun and wind and, in the case of his early house in Carthage, could have been inspired by the indigenous building of Tunisia.[14] Corbusier's "*brises-soleil*" (shading devices) and his use of "thick-walls" and double-height spaces have precedents in vernacular building throughout the Mediterranean, where they offer appropriate responses to warm climate requirements.

Sun control was developed into an architectural science by the Olgyay brothers in the early 1950s; their subsequent publications are classics still in print today.[15] Concurrently, work in building climatology by researchers and designers was published in professional journals and popular housing magazines.[16]

The connection between design and climate control is thus a complex theme that follows the entire history of building technology. Extended analysis of this connection would have to trace not only the development of energy resources for buildings and the technical knowledge of how to apply them, but the often

12. Nevin Summers: "Analyzing the Gropius House as Energy Conscious Design," *AIA Journal*, February 1977.
13. Robert W. Marks: *The Dymaxion World of Buckminster Fuller*, Southern Illinois University Press, Carbondale, IL, 1960.
14. *L'Architecture d'Aujourd'hui*, October, 1948.
15. Aladar Olgyay and Victor Olgyay: *Sun Control and Shading Devices*, Princeton University Press, 1957; Victor Olgyay: *Design with Climate*, Princeton University Press, 1963.
16. "Climate Control Project," *AIA Bulletin*, September 1949 (published in alternate issues until January 1952), available from University Microfilms, Ann Arbor, MI, order number PB272; *House Beautiful* (numerous issues from October 1949 to February 1952).

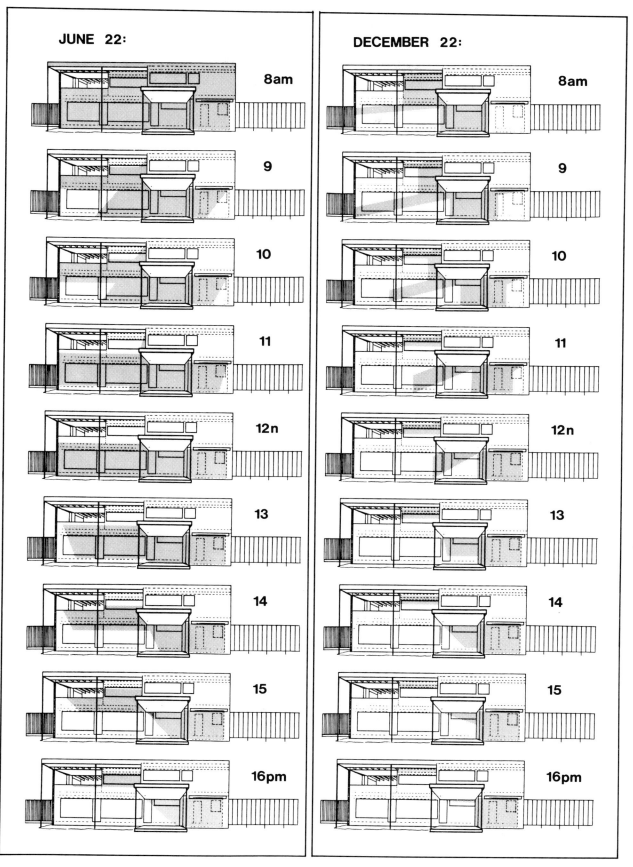

Fig. 5 Analysis of window wall shading of the Gropius House. (From Nevin Summers, *AIA Journal,* February 1977.)

ambivalent cultural and aesthetic attitudes about the relationship between nature and machine technology.

Contemporary architects have used the relative freedom of expression offered by modern technology to pursue design styles of their own invention. Recently, energy design has been used as the rationale for aesthetic gymnastics, putting buildings up in the air or underground (*Figure 6*).

Presently, some commentators predict that energy conservation may provide impetus to a rethinking of architectural styles and methods as dramatic as that which followed the emergence of industrialization. As argued in the *New York Times* editorial of November 30, 1973:

The job is not going to be done by removing light bulbs. What is required is a radical design approach to declining resources. There was an architectural revolution near the beginning of this century, and it now appears that there may have to be another one before the end. It will profoundly affect the way we build and live.

Whether the form of architecture is dramatic or modest, it is hoped that solutions will emerge with a depth and subtlety equal to the technical understanding of buildings that energy studies provide us. If economic and environmental perspectives extend the science of building, historical and cultural perspectives reassert its art. It may return us to familiar forms, as in a thoughtful design submission for a recent California state office building competition (*Figure 7*), modeled after warm-dry–climate courtyard housing. Perhaps· as shown in Paolo Soleri's proposal for an urban village (*Figure 8*), we have come, 1,000 years after Pueblo Bonito, full circle.

An Economic Perspective

As discussed in the previous section, energy considerations should extend our design studies to the historical origins of architecture and building technology. Energy implications also extend the boundaries of the designer's concern to topics of planning, economics, and the entire range of environmental impacts implicit in building design and construction. Energy studies cross borders and engage many professional and research disciplines.

To begin with the first questions asked: What is the energy crisis and how does it affect building design?

The projections of future fossil fuel supplies vary, being based more on assumptions than on substantiated fact. But in an authoritative summary of recent fuel availability projections, V. E. McKelvey, director of the U.S. Geological Survey, presents the conclusion that known reserves of all recoverable world fuel

Fig. 6 Three buildings based upon three different climatic contexts: (a) Social Studies Building, Hebrew University, Jerusalem (photo courtesy of Hanna Shapira); (b) Office Building, Raleigh, North Carolina (photo courtesy of Odell Associates, Architects); (c) Scanticon Conference Center Housing, Aarhus, Denmark (photo courtesy of K. Friis and E. Moltke, Architects).

(a)

(c)

resources (oil, gas, and coal) would last 34 years if world consumption continues at an annual growth rate of 5% (the average for 1960 to 1973). If the consumption rate were reduced to 2% per year, the time to exhaustion would be extended to 90 years.[17] The projections are based only on known reserves and do not include total world resources that are thought to exist, but have not been proven. But, counting the number of years to depletion is, hopefully, not a relevant exercise once it has properly alerted us to the social and political implications of fuel resource scarcity. The important points are that supplying additional energy will become increasingly costly no matter what the future source is to be, and that continuing to increase energy demand involves unprecedented economic risk due to trade imbalances and their domestic repercussions, as well as social and environmental stress due to loss of natural resources, pollution, and related health and safety costs associated with the energy-intensive development required by profligate energy use.

All of these points could be true, but why the connection with

17. V. E. McKelvey: "World Energy—The Resource Picture," in R. Fazzolare and C. B. Smith, eds.: *Energy Use Management Conference Proceedings*, Pergammon Press, New York, 1977.

Fig. 7 California State Office Building competition entry (second-place award): SOL-ARC/ELS Design Group, Architects.

Fig. 8 Design for an Arcology village to meet climate conditions of India-Pakistan: Paolo Soleri, Architect (photo: Ivan Pinter).

building design? The relationship exists because of the combination of several facts. Firstly, around 40% of our national energy consumption is used in the building sector to heat, cool, and illuminate our buildings; to manufacture building products; and to construct buildings.[18] Secondly, as much as one-half of this energy could be saved by proper building design, construction, and use management. Energy waste in the building sector has obvious economic impact to building owners and, beyond that, aggravates indirect environmental and health costs borne by future generations. The urgent decision is when to invest in energy conservation in the building sector; the longer the decision is delayed, the more difficult that option will be, as a greater portion of available capital is assigned each year to escalating energy expenditures to operate buildings.

These points are argued in several reports by the American Institute of Architects Energy Committee, which conclude that the amount of energy that could be saved by energy conservation through building design is approximately equal to that projected to be available from any one of the major domestic energy sources in 1990[19] (*Figure 9*).

These facts build the case for the energy conservation alternative: an effort, equal to or greater than that now projected for energy development, should be devoted to conserve energy by improved design of buildings, transport, and other energy-intensive consumer products. The argument has been taken up by many authors that, due to energy waste in conversion and transmission, a Btu saved is worth two Btu produced, or put in other terms, a dollar spent in energy conservation at the building scale could save twice the energy produced by an equivalent investment in power supply and production capacity.[20]

The implications of the conservation alternative are thus enormously important to the design professions, as well as to the entire building industry; the more so because, as coherent as the arguments for conservation may be, relatively little has been actually accomplished to implement energy conservation practices compared to the range and magnitude of existing possibilities.

To put the promise of the conservation alternative in a realistic framework, the difficulties of actually carrying out a large energy conservation program at the building scale need to be faced. For if energy-conserving building design is ethical, wise, and economical, why then is it not inevitable?

The reasons, which are discussed at length in the concluding chapter of this book, come down to the fact that it is extremely difficult to change one's habits. Energy conservation requires changes in the way buildings are financed, designed, built, and used.

The most common argument offered against energy conservation design is that it is too costly, it cannot be financed, it cannot be marketed, it doesn't "pay back" quickly enough. In many

18. "Technical Options for Energy Conservation in Buildings," National Bureau of Standards Technical Note 789, July 1973; Richard G. Stein: *Architecture and Energy,* Anchor Press/Doubleday, New York, 1977.
19. "Energy and the Built Environment: A Gap in Current Strategies," May 1974; "A Nation of Energy Efficient Buildings by 1990," *American Institute of Architects,* Washington, DC, n.d.
20. Denis Hayes: *Rays of Hope,* W. W. Norton, New York, 1977; Amory B. Lovins: *Soft Energy Paths,* Ballinger Publishing Company, Cambridge, MA, 1977 (hereafter cited as *Energy Paths*).

cases, this economic reasoning can be faulted, but in other cases, it cannot. Energy conservation does involve improved building quality which requires a larger economic investment than the "build cheap now—pay later" approach. The question that needs to be discussed, however, each time the economic criterion is applied, is, what are we saving by not investing in energy conservation? If it is capital or cash liquidity, what will that capital buy instead? Isn't there an increased price that everyone is willing to pay for stability of energy costs, for improved environmental quality, for increased economic and social well-being?

The point is that the market cost of energy does not now reflect its real cost, whether to produce and supply energy in the first place (plant costs are partly subsidized by tax credits and allowances, and energy charges are lower for large energy consumers); to clean up the environmental pollution and waste that results when energy is converted and transported (environmental clean-up costs are indirectly passed on to the general public or to future generations); or to replace the energy resource once it is depleted (in which case the replacement cost must include the entire capital expenditure required to supply an alternate source for equivalent energy).

Fig. 9 Comparison of potential U.S. energy supply projected to be available in 1990 with potential energy saved through energy conservation in buildings. Units are Million Barrel per Day Oil Equivalent (bbl/d). A bbl is equal to 42 U.S. gallons of 5.5×10^6 Btu. A bbl/d is a measure of thermal energy producing capacity equal to 67.1 kW. ("Energy and the Built Environment: A Gap in Current Strategies," American Institute of Architects.)

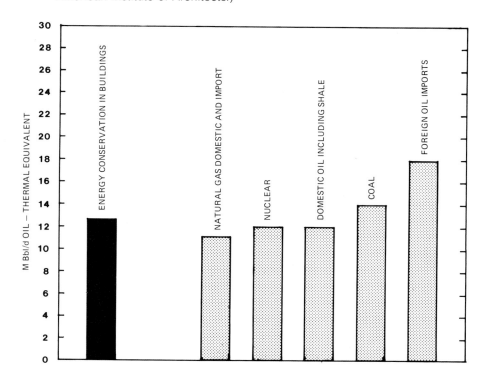

We need mechanisms by which the true costs of energy use are reflected in our design decisions, either by marketplace corrections, which inevitably mean higher energy costs or—and here the ultimate economic advantage of energy conservation needs to be made emphatic—by reducing energy waste and consumption by conservation design.

The remainder of this section reviews energy cost concepts that help account for the true, or "net," energy implications of building design.

Embodied Energy Cost   Energy is used in constructing buildings and in producing construction materials and components. Richard Stein and Diane Serber propose, in Chapter 10, the concept of "embodied energy" as a measure of energy required to manufacture and put into place a particular building component or construction system. Because manufacturing energy costs are subsidized or are otherwise accounted for at rates different from those charged other consumers, the market price of a product used in construction may not be a true measure of the energy embodied in its manufacture. Up to 5% of the United States' energy consumption has been ascribed to energy embodied in construction, and this can be readily reduced by improvements in design and manufacturing processes.

Source Energy Cost   "End-use" energy, that required at the building to operate its systems, is usually accounted for by the "purchased" cost of fuel and electricity. It is purchased energy costs, the costs in the marketplace, that are used in life-cycle costing, the technique by which building operational costs are calculated over an extended period to determine whether or not a particular energy conservation feature is cost-justified. But here again, the market cost of energy may not accurately represent differences in the primary expenditure of "source energy" required to produce, convert, and transport that energy to the building. For example, to produce electricity at a power plant by conventional fossil fuels and supply it to the building for electric resistance heating requires three to four times the source energy as that used by a gas- or oil-fired burner at the building itself.

The accurate accounting of differences between purchased-energy cost and source-energy expenditure is greatly complicated by the capital expenditure required to produce and market energy. In the case of the electric power plant, the capital cost of constructing the plant would be much the same whether or not electric consumption is increased by electric resistance heating devices in the buildings. In fact, energy conservation reduces the market for the utility companies who are left with the amortization costs of the original investment (although they will have received public subsidies in the form of investment tax credits). As an inevitable result, the purchased rate of a unit of energy is increased, whether it is electricity or any other utility. For example, in California, in the recent water conservation program, although water was conserved, the unit cost of purchased metered water was raised so that the water bill to the consumer was the same or greater than before the conservation effort.

Marginal Cost of Energy   Whether it saves energy, such as by improved insulation, or actually produces energy, such as by solar panels, the cost of constructing energy features on a building should be compared to the capital cost of the energy infrastructure that would otherwise be required. From this standpoint, one can see that the eventual costs that will be charged to the public to convert or build power plants to produce energy may greatly exceed the cost of conservation at the building scale.

Amory Lovins has proposed that energy alternatives be analyzed in terms of the replacement, or "marginal" cost, the economists' term for the future increment in costs anticipated to supply a commodity. *Table 1,* the calculation method for which is given in Lovins' book, *Soft Energy Paths,* compares the marginal costs of various energy systems, including energy conservation alternatives which are less expensive than the energy-intensive options by a startling order of magnitude that is not reflected in current market costs.[21] Other analysis methods by which to properly assign economic values to nonreplenishable resources have been proposed and are being developed.[22]

Transportation Energy Costs   Just as building design decisions have an impact on the demand for energy placed on the energy production and supply infrastructure, planning and building layout affect the resulting transportation energy costs as a function of building density and activity-use zoning. The mode and number of people per vehicle are key variables critical to the energy cost-effectiveness of transportation. In a comparison of all energy costs related to manufacture, construction, and operation of urban transportation modes, Margaret Fulton Fels has shown that the relative order of merit between alternatives may change depending upon the criterion used for evaluation (*Figure 10*). Furthermore, the commonly assumed energy efficiency of "mass transit" depends upon its being used. This variable is particularly sensitive to planning, layout, and activity location decisions.

Indirect Social and Environmental Costs   In all cases, building, energy infrastructure, and transportation systems require energy for their construction and operation, as well as for their eventual demolition or replacement. Wherever energy is converted and consumed, there is an impact on the environment. Negative impacts include loss of land and seashore to energy recovery, transport, and storage facilities, and degradation of air and water resources by pollution or accidents. These, then, impact on social welfare, safety, and health costs in ways that are delayed and indirect. As a result, they are difficult to trace, except by gross statistical analysis, which requires time, and even then, is subject to wide variation of interpretation. But the indirect costs of different energy sources should be compared in evaluating the

21. Lovins, *Energy Paths,* p. 134.
22. Stephen F. Weber: "The Effect of 'Resource Impact Factors' on Energy Conservation Standards for Buildings," National Bureau of Standards, NBSIR 77-1199 (R), February 1977.

TABLE 1

INTRODUCTION:
ENERGY
CONSERVATION
THROUGH
BUILDING
DESIGN

17

Approximate marginal capital investment (1976 dollars) needed to build complete energy systems to deliver energy to U.S. consumers at a rate of one bbl/day. (Amory B. Lovins: "Re-examining the Nature of the ECE Energy Problem," United Nations Economic Commission for Europe, Geneva, secretariat document number ECE (XXXIII)/2/I.G., February 1978.)

Energy system	Date of operation	Capital cost[a] 1976 $/bbl·d	1976 $/kW	Form supplied
"Hard" technologies				
Traditional direct fuels	1950s–60s	2–3,000	30– 45	fuel
Direct coal	1970s			
North Sea oil	late 1970s	10,000	150	fuel
U.S. frontier oil & gas	1980s	10–25,000	150–370	fuel
Synthetics from coal or shale	1980s	20–40,000+	300–600+	fuel
Central coal-electric + scrubbers	1980s	170,000	2530	electricity
Nuclear-electric (LWR)	mid-1980s	235,000	3500+	electricity
"Technical fixes" to improve end-use efficiency				
New commercial buildings	1978	−3,000	−45	heat & elec.
Common industrial & architectural leak-plugging; better domestic appliances	1978	0– 5,000	0–75	heat & elec.
Most heat-recovery systems	1978	5–15,000	75–225	heat
Bottoming cycles; better motors	1978	20,000	300	electricity
Very thorough building retrofits	1978	30,000	450	heat
Transitional fossil-fuel technologies				
Coal-fired fluidized-bed gas turbine with district heating and heat pumps (COP = 2)	1982	30,000	450	heat
Most industrial cogeneration	1979	60,000	900	elec. & heat
"Soft" technologies				
Passive solar heating (≤100%)	1978	<0–20,000	<0–300	heat
Retrofitted 100%-solar space & water heat, 10²-unit neighborhood	1985	20–40,000	300–600	heat
Same, single house	1985	50–70,000	750–1050	heat
300°C solar process heat	1980	120,000	1790	heat
Bioconversion of farm & forestry wastes to alcohols	1980	15– 25,000+	225–370+	fuel
Pyrolysis of municipal wastes	1980	30,000[b]	450[b]	fuel
Microhydroelectric plants		30–140,000	450–3000	electricity
Wind-electric plants		90–200,000	1340–3000	electricity

[a]Empirical data except for synfuels (industry projections), fluidized-bed gas turbine system (turnkey offering price), and solar neighborhood heating representative values; actual values may be sensitive to date and site. U.S. conditions except as noted. Cost is per bbl·day (67.1 kW(t), as 1 bbl = 5.8 GJ) or per kW(t) of enthalpy delivered to final user.
[b]Excludes investment credit for by-products (e.g., materials recovery) and for waste disposal services replaced.

cost effectiveness of the energy conservation alternative. There are also positive environmental benefits that can be served by planning and design, including reclamation of open land for food production, water and air purification, and wildlife preservation, not to mention physical and spiritual recreation for urban-bound citizens. As a qualitative measure of these values, Malcomb Wells

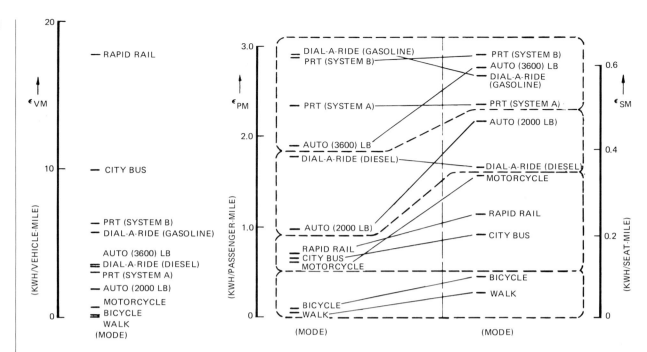

Fig. 10 A comparison of the net energy requirements in kWh (embodied plus operating energy) of transportation systems based on three different criteria: vehicle-mile, passenger-mile, and seat-mile. (Margaret Fulton Fels: "Comparative Energy Costs of Urban Transportation Systems," *Transportation Research Journal*, October 1975.)

proposes that the "wilderness scale" be applied to building design alternatives[23] (*Figure 11*).

Similar terms of cost/benefit should be used to evaluate building design options, rather than a strict determination based on the market cost of energy, which, as we have seen, does not accurately reflect real energy value (*Figure 12*). Towards this end, energy cost methods must be increasingly refined.

A Cultural Perspective

The interrelationship between building design and environmental quality should be recognized: it connects the act of design directly to the quality of life that is to be sustained in the future. If design is the preparation by our generation for the world of our children and for the unborn, what will their inheritance be?

In the face of specious arguments that energy saving must result in lower environmental quality standards and reduced comfort and convenience, it needs to be clearly stated that the allocation of economic, energy, and environmental resources is part of the same solution to maintain and improve the quality of life.

In this respect, the potential of design—to anticipate change, to correct imbalance, to prepare solutions that are efficient and elegant—is our most valuable resource. The question is whether

23. "Environmental Impact," *Progressive Architecture,* June 1974.

we can, in fact, use and improve our design abilities to create and sustain our cultural choices. As put by M. King Hubbert, a scientist now retired from a career in the Shell Oil Company and the U.S. Geological Survey and an early prognosticator of the current energy shortages:

The foremost problem confronting humanity today is how to make the transition from the precarious state we are now in to

INTRODUCTION: | **19**
ENERGY
CONSERVATION
THROUGH
BUILDING
DESIGN

(a)

Fig. 11 (a) Malcomb Wells' underground office building and (b) its evaluation in terms of environmental impact qualities (natural environment ideal = + 1500).

(b) **Wells' Underground Office**

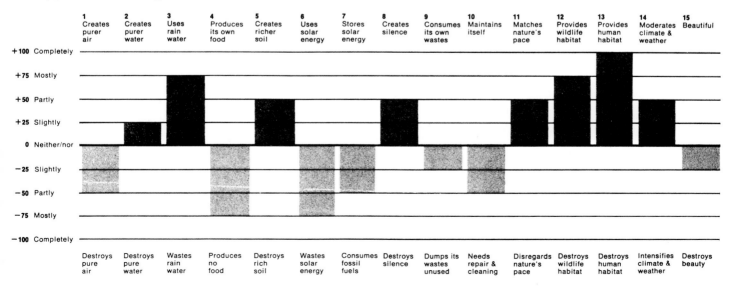

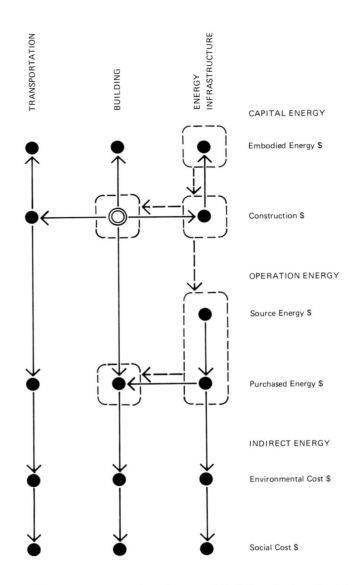

Fig. 12 Summary: Energy Cost Impact of Building Design Decisions. Solid lines indicate how building construction cost factors influence second- and third-order energy costs. Dotted line indicates how marginal costs of energy infrastructure influence life-cycle building costs.

an optimum future state by the least catastrophic progression. Our principal impediments at present are neither lack of energy or material resources nor of essential physical and biological knowledge. Our principal constraints are cultural.[24]

But cultural change is difficult, the more so as it requires change in underlying social and institutional structures. In a 1970 lecture, "Environments at Risk," anthropologist Mary Douglas draws a parallel between the contemporary environmental movement and the movement that began a century earlier for the abolition of slavery. She sees it as one that is equally profound in its potential

24. As quoted in the *New York Times,* December 2, 1976.

impact upon our economic and social assumptions and that can be expected to have to overcome resistance to what is an equally difficult, but inevitable process of cultural evolution:

> *The abolitionists succeeded in revolutionizing the image of man. In the same way, the ecology movement will succeed in changing the idea of nature. It will succeed in raising a tide of opinion that will put abuses of the environment under close surveillance. Strong sanctions against particular pollutions will come into force. It will succeed in these necessary changes for the same reason as the slavery abolition movement, partly by sheer dedication and mostly because the time is ripe.*[25]

The energy issue has thus impelled design professionals into perhaps an unprecedented role as those most able to help solve emerging resource and cultural problems *by design.* And rather than eliminate the aesthetic component of design, the cultural perspective shows how necessary it is as the ultimate embodiment of our aspirations and commitment.

Architects once studied the rules of proportion for the styles and orders of the classic temples of antiquity. The earth is now that temple: the rules are those of building and living within the limits of the world's balance of resources and energy.

25. Mary Douglas: "Environments at Risk," *Times Literary Supplement,* London, October 30, 1970.

2

ARCHITECTURE CONFRONTS ENVIRONMENTAL TECHNOLOGY: AN HISTORICAL PERSPECTIVE

Robert Bruegmann and Donald Prowler

The origins of the current energy dilemma in architecture may date to the first half of the nineteenth century, when architects and engineers laid the basis for modern environmental technology. Today, when much of this legacy is being reexamined, it is appropriate to look at the pioneering efforts in central heating and forced ventilation in order to observe some vigorous, if often confused, responses which nineteenth-century designers made when faced with new environmental and technological challenges.[1]

Before the nineteenth century, virtually the only means of heating buildings were the open fireplace and the closed stove. Although each had been refined considerably, they remained, in many ways, highly unsatisfactory in use and appearance (*Figure 1*). It should be remembered how restrictive the resulting heating and ventilation requirements were on the configuration of any large building. The designer was obliged to include a fireplace or stove in every inhabited room, and a flue to carry away the products of combustion. Any area designed to hold a large number of people had to contain a very large volume of air. Even as vast a space as the interior of Notre Dame Cathedral in Paris was apparently insufficient when enough people crowded into it. Eugene Péclet, the noted French writer on heating and ventilation, reported that at a funeral service which he attended in the church, the heat generated by the 6,000 spectators became so intense without sufficient air movement to carry it away, the candles around the catafalque drooped and many people fainted. On the other hand, heating large spaces usually meant encumbering the room with stoves and lengthy exposed flues. The placement of

Fig. 1 One of two Arnott stoves installed about 1840 in the Long Room of the Custom House, London. Architect Charles Fowler explained their elaborate ornamentation: "It was deemed proper and consistent that the stoves should be rendered suitable in their external appearance to the situation they were to occupy as appendages to so noble an apartment." (From Charles Fowler, "On Warming and Ventilating the Long Room of the Custom House, London," *Transactions of the Royal Institute of British Architects*, vol. 1, 1842.)

1. Robert Bruegmann: "The Origins of Central Heating and Forced Ventilation and Their Effect on Architectural Design," *Society of Architectural Historians Journal*, October 1978.

ENERGY
CONSERVATION
THROUGH
BUILDING
DESIGN

2 Eugene Péclet, *Traite sur la Chaleur*, Paris, 1843 edition.

3. A very good illustration of a hypocaust-heated greenhouse can be found in William Chambers, *Plans and Elevations of the Gardens and Buildings at Kew*, London, 1763, plate vii.

4. These installations are recorded in the pioneer works on steam heating: Robertson Buchanon, *Treatise on the Economy of Fuel*, Glasgow, 1815; Thomas Tredgold, *Principles of Warming and Ventilation*, London, 1824; and Walter Bernan, (pseud. Robert Meikleham) *On the History and Art of Warming and Ventilating*, London, 1845.

5. On the Derbyshire Infirmary see Charles Sylvester, *Philosophy of Domestic Economy as Exemplified in the Mode of Warming, Ventilating, and Cooking Adopted in the Derbyshire General Infirmary*, London, 1819.

6. The pioneer text on low-pressure hot-water heating is Charles Hood, *Practical Treatise on Heating Buildings by Hot Water*, London, 1837. For high-pressure hot-water heating, the most important early source is Charles Richardson, *Practical Treatise on the Warming and Ventilation of Buildings*, London, 1837. On Bonnemain, see the article by M. Payen, in *Annales de l'industrie*, June 1827.

water closets and kitchens outside the main building block was dictated by the necessity of preventing odors from reaching public areas.[2]

Attempts to develop central heating go back at least to the late seventeenth century. Possibly, the Roman hypocaust system, in which radiant surfaces were heated by flues in the floors and walls, survived in some form from antiquity. It was certainly a common means of warming greenhouses in the eighteenth century and was revived occasionally in the nineteenth, although fire hazards prevented it from becoming widespread before the introduction of the electric radiant panel in the mid-twentieth century.[3]

Not until the 1790s, however, was a sustained effort made to develop central heating and mechanical ventilation. The major center of invention in early central heating technology was the British midlands where an extraordinary group of scientists and industrialists developed a wide range of innovations in architectural technology. In addition to heating and ventilation, these new techniques included metal framing, hollow-pot vaulting and gas lighting. Two central figures in the group, Matthew Boulton and James Watt, were among the first and most extensive experimenters with steam central heating. They used it first in their homes and then on a larger scale in their mills and in those of their friends. At the Lee spinning mill in Salford, about 1800, they united steam heating with the equally new structural technique of iron skeletal framing by passing steam through hollow structural columns of the building (*Figure 2*).[4]

In 1792, William Strutt, also a mill owner from the midlands, was the first to develop large-scale hot-air central heating in a mill in Derby. The first early monument of this kind of heating was the Derbyshire Infirmary, whose design and ingenious equipment were all of Strutt's devising. Besides the hot-air system (*Figure 3*), the building design included hollow-pot vaulting for the baths and boasted a toilet with provisions for ventilation and automatic flushing (*Figure 4*).[5]

Of these early techniques, central hot-water heating was the last to develop. Although used successfully by the Frenchman Bonnemain in a chicken incubator near Paris in the 1770s (*Figure 5*), it was not until the 1830s that any further systematic development took place. At that time, two rival systems came into being, one based on low pressure with large-diameter pipes, and the other, developed by Jacob Perkins, consisting of a sealed high-pressure circuit of small-bore pipes (*Figure 6*).[6]

The earliest form of forced ventilation was based on the induced extraction of air from a space by placing a fire at the base of a shaft or flue. The heated air rose in the shaft as it became less dense and allowed cooler air to replace it. This principle, called the chimney "stack effect," had long been known, having been a common practice for centuries for mine ventilation. The Marquis

Fig. 2   Section of mill building heated by steam carried in structural iron columns. This system, proposed in a publication of 1806, probably resembles very closely the system c. 1800 at the Lee mill in Salford. (From *Transactions of the Royal Society of Arts,* vol. 24, 1806.)

Fig. 3   Section of the hot-air furnace devised by William Strutt for the Derbyshire Infirmary, erected 1806–1810. The fire in the central area of the furnace heated the metal surface of the domed "cockle." The cockle was surrounded by a large air space enclosed by bricks. Cold air entered the cavity space at the bottom under "D" and was brought into contact with the hot metal surfaces through ceramic tubes. The warmed air passed up the side of the metal cockle and back out of the tubes above "D" into the hot-air chamber. It then flowed into the building through the great brick duct at the top. (From Charles Sylvester, *Philosophy of Domestic Economy,* London, 1819.)

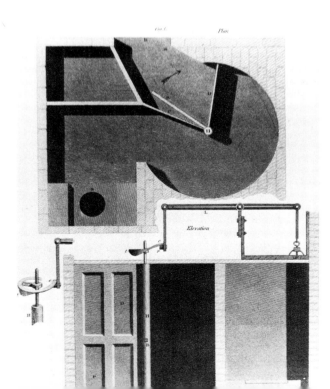

Fig. 4   Plan and section of the water closet at the Derbyshire Infirmary, 1806. In this arrangement a revolving door prevented the escape of air from the water closet to the rest of the asylum. Every time the door was turned the toilet was automatically flushed and the air in the chamber was expelled through the hole above the toilet, "S." This arrangement allowed William Strutt, the designer of the hospital, to place it in a position convenient for patients, near the center of the plan instead of in an outbuilding. (From Charles Sylvester, *The Philosophy of Domestic Economy,* London, 1819.)

ENERGY
CONSERVATION
THROUGH
BUILDING
DESIGN

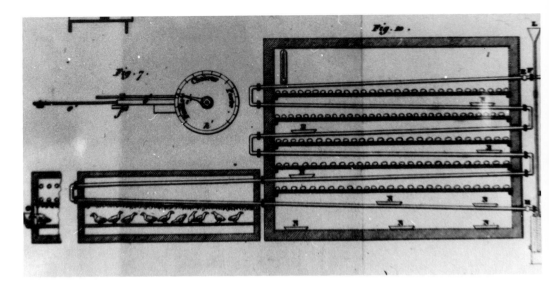

Fig. 5 Heating system designed in the 1770s for Bonnemain's chicken incubator near Paris. This was the first widely published hot-water heating system. Strangely enough, it was not until the 1830s that the method was revived on any scale. (From M. Payen, *Annales de l'Industrie*, June 1827.)

de Chabannes made extensive use of this principle in buildings. Chabannes, who dabbled in all branches of the new heating and ventilation systems before going broke, used specially constructed ventilation fires, steam cylinders, and gas chandeliers to provide sufficient heat to maintain an upward air movement to ventilate rooms. Subsequently, his system became very common in the early nineteenth century (*Figure 7*). An alternative method of ventilation involved forcing the air into a space by mechanical means. This system, too, had been used for centuries, but it was not until the mid-nineteenth century that the steam engine was harnessed to the fan to offer sufficient power to ventilate large buildings. The first really large-scale installation was designed by David Boswell Reid in the 1850s for use in Harvey Lonsdale Elme's splendid St. George's Hall in Liverpool (*Figure 8*).[7]

By 1860, the new central heating and ventilating technologies had reached a state of maturity. Fresh air could be delivered, at any velocity, in theory at least, then cleaned, filtered, and warmed to any temperature (*Figure 9*). When a problem arose, a frequent remedy was simply to make more sophisticated devices to solve it. When the problem of maintaining acceptable air flow in buildings became crucial and an opening door or window could upset the balance of the mechanical system, one remedy was to seal the building. As early as the 1820s, John Vallance patented a system in which mechanical ventilation, sealed windows, and a revolving door were used to completely control the climate of a room. The editor of the *London Journal of Arts and Sciences* commented, "Among the many wild schemes and theories which

7. Chabannes published *On Conducting Air by Forced Ventilation* and an *Appendix*, both apparently about 1818. On St. George's Hall see William MacKenzie, "The Mechanical Ventilation and Warming of St. George's Hall, Liverpool," *Civil Engineer and Architect's Journal*, 1964, pp. 136–139; see also Quentin Hughes, "Neo-Classical Ideas and Practice: St. George's Hall, Liverpool," *Architectural Association Quarterly*, vol. 5, no. 2, pp. 36–44.

ARCHITECTURE
CONFRONTS
ENVIRONMENTAL
TECHNOLOGY:
AN HISTORICAL
PERSPECTIVE

27

Fig. 6 John Soane's Museum, London. Section showing the Perkins' high-pressure hot-water system installed about 1831 which operated well into the twentieth century. Soane had tried to warm his complex maze of spaces by a number of heating schemes, but none were satisfactory until he installed this system. The very high temperatures possible in this kind of heating system allowed the use of small-bore pipes which could be easily concealed. The boiler was located in the stairhall in front of the plane of this section. The expansion tube can be seen at "*b*" in the upper right of the old office. A heating coil is concealed below the table in the monk's room. In the Belzoni Chamber the heating tubes were placed under the bases of the marble antiquities. Around the base of each of the skylights seen here, Soane also ran coils to counteract the fall of cold air. (From Richardson, *A Popular Treatise of the Warming and Ventilation of Buildings*, London, 1839.)

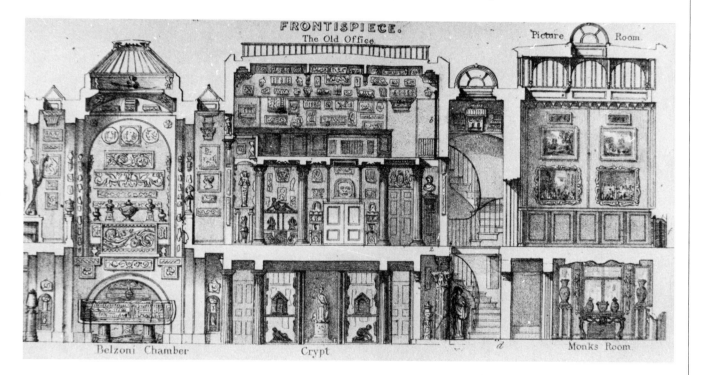

are occasionally dignified with the title of patent, we have rarely met with any more impracticable and ridiculous." Yet this scheme, referred to so often to typify mid-twentieth–century building design, was in fact widely used in the last century.[8]

One of the most compelling reasons for the rapid growth of the new technologies was economic. To heat with one fire requiring one attendant was cheaper than using many individual fires needing many attendants. Ventilation was found to be economically beneficial. Morill Wyman, author of an early treatise on ventilation, reported the story of a Manchester factory where the industrialist was quite pleased with his system because it increased productivity. But his workers were dissatisfied because they

8. On Vallance see *London Journal of Arts and Sciences*, vol. 2, p. 120 and vol. 3, p. 292.

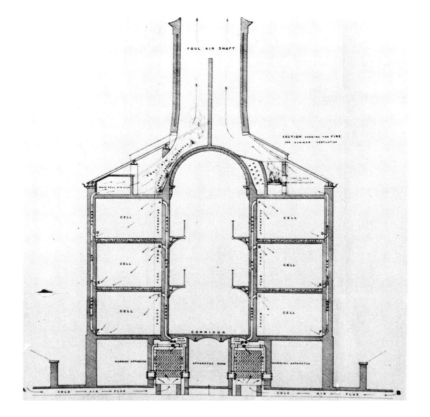

Fig. 7 Pentonville Prison, London, 1841–1842. Section of cell wing showing the heating and ventilating system installed by engineer Joshua Jebb who was mainly responsible for the design of the building. In this scheme, the air entered the building through a large underground flue, was heated as it passed through large boilers in the basement, then passed through a series of flues within the thickness of the corridor walls, and finally, entered the cells near the ceiling. Air was extracted near the floor and drawn up flues in the exterior wall to a special ventilating fire in the attic which forced it to rise through the "foul air shaft" into the atmosphere. In summer the boilers were not used, but the ventilation fires still assured a continuous flow of air through the cells. (From "Report of the Surveyor General of Prisons on the Construction, Ventilation and Details of Pentonville Prison," London, 1844.)

became healthier and worked up a bigger appetite which they could not satisfy with their unchanged wages![9]

The new systems undoubtedly produced higher levels of comfort. Wyman reported on the case of an Edinburgh club where a new ventilation system was installed:

> *Gentlemen of sober, quiet habits, who usually confined themselves to a couple of glasses, were not satisfied with less than half a bottle; others who took half a bottle, now extended their potations to a bottle and a half. In fact, the hotel keeper was drunk dry. That gentlemen who had indulged so freely were not aware of it at the time is not wonderful; but that they felt no unpleasant sensations the following morning, which they did not, is certainly quite so.*[10]

9. Merrill Wyman, *Practical Treatise on Ventilation*, London, 1846 (hereafter cited as *Ventilation Treatise*).
10. Wyman, *Ventilation Treatise*.

There were also great advantages for the architect. Central heating allowed him to ignore building orientation when necessary and to suppress chimneys and fireplaces. The first major steam heating system in France was installed at the Bourse in Paris in 1828, in great measure, to avoid the multiplicity of small stacks which had proven incongruous on A. T. Brongniart's Greek revival design. The architect could also use greatly expanded areas of glass. The Crystal Palace, for example, while not originally heated because the exhibition was to last only one summer, was given a hot-water system by Paxton when it was moved to Sydenham for permanent use. Forced ventilation allowed the designer to

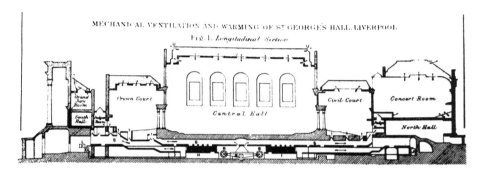

Fig. 8 St. George's Hall, Liverpool, constructed 1841–1854. Longitudinal section showing David Boswell Reid's mechanical ventilation. The fresh air was brought in at the basement level, warmed by coils of steam pipes, then forced into all parts of the building by giant fans. The pressure created by the fans was sufficient to force air already in the building out through the openings in the ceilings, into the attic spaces, and then out into the atmosphere. (From William MacKenzie, "The Mechanical Ventilation of St. George's Hall, Liverpool," *Civil Engineer and Architects' Journal,* 1864.)

Fig. 9 Temporary House of Lords, London. Basement plan showing the use of water sprinklers for the filtering of intake air. Designed by David Boswell Reid about 1839. (From Reid, *Illustrations of the Theory and Practice of Ventilation,* London, 1844.)

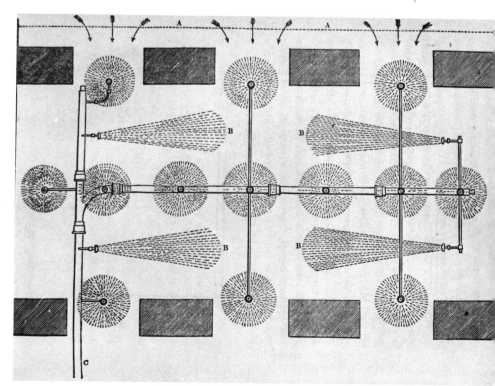

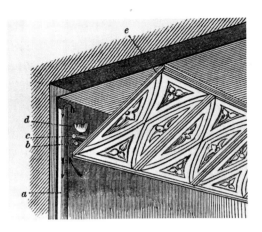

Fig. 10 David Boswell Reid's system of "exclusive lighting." In this system, which Reid applied to the Temporary House of Commons, the major problem with gas lighting, that of keeping the combustion products out of the chamber, was solved by placing the gas pipes and jets behind a tracery panel filled with glass. The heat produced by these lights also helped extract air from the chamber. (From Reid, *Illustrations of the Theory and Practice of Ventilation,* London, 1844.)

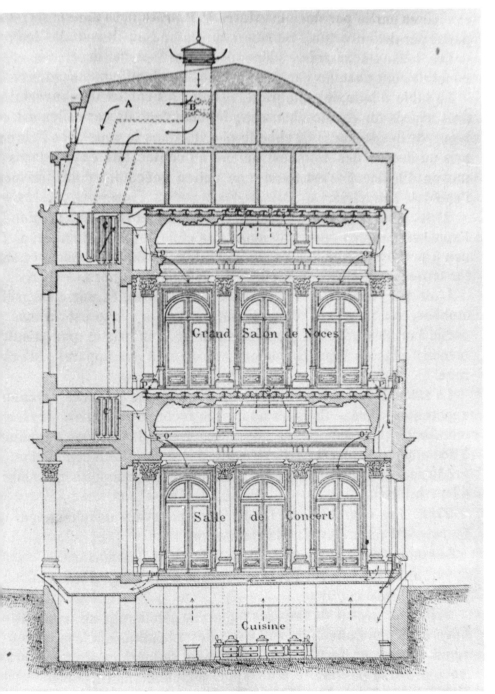

Fig. 11 (Left) Hotel Continental, Paris. Section showing heating and ventilation installation by Geneste and Herscher, engineers, of Paris. This section shows how the ventilation system was ingeniously threaded through the walls of the richly decorated public rooms. The air was taken from a louvered cupola at the top of the building where the atmosphere was thought to be purest, driven by fans at "B" to the steam heating coils at "C," and from there injected into the Grand Salon de Noces and the Salle de Concert through ornamental cornices. The evacuated air was taken at floor level, "P," and secondarily from above the gas fixtures at "S," and expelled by a second set of fans not visible in this section. The kitchen was ventilated separately, and thermally insulated from the rooms above by a double ceiling which also served as ventilation space for the Salle de Concert. (From Eugene Peclet, *Traité de la Chaleur,* 1878 edition.)

build much deeper buildings, to lower ceiling heights, to design interior spaces with no windows, and to arrange complex, flowing spaces. It permitted a significant increase in the level of lighting by the introduction of gas lamps (*Figure 10*), and no less revolutionary, to bring kitchen and toilet into the main block of the building (*Figure 11*).

In the early nineteenth century, there was frequently a lively interchange among architect and engineer caused by the need to reconcile heating, ventilation, and architectural design. In some buildings, the architectural effects were considered primary and the equipment had to be ingeniously accommodated (Figures 6, 11). In other cases, particularly in more utilitarian buildings, the efficiency of equipment became an overriding factor, and the building constructed around it. This produced buildings where the section was almost an air-flow diagram (*Figure 7*). At the Wakefield Lunatic Asylum the heating system was integrated with surveillance, another prime concern (*Figure 12*). In residential construction, more than one designer proposed house designs built around the idea of supplying a comfortable interior atmosphere (*Figures 13* and *14*).[12]

Some architects were interested in the aesthetic and symbolic expression and articulation of the new equipment. A good example of this can be found in the works of John Claudius Loudon, who

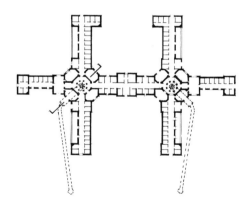

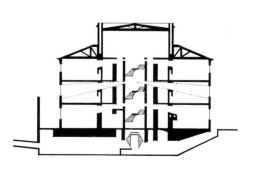

Fig. 12 Ground-floor plan and section of the Wakefield Infirmary, 1816–18, showing heating system designed by Charles Sylvester. In this building, fresh air was conducted into the building through great underground tunnels, shown in the plan in dotted lines, which pre-heated the air in winter and cooled it in summer. The air was then heated by a "cockle" furnace at the base of the two central staircases from which the asylum wings radiated. The air rose in a well in the center of the staircases and was dispersed to the wards through a series of transoms. These openings were also designed to allow easy surveillance of the wards from the central staircase. The path of the air, as well as the line of sight from a stair landing into the wards on the second floor, is shown in the section in dotted lines. (Redrawn from Watson and Pritchett, *Plans, Elevations, and Descriptions of the Pauper Lunatic Asylum Lately Erected at Wakefield*, York, 1819.)

11. On the Bourse see *Bulletin de la Societe d'Encouragement*, vol. 2, p. 120 and vol. 3, p. 292. On the Crystal Palace Heating see *Tallis' History and Description of the Crystal Palace*, London, n.d., p. 446. 12. On the Wakefield Infirmary see C. Watson and J. P. Pritchett, *Plans, Elevations, and Descriptions of the Pauper Lunatic Asylum Lately Erected at Wakefield*, York, 1819.

32

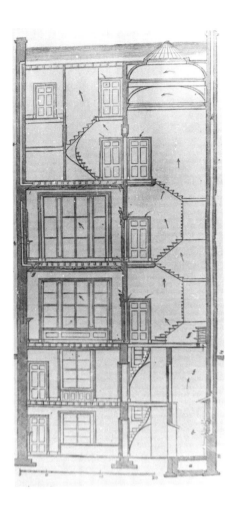

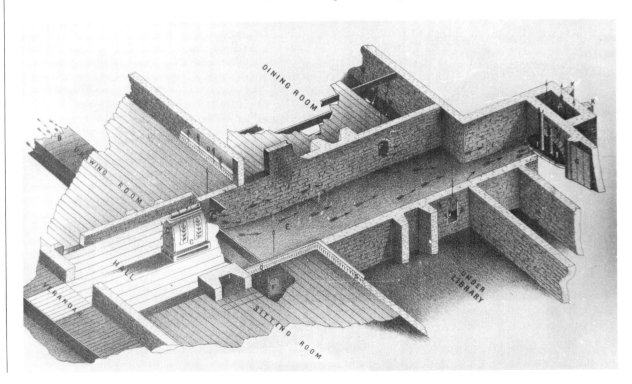

Fig. 13 Section of John Robinson house, Edinburgh, showing heating and ventilating system, c. 1839, installed by John Sylvester. In this house, a cockle stove, like that at the Derbyshire Infirmary, was placed at the bottom of the stairwell. The warm air rose in the well and into all of the rooms through perforated moldings over doors and in the ceiling cornices. (From Loudon, *Encyclopedia of Cottage, Farm, and Villa Architecture,* London, 1833.)

Fig. 14 Henry Ruttan's scheme for a house which could be efficiently heated and ventilated, one of many proposed in the nineteenth century. In this design the area below the floor was almost entirely devoted to air circulation. The fresh air entered under the drawing room, was heated by the air heater at "C," and spread throughout the building. Air was extracted through perforated cornices and baseboards, for example at "D" in the sitting and drawing rooms, and drawn from the shallow areas under the rooms through sliding registers at "F" into the main foul air channel "E," and finally to the exhaust stack "A," which was powered by the kitchen stove "K." By this method the ventilation of the water-closet pipes, which ran immediately behind the exhaust stack, was also assured. (From Henry Ruttan, *Ventilation and Warming of Buildings,* New York, 1862.)

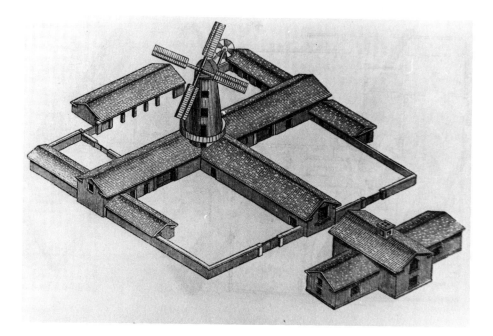

ARCHITECTURE
CONFRONTS
ENVIRONMENTAL
TECHNOLOGY:
AN HISTORICAL
PERSPECTIVE

33

Fig. 15 Design of a farmhouse with the energy source, in this case a windmill, at the center. (From Loudon, *An Encyclopedia of Cottage, Farm, and Villa Architecture*, London, 1833.)

was fascinated by new building technology of every sort. He proposed a farmhouse design in which the energy source, a windmill, was placed at the center of the composition (*Figure 15*). On a much larger scale, he designed a quadrangular complex of 80 cottages which were to be heated by a single fire, a scheme which predated, by decades, Birdshill Holly's first successful district heating. He placed the fire in a building at the center of the quadrangle with the great stack precisely at the crossing of the axes (*Figure 16*).[13]

Other men were interested in alternative ways of servicing buildings. One rudimentary proposal, dating from about 1800, involved the ventilation of a milk house by the use of solar energy (*Figure 17*). A more seriously considered proposal was put forth by Loudon, who, in 1830, published a design for a model cottage which was intended to be as self-sufficient and as energy-conscious as possible. Water was to be collected on the roof, stored in a large cistern, then filtered and pumped into the house. The liquid manure produced by the animals housed in the rear portion of the building was collected in a central cesspool where it was allowed to ferment before being used as fertilizer. Finally, Loudon designed a hypocaust system which he felt would be so efficient that the house could be heated with the wood which could be recovered by each family from one acre of forest land (*Figure 18*). To conserve heat, he stipulated cavity-wall brick construction and avoided north-facing windows and doors.[14]

13. John Claudius Loudon, *An Encyclopedia of Cottage, Farm and Villa Architecture*, London, 1833, with many later editions (hereafter cited as *Architecture Encyclopedia*).
14. Loudon, *Architecture Encyclopedia*, pp. 8–21.

A final example of the exploration of alternative heating and ventilating practices was the work of Edward S. Morse. In 1885 he made public the methods he used to heat and ventilate a room in his house, part of a museum in Salem, and a room at the Boston Athenaeum, using solar energy. His diagram shows that he employed a glass-fronted box-like device which is the earliest known example of a passive "solar-wall" system, a plan that has received renewed attention in the past few years (*Figure 19*).[15]

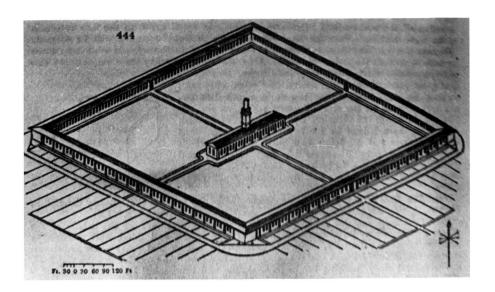

Fig. 16 Loudon's scheme for a quadrangle of 80 cottages heated by a single fire in the center. (From Loudon, *An Encyclopedia of Cottage, Farm, and Villa Architecture*, London, 1833.)

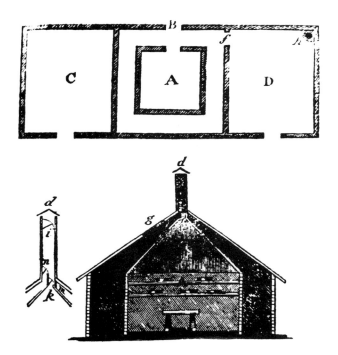

Fig. 17 Scheme for the ventilation of a milk house by solar energy, c. 1800. The interior chamber was to be enclosed in a larger exterior structure and lit by a pair of corresponding windows in the two roofs. The peaks of both gables would lead to a ventilating shaft which was to have three solid sides, but one glass side facing south. Depending on the season, one could regulate dampers in the shaft so that air would be drawn out of the inner room or from the passage around it. The sun shining through the south glazing warms the interior surface of the shaft which, in turn, warms the air, causing it to rise and induce fresh air from openings below. By this method, various combinations of ventilation and temperature control were possible. (From "Practical Remarks on the Management of the Dairy," *Recreations in Agriculture*, vol. 3, 1800.)

Integrating technology and architectural design posed a great many problems. As the new technologies passed out of the rudimentary stage, it became too complicated for the architect alone to design them, and this occasioned the rise of a new design professional, the heating and ventilating engineer. While some architects worked with their new colleagues, a sizable number instead renounced all responsibility in the matter and retreated to the "aesthetic" aspect of their work. In a number of cases, the

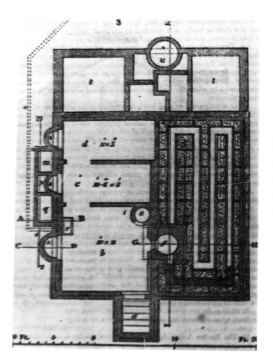

Fig. 18 Basement plan and section I–K of Loudon's model cottage, c. 1830, heated by hypocaust. In this design, the combustion products from the bake oven, "f" in plan, "r" in section, would be channeled through a long series of flues under rooms of the house. The rear rooms were to be used to store grain and to house the farm animals. The large tank, "g," was used to collect rain water from the roofs for use in the cottage. (From Loudon, *An Encyclopedia of Cottage, Farm, and Villa Architecture,* London, 1833.)

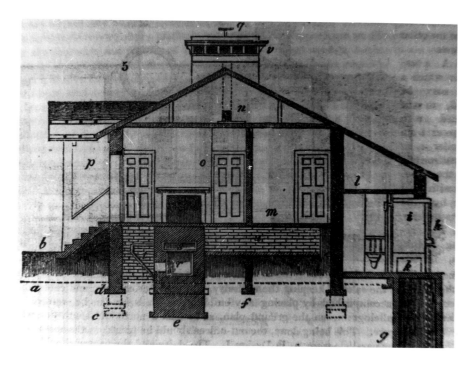

15. Edward S. Morse, *Abstracts of the Society of Arts,* Massachusetts Institute of Technology, Meeting 331, 1885, pp. 115–120.

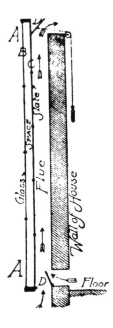

Fig. 19 System of solar heating and ventilation of Edward S. Morse. Morse placed a box with a slate panel (C) and glass front panel (B) several inches from the wall of a building. The area between the wall and the bottom box was vented at the top and bottom into the building interior. By controlling the valves in these passages (D), it was possible to heat or ventilate, or do both at once. When both valves shut off contact with outside air, for example, the air behind the box would be heated, rise, and enter the room near the ceiling, drawing into the flue space the cooler air near the floor.

buildings were designed and even built before a heating contractor was called in to arrange boilers and pipes. As might be expected, the usual result was unsatisfactory to all parties. By mid-century it was realized that the engineer had to be involved from the beginning, but defining his exact role was difficult and often led to disputes.

An extreme example occurred at the new Houses of Parliament in London. The architect, Sir Charles Barry, was at first quite agreeable to working with the independently appointed heating and ventilating engineer, David Boswell Reid. Reid, who had been a successful physician before becoming the prime authority in Europe on ventilation, demanded large amounts of space in the building for his apparatus and called for an enormous central tower to serve as an air intake. Barry agreed to the demands, in fact delighted with this excuse to build yet another tower. For five years Reid and Barry worked together installing thousands of miles of pipe, cavernous air passages, and thousands of valves in what was probably the most ambitious and costly mechanical system of the century.[16]

By 1846, however, tempers began to flare over delays in construction, the high cost of the equipment, and doubts about the compatability of the Reid installations with the fireproofing of the building. Each man had authority over distinct parts of the building. Reid complained that Barry would not allow him to use certain air intake and exhaust channels. Barry stated that Reid systematically removed his structural supports to install ducts, endangering the solidity of the building, and had usurped a full third of the building's cubic footage.

Although Reid has been frequently called the villain in the piece, this opinion was largely the verdict rendered by the architectural press and does not do Reid justice. He was a very competent technician and his methods soon became almost universally accepted. Part of the problem was Reid's difficult

16. On the Houses of Parliament see David Boswell Reid, *Illustrations of the Theory and Practice of Ventilation*, London, 1844 (hereafter cited as *Illustrations*); and the introduction of Reid's *Ventilation In American Dwellings*, New York, 1858. For the other side of the story see Alfred Barry, *Life and Works of Sir Charles Barry*, London, 1867, pp. 161–181; and, more recently, M. H. Port, *The Houses of Parliament*, New Haven, 1976.

personality; part was the scale of the undertaking; probably most important, however, was a fundamental disagreement in goals. Reid sincerely believed, and many of the Members of Parliament were in complete accord, that the primary purpose of the Parliament building was to provide a comfortable interior atmosphere. At one point, he actually called the masonry and wood of the Commons chamber a "piece of apparatus" in his air moving system. Barry obviously could not agree with this startlingly modern, but very narrow, definition of architecture and, backed by the architectural press, he demanded repeatedly that the architect be given unequivocal final authority over all design decisions.[17]

In the end, after years of debate, the authorities finally agreed and Reid departed. This decision was probably a necessary and beneficial step. This incident, while little known, is certainly a very important episode in the consolidation of the architectural profession in the nineteenth century.

The insistence on the primacy of the architect had a side effect, however, the ramifications of which are becoming fully apparent only now: it relegated the engineer to a secondary position. His job became to thread the necessary equipment through the architect's building instead of collaborating on a single unified design. Charles Garnier, architect of the Paris Opera, reported later that his engineer, Hamelincourt, thought of the opera as one long air tube with a wider portion in the middle to accommodate the stage and audience, and battled for every square centimeter of flue section. However, Garnier clearly had ultimate control and the engineer was forced to compromise.[18]

By the late nineteenth century, the new technology had been codified, explained clearly in textbooks, and had entered into architectural training. It enabled the architect to grasp the essentials with relative ease and to establish his role as the head of a team of experts. In the end, the architect found himself more than ever obliged to depend on others for supplying the technical expertise, but he had gained sufficient understanding of it to coordinate the over-all building design. Unfortunately, this process required design standardization which discouraged any fundamental reexamination of the technology. Thus, while the architects and engineers of the early nineteenth century were frequently aware of the problems and challenges presented by their new methods, their very success in meeting these problems allowed their successors to take the technology for granted and to reduce it to pieces of hardware and pages of engineering tabulations.

For much of the later nineteenth century and well into the twentieth, the story of the development of heating and ventilation is essentially the further perfection of techniques introduced by early-nineteenth-century pioneers and the adaptation of the then-established technology to changing architectural forms. The increasingly sophisticated equipment and abundant energy sup-

17. Reid, *Illustrations*, p. 275.
18. Charles Garnier, *Le Nouvel Opera de Paris*, Paris, 1870–71, p. 118.

plies allowed designers to build ever larger, more complex, but also inefficient and poorly oriented, buildings. The story of twentieth-century architecture follows this progressive abolition of traditional environmental design restraints, always achieved, however, with a compensating increase in the building's energy requirements.

With the energy crunch of recent years, the immediate reaction was to apply new layers of technology on top of existing ones, perhaps because the lessons of the nineteenth century had been so well accepted and assimilated. More complicated zoning, computers, flat-plate solar collectors, and heat pumps are being developed as technical ''add-ons'' to existing systems. However, these rote assumptions about the relationship between technology and architecture are being questioned. Designers are faced with many of the same questions of basic design which confronted the architects of the early nineteenth century. It remains to be seen if contemporary architects can grasp the essentials of environmental and energy imperatives and respond to the new formal and aesthetic challenges that they offer.

Further Notes

The history of modern central heating and mechanical ventilation remains to be written. The heating and ventilation textbooks of the nineteenth century invariably contained a good section on history. Excellent examples can be found in Eugene Péclet, *Traité de la Chaleur,* Paris, 1828, and later editions; Morill Wyman, *Practical Treatise on Ventilation,* London, 1846; Charles Tomlinson, *Rudimentary Treatise on Warming and Ventilation,* London, 1850; and John S. Billings, *Ventilation and Heating,* New York, 1893. This historical consciousness has been completely lost by writers of engineering texts in the twentieth century, however. No one in this century has more than scratched the surface in compiling the available information. Several articles, including A. E. Dufton, ''Early Application of Engineering to the Warming of Buildings,'' *Newcomen Society Transactions,* vol. 21, pp. 90–107; N. S. Billington, ''A Historical Review of Heating and Ventilation,'' *Architectural Science Review,* vol. 2, pp. 118–130; *Home Fires Burning,* Lawrence Wright, London, 1964; as well as a section in Maurice Daumas, *Histoire Générale des Techniques,* Paris, 1968, deal with the subject, but in very summary fashion. More important is Eugene Ferguson's, ''A Historical Sketch of Central Heating 1800–1860,'' in *Building Early America,* Charles Peterson, ed., Philadelphia, 1976. The most important studies of the subject have come from architectural historians treating specific building types. The most notable are the excellent chapters in John Hix, *The Glass House,* London, 1974; Jennifer Tann, *The Development of the Factory,* London, 1970; and Mark Girouard, *The Victorian Country House,* Oxford, 1971.

3

OBSERVATIONS ON ENERGY USE IN BUILDINGS

Richard G. Stein

This chapter is adapted from an article of the same title from the *Journal of Architectural Education,* February 1977, and summarizes topics discussed in detail in Richard G. Stein: *Architecture and Energy: Conserving Energy through Rational Design,* Anchor Press/Doubleday, New York, 1977.

ENERGY
CONSERVATION
THROUGH
BUILDING
DESIGN

The idea propagated at the end of World War II—that we were on the threshold of a period in which humankind would be set free from traditional restraints imposed by natural systems—was a very heady idea; the Icarus legend brought up to date. It has resulted, in the last 25 years, in a decided direction in the path that architects were to follow. The architectural press, the critics, the schools, all encouraged an architecture that was different for its own sake and in many ways diametrically opposite to the view that had shaped the new architecture of the 1920s, '30s and '40s. Brought with it was a marked difference in the energy performance of buildings—in the amount of heating, cooling, lighting, ventilation, and other mechanically controlled environmental conditions on which the buildings depended to achieve human comfort. The figures that resulted from this approach to building design are indeed alarming, particularly in view of their implications in terms of depletable resources; an increasingly polluted environment; the exhaustion of vast acreage of land for coal strip-mines and of seabeds and ocean-front for oil and gas exploration and depots— all in order to have energy to operate our buildings.

This chapter will point out the misuse and overuse of energy in all areas of building construction to demonstrate that there are options available for across-the-board reduction in energy use through building design and operation that far exceed, in cost effectiveness, the potential of new energy technologies that might be developed during the next quarter-century. More importantly, these options apply as much to existing buildings as to new ones.

To understand the problem, consider high-rise office buildings, probably the most characteristic building form of the post–World War II era. In the past decades, the average requirement for energy use within these buildings has more than doubled, while there has been no fundamental change in the way business is carried on inside. In fact, in New York and other large cities, the same kinds of activities are carried on equally effectively or ineffectively in buildings that may have been built 50 years apart. The oldest building has the same kind of corporate tenant as its recently completed neighbors.

When New York City was faced with continuing brown-outs and limited electricity to supply its buildings, John Lindsay, mayor at the time, established a bureau to look into the energy problems in the city's buildings, and Dr. Charles Lawrence, an engineer and conscientious student of energy use in buildings, was appointed public utility specialist. With the assistance of the New York City Real Estate Board, questionnaires were sent to the owners of 180 buildings built since World War II, primarily in the two decades from 1950 to 1970.[1] The owners were requested to indicate the amount of energy from electricity and other sources, such as steam, oil, or coal, that went into the heating and cooling of their buildings. These figures were related to the square feet of rentable space and the total square feet within the building, and

1. D. E. Abrahamson, and S. Emmings, eds.: *Energy Conservation: Implications for Building Design and Operation: Conference Proceedings,* University of Minnesota, May 1973.

then compared on the basis of energy per gross square foot. The results give an indication of how buildings really function and what the range is in their energy demand. The basis for the study was the 86 questionnaires which were returned. The figures were all end-use figures, and it is necessary to apply certain conversion factors to understand their true source-energy use. (All of the studies conducted by my office have gone back to source use, since ultimately, if the same end-use energy can be provided by several interchangeable means, the efficiency of the energy *producer* is decisive. This is particularly true when applied to electric heating as opposed to heating with other sources. After a building's heat load has been determined, electric heat requires almost four times that amount at the generating plant, while a fossil fuel burner may require 1½ to 2 times that amount.)

In the study of New York City office buildings, the results are as follows (with kilowatt hours tabulated at 3,412 Btu/kWh). In the first five years covered in the survey, 1950 through 1954, converting figures back to Btu per square foot per year, there was an average of 50,500 Btu of electricity and 78,400 Btu of steam for heating—for a total energy use of 128.9 thousand Btu/ft². In the subsequent five-year period from 1955 to 1959, electricity required 56,300 Btu, and steam 108,100 Btu, for a total of 164,400 Btu—an increase of 40,000 Btu/ft² over the previous five years. In the third five-year period there was an additional jump. Electricity now consumed 60,400 Btu and steam 154,100 Btu for a total of 214,500 Btu. In the fourth five-year period, from 1965 through 1969, electricity had gone up to 78,400 Btu/ft², and steam 188,000, for a total of 266,400 Btu/ft², making it obvious that the total energy use in this period had more than doubled.

If we consider the source energy necessary for the electricity, the figures are even more startling. (The figures are based on Con Edison's heat rate of about 12,500 Btu/kWh with no added factor for transmission losses.) Of the four five-year periods, the first used a total of 263,400 Btu/ft²; 1955 to 1959 required 314,400; and 1965 through 1969, 553,900 Btu/ft². The last figure is the equivalent of 3.8 gallons of oil per square foot per year. With these figures and oil costs currently in the neighborhood of 50¢ a gallon and rising, it is not surprising that there is concern about the cost of energy use in these buildings, not to speak of the moral question of why such extravagance has entered the building process itself and why it is tolerated. What is more disturbing, however, is that the figures given are averages. By no means are they the most extreme examples of excessive energy use.

Of all the buildings considered in the Lawrence study, the greatest energy use reported was 403,000 Btu/ft²/year of on-site energy use. The lowest was 72,000 Btu. Thus, the highest energy use is 5½ times the lowest. It must be remembered that these are office buildings that serve approximately the same kinds of use and a common building type in the same climate area. The difference in energy use could be considered to result from the physical design solutions and the methods of using the buildings. If one uses the figure for source energy for electricity, the total energy requirement for the building approximately doubles. Applying that rule of thumb to the figures in the published reports (since these figures are not broken down into steam and electricity, nor is the source of the steam identified), one can assume that the high-energy user uses 800,000 Btu/ft², or 5½ gallons of oil per square foot per year.

To understand these statistics it is necessary to specify the ways in which buildings use energy. Each building type has a characteristic pattern, but each building varies within it. *Figure 1* summarizes the findings of a detailed study commissioned by the New York State Office of General Services to see what could be done to reduce energy use in two existing state-owned office buildings.[2] Typical of many buildings built in the 1960s, they have undifferentiated facades, regardless of orientation. One building has a glass and aluminum curtain-wall skin, the other a glass, aluminum, and face-brick facade. The glazing in each case is tinted, single-thickness glass in inoperative windows (opened only for window cleaning). Both have about 100 to 110 footcandles (fc) of uniform distributed light produced by lighting installations that vary around 4 watts/ft². Both buildings have terminal reheat systems—that is, systems that add heat to super-chilled air in order to modify it to the varying temperature requirements in different parts of the building. Each building contains about 600,000 ft² in total area. One building has a square plan with about an acre of floor space per floor and a height of 12 stories; the other has about 100,000 ft² per floor for five stories. Both have additional usable space below grade.

Figure 1 gives their energy use in millions of gallons of oil equivalent. The source energy to generate the electricity is computed in Btu, which is then converted to equivalent gallons of oil at 146,000 Btu/gal, whether the electricity is used directly in the building or in the central boiler plant, which also houses the central electric chillers. This is added to the actual oil burned in the boiler plant to produce steam, prorated to the two buildings.

Both buildings operate within the energy use limits of the typical office buildings built in New York City during a comparable five-year period as described in the Lawrence study. Both buildings are located in Albany, which has a slightly colder winter, but a summer temperature comparable to that of New York City. They are representative of neither the most efficient nor the most extravagant of the buildings built. In other words, they can be considered typical, average buildings of their type.

Electricity is by far the largest energy user when one goes back to source energy. Chilled water is provided by electric compressors at the central mechanical plant. The rest of the electricity is utilized at the building. Of all of the electricity, well over half of

2. Pope, Evans, and Robbins, Inc., with Richard G. Stein and Associates: "Energy Conservation Study: State Office Building Campus, Buildings 8 and 12," 1975.

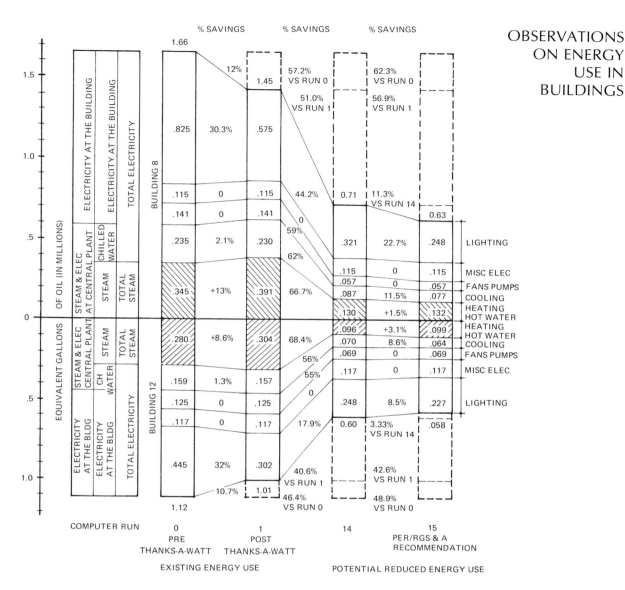

Fig. 1 Annual energy use and potential energy savings in million gallons of source-energy fuel oil (shaded areas represent anticipated savings).

it (in fact, half of all energy) goes into the lighting in one building; in the other about 40% of total energy is in the lighting system.

The state-instituted energy conservation program on its own— turning off some of the lights, being more disciplined in the way the systems were used—has resulted in a 12% energy savings in one case and 10% in the other. However, in analyzing the buildings more closely, it was found that even this significant savings is but the tip of the iceberg. With a time of less than two years to pay back the capital costs with savings, one of them could have a further reduction of 57% and the other an additional reduction of 42%. With a longer payback time, there are other

ENERGY
CONSERVATION
THROUGH
BUILDING
DESIGN

things that can be done to further reduce conventional energy requirements by an additional 7% or 8%, such as introducing double glazing, adding solar collectors and removing the ballasts in the lamps that have been deactivated.

When one looks to see how energy is used, one finds that, as the building systems now operate, the skin of a building is not the greatest consumer, but is responsible only for a little less than a quarter of the total requirements as represented by the heating load (which also includes heating for the terminal reheat systems). Cooling requires about 14%, mostly to remove internally generated heat. Thus, the improvement of the thermal performance of the wall alone does not produce the largest savings.

Before proposing a more rational energy use, one must understand what has become characteristic in this kind of building. Over the last 20 years, the mechanical systems have required a constantly increasing share of the total building dollar. As architects have simplified the facade of the building, complex mechanical systems have increasingly become more extensive and expensive, to compensate for the less selective performance of the skin. If one designs a building with a more sophisticated and differentiated skin, based on its orientation and climatic performance, the additional cost in architectural work and construction work is often far less than the savings achieved by being able to reduce the size of the mechanical system. From our recent office experience, with only a slight increase in cost for the skin of college buildings, the mechanical plant—the size of the steam boilers, electrical generating capacity, and number of tons of refrigeration required—was reduced by 20% to 40% below those normally estimated, based on previous experience of buildings with similar area and volume.

Further, if only the thermal performance of the skin is considered to be the determinant of energy use in the buildings, the assumption is commonly made that the minimum-surface building, which has the least area for energy transfer, will be the most energy efficient. But of these two buildings, Building 12, which has a considerably larger surface area, starts out with about two-thirds the energy use of the building that more nearly resembles a cube, the difference attributable, in part, to reduced electric lighting energy required with proper use of natural illumination.

After all the easily available energy reductions have been made, they will both use about the same amount of energy per square foot—in source energy, almost exactly the equivalent of one gallon of oil, or roughly 150,000 Btu/ft²/year, including electricity. If one converts back to end-use on-site energy, this is in the neighborhood of 70,000 to 75,000 Btu.

Now let us look at the statistics on household electrical use. Starting with 1959 United States figures, there were about 180 billion kWh sold for residential use by about 50,400,000 customers. This means that each residential customer bought an average of 3,570 kWh of electricity a year. In 15 years the amount of electricity sold for residential use has tripled. The number of families served has increased 40%, but the use per family has increased by 100%, bringing the current total to about 555 billion kWh/year.

Investigations of other building types—stores, hospitals, recreational facilities, schools—all demonstrate similar increases in energy dependency in the short periods bounded by the last two decades.

Fig. 2 Current energy use in school buildings and anticipated savings.

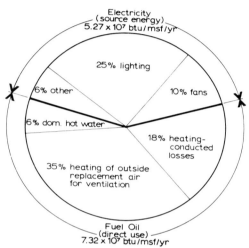

2a   Present energy use pattern.

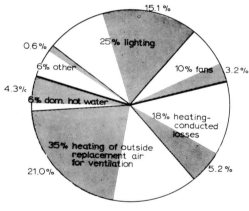

2b   Projected savings (new buildings), 49.4% total.

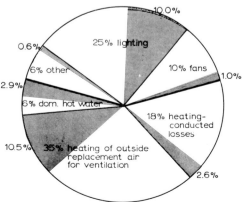

2c   Projected savings (retrofit), 27.7% total.

ENERGY
CONSERVATION
THROUGH
BUILDING
DESIGN

In a recent study, the energy use in some thousand schools in the New York City school system was analyzed in detail.[3] General statistics were studied and a number of buildings examined extensively. The educational standards and requirements that determined the level of services were reexamined to ascertain whether the kinds of installations called for were required for effective performance of the school function.

There were some significant results of this study (*Figure 2*). First, school buildings in New York City have a characteristic energy use and distribution of energy requirements different from either the typical office building or schools in other areas, particularly those dependent on air conditioning. Second, the New York City schools operate on a lower use of energy per square foot than do schools in any other area we examined. The average amount of source energy for all the schools was approximately 125,000 Btu/ft² for all purposes. This figure, based on present operation, is a little less than a gallon of oil per square foot per year.

In Figure 2, showing the distribution of uses, it can be seen that lighting represents about 65% of electrical usage, but in this case it is only about 40% of total usage. Of the remaining 60%, which is used for heating directly, more than half is used to heat outside air to replace the air that is exhausted for ventilation code requirements. About half as much is expended to make up the heat lost through the walls and roof of the building, and, of course, from infiltration at doors and other openings. About 6% in total is used for domestic hot water. Half of this energy use is unnecessary in new buildings and at least one-fourth can be readily eliminated in existing buildings.

These specific findings may have general implications: in investigating lighting we found that the lighting that was specified and provided did not perform as designated. In the newer schools, uniform lighting levels of 60 to 70 fc were designed. In actuality, the contribution of outside light through the windows creates enormous light-level variations, in some cases as high as 1,500 fc near the windows and as low as 12 fc at the far corner of the room. This more than 100:1 light-level differential was not noticed by the people in the room, nor was it found to be disturbing to them.

The schools had a typical oil and electrical use curve that was characteristic of almost all the schools. The only school that varied sharply was a windowless school, presumably with very efficient mechanical systems and high thermal performance in the walls and roof. Yet, it required more than twice the average electrical requirement because of the necessity for using mechanical systems and lighting at all times during building use. This underscores an important point that runs counter to a good deal of current practice: a building that uses its mechanical systems only when natural methods are inadequate will, in general, be more economical in energy use than a building that

3. Richard G. Stein, and Carl Stein: "Low Energy Utilization School," Report for Board of Education, City of New York, NSF-RANN Grant GI-39612, 1974.

is always completely dependent on mechanical systems for its light, air, heating, and cooling.

We examined the success of the schools' education when light levels were increased by checking some 30,000 reading achievement scores over a period of six years, both in schools that had their light levels increased and in schools that were unchanged through the six-year period. The results indicated a lack of correlation between increased light levels and academic performance. This agrees with observed information from England on light levels, and is consistent with pre-fluorescent standards that recommended 20 to 30 fc as being adequate for classroom work.

Using existing buildings as laboratories is particularly instructive since so much of our overuse of energy has been institutionalized in codes, recommendations, and high-technology solutions to what are, in fact, low-technology or no-technology problems.

Since what we are seeking is a realistic basis for evaluating the alternatives available for energy conservation in buildings, we must understand the potential contribution and limitations of new solar technology, such as the flat-plate collector, which in the public mind has become the most visible and attractive symbol of good ecological intentions and of the way to solve our energy problems. To gauge its potential, a study was carried out wherein a number of assumptions were made for the most optimistic "scenario" that one could expect for the implementation of solar technology for buildings.[4] These included incentives of government support, funding, and compatibility with existing construction and mechanical systems, all of which might result in the maximum possible use of solar-collector technology within a 10-year period.

The assumptions made based on the most optimistic situation were as follows. Solar collectors will be installed on single-family and low-rise residences, including 25% of existing houses and 50% of new houses. They will provide 75% of the total heat requirement of these houses and have, on the average, a collector area equal to 50% of the heated floor space. The total installed cost for new residences is assumed to be $20/ft² of collector for new residences and $25/ft² for existing structures; this price includes all piping, storage, and controls. At the end of 10 years, 25 million out of 75 million housing units will be so equipped. The total installation cost required is $345 billion for the 15 billion ft² of collectors, assuming constant 1976 dollars.

Now what will the results be? Approximately 20% of our total national energy use is used directly for fossil fuel heating and hot water, about 60% of which is used for residential purposes. Thus, 12% of our total energy use becomes the target for the solar substitute that we have just described, which if used on one-third of all residential units, ends up to be one-third of 12%, or 4%. If 75% of the energy requirements of these units will be provided by the solar installations, the potential fossil fuel energy reduction becomes 3% of the total.

4. Center for Advanced Computation, University of Illinois, and Richard G. Stein and Associates: "Energy in Building Construction," Report of Study under ERDA Contract E(11-1)-2791, December 1976.

Let us project a very low figure for the estimated increase in national energy use—10% in the next 10 years. We can then conclude that if the introduction of solar-collector technology is the only energy shift we achieve, and if we do not make some drastic changes in the basic way we use energy in buildings, we would only be 7% worse off at that time than we are now, instead of 10%.

Figure 3 indicates other possibilities that are readily available for energy savings in building and in that part of industry that serves it. As shown in "Bar Graph A" of Figure 3, basic divisions of total energy use in the United States are: source energy for electrical generation, 25%; transportation, 25%; heating and hot water, 20%; and direct use of fossil fuel in industry, 30%. In addition, a part of the electrical figure represents industrial use of electricity. Approximately 40% of electric energy generation sold is in a category listed as "Commercial and Industrial Large Light and Power"; not included in these figures is an additional use of electricity, generated by industry for its own use.

This summary describes only the energy use that results from the systems that are built into buildings and does not include optional energy use resulting from electrical accessories, gadgets, television sets, or even such necessities as refrigerators and ranges. The statistics refer only to systems that are incorporated into building construction—heating systems, cooling systems, ventilating systems, vertical transportation systems, and pumps and motors that operate such features as water supply and sewage. Included, of course, are the lighting systems, which are very large energy users. Our investigations indicate further that, of the total industrial energy use, 6.25% is the energy used by the new-building construction industry, which is significant in the analysis of energy embodied in building construction, as discussed in detail in Chapter 10.

A certain amount is also used in each category either through the construction of buildings or through their operation and maintenance: over 15% of industrial, all of the heating, about 50% of electrical, and possibly 20% of the transportation (which may be considered to result from the way buildings are built and located, making necessary an excessive use of the automobile in order for people to take care of their shopping needs, their travel to and from business, jobs, schools, and such).

"Bar Graph B" in Figure 3 consolidates all of these building-related energy uses, not including the secondary energy use for transportation. We find that almost 40% of the total national energy budget is committed through the building process. Shown hatched in each of the categories is the amount that can be eliminated through readily available conservation techniques and through the widespread introduction of solar heating. Solar heating must be considered as having a considerably longer lead time for installation; nevertheless, we are now grouping these together

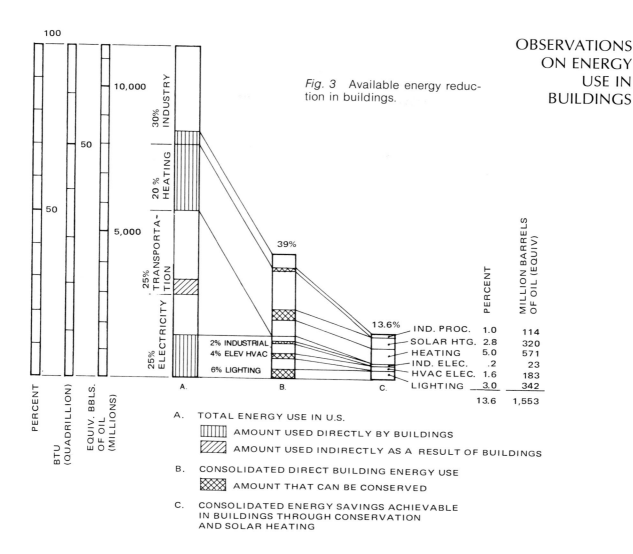

Fig. 3 Available energy reduction in buildings.

	PERCENT	MILLION BARRELS OF OIL (EQUIV)
IND. PROC.	1.0	114
SOLAR HTG.	2.8	320
HEATING	5.0	571
IND. ELEC.	.2	23
HVAC ELEC.	1.6	183
LIGHTING	3.0	342
	13.6	1,553

2% INDUSTRIAL
4% ELEV HVAC
6% LIGHTING

A. TOTAL ENERGY USE IN U.S.
  ||||||| AMOUNT USED DIRECTLY BY BUILDINGS
  ///// AMOUNT USED INDIRECTLY AS A RESULT OF BUILDINGS

B. CONSOLIDATED DIRECT BUILDING ENERGY USE
  XXXX AMOUNT THAT CAN BE CONSERVED

C. CONSOLIDATED ENERGY SAVINGS ACHIEVABLE
  IN BUILDINGS THROUGH CONSERVATION
  AND SOLAR HEATING

and we find that 13.6% of the *entire* present energy use can be eliminated rapidly, assuming a desire to do it and the cooperation of the American people.

Over one-third of the energy now directly used through the building process can be dispensed with, as evidenced by the studies described above. This is the equivalent of 9.5 quadrillion Btu of national energy use. If this amount of end-use energy were produced electrically, it would require 520 1,000-megawatt (MW) electrical plants. In other words, if we produced a new 1,000-MW electrical plant every two weeks for the next 20 years, we would achieve the same end result, except that the amount of site damage, resource exhaustion, and environmental degradation that would go with the production of electricity would be entirely eliminated simply by pursuing the course of energy-use reduction that is available to us in building design and use.

To reestablish perspective, we must look at United States figures in their global context. There are about 210 million people in the United States. The accepted world population in 1970 was 3¾ billion. Of these, 210 million people use 70 million billion Btu (or 70 quads). The rest of the 3¾ billion use 130 quads. Individually, on the average, the people in the United States each use about 333 million Btu/year compared with an average per capita in the rest of the world of about 39 million Btu, about one-ninth as much. Our measure of 1 million Btu does not represent much energy. It will produce and deliver only about 90 kWh of electricity for instance, and 90 kWh of electricity is less than 1/50th of the average American's yearly electrical purchase and less than 1/250th of the average heating bill of an electrically heated house.

After the United States has used 35% of the world's energy, not everyone who is left participates equally in the remaining 65%. For example, let us consider the underdeveloped countries with their population of 2¾ billion—about two-thirds the total population of the world. Their combined total energy use is 34 quads—about half of the total energy that is used in the United States—and the per capita energy use based on 1969 figures is about 12 million Btu/year, compared with about 333 million in the United States—about 1/30th as much. These are average figures which means, of course, that many countries and millions of families are operating with considerably less energy per capita.

This is not energy that is expended by the individual. It includes all of the manufacturing uses, all of the non-personal transport uses, all of the energy lost in the generation of electricity, all of the energy to maintain and keep military and governmental apparatuses operating. After these uses have been prorated to the individuals and subtracted from the average of the 12 million Btu per person per year, the remainder can be considered available for personal use—light, heat, transportation, cooling, hot water, refrigeration, and such.

Moreover, we know that the prevailing pattern in all the countries that are experiencing the most rapid growth is that virtually all of the new population settles in cities or forms new cities, and that problems of housing and building are compounded by the greater complexity of services required in the first shift from rural living to urban living. The rural dwelling can provide basic shelter through the use of available local materials. If there is a potable water supply—a spring or a clean stream—and enough distance between structures, the primary sanitary provisions will have been met. While lighting systems, refrigeration, and sewage disposal are desirable, they are not absolutely essential for survival. However, when an individual or family moves to a city or becomes a part of a new, closely integrated community, a number of additional necessities will have to be provided—a central water and sewage system, some means of transportation, fuel for cooking, a method of disposing of solid waste, and desirably, an access to electricity. All of these requirements increase the base amount of energy per capita so that even more is required for new populations than for the stabilized population in these areas of the world.

Realizing this, what is imperative is not the further development of gadgetry, but a fundamental reassessment of how we can live, how we can develop a life style that will not be based on the deprivations of vast areas of the rest of the world where, as in the United States, there are still enormous building requirements which must be provided for simply and beautifully.

We must now address the problem as one requiring a different method and scale of building. I think the ultimate result will be a subtle enrichment of the quality and texture of our lives, a reintroduction into the cities of the desirable characteristics being lost through our overscale construction and energy profligacy. Redirecting our architectural objectives to solve these new problems is our major task today.

4

HOW AND WHY BUILDINGS USE ENERGY

Lawrence G. Spielvogel

Portions of this chapter are taken from articles by the author that previously appeared in *ASHRAE Journal,* January 1974 and *Architectural Record,* February 1976.

The one factor that, more than any other, determines energy consumption of a building is how it is used. How it is used has more impact than the type or capacity of the HVAC system, or the boilers, or the chillers, or the energy source; more than how much glass, or insulation, or lighting a building has. It is the people who occupy a building that place the demands on systems that use energy. It is the *hours of operation* of systems and components that are the major determinant of energy consumption. What runs most of the time and typically at full load? Prime examples are lighting, fans, and pumps. In many buildings the

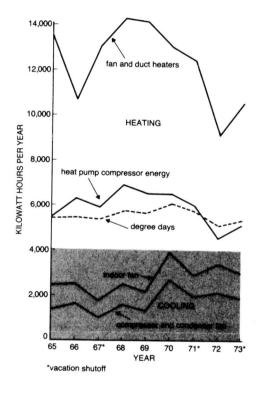

Fig. 1 Annual variation in heating and cooling energy use for a single-family house with heat pump.

fans and pumps use more energy in a year than the chillers do.

While such statements may sound obvious, their reality is often ignored in many studies and projections of building energy use. Comparisons of buildings on the basis of installed capacities of HVAC, lighting, and other electrical equipment can be misleading, because the quantity of energy used is not necessarily related either to design load or to installed equipment capacity.

The importance of the "occupant" factor is demonstrated by studies on energy use by Princeton University in "what would appear to be identical dwellings" showing that during a given period of time, "a ratio of better than 2:1 in energy consumption exists between the highest and lowest users."[1]

Furthermore, energy use can vary widely from year to year in dwellings, as demonstrated by *Figure 1*, which shows metered energy for heating and cooling of a single-family dwelling in Indiana over a nine-year period.

1. David T. Harrje, et al.: "Residential Eenergy Conservation: The Twin-Rivers Project," *ASHRAE Transactions*, part 1 (1977).

Only a Small Fraction of Annual Energy Use Occurs During the Extremes of Weather

Most energy use in buildings occurs when the outdoor temperatures are moderate, which means that the HVAC systems operate at part load most of the time. Only a small fraction of the energy use occurs during temperature extremes.

Take a hypothetical building located in Washington, DC. In *Figure 2,* the lowest curve shows the load; heating, lighting, cooling, call it what you will. As you would expect, there is a peak at around 100F and at around 0F, and the load in between is less. The middle curve shows the number of hours in a year at these outdoor temperatures in the Washington, DC metropolitan area. You can see that, for most of the year, the temperature is between 30F and 70F. What is energy in this case? "Energy" is shown in Figure 2 as the product of load times hours, the top curve in the figure. It shows that virtually two-thirds of the annual energy consumption occurs when outdoor temperatures are between 30F and 70F.

As designers and owners of buildings, we have been concerned about how efficient our boilers and chillers are when it is 0F or

Fig. 2 Annual energy consumption for a house in Washington, DC as a function of load.

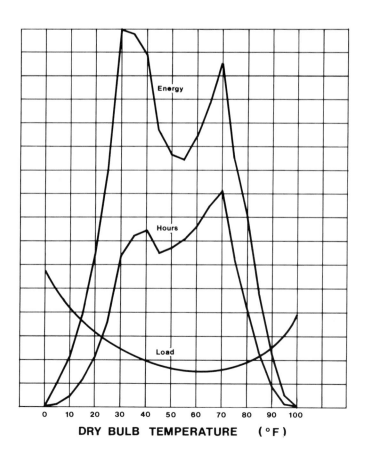

DRY BULB TEMPERATURE (°F)

100F outside. We should care little about how equipment performs at these temperatures, because, theoretically, these conditions exist for only one hour per year. When is most of the energy used? When it is between 30F and 70F outside, because those temperatures occur during most of the hours each year. We should be far more concerned about how efficiently our buildings and their systems operate when it is 50F, because that is when the energy is used—when these intermediate conditions exist. Designers are always concerned about making sure that the boilers and chillers are big enough to meet extreme conditions. But, from an energy standpoint, they should be looked at in a totally different way: what happens in the middle? What happens when the building is operating under a light load? That is when the energy is used.

When looking at the energy consumption in a building, one has to discriminate between those items of equipment that will be used frequently and those that will not. The best way to describe this is with the term "load factor." Load factor is a convenient way of describing how much anything is used. A 1,000-watt light bulb used 724 hours per month gives a 100% load factor. But in an office building, chances are that that light bulb will only be used 200 or 300 hours per month, giving a load factor of 30% or 40%. When evaluating energy use, it is most beneficial to analyze those energy-consuming items that have the highest load factors.

Space Allocation Directly Affects Efficiency of Energy-Using Systems in Buildings

Some of the most significant decisions affecting eventual energy use of a building are made in the very early programming stage. Energy use is important enough to be included as one of the criteria in the spatial organization of buildings. This means, for example, that particular attention must be paid to spaces that have only part-time occupancy, such as conference rooms and auditoriums, and to spaces that are used around the clock, such as computer rooms.

A recent study[2] on the energy use of 50 office buildings in Philadelphia concluded that, "the single most important finding is that the variables most affecting energy consumption are the extent and type of building use, as determined . . . by presence or absence of computers, data-processing equipment and support facilities," in which case the energy use was 50% higher than buildings without this equipment.

Virtually every one of these buildings was designed without thought being given to where computers would be located. While most of the 50% premium in energy use can be attributed to the computers and their air conditioning, the fact that support facilities have to be provided for people working in these facilities is of major significance.

2. Enviro-Management and Research, Inc.: "Energy Consumption in Commercial Buildings in Philadelphia," National Electrical Manufacturers Association, New York, 1975.

ENERGY
CONSERVATION
THROUGH
BUILDING
DESIGN

Most office-related energy systems are operated for 50 to 60 hours a week, while most computers are used for as much as 168 hours a week (24 hours a day). This means that it is necessary to provide lighting in the lobby, stairwells, corridors, lounges, and toilet rooms, as well as elevator service, vending machines, and so forth, for people working in these facilities. It may be necessary to provide almost as much energy for these services in the "spine" of the building as when the building is fully occupied.

There have been cases where computer rooms occupying less than 10% of the floor space of an office building consumed more than two-thirds of the annual electricity.

Big Variations in Energy Budgets Can Result From Changes In Design and Operation

Strikingly, studies of projected energy usage in buildings, using commonly accepted design practices, have shown variations as high as 5:1 or even 10:1, depending upon the systems selected and their operation.

While this is not usual, it is relatively easily to demonstrate variations on the order of 2:1, as in *Table 1* which lists energy budgets for a variety of system design and operations options for a proposed office building.[3] Some of the items having significant impact in this example include amount of ventilation air, hours of fan operation, and control and capacity of perimeter radiation.

Even in buildings having reasonable energy consumption, it is

TABLE 1

Energy Use Variations with Alternate Designs for a Three-Story Building

Alternatives	Estimated gas use, Mcf	Equivalent electricity MkWh	Approximate energy budget Btu/ft²/year
1* Base case 0.1 cfm/ft²	10,127	2,415	73,400
2* Increased ventilation air	12,913	2,498	85,800
3 Single glass used	14,287	2,515	91,500
4* 68F-winter (20% relative humidity), 80F-summer	7,324	2,226	59,700
5* Heat recovery	9,165	2,856	75,700
6 Only 75% perimeter radiation installed	8,949	2,396	68,500
7 Modular radiation control	6,729	2,353	59,000
8 Perimeter radiation shutoff at night	6,749	2,356	59,200
9 Heat off over 50F	8,799	2,364	67,500
10* Reduced operation of air handlers	9,005	2,388	68,600
11* Increased operation of air handlers	17,851	2,869	110,600
12* Combined features	4,715	2,240	49,400

This table gives energy budgets for a three-story building with a central chilled-water system and a steam boiler, with a medium-velocity, variable-air-volume air-distribution system and perimeter radiation.
*1. The base case assumes the use of double glazing. 2. Ventilation air is increased to 0.25 cfm.
4. Base case (1) assumes 72F in winter and 75F in summer. 5. Heat recovery used, economy cycle (viz, outdoor air used for cooling) is turned off. 10. Startup is delayed until 8:00 am, and the system is shut off at 5:00 pm, reducing operation by three hours. 11. The air-handling system is operated 24 hours a day, but outside air is shut off when the building is unoccupied. 12. Several of the energy-saving features are combined. They are not cumulative however, so energy saved is somewhat less than the sum total.

3. Lawrence G. Spielvogel: "Computer Energy Analysis for Existing Buildings," *ASHRAE Journal,* August 1975.

possible to find further substantial reductions as demonstrated by *Table 2*. This 1 million ft² building has a perimeter induction system and interior zone reheat, and during one particular year had a measured energy consumption of about 70,000 Btu/ft²/year. Through a combination of design, operational, and schedule changes, computer simulation indicated a possible reduction of 20%.

TABLE 2

Effects of Design, Operation and Schedule Changes on a Million Square Foot Building

	Annual energy use/ft²					Percent savings		
	kWh	Btu	Steam (lb)	Btu	Total Btu	Heat	Cool	Elec
1 Building as is	7.9	26,963	42.3	42,300	69,263	0.0	0.0	0.0
2* Schedule changes								
a) 4-day week	7.7	26,280	40.3	40,300	66,580	8.5	3.7	3.4
b) daylight time	7.9	26,963	41.6	41,600	68,563	−1.6	4.3	0.3
3* Temperatures								
76-65F vs. 80-70F	7.9	26,963	39.2	39,200	66,163	30.5	−4.2	0.4
4 Skin changes								
double glass	7.9	26,963	40.4	40,400	67,363	14.0	1.1	0.0
5* Air system changes								
a) reduced airflow	6.3	21,502	40.8	40,800	62,302	−4.3	11.8	20.6
b) vav + recirculate								
primary air	6.7	22,867	39.7	39,700	62,567	1.9	14.6	16.1
6* Central plant changes						Steam		
a) base-load 500-ton chiller	7.6	25,939	38.2	38,200	64,139	9.7		4.5
b) electric 500-ton chiller	8.2	27,987	27.6	27,600	55,587	35.0		−3.2
c) electric 200-ton chiller	7.9	26,963	32.5	32,500	59,463	23.0		0.2
7 Combination of reduced airflow + recirculation + base-load 500-ton chiller	6.0	20,478	35.6	35,600	56,078	16.0		25.0

The values in the table are the results of a computer analysis of an existing building with steam-turbine cooling.
*2a. Energy savings due primarily to reduction in number of startup and shutdown hours per week.
2b. Daylight saving time reduced cooling energy but required more heating energy due to a one-hour earlier startup in mornings and the heating of ventilation air. The extra heating energy almost cancelled the cooling-energy saving. 3. Saving achieved by setting thermostat in winter at 65F instead of 76F, and 80F in summer instead of 70F. 5a. Savings due to reduction of air flow on both perimeter and interior systems to match actual load. 5b. Savings due to replacement of interior reheat coils with variable-air-volume boxes, and recirculating primary air for perimeter induction system in excess of that required for ventilation alone. 6. The central chilled-water plant consists of small, medium (500-ton), and large turbine-driven chillers. The medium-size chiller was used for the base load. Three of the alternatives included: 1) base loading the 500-ton turbine chiller; 2) substituting a 500-ton electric base-load chiller; and 3) installing a 200-ton electric base-load chiller.

Energy Budgets

In the process of determining how a building uses energy, how much it uses, and how it compares with other buildings in the same category, the term "energy budget" arises. An energy budget is a description of how much energy a building uses. The most common definition of the energy budget is the Btu in the purchased fuel plus the Btu in the purchased electricity, divided by the square footage of the building. For a new federal office building, which is a unique class of building, the General Services Administration suggests that a design target should be 55,000 Btu/ft²/

year, and for existing buildings, 75,000 Btu/ft²/year.[4] However, if one looks at the energy budget for an actual office building, it is generally found to be operating at between 75,000 and 500,000 Btu/ft²/year. Most office buildings fall in the range of 100,000 to 200,000 Btu/ft²/year.

Many other types of buildings are far more energy intensive. Most food service operations use 300,000 to 500,000 Btu/ft²/year, while research laboratories can use from 500,000 to 1,000,000. Energy budgets cover a wide range.

A word of caution, though, about interpretations and inferences, drawn from reported measured data (annual energy budgets). Good-quality energy consumption data and adequate information on buildings and their use is difficult and expensive to obtain. Scarcely any buildings are monitored by anything more than a single kWh meter, and bills for fuel oil, gas, or steam. Seldom are individual pieces of equipment metered. For these reasons, when reported data is being used as a basis for comparison, the quality of the data must be examined and used carefully, taking into account the presumed accuracy and knowledge of the people reporting the data, who is presenting the data and why, the validity of the sample, and so forth.

Reasons for Energy Consumption

In residential buildings, the vast majority of energy use is for climate control, so that the thermal quality of the building and the severity of the weather become the predominant influences on energy use.

In nonresidential buildings the reasons for energy use become far more complex. The general reasons, in descending order of energy influence, are:

1. Function of Building

2. Type of Control

3. Energy Distribution Energy

4. Hours of Operation

5. Ventilation Rate

6. Thermal Quality of Building

Building Function   The function of the building determines the energy-consuming equipment within the building, and secondarily, can influence the heating and/or cooling system type and thereby its energy intensity. *Table 3* shows the range of energy budgets in identically constructed stores in an enclosed-mall shopping center with identical hours of operation.

4. *Energy Conservation Design Guidelines for New Office Buildings,* 2nd ed., July 1975; *Energy Conservation Design Guidelines For Existing Buildings,* February 1975, U.S. General Services Administration.

TABLE 3

Energy Usage in a Shopping Mall

	Btu/ft²/year
Auto center	74,000
Department store	114,000
Department store	102,000
Variety store	100,000
Restaurant	409,000
Bank	131,000
Drug store	129,000
Food market	205,000
Dry cleaner	688,000
Book store	104,000
Doughnut store	326,000

Control The type of control of the heating and cooling systems (and many process systems) can influence energy use to a great extent. These control systems can generally be considered as either direct or indirect, depending upon how the net need for climate control determines energy consumption.

Direct control implies that energy is supplied or consumed to meet a need at almost exactly the rate that the need exists. One example of this is a house where a thermostat in the living room or dining room senses a need for heat and turns on the furnace. That is direct control in a way, but not entirely, because direct control should be room by room. Tests have shown that, in a house, room-by-room thermostatic control will save 20% to 30% of the energy that a single thermostatic control uses.[5] Direct control exists where the need for energy is in proportion to the amount of energy supplied, or vice versa.

Indirect control abounds in all kinds of buildings, other than residential. Indirect control includes such things as fixed cooling-coil supply-air temperature or outdoor-temperature reset schedules. Many consider that to be a wonderful idea: the colder it gets outside, the hotter the water is. But what has actually happened is that someone, the engineer or the control designer, has predicted the need for a certain amount of energy when it is a certain temperature outside. That is artificial. That is indirect control—where more energy than is needed is provided all the time to assure that it is there if it is needed or to satisfy the most extreme conditions.

The difference between direct and indirect control is that the energy waste associated with indirect control is probably 10 times greater than that with direct control. Yet, the direct controls are the ones that are obvious: they are the ones there on the walls. The indirect controls are the ones that are causing large quantities of energy to be consumed. Those are the ones in the ducts, in the piping, and in the heat exchangers. Indirect controls are the ones in which the energy delivered or consumed is not directly related to the needs down at the end of the line in the occupied spaces in the building.

5. W. S. Harris, and C. H. Fitch: "Performance of a Seven Zone Residential Hydronic Heating System," *ASHRAE Transactions*, part 1, 1967.

Energy Distribution Energy Energy distribution energy is that which is used to move heating and/or cooling energy through a building from its source to its end-use, usually the occupied spaces.

If one looks at the heating process in a building, one can see that most often that heating process consists of taking some reasonably raw form of energy, be it steam or gas or oil or electricity, and converting or combusting it typically at one or more locations in the building; but, inevitably the location at which that energy is converted or transformed is not the location where it is eventually used—namely, the occupied space. So what is done with it? Well, it is made into steam or into hot water and pushed or pumped around the building. That takes energy to accomplish. And then, in order to get that heat into the occupied space, it may be necessary to use a secondary pump, or possibly a fan, in order to blow that heat into the space. So it takes some energy for the fan to do that. This energy tends to be forgotten all too often, but frequently turns out to be quite significant. And it turns out to be even more significant in air-conditioning systems or in combination heating and cooling systems.

To look at the air-conditioning process from an energy distribution standpoint in reverse: what is air conditioning but the removal of heat that is generated in a space? How is that done? Air is blown into the space; it takes a fan to do that. The air is then taken back over a cooling coil where it is cooled, the heat is taken out with chilled water, and the chilled water must be pumped around. That takes energy. Then the chilled water is taken back to a chiller and the chiller requires some energy (but that is not a concern at the moment). Then it is necessary to pump condenser water up to a cooling tower somewhere, and it takes some energy to do that pumping, and finally at the cooling tower it takes energy to blow the heat to the atmosphere.

The reason for the emphasis on energy distribution energy is that even though it may be small in magnitude, it is typically large in duration, in that the fans and pumps run (with the exception of a cooling tower or a variable volume system) at full load for every occupied hour. At least chillers modulate in accordance with load. But energy distribution energy most often tends to be a constant load. The reason it is a high load factor is because of its long hours of operation.

Hours of Operation Since most nonresidential (and many residential) buildings are not used 24 hours per day, the hours of operation for the heating and cooling systems will have a significant influence on energy use. Even the most efficient system that operates when the space it serves is not in use is causing the energy consumption of the building to go up almost in proportion to the hours of operation.

Ventilation and Thermal Quality Finally, things like the ventilation rate and thermal quality of the building, while very significant energy determinants in residential buildings, will be of lesser significance than those considerations discussed above. Frequently they can exhibit the opposite influence, as detailed in the Technical Note at the end of this chapter.

Energy Budgets Vary from Building Type to Building Type, and Building to Building

Seemingly there is little consistency in annual energy consumption of buildings within given building types. And paradoxical as it might seem at first, statistics show that climate, itself, is not much of a factor. All of which tends to confirm the thesis that it is how a building is used and how much the systems are used that determine annual energy consumption.

Office Buildings   Every year the Building Owners' and Managers' Association (BOMA) reports the air-conditioning operating costs of over 125 million ft² of office buildings on a city-by-city basis.

If air-conditioning operating cost, which in itself is fairly crude (how does one apportion the electrical energy usage among the various systems?), is plotted against cooling degree days, which also is fairly crude, on a city-by-city-basis, the plot is a scatter of points all over the place (*Figure 3*). In other words, no consistent pattern develops. What one might expect would be a series of points forming a diagonal line, starting low at the lowest degree days, and being high at the highest degree days. But this graph shows that cooling cost of office buildings has little relationship to climate. The reason is that most of the air-conditioning energy is used to offset heat gains from people, lights, and equipment, which are the same for office buildings in Fairbanks as they are in Miami.

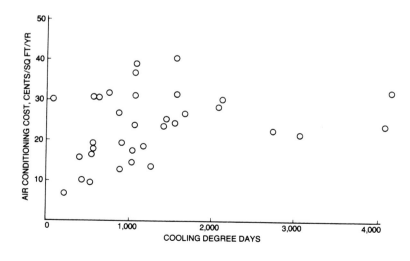

Fig. 3 Plot of air-conditioning cost versus cooling degree days for 125 million square feet of office space.

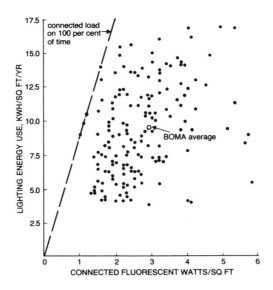

Fig. 4 Plot of office building lighting energy consumption versus installed capacities.

Another misconception is that the efficiency of equipment at full load is an index of how efficiently a building will be operated; but this is not necessarily so. Again, it is how the building is used. Take an example: a centrifugal chiller for a high-rise office building might have an efficiency of 0.7 kW/ton, while some smaller low-efficiency units might take 2 kW/ton. But if one tenant wants to work late in an office building with a central system, it is necessary to turn on, say, one 500-ton chiller, a couple of 100-hp (horsepower) pumps, a 50-hp cooling tower fan, one 400-hp primary air fan, and a 100-hp return fan. Before you know it, almost 1,000 kW are being used. Unitary air conditioners, on the other hand, would take only about 2kW per person to keep late workers comfortable.

The case is not being made for unitary equipment, per se; not at all. Obviously, a central system is more efficient where occupancy is uniform and consistent in a large building. The point is again, however, that actual building use is a primary factor in energy use.

Earlier the statement was made that there is no direct relationship between installed capacity and energy consumption. This is borne out by data on lighting energy use in 307 office buildings across the country, as collected by BOMA[6] (*Figure 4*). There is no pattern whatever between installed capacity and annual energy use.

Schools and Colleges This inconsistency we've been demonstrating is true of schools, too. This is shown in *Table 4*, an energy-use study of schools in Fairfax County, Virginia.[7] All the schools in this county operate under nearly identical weather conditions, and generally speaking, the architecture is similar. But note, for example, how electrical consumption varies from

6. Ross and Baruzzini, Inc.: "Energy Conservation Applied to Office Lighting," Federal Energy Administration, Washington, DC, April 15, 1975.
7. "Energy Study—Fairfax County Public Schools," Educational Facilities Laboratories, New York, 1973.

TABLE 4

Energy Consumption Cost of 17 Elementary Schools in the Same County

Schools	Area (ft²)	Cost of electricity per ft²	Cost of fuel oil per ft²
Greenbriar East	59,483	.135	.059
Fort Hunt	66,992	.131	.061
Brookfield	43,794	.127	.062
Kings Glen	64,023	.107	.073
Camelot	76,853	.100	.076
Forest Edge	80,843	.094	.050
Mt. Vernon Woods	40,051	.094	.066
Oak View	77,254	.092	.079
Wolftrap	49,082	.086	.056
Floris	19,637	.079	.089
Little Run	40,035	.074	.070
Quander Road	40,033	.062	.091
Cedar Lane	37,194	.061	.088
Beech Tree	40,333	.060	.070
Sleepy Hollow	39,045	.049	.101
Oak Grove	10,349	.039	.188
Crestwood	46,983	.038	.108

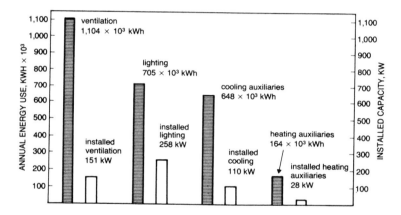

Fig. 5 Relationships between installed capacities of equipment and energy consumption at an Ohio university.

school to school. Yearly costs range from 13.5¢/ft² to 3.8¢/ft²: a ratio of 4:1!

These schools are in an area where the utility company had an electric rate of a flat 1¢/kWh with no demand charge, so the cost is directly related to the actual energy use. All the schools also pay the same price for fuel oil. So the cost figures are directly related to energy consumption.

Figure 5 again confirms the precept that says, "I don't want to know so much how big the equipment is, I want to know how much it's used." This is a building at Ohio State University that has absorption cooling with a gas-fired boiler, which is also used for space heating.[8]

Installed capacity of the ventilation equipment is only 151 kW,

8. *Proceedings of the Conference on Energy Conservation in Commercial, Residential and Industrial Buildings*, Ohio State University, Columbus, Ohio, May 1974.

TABLE 5

Energy Usage of University Buildings in Utah

Building	Institution	Building area, ft²	Heat	Energy budgets MBtu/ft²/year	
				Electric	Total
Law	U of U	57,286	207	180	387
Pharmacy	U of U	57,790	129	51	180
Chemistry	U of U	95,160	429	158	587
Library	U of U	248,480	117	134	251
Fine Arts	USU	132,435	148	52	200
Eng. & Phys. Science	USU	142,580	119	30	149
Forestry & Bio. Science	USU	118,827	128	54	182
Fine Arts	SUSC	18,849	95	39	134
Library	SUSC	45,168	70	70	140
Phys. Ed.	SUSC	50,349	227	24	251
Science	SUSC	45,609	147	24	171
Range			70 to 429	24 to 180	134 to 587
			6.1:1	7.5:1	4.4:1

TABLE 6

Utah Universities—Hours-Use of Installed Capacity

Building	Institution	Building area, ft²	Heat	Mech. elec.	Light elec.
Law	U of U	57,286	5227	3471	5439
Pharmacy	U of U	57,790	3856	2250	1915
Chemistry	U of U	95,160	2723	2468	3694
Library	U of U	248,480	4022	2227	9155
Fine Arts	USU	132,435	2425	2664	1491
Eng. & Phys. Science	USU	142,580	2335	1872	3660
Forestry & Bio. Science	USU	118,827	4246	1473	3933
Fine Arts	SUSC	18,849	1860	1065	2558
Library	SUSC	45,168	441	2878	3386
Phys. Ed.	SUSC	50,349	2866	2512	2362
Science	SUSC	45,609	4018	2906	1964
Range			441 to 5227	1065 to 3471	1491 to 9155
			11.8:1	3.3:1	6.1:1

but look at the amount of energy it uses. In contrast, the lighting load is almost twice the installed capacity of the ventilation, but it uses only two-thirds as much energy.

University buildings of various types have been shown to vary by more than 4:1 in energy use[9] (*Table 5*). Obviously, a chemistry building will use a lot more than a fine arts building due to function. But the table shows that energy use of fine arts buildings at two different universities in Utah varied by 50%.

Table 6 shows the data from these same buildings rearranged in terms of load factor—in hours-use of installed capacity which were obtained by dividing the measured energy consumption by the installed capacity. These are shown for the electricity used for cooling, the electricity for lighting, and the high-temperature hot

9. B. O. Furner: ''Campus Utility Costs,'' *Heating, Piping and Air-Conditioning*, November 1973.

water used for heating. If energy consumption were at all related to installed capacity or peak load, then all of the load factors in any category would be equal, which obviously, they are not.

Hospitals   Energy use in hospitals is intensive, as is shown in *Table 7*, from a study of three Veterans Administration hospital buildings in different parts of the country.[10]

But climatic comparisons are also interesting. In Buffalo, where the winter design temperature is −10F, one would expect the

TABLE 7

Energy Usage of Three V.A. Hospitals

Hospital	Btu/ft²/year
Lake City, FL	
Fuel	189,000
Electricity	73,000
Total	262,000
San Diego, CA	
Fuel	285,000
Electricity	122,000
Total	407,000
Buffalo, NY	
Fuel	176,000
Electricity	41,000
Total	217,000

TABLE 8

Government Building Energy Budgets after Energy Conservation Program

Department/Agency	ft² × 10³	Btu × 10⁹	Btu/ft²/year
Commerce	3,874	2,366	610,000
Defense	1,818,371	478,347	268,000
ERDA	79,895	81,289	1,017,000
GSA	190,935	44,414	232,000
NASA	31,500	25,455	808,000
Postal Service	67,713	44,275	654,000
VA	109,871	37,243	339,000
Total Government	2,476,884	762,802	308,000

fossil fuel requirements to be a lot higher than in Florida or California, where the design temperatures are 30F to 40F. But not so. This table again says when it comes to the amount of energy used, regardless of source, factors other than climate are the prime determinants.

Table 8 shows federal government building energy budgets by agency for the major energy-using agencies.[11] To some degree, these energy budgets reflect the function of the buildings used by each agency.

10. Reynolds, Smith and Hills: "Energy Conservation Study of V.A. Hospitals," Veterans Administration, Washington, DC, 1974.
11. Testimony of FEA Before the U.S. House Government Operations Committee on July 27, 1976.

Design Concept More Important Than Efficiency

All other things being equal, anything which improves the energy efficiency of the products and systems that we use in buildings is certainly to be encouraged. However, it should be stressed that in many cases in the real world of buildings, all other things are not always equal.

As an example, assume three identical houses with three identical families. House A has a central air-conditioning system with an energy efficiency ratio (EER) of 12 Btu/watt. House B has a central air-conditioning system with an EER of 8 Btu/watt, while House C has individual window air-conditioning units with an EER of 4 Btu/watt. Which house will use the least amount of energy for air conditioning?

The strict technological approach would answer that House A would use the least amount of energy. The engineering approach would say that it would be either House A or House B depending upon the particular performance of the central air-conditioning systems. If the air-conditioning system in House A achieved its EER by doing far more latent cooling than necessary, while the air-conditioning system in House B did only sensible cooling, there is a very good chance that House B would use less energy than House A. The reason for this would be that the air-conditioning system in House A would do far more total cooling than the system in House B. However, the question becomes not one of which does more cooling, but which one does the kind of cooling, namely sensible cooling, that is really necessary to maintain comfort in the house.

The answer to this problem would probably be that House C would use the least energy. Even though the EER of the window units is far lower than that of the central systems in Houses A and B, the units in each room would be used only during the periods when cooling was desired in each room. When cooling is desired in any one room in House A or B, the entire house must be cooled, and therefore, more energy is consumed.

Another example involves domestic hot-water systems. In many domestic hot-water systems, more energy is used to keep the pipes hot than to heat the water. Take a simple case of two toilet

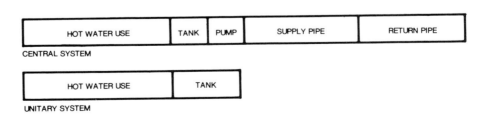

Fig. 6 Heat losses from the piping plus the pumping energy in a constantly circulating domestic hot-water system can consume more energy than local water heaters installed at the point of use.

rooms 100 ft apart. There are two options: put a water heater in each room, or install a single water heater in one room and circulate hot water to the other. The central hot-water system ends up using about 2½ times as much energy as the two individual water-heating systems, even though the heat losses from the tanks are greater with the individual systems because there are two tanks. The heat losses from the piping plus the energy required to run the circulating pump is far greater than both the heat losses from the tanks and the amount of energy in the hot water (*Figure 6*).

These examples show that we must consider not only available technology, but also how it is applied to buildings, and how users will operate the systems and equipment. While use of improved technology can result in lower energy consumption with all other things being equal, we must go further to consider how this technology is applied to buildings, and then further still, to look at how people use them.

Selection of the proper design concept in terms of how energy is used can have a much greater impact on energy use than the efficiency of the equipment used. One of the key factors which can dominate the energy use of a building is providing the means by which it can be operated efficiently. Even an inefficient system that is turned off when not needed will use far less energy than an efficient system that can't be turned off.

Low Life-Cycle Costs and Low Energy Use Do Not Necessarily Go Hand in Hand

It may seem surprising, but there is no basic or implied relationship between low life-cycle cost and low energy consumption that holds true in all cases.

For example, a recent study on a large high-rise office building recommended adoption of the system that had the highest annual energy requirement because it had the lowest annual operating cost. Reason for this apparent anomaly was that the district energy company had a 100% demand ratchet charge for 12 months based upon maximum demand.

The system with the highest capacity, though more efficient than a lower capacity (and lower cost) system, had the highest demand charge, and consequently, the highest operating cost. The cost for the actual energy used amounted to less than one-third of the annual energy bill; the remaining two-thirds was demand charge.

The subject of life-cycle cost is used today, on the very patriotic assumption that anything we consider that has a low life-cycle cost will automatically have low energy consumption. That, of course, is false. Low life-cycle cost does not necessarily yield low energy consumption. Life-cycle costing is based on assumptions about what will happen in the future to such things as taxes,

TABLE 9

Summary of Life Cycle Costs

System number	First cost $	Annual energy cost $	Life-cycle cost $	Energy budget MBtu/ft²/yr
1	+ 50,000	+14,135	+643,767	82.5
2	+125,000	+10,044	+605,087	79.0
3	+175,000	+ 5,106	–0–	48.9
4	+375,000	–0–	+186,121	45.6
5	–0–	+22,422	+109,093	59.5
6	+125,000	+ 2,946	+381,558	70.9

inflation, and the like. A life-cycle cost can often be made to come out showing whatever is wanted, just by juggling the assumptions.

As an example, *Table 9* shows a presentation to a conservative private corporation of the life-cycle cost analysis for six energy-related alternatives. All costs are grouped incrementally, so that each column shows all costs related to a zero base. For the six alternatives being considered, there are first-cost premiums that go as high as $375,000, energy-cost premiums that go as high as $22,000 per year, and life-cycle cost premiums that go as high as $643,000. Associated with each is an annual energy consumption. Note that the system with the lowest first cost does not have the highest energy consumption, meaning that the cheapest building does not necessarily use the most energy. And note that the building with the lowest life-cycle cost does not have the lowest energy consumption.

Minor changes in any of the assumptions in the life-cycle cost technique will change the relative life-cycle costs considerably, but the energy consumption will not change. Therefore, it is possible to make the life-cycle cost turn out to be just about anything. This is not to say that it is not a reasonable means for

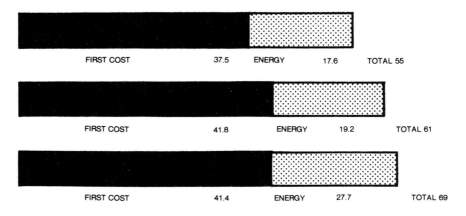

FIRST COST	37.5	ENERGY	17.6	TOTAL 55
FIRST COST	41.8	ENERGY	19.2	TOTAL 61
FIRST COST	41.4	ENERGY	27.7	TOTAL 69

Fig. 7 First costs and life-cycle energy costs for three bids on GSA Social Security project, May 1976 (in millions of dollars).

businesses to evaluate alternatives. But don't place 100% reliance on a conclusion that low life-cycle cost and low energy consumption are directly related.

Figure 7 presents another example. The General Services Administration took bids on a new Social Security Center in Baltimore. Prior to the bidding, each one of the three competitors had a life-cycle energy cost analysis done by the government, and they were told that the basis for award would be lowest total of the bid price plus the life-cycle energy cost. They each knew their life-cycle energy cost before submitting their bids. The U.S. Steel and Owens-Corning joint venture had not only the lowest first cost, but also the lowest life-cycle cost, and was granted the award. In this case, life-cycle costing was one of the means of choosing among alternatives, but it also shows that the system with the lowest life-cycle cost can also have the lowest first cost.

With Computer Simulation, How the Building is Used Influences Accuracy of Results

From what has been said so far, one might be overwhelmed with the thought of predicting building energy use. There are, however, a number of computer programs available for this purpose. They have a wide range of capabilities and costs. No one computer program will be applicable in all situations. The key factor in selecting a program is its ability to handle the specifics of the building being evaluated in sufficient detail and with sufficient flexibility to permit study of alternatives in adequate depth.

The cost of using these programs for new building design can range from less than one hundred dollars to several thousand dollars, plus about 1 to 10 professional man-days. Once a particular program has been selected, the main items of cost are the number of alternatives to be evaluated, and the complexity of the building and its systems.

Several comparisons of available computer programs have concluded that:[12]

1. The results to be obtained by using several computer programs on the same building will range from very good agreement to no agreement at all. The degree of agreement is dependent upon the interpretations made by the computer programs to handle the building in question.

2. Several people using several programs on the same building will probably not get good agreement on the results of an energy analysis.

3. The same person using several programs on the same building may or may not get good agreement, depending

12. Lawrence G. Spielvogel: "Comparisons of Energy Analysis Computer Programs," *ASHRAE Journal,* January 1978.

upon the complexity of the building and its systems and the ability of the computer programs to handle the specific conditions in the building.

How accurate are the results? Frequently, there are wide discrepancies between predicted and actual energy use because the use of the building turned out not to be what was presumed in the computer simulation. Then adjustments to the initial assumptions regarding hours of occupancy, night and weekend use, mechanical system operation, and so forth, are necessary to more closely match the predicted to the actual energy consumption.

Building Owners Must be Able to Control Building Energy Consumption for Efficiency

While the variations in building energy consumption that have been demonstrated are probably best explained by use of buildings more than by their physical characteristics, this by no means implies that buildings and their systems should not be optimized for efficient use of energy in themselves. But the overriding factor still is the ability of the owner to efficiently control the energy consumption of the building, whether this be provision for switching lights off and on within reasonable building modules, allowance for part-load operation of systems, design for part-time occupancy of spaces, or other strategies addressed particularly to use factors.

Technical Note: Determination of Optimum Insulation in Buildings

We have long been under the impression that some insulation in buildings is good and that more is better. This generally holds true for residential buildings, but is not necessarily true for commercial, industrial, and institutional buildings.

A residential building is what I would call a thermally "light" structure, which may be defined as one in which the heating and cooling requirements are roughly proportional to the difference between indoor and outdoor temperature. Other examples of a thermally light building would include structures that are heated only with little or no internal gains, such as warehouses.

A thermally "heavy" structure is one in which the heating and cooling requirements are not directly proportional to the difference between indoor and outdoor temperature due to the presence of cooling and internal or solar heat gains. Examples of this type of thermally heavy structure include most any commercial, industrial, or institutional building.

The purpose of this Technical Note is to demonstrate a technique for determining the optimum *U*-values for walls, roofs, etc., in thermally heavy structures. It is recognized that the energy requirements for these structures vary so widely that there can be no generalizations made with regard to the use of insulation. This is quite contrary to the generalizations regarding insulation used in the design of light thermal structures, which say more insulation will reduce energy consumption.

Other factors to be considered in any analysis are the equipment capacity and thermal comfort associated with changes in *U*-value. The higher the *U*-value, the greater the equipment capacity. These must be taken into account in the course of any analysis. The subject of discussion here is only energy requirements and not equipment capacities or comfort. Generally speaking, the incremental cost of heating and cooling equipment capacity is relatively small for the loads imposed by walls and roofs compared with operating cost.

Methodology I have selected as an example, a building located in Columbus, Ohio, and have used weather data from *U.S. Air Force Manual 88-8,* Chapter 6, 1967, along with the "bin" method of energy analysis as described in Chapters 11 and 43 of *ASHRAE Handbook & Product Directory* (1973 *Systems* Volume).

In order to simplify the analysis, I have selected a 10-ft by 15-ft perimeter module of a building with a perimeter wall 10 ft wide by 10 ft high. The *U*-values that are investigated are those that apply to the over-all combination of materials in this 100 ft² of wall so that the percentage of glass and other materials is left up to the designer. For example, when I select a wall having a *U*-value of 0.6, it could be 100% double glass or some combination of single glass plus other materials, such that the over-all average *U*-value is 0.6.

I have also assumed that solar heat gain does not enter into the analysis, which would be similar to assuming a north-facing wall. Consideration of solar heat gain can certainly affect the results of the analysis either way; however, my purpose here is to demonstrate the principles involved. Likewise, I have assumed no gains or losses to the space due to floor or roof, ventilation and infiltration. These are best considered in a computer analysis.

I have assumed that the building is in operation continuously, such as might be the case with a municipal building, and that direct electric resistance heating is used. This again simplifies the calculations and permits the use of a common unit of energy consumption, namely, the kilowatt hour, (kWh). This type of analysis works just as well with any type of fuel or any other hours of operation. Only the results change.

Cooling Systems Two types of cooling systems are analyzed, both of which are assumed to have an energy requirement of 1,000 watts/ton/hour. One type of cooling system operates whenever there is a net positive heat gain to the space regardless of outdoor temperature. This type of system might be a through-the-wall unit, a fan coil unit, or heat pump.

The second type of system is an all-air system which employs the "economy cycle" and is so arranged that outdoor air can be used for cooling whenever its temperature is below 50F. More complex heating- and cooling-system analysis can be accomplished by computer simulation.

Since one of the basic premises of this analysis is that buildings with internal gains do not exhibit the same energy consumption characteristics for heating and cooling that simple buildings do, I have selected internal gains at two levels: 2.44 watts/ft² and 4.88 watts/ft². These levels of internal gains are quite consistent with current practice in building design.

Calculations Sample calculations are shown in *Table 10,* in which I have used the "bin" method in five-degree increments. At each five-degree level, I have shown the annual number of hours which occur in the five-degree bin. Column 3 shows the internal gains based on either 2.44 or 4.88 watts/ft². Column 4 shows the transmission heat gain or loss that occurs at each of these outdoor temperatures with the U-value under consideration. Columns 5 and 6 show the net cooling or heating requirement at each temperature level. Columns 7 and 8 show the hourly energy requirement for heating or cooling.

TABLE 10

Energy Consumption at $U = 0.5$ and 4.88 watts/ft²

1	2	3	4	5	6	7	8	9	10	11
								No econ.	Econ.	
	Ann.	Btu/h int.	Btu/h	Btu/h	Btu/h	kW	kW	kWh	kWh	kWh
F	hrs.	gains	trans.	cool	heat	cool	heat	cool	cool	heat
95	14	2500	1000	3500		.30		4	4	
90	77	2500	750	3250		.27		21	21	
85	215	2500	500	3000		.25		54	54	
80	367	2500	250	2750		.23		84	84	
75	559	2500	0	2500		.21		117	117	
70	804	2500	−250	2250		.19		153	153	
65	846	2500	−500	2000		.17		144	144	
60	804	2500	−750	1750		.15		121	121	
55	792	2500	−1000	1500		.12		95	95	
50	668	2500	−1250	1250		.10		67	67	
45	650	2500	−1500	1000		.08		52		
40	672	2500	−1750	750		.06		40		
35	705	2500	−2000	500		.04		28		
30	689	2500	−2250	250		.02		14		
25	477	2500	−2500	0		0		0		
20	230	2500	−2750		250		.07			16
15	98	2500	−3000		500		.15			15
10	51	2500	−3250		750		.22			11
5	18	2500	−3500		1000		.30			5
0	10	2500	−3750		1250		.37			4
−5	14	2500	−4000		1500		.44			6
Totals 8760								994	860	57

Col. 3 + Col. 4 = Col. 5 or Col. 6
Col. 2 × Col. 7 or Col. 8 = Col. 9, 10 or 11

Column 9 shows the annual kilowatt hours required for cooling without the economy cycle, while Column 10 shows the annual kilowatt hours when using the economy cycle. All cooling kilowatt hours below 50F were simply dropped. Column 11 shows the annual kilowatt hours for heating. These kilowatt hours for cooling and heating are obtained by multiplying the kilowatts in Columns 7 and 8 by the number of hours at each temperature level in Column 2.

This calculation procedure is then repeated for various levels of internal gains and for various U-values. The results are plotted in *Figures 8* and *9*. Figure 8 shows that with internal gains of 2.44 watts/ft^2 no heating energy is required at U-values below 0.17, and that above that U-value, the annual heating energy requirement rises quite rapidly, as one would expect. The annual cooling energy required will be quite different, depending upon whether or not the economy cycle is used at least below U-values of 0.4.

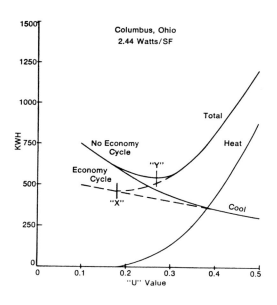

Fig. 8

At U-values of 0.4 and greater, the building itself becomes a natural cooling machine, or "free" economy cycle. The total annual requirement for energy is then the sum of the heating plus the cooling energy.

When using the economy cycle and internal gains of 2.44 watts/ft^2, the minimum annual energy requirement shown at point "X" represents a U-value of 0.18, which is also the point at which almost no heating energy is required. With no economy cycle, the minimum total annual energy requirement occurs at point "Y," with a U-value of 0.27.

Figure 9 shows a similar set of curves for internal gains of 4.88 watts/ft^2. For the circumstances of this example, it can be said that the higher the internal gains, the higher the U-value desired.

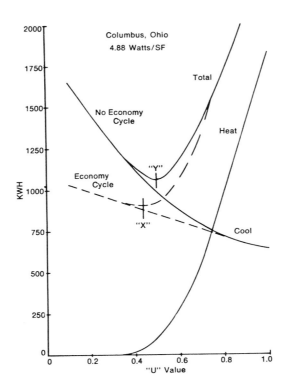

Fig. 9

Note that in this example, without the economy cycle, the annual energy requirement at a U-value of 0.1 is approximately 60% greater than at a U-value of 0.5.

The basic reason that these results occur is that, in most cities, there are far more hours per year at outdoor temperatures of 50F to 75F than there are between 75F and 100F. At temperatures between 75F and 100F, low U-values do result in less energy consumption; however, at temperatures between 50F and 75F these low U-values inhibit the flow of internal heat gains out of the building, thereby creating higher cooling loads, and therefore, higher energy requirements than those which would occur with the higher U-values. Since there are far more hours during which the temperature is between 50F and 75F than between 75F and

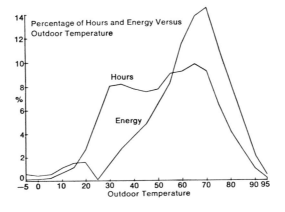

Fig. 10

100F, what you might save in the way of energy at outdoor temperatures over 75F can be more than spent in additional cooling energy during the greater number of hours at temperatures below 75F. *Figure 10* shows this comparison using the data in Table 10.

Important considerations in this type of analysis include the level and duration of internal gains, and the nature of the energy consumption of the types of heating and cooling systems to be employed. In this example, I have looked at a relatively simple situation. In the case of a real building, there would be a multiplicity of situations to be evaluated, such as walls, roofs, and floors. The use of computer programs makes these more complex analyses practical.

If energy consumption were related to *U*-value, then a "glass box" would have several times the energy consumption of a "windowless" building for HVAC. Experience shows that this is not the case and that the differences in energy consumption are small. In all probability, the energy consumptions lie on either side of the "optimum" point in Figures 8 and 9.

For buildings having internal or solar heat gains higher than 1 watt/ft², lower *U*-values will not necessarily reduce energy consumption over the course of the year, and will usually increase energy consumption. Due to the wide diversity of building types, internal gains, system types, and operating conditions, no rules of thumb can be used to establish *U*-values that will result in minimum energy consumption.

5

PASSIVE
SOLAR HEATING
OF BUILDINGS

D. Balcomb,
J. C. Hedstrom and
R. D. McFarland

This chapter is based on the work of the authors at the Los Alamos Scientific
Laboratory under the auspices of the U.S. Department of Energy and enlarges
upon results previously reported in "Simulation Analysis of Passive Solar Heated
Buildings," *Solar Energy,* vol. 3, no. 3 (1977); and "Passive Solar Heating of
Buildings," Associated Universities, Inc., July 1977; and "Passive Residential
Design Competition and Demonstration," U.S. Department of Housing and
Urban Development Document HUD-PRD-311, May 1978.

Solar heat gain through windows, walls, modified walls, sky-lights, clerestory windows, and roof sections provide an opportunity to reduce dramatically the purchased energy requirements of a building. To the extent that the thermal energy flow is wholly by natural means, such as radiation, conduction, and natural convection, and solar energy contributes a significant portion of the total outside energy requirements (say, more than one-half), the building can be referred to as a passive solar-heated structure.[1]

Passive solar heating works very well, more so than is generally recognized in conventional building design practice. The effectiveness of passive systems has been demonstrated in a variety of buildings located in different climates. The occupants of these buildings testify to their comfort, to the ease of operation, and especially to their low fuel bills. A principal problem, however, has been the lack of a quantitative basis by which to incorporate passive concepts into architectural and engineering design.

To provide the needed quantitative basis for passive system design, the Los Alamos Scientific Laboratory (LASL) has been evaluating passive solar heating under the Department of Energy Solar Heating and Cooling Research and Development Branch. Fourteen test rooms have been set up at Los Alamos to study the performance of passive solar heating elements under controlled conditions. At the time of this writing, test data for one year have been obtained on a pair of test rooms which utilize thermal storage-wall concepts, one with cylindrical water storage tubes and the other with a thick masonry wall, each located behind a vertical double-glazed window, but with no additional provision against heat loss. The temperature histories in these rooms were predicted by what proved to be an accurate simulation analysis technique developed at LASL: during the mid-winter months each of these rooms have evidenced an average inside temperature 60F to 70F *above* the ambient temperature with no additional heating than that from the solar storage walls. Most recently, 15 buildings have been instrumented in order to study passive solar heating elements in different configurations, the data from which are being used to validate the simulation analysis technique.[2]

A comprehensive simulation analysis computer code, written to predict the performance of passive solar-heated buildings, has been partially validated against test-room results and has been used to predict the performance of several building geometries. The results of geographic studies done with this code are reported in this chapter and demonstrate that passive solar heating systems can be expected to work effectively in all United States climates, and thus warrant major emphasis as an essential element of energy conservation design.

Types of Passive Systems

The simplest type of passive system is the *direct gain* approach through windows, usually double glass, ideally facing south. To

1. Some variations rely upon electric power for insulation and shading controls or for fans to move air and are often referred to as "hybrid systems." Designs in which solar energy makes only a partial contribution (say 30% to 50%) might best be referred to as "sun-tempered."

2. These are the Doug Kelbaugh residence in Princeton, NJ; the Benedictine Monastery Dove Publications Building in Pecos, NM; four small buildings at the Ghost Ranch in Abiquiu, NM; the Bernardo Chavez solar greenhouse in Anton Chico, NM; the Santa Fe First Village Units #1 and #4, which are the residences of Bruce Hunn, Carl Newton, and Tom Shankland in Los Alamos, NM, and of Ralph Williamson and Mark Jones in Santa Fe, NM.

help store the heat, such a building design should include considerable thermal mass, such as poured concrete floors or massive masonry construction in the walls or ceiling with insulation on the outside. In a sense, the building becomes a live-in solar collector. The south orientation offers seasonal control automatically, since the south face is exposed to a maximum amount of solar energy in the cold winter months when sun angles are low, and a minimum in the summer when sun angles are high.

One of the best examples of a direct gain system is the Wallasey School.[3] Built in 1962, in Liverpool, England, near the sea at a latitude of 53°N, it is possibly one of the largest passive solar-heated structures in the world to date and the first use of the direct-gain system in a school. The construction consists of 7 to 10 in. of concrete in the roof, floor, and three walls, with 5 in. of expanded polystyrene as exterior insulation. The south-facing solar wall itself is an expanse of glass, 27 ft tall and approximately 230 ft long. There are two sheets of glass: the one on the outside clear, and, about 2 ft inside of that, a layer of diffusing glass which refracts the solar rays so that they uniformly irradiate the ceiling and floor. The structure is heated to about 50% by the sun, the remaining energy for heating coming from the lighting and from the occupants. The auxiliary system originally installed has not been needed.

A second type of passive solar heating system is the *thermal storage wall* in which a glass-covered wall, heated by the direct solar rays, then re-radiates the stored heat to the building interior. The storage wall can be composed of water-filled containers or masonry. To be a good absorber, the outer surface of the wall is painted black or a dark color. (A small section of concrete thermal storage wall was used in the Wallasey school.)

The Steve Baer house, built in Albuquerque, New Mexico in 1973, is the first and best-known of the water-container variation, in which the thermal storage wall consists of 55-gal drums filled with water, arranged on their side in a vertical rack. In winter, exterior panels are raised at night for insulation and lowered during the day to allow the sun in and, due to an aluminized coating on the panels, reflect additional sun onto the storage.

A well-known example of the concrete storage-wall concept is a group of houses in Odeillo, France, by engineer Felix Trombe. In the earliest Trombe house built in 1967, the wall is about 2 ft thick. The primary heating of the house is by radiation of heat passing through the wall and by convection along the interior of the wall. About 30% of the energy is by a thermocirculation path which operates during the day by natural convection through openings at the bottom and top of the wall. Data taken on this system for a period of four days in December 1974 show its performance in a situation in which the ambient temperature is slightly above freezing and there are two sunny days, a cloudy

3. J. E. Perry: "The Wallasey School," *Passive Solar Heating and Cooling,* Conference and Workshop Proceedings, May 1976, Albuquerque, NM (available from NTIS, Springfield, VA 22161—$10.50) (hereafter cited as *Solar Heating*).

day, and then another sunny day.[4] The outside surface of the concrete, covered with one layer of glass, heats up to about 140F to 150F during the day. The inside temperature remains at about 85F fairly uniformly, providing radiant and convective heat to the room.

Data taken over a period of one year (1974) indicate that about 36% of the total energy incident on the wall is effective in heating the building during the winter months, which would be typical of a good active solar heating system (*Figure 1*). Of the total thermal energy required by the building (which is controlled at a temperature of 68F), about 70% was provided by solar energy during the one-year period (*Figure 2*).

A combination of the direct-gain and storage-wall concepts is the *solar greenhouse*, in which a greenhouse is located on the south side of a building with some kind of thermal storage wall between the greenhouse and the building itself. The temperature in the greenhouse does not require precise control as long as plants do not freeze. Solar energy could provide, typically, all of the required heat for the greenhouse as well as a substantial portion for the building it serves.[5]

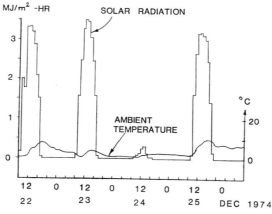

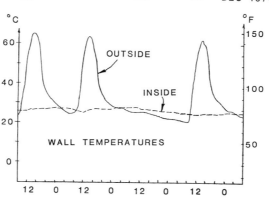

Fig. 1 Measured performance of the 1967 Trombe house during four winter days, December 1974.

4. F. Trombe, J. F. Roberts, M. Cabanat and B. Sesolis: "Some Performance Characteristics of the CNRS Solar House Collectors," *Solar Heating*.
5. F. Fisher and W. F. Yanda: *Solar Greenhouses*, John Muir Press, Santa Fe, NM, 1976.

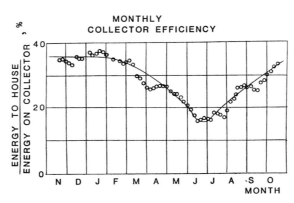

Fig. 2 Efficiency of the 1967 Trombe house thermal storage wall.

Another type of passive system is offered by the *roof pond* in which thermal storage is located on the roof of the building. Insulating panels in this case are located on a flat roof and slide back and forth on tracks to either expose or cover the roof pond, which might typically be a transparent water bag placed directly on a black painted roof surface. The water bags, or "thermoponds" as they are often referred to, are left exposed to the sky during the day in the winter and during the night in summer. This allows heat input from the sun on a winter day and heat loss by radiant cooling on a summer night. The insulation is placed over the roof pond during a winter night to conserve heat, and during a summer day to exclude the sun. Known as the "Skytherm System" and originally developed by Harold Hay with John Yellott and built in a test model in Arizona in 1967, this system has most recently been used in a live-in prototype in Atascadero, CA, where it has worked very well, having operated for several years without any back-up energy.[6]

A fifth type of passive system is a *natural convective loop*. The classic thermosiphon water heater fits into this category, where a solar collector is placed below the hot-water storage so that the storage is heated simply by the natural upward flow of heated water from the collector, with the cooler water from the bottom of storage dropping to the bottom of the collector. Natural convective loops which use air as the heat transport fluid for space heating have been built and work well, an excellent example of which is the Paul Davis house in Corrales, New Mexico.[7]

Mathematical Simulation Analysis

Thermal network analysis techniques can be used to predict the performance of passive solar-heated buildings in which the building temperatures are described at different locations, including air temperature, surface temperatures, glass temperatures, and the temperature of thermal storage materials at various depths. Energy balance equations are set down for each location, accounting for thermal energy transport by radiation, conduction,

6. P. W. Niles: "Research Evaluation of a System of Natural Air Conditioning," 1976, NTIS, Springfield, VA.
7. P. Davis: "To Air is Human," *Solar Heating*.

and convection; energy sources from the sun, lights, people, and auxiliary heaters; and sensible thermal energy storage in the building materials. The temperature history of each location is then simulated by solving these equations for given inputs of solar radiation, ambient air temperatures, and wind. As described in the remainder of this chapter, this technique is used to predict the performance of various passive solar heating concepts which use solar gain through windows and thermal storage mass walls. The influence of design variables is studied by successive computations made with different parameters. *Reference 8* details the mathematical basis of the thermal performance model. Various passive system options can thus be compared:

1. Solid Wall: No thermocirculation is allowed.

2. Trombe Wall: Thermocirculation is allowed only in the normal direction as described above. Reverse thermocirculation, as would normally occur at night, is prevented by installing a thin plastic-film damper over the inside of the top opening. If reverse thermocirculation is not prohibited, the vents are a net thermal disadvantage to the building.

3. Trombe Wall with Control: Frequently, the result of the normal thermocirculation is to overheat the building during the day. In this option, the vents are closed whenever the building temperature is 75F or greater. This greatly reduces the required cooling. This presumably would require some passive or active mechanism.

Another configuration analyzed is the "water wall." This might consist of drums of water stacked to form a thermal storage wall as described above in the Steve Baer house. Alternatively, vertical freestanding cylindrical tubes or any other means of containing water in a thermal storage wall could be used. When heated by the sun on one side, the water will convect to transport the heat

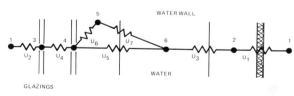

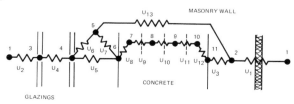

Fig. 3 Simulation schematic (Reference 9).

8. J. D. Balcomb, J. Hedstrom and R. McFarland: "Passive Solar Heating of Buildings," Los Alamos Scientific Laboratory (LA-UR-77-1162), 1977.

across the wall horizontally, and thus temperature gradients across the wall will be very small.

In the analysis, the room temperature (Node 2 in *Figure 3*) is always maintained within bounds T_{min} and T_{max}, which are set at 65F and 75F respectively. In the solution of the equations, two possible situations can result:

1. The calculated room temperature falls within the prescribed bounds T_{min} and T_{max}

2. The calculated room temperature is above T_{max} or below T_{min}.

In the first situation, the room temperature assumes the calculated value. The second situation results in two further possibilities:

1. The calculated room temperature is less than T_{min}. In this instance, auxiliary energy is calculated as required to hold the room at T_{min}.

2. The calculated room temperature is greater than T_{max}. In this instance, excess heat is dumped to the outside air, presumably by ventilation in order to hold the room at T_{max}.

Comparison with Test-Room Results The validity of the simulation analysis techniques for these two simple concepts was established by demonstrating that they adequately predict the temperature behavior of several small, passive, test rooms located in Los Alamos (*Figure 4*). These test rooms are small insulated structures measuring 5 ft wide by 8 ft deep by 10 ft high. The entire 50 ft² south wall of each test room is glazed with two

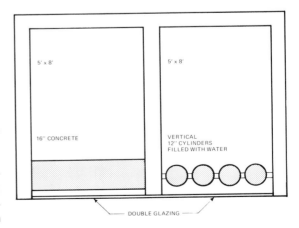

Fig. 4 A plan view of the passive test rooms. The walls, floor, and ceiling are 2 × 4 in. stud-wall construction with 3½-in. fiberglass insulation. The exterior is covered with plywood and the interior lined with 1-in. polystyrene insulation. The building interior mass is negligible compared with that of the various thermal storage elements added for the tests. The net calculated thermal conduction coefficient (exclusive of the south wall and the common wall) between the building interior and the ambient exterior temperature is 0.23 Btu/F hr ft² of south glazing.

sheets of ⅛-in. plexiglas separated by a ½-in. air gap. The rooms are oriented with the south wall facing 13° east of due south.

One test room contains four fiberglass tubes 12 in. in diameter and 8 ft high, which stand directly behind the glass, separated slightly from one another and the side walls. During most of the winter, the spaces between tubes and the 2-ft space above the tubes were blocked with 2-in.-thick polystyrene insulation cut to fit. The tubes are blackened to absorb solar radiation and filled with 188 gal of water.

A second test room contains a 16-in. solid concrete block wall, blackened on the outer surface. Three 3-in. by 8-in. holes were left open near the bottom and also near the top to allow air to thermocirculate from the room floor level up through the 6-in. space between the wall and the glazing, and return at the room ceiling level. During portions of the test year, the holes were alternately blocked or left open day and night or opened only during the day.

On a typical mid-winter clear day with an average ambient temperature of 23F, the water temperature at mid-height varied from 82F to 101F, and the room interior globe temperature varied from 74F to 94F. Stratification of water temperature of up to 32F was observed from the bottom of the tube to the top of the tube. In the second test cell, the exterior wall surface temperature varied from 93F to 153F, the interior wall surface temperature varied from 84F to 96F, the top vent temperature varied from 84F to 132F, and the room interior globe temperature varied from 74F to 98F. During the longest stormy period of the winter, for which the ambient temperature held at roughly 20F, the interior temperature of both rooms dropped to the yearly minimum of 48F.

Resulting storage masses were as follows:

	Thermal Storage/Glazed Area Btu/Ft²$_g$
Water wall	35.0
Masonry wall	32.5

Based on performance during the test year, the test rooms were very well heated by the sun. Average room temperatures were 60F to 70F *above* the ambient average temperature during typical sunny mid-winter days. The minimum temperature in the one room was very nearly equal to the minimum temperature in the other room each night throughout the winter. Daily room temperature variations were approximately as follows:

Water wall:	20F
Masonry wall:	
Vents closed	11F
Vents open	24F

Thus the main effect of the thermocirculation vents is to provide direct heat to the room during the day. This increases the daily temperature swing, and although the daily average room temperature is larger by about 5F, it does not noticeably change the minimum room temperature. The maximum inside wall surface temperature occurs at roughly 4:00 pm on the water wall, and at 8:00 pm to 10:00 pm on the masonry wall.

Comparison of calculated and measured temperatures have been made for the period December 31, 1976 to January 6, 1977, during which the thermocirculation vents were open, and during the period January 18 to January 21, when the vents were blocked. The first interval is a period of erratic weather with three separate snowfalls and some bright sunny intervals. The second period starts with a sunny day followed by three days of partial sun.

The simulation model quite accurately predicts the temperature during most of the time—generally within 2F. The largest errors occur during strong heating periods when discrepancies up to 8F are observed. As a result, it was concluded that these particular passive collector-storage elements are quite amenable to accurate representation using the type and level of simulation models employed.

Simulation Analysis for Los Alamos For much of the preliminary analysis done to date, the solar and weather data used were for Los Alamos, from September 1972 to August 1973. For this year, the total radiation on a horizontal surface was 518,000 Btu/ft² and the space heating load (base: 65F) was 7,350 degree days (18% colder than normal for Los Alamos). This is a severe test. For these initial studies, the glass conductance was characterized

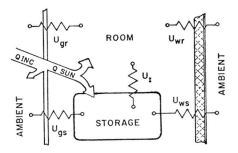

Fig. 5 Passive Solar Heating Model used for the Los Alamos simulation of four passive systems (Cases 1 through 4).

by a single constant term rather than the non-linear, two-term representation shown in Figure 3. The results are useful to determine general effects, but the simple model over-predicts the total performance by about 12%. Five different cases have been studied as follows (see *Figure 5* for designation of symbols):

Case 0: The room and storage are the same temperature. (U_1 is infinite.)

Case 1: Storage is coupled thermally only to the room. This case would represent massive internal walls or furniture placed out of the direct sunlight.

$$(U_{gs} = 0, U_{ws} = 0)$$

Case 2: Storage is placed directly in front of the glass. The sun shines on and is absorbed by storage. Storage is thermally coupled to the environment (ambient air temperature) through the glass and also to the room.

$$(U_{gr} = 0, U_{ws} = 0)$$

Case 3: Storage is placed against the back wall out of the direct sun. This case would represent massive walls or roof insulated on the outside.

$$(U_{gs} = 0, U_{wr} = 0)$$

Case 4: Storage is placed in the room in the direct sun but loses heat only to the room.

$$(U_{gs} = 0, U_{ws} = 0)$$

These cases are intended to represent extremes. Any real design, while tending toward one or another case, probably will be a mixture. For the preliminary study, the *U*-values were held constant, although in reality, they will vary with temperature difference, wind, and other influences. The glass was assumed to be vertical, to face due south, and to be unshaded. Three glazings were studied:

1. Single glazing: $U_g = 1.1$ Btu/hr ft² F
2. Double glazing: $U_g = 0.50$ Btu/hr ft² F
3. Night insulated double glazing: $U_g = 0.1$, 5:00 pm to 8:00 am

A value of U_{wr} of 0.5 Btu/ft²$_g$ F was chosen initially.

A storage mass of 30 Btu/ft²$_g$ F was chosen. This is equivalent to 30 lb of water per square foot of glass or 150 lb of concrete.

Lastly, the room temperature was allowed to vary 5F around a desired value of 70F. Therefore $T_{min} = 65F$ and $T_{max} = 75F$.

Simulation Results for a Case with Water Storage It is instructive to observe the simulation results for a few days of cold weather. *Figure 6* shows the seven-day interval between the 31st of December and the 6th of January. Case 2 was chosen for this calculation with a value of $U_I = 1.0$ Btu/hr ft²$_g$ F. There was snow on New Year's Eve followed by two days of cloudy weather, and then cold but sunny weather. A summary for the entire year is shown in *Table 1* for this same Case 2 example.

In the following discussion, the effect of variations in different parameters will be shown. In each case the simulation model was run repeatedly, each time varying one parameter while holding

TABLE 1

Annual Solar Performance Summary for Case 2 Simulation (Water Wall)

Btu/ft² of glass

Month	Building load	Incident solar energy on glass wall	Solar energy trans-mitted through glass wall	Excess energy ventilated	Auxiliary energy required	Degree days (F) (65° base)	Percent of solar heating
9	6073	36882	25311	6183	48	208	99.20
10	8447	31623	22044	3479	2149	506	74.56
11	13617	40108	29331	638	4300	1032	68.42
12	15006	39693	29638	762	5788	1144	61.43
1	15865	46150	34353	817	4573	1202	71.17
2	13066	38830	27956	961	4053	982	68.98
3	12650	34802	23904	472	5377	980	57.49
4	10451	34288	22682	650	3081	759	70.52
5	6861	30510	19856	2583	842	366	87.72
6	4147	33966	22162	8321	1	123	99.96
7	3520	28398	18686	7413	0	28	100.00
8	3252	31298	20660	8873	0	16	100.00
Yearly Summary							
	112964	426547	296582	41152	30214	7350	73.25

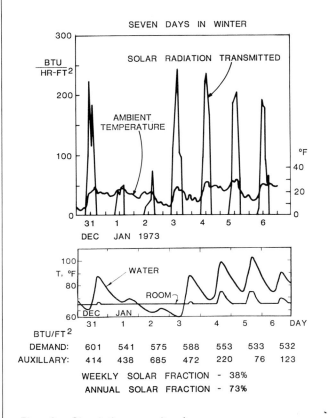

Fig. 6 Simulation results for seven consecutive winter days.

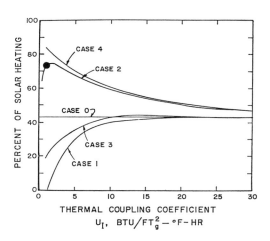

Fig. 7 Effect of thermal coupling between room and storage.

the others constant at the nominal values given above. The circled point on the graphs in *Figures 6* through *10* represents the nominal case.

Figure 7 shows the yearly results for all five cases as a function of the room-to-storage thermal coupling factor, U_l. All cases become equivalent for large values of U_l, which is to say, as the difference between storage temperature and room temperature increases, Cases 2 and 4 are appreciably better in performance than the others. These two cases are for a wall directly heated by the sun, which is clearly an enormous advantage. Case 4 is unrealistic for low values of U_l because the sun must shine through the room to reach storage and this implies transparent insulation. Case 2 is similar to a Drumwall, with the thermal storage in water contained in cans placed in front of the glass wall.

It is significant to note that there exists an optimum value of U_l for Case 2. The optimum value is approximately 1.5 Btu/hr ft²$_g$ F. The reason for the optimum is as follows: at higher values of U_l, storage loses too much heat to the room during charging periods. This prevents storage from attaining higher temperatures and storing greater amounts of heat. At lower values of U_l, storage attains such high temperatures during charging periods that it loses too much heat through the glass to the environment. Clearly the optimum value of U_l will depend on the amount of storage heat capacity that is provided for.

The effect of varying the values for storage heat capacity and for glass insulation is shown in *Figure 8*. Most of the benefits of storage are obtained at a value of 30 Btu/F ft²$_g$. The improvement obtained with double glazing is very dramatic. In fact, a single glazed wall without night insulation can hardly be considered a viable passive solar heating element since only 30% of solar heating can be achieved even with large storage, and the glass is a net loser with small storage. The increased effectiveness of insulating the glass at night (for example, as in a Beadwall) is impressive. The cost-effectiveness of various insulation strategies deserves further study. Night insulation with single glazing can be seen to be more "cost effective" in the amount of heating energy that is saved than when compared to its use with double glazing. In fact, single glazing becomes viable *only* with night insulation. A strategy of placing night insulation based on observed conditions rather than a timeclock would result in only a small increase in performance ($\sim$2%).

The effect of varying the glass area is inverse to the effect of varying the building thermal load U_w. This is shown in *Figure 9*.

The effect of the allowable temperature swing is shown in *Figure 10*. A variation of 5F may be reasonable for a residence, whereas a much larger variation may be tolerable in other buildings, such as a warehouse or greenhouse. The effect of mass is also shown for both Cases 2 and 4.

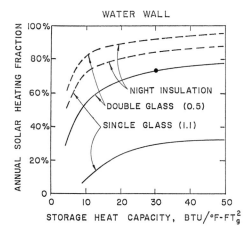

Fig. 8 Effect of storage mass.

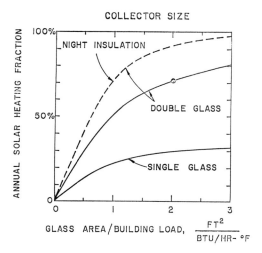

Fig. 9 Effect of glass area.

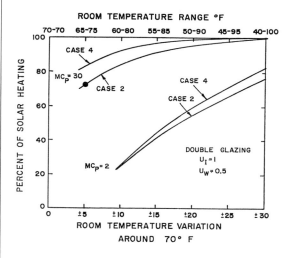

Fig. 10 Effect of allowable room-temperature variation.

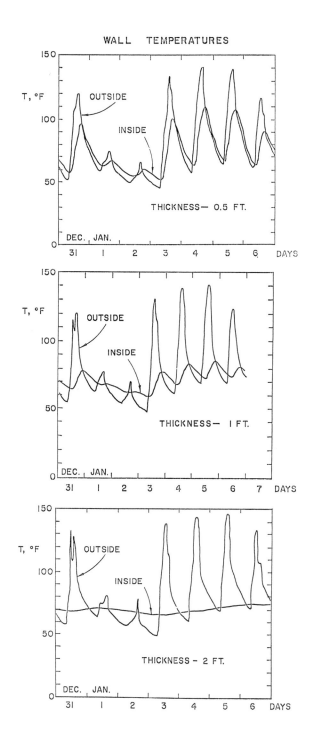

Fig. 11 Time response of a masonry wall for a one-week period.

Simulation with a Masonry Wall   The example of Case 2 is somewhat representative of the concept utilizing a concrete wall, developed at Odeillo, France by Trombe and his colleagues. In the French concept, a thermocirculation path was provided by perforations extending through the wall at the top and bottom. The positive value of these perforations had not yet been established and this effect was not simulated.

In order to study the basic performance characteristics of such a wall, as compared to the case of the water wall studied earlier, the mathematical model was modified to describe the time- and space-dependent thermal transport of heat through the wall, by simulation of the masonry temperature at the wall surfaces and at several different distances into the wall.

The thermal properties used for the masonry were as follows (typical of dense concrete):

Heat Capacity: 30 Btu/ft³ F
Thermal Conductivity: 1 Btu/ft F hr

The calculated wall temperatures shown in *Figure 11* are for the same seven-day period shown in Figure 5 for three different wall thicknesses: .5 ft, 1 ft, and 2 ft. The daily fluctuations felt on the inside wall surface are markedly different for the three cases, being very pronounced (~45F) for the thin wall and almost non-existent for the thick wall. The longer-term effect of the storm is observed on the inside of the thick wall as a 10F variation.

The net annual results of several such calculations are summarized in *Figure 12*. The net annual thermal contribution of the three different thicknesses of walls are not markedly different. In fact, the 1-ft-thick wall is the best of the three—giving an annual

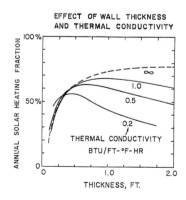

Fig. 12   Yearly performance of a passive masonry wall as a function of thickness for various thermal conductivities.

solar heating contribution of 68%. This compares with a value of 73% for a water wall with the same heat capacity. In each case, auxiliary cooling or heating was assumed to maintain the room temperature within the bounds given previously. Although the net thermal contribution of the thin-wall and thick-wall cases are nearly the same, both the amount of control required for the thick wall, as well as the variation in room temperature within the set bounds, are much less.

The effect of variations in wall thermal conductivity is also shown in Figure 12. It can be seen that for each conductivity, there exists a thickness which will give a maximum yearly solar energy yield. The optimum thickness decreases as the thermal conductivity decreases. Annual heating performance, of course, is only one consideration in the selection of wall materials and wall thickness.

Results for Other Climates

In the analysis for other climates, the more detailed simulation model of the glazing layers was used as shown in Figure 3. The more accurate representation makes a significant difference—the annual solar heating fraction for Los Alamos was reduced from 68% to 56% in one case. Since the more complex model has been validated against the test-room data, it is more to be believed. Several changes in the model are responsible for the change. Probably the most significant is a more detailed accounting of the transmission of diffuse and reflected solar energy.

Hourly values of solar radiation and weather data were obtained from the National Weather Service. A specific one-year period was selected for the hour-by-hour simulation analysis. For Madison, Wisconsin the year chosen was July 1961 through June 1962. The results of a parametric study of the effect of thermal storage mass is shown in *Figure 13* for the four cases studied. As had been noted in a previous preliminary analysis, there is an

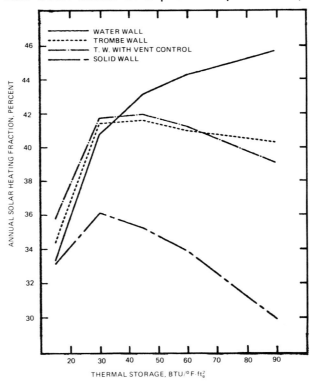

Fig. 13 Effect of storage mass and wall type on the performance of four thermal storage wall systems for Madison, WI. Weather data used are for 1961–62 (7,838 degree-days). Load = .5 Btu/hr ft² F

TABLE 2

Annual results for five thermal storage wall alternatives: WW—water wall; SW—solid wall (no vents); TW—Trombe wall (no reverse vent flow); TW(A)—Trombe wall with vents open at all times; TW(B)—Trombe wall with thermostatic vent control. Thermal storage mass = 45 Btu/F ft_g^2.

| City | Annual percent solar heating | | | | |
	WW	SW	TW	TW(A)	TW(B)
Santa Maria, CA	99.0	98.0	97.9	97.3	98.0
Dodge City, KS	77.6	69.1	71.8	62.8	73.6
Bismarck, ND	49.8	41.3	46.4	31.1	47.6
Boston, MA	60.0	49.8	56.8	44.9	56.7
Albuquerque, NM	90.8	84.4	84.1	81.8	87.5
Fresno, CA	85.5	82.4	83.3	78.0	83.4
Madison, WI	43.1	35.2	41.6	24.7	42.0
Nashville, TN	68.2	60.7	65.2	54.1	65.4
Medford, OR	59.0	53.3	56.1	42.2	56.8

TABLE 3

Annual results for 29 locations. Trombe wall system (18 in. thick); Thermal conductivity = 1 Btu/ft hr F; Heat capacity = 30 Btu/ft³ F; Vent size = .074 ft² per foot of length (each vent); No reverse thermocirculation; Load (U_1) = .5 Btu/hr ft² F; Temperature variation 65F to 75F.

City	Year starting	Heating degree days	Latitude	Solar heating,* Btu/ft_g^2	Solar heating fraction, percent
Los Alamos, NM	9/1/72	7350	35.8	60,200	56.5
El Paso, TX	7/1/54	2496	31.8	50,000	97.5
Ft. Worth, TX	7/1/60	2467	32.8	38,200	80.8
Madison, WI	7/1/61	7838	43.0	44,900	41.6
Albuquerque, NM	7/1/62	4253	35.0	63,600	84.1
Phoenix, AZ	7/1/62	1278	35.5	38,300	99.0
Lake Charles, LA	7/1/57	1694	30.1	34,300	90.5
Fresno, CA	7/1/57	2622	36.8	43,200	83.3
Medford, OR	7/1/61	5275	42.3	47,400	56.1
Bismarck, ND	7/1/54	8238	46.8	53,900	46.4
New York, NY	6/1/58	5254	40.6	48,000	60.2
Tallahassee, FL	7/1/59	1788	30.3	40,700	97.3
Dodge City, KS	7/1/55	5199	37.8	58,900	71.8
Nashville, TN	7/1/55	3805	36.1	39,500	65.2
Santa Maria, CA	7/1/56	3065	34.8	69,800	97.9
Boston, MA	7/1/57	5535	42.3	47,100	56.8
Charleston, SC	7/1/63	2279	32.8	47,900	89.3
Los Angeles, CA	7/1/63	1700	34.0	53,700	99.9
Seattle, WA	7/1/63	5204	47.5	42,400	52.2
Lincoln, NE	7/1/58	5995	40.8	53,500	59.1
Boulder, CO	1/1/56	5671	40.0	62,500	70.0
Vancouver, BC	1/1/70	5904	49.1	46,000	52.7
Edmonton, Alb.	1/1/70	11679	53.5	37,700	24.7
Winnipeg, Man.	1/1/70	11490	49.8	33,700	22.6
Ottawa, Ont.	1/1/70	8838	45.3	37,900	31.9
Fredericton, NB	1/1/70	8834	45.8	40,100	33.9
Hamburg, Germany	1/1/73	6512	53.2	24,900	27.5
Denmark	?	6843	56.0	43,100	43.8
Tokyo, Japan	?	3287	34.6	50,300	85.8

*The values in the solar heating column are the net energy flow through the inner face of the wall into the building.

optimum thickness of about 1 ft for the masonry wall. From calculations done for other locations, it was determined that this optimum does not depend on climate.

A study of the effect of climate on performance is given in *Table 2*. These calculations are all for a thermal storage mass of 45 Btu/F ft²$_g$(~18 in. of concrete or 8.6 in. of water). Although some cases are clearly better than others, all seem to be viable approaches to solar heating in all the climates studied. The effectiveness of the thermocirculation vents is pronounced in the colder climates.

The ultimate measure of cost-effectiveness of these concepts will be the heating energy delivered to the building by the solar wall. These annual values are given in *Table 3* for the particular case of the 18-in. Trombe wall.

These results from work in progress at LASL, while limited to the particular examples that have been studied, show the value of simulation and performance analyses of passive systems that, in time, will yield quantitative data and rules of thumb for passive architectural and engineering design. A long-hand method for estimating the performance of the passive systems discussed in this chapter is given in the Technical Note that follows.

The examples reported in this chapter do show that passive design deserves a greater emphasis in environmental control engineering and, indeed, should provide the starting point on which energy conservation building design is based.

Technical Note: Performance Estimate Technique for Solar Storage Walls

The estimation technique outlined below has been developed at the Los Alamos Scientific Laboratory from the computer simulations for the specific passive systems discussed in this chapter and requires only monthly solar radiation and degree-day data. The method is appropriate for the preliminary design calculations of small buildings, such as houses, where computer-based programs are not available. The result obtained by completing the calculations is the total annual heating energy required to maintain the building at 65F. This number, when divided by the building floor area and divided by the heating degree days, provides a basis for comparing designs in different locations.

The technique thus allows the designer to estimate, by simple long-hand calculation, the relative performance of designs that utilize solar storage walls. A calculation form is provided, *Table A*, by which to tabulate the results, as follows:

Table A Columns 1 and 2 summarize the building thermal load for each month of the year. This load profile can be based on a simplified degree-day analysis, assuming a single building loss coefficient from the building heated space to the outside, in the absence of solar gains. Columns 3 through 9 summarize the

TABLE A

Building Thermal Load Profile

Month	(1) Monthly Degree Days	(2) Thermal Load	(3) Solar Radiation on a Horizontal Surface	(4) Solar Declination at Mid-Month (D)	(5) L − D	(6) Solar Radiation Absorbed	(7) Solar Load Ratio (SLR)	(8) Solar Heating Fraction (SHF)	(9) Auxiliary Heating Energy
		MBtu/ mo.	Btu/ mo. ft²			MBtu/ mo.			MBtu/ mo.
Aug.				14.0					
Sept.				2.8					
Oct.				−9.1					
Nov.				−18.6					
Dec.				−23.1					
Jan.				−21.4					
Feb.				−14.0					
Mar.				−2.8					
Apr.				9.1					
May				18.6					
Jun.				23.1					
Jul.				21.4					
Total									

auxiliary load based on the Solar Load Ratio method. The total monthly solar energy transmitted through the solar collection surface is determined and this is divided by the total monthly thermal load to determine the monthly Solar Load Ratio (SLR). The monthly Solar Heating Fraction (SHF) is then determined from a selected curve and the monthly auxiliary energy requirement is calculated.

Step 1: Determine the Modified Building Loss Coefficient. This can be calculated in either one of two ways.

Method 1: If the design load has been determined, based upon an assumed design temperature, then the Modified Building Loss Coefficient is calculated as follows:

$$\text{Modified Building Loss Coefficient, Btu/Degree Day} = \frac{24 \times \left(\begin{array}{c}\text{Design Heating}\\\text{Load, Btu/hr}\end{array}\right)}{\left(\begin{array}{c}\text{Inside Temperature}\\\text{Assumed, F}\end{array}\right) - \left(\begin{array}{c}\text{Outside Design}\\\text{Temperature, F}\end{array}\right)}$$

Method 2: Alternatively, the Modified Building Loss Coefficient can be determined directly from the building outside envelope areas and calculated U-values. Compute the area of each window, wall section, roof, etc. Then multiply the appropriate

U-value by the area and sum the U × A products (Btu/hr F). The sum of the U × A products is the Building Skin Conductance (Btu/hr F).

The infiltration load is now computed, as the product of the building volume (ft³), the heat capacity of air (0.018 Btu/ft³ F at sea level), and the number of air changes per hour assumed in the calculations:

$$\frac{\text{Infiltration}}{\text{Load, Btu/hr F}} = \text{Volume} \times \text{Specific Heat} \times \frac{\text{Air Changes}}{\text{per Hour}}$$

Finally,

$$\begin{array}{l}\text{Modified Building}\\ \text{Loss Coefficient,}\\ \text{Btu/Degree Day}\end{array} = 24 \text{ (hours)} \times \left[\frac{\text{Building Skin}}{\text{Conductance}} + \frac{\text{Infiltration}}{\text{Load}}\right]$$

Step 2: Tabulate the Monthly Heating Degree Days in Column 1.
Step 3: Multiply Column 1 by the Modified Building Loss Coefficient to obtain the Monthly Load (Btu/month) and list in Column 2.
Step 4: Total Columns 1 and 2.
Step 5: List in Column 3 the monthly solar radiation incident on a horizontal surface for the proposed site (Btu/month ft²). These values should be based upon National Weather Service measured data or other reliable measured data.[9]
Step 6: Subtract the Solar Declination at mid-month (given in Column 4) from the latitude at the building site and list in Column 5. This is L − D.
Step 7: List in Column 6 the Solar Radiation Absorbed. For vertical south-facing double glazing (normal transmittance = 0.74), this value can be determined from the following equation:

$$\begin{array}{l}\text{Solar Radiation}\\ \text{Absorbed,}\\ \text{Btu/month}\end{array} = \left[\begin{array}{l}\text{Horizontal}\\ \text{Solar Radiation}\\ \text{(Column 3)}\\ \text{Btu/month ft}^2\end{array}\right] \times \left[\begin{array}{l}\text{Net Solar}\\ \text{Collection}\\ \text{Area, ft}^2\end{array}\right] \times \left[\begin{array}{l}\text{Solar}\\ \text{Absorptance}\\ \text{of}\\ \text{Collection}\\ \text{Surface}\end{array}\right]$$

$$\times [(0.226) - (.002512)(L - D) + (.0003075)(L - D)^2]$$

Figure 14 can be used to more simply obtain the value for the last term in this equation for Latitude Correction for each month.
Step 8: Divide Column 6 (Solar Radiation Absorbed) by Column 2 (Thermal Load) to obtain the Solar Load Ratio (SLR) and tabulate in Column 7.
Step 9: Using the Solar Load Ratio from Step 7, obtain the value for the monthly Solar Heating Fraction (SHF) from *Figure 15*. Tabulate these values in Column 8.

9. *Hourly Solar Radiation Data for Vertical and Horizontal Surfaces on Average Days in the United States and Canada,* NBS Building Science Series 96, Government Printing Office, Stock Number 003-003-01698-5.

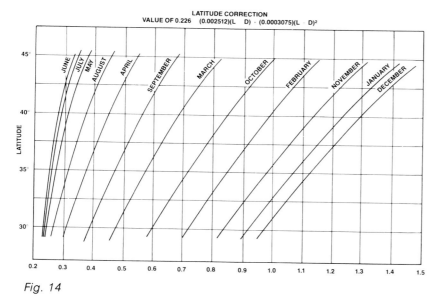

Fig. 14

Step 10: In Column 9, tabulate the Monthly Auxiliary Energy required, as calculated from the formula:

$$\begin{array}{l}\text{Monthly Auxiliary}\\ \text{Energy, Btu/month}\end{array} = (1 - \text{SHF}) \times \left[\begin{array}{l}\text{Monthly}\\ \text{Load (Column 2)}\\ \text{Btu/month}\end{array}\right]$$

Step 11: To compare a building design in different heating zones, obtain the estimated heating energy requirement for auxiliary energy per degree day per ft² by dividing the total of Column 9 (auxiliary heating) by the product of the heating degree days (total of Column 1) and the building floor area:

$$\begin{array}{l}\text{Heating Energy}\\ \text{Required,}\\ \text{Btu/DD ft}^2\end{array} = \frac{(\text{Auxiliary Heating})}{(\text{Degree Days}) \times (\text{Floor Area})}$$

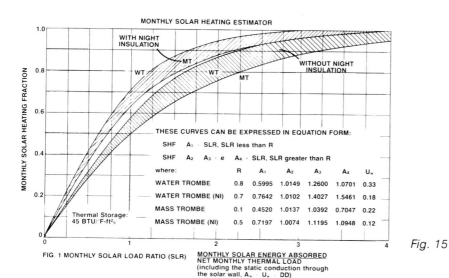

Fig. 15

6
ARCHITECTURAL DESIGN BASED ON CLIMATE

Murray Milne and Baruch Givoni

This chapter is based upon material reported in part in B. Givoni: *Man, Climate and Architecture*, 2nd ed., Applied Science Publishers, Ltd., London, 1976, chap. 16.

The process by which architectural design is developed in response to specific climatic requirements was given the name "bioclimatic" design by the Olgyay brothers nearly 20 years ago, at a time when architects and researchers showed a great interest in climate as a basis of building design.[1] A method similar to the Olgyay's was proposed in the 1969 edition of *Man, Climate and Architecture*, based on the psychrometric chart, which gives the designer an accurate representation of the potential effect of the building envelope, as well as other environmental control strategies, on achieving human comfort in buildings, given data on ambient climate conditions.

This chapter describes the use of the psychrometric chart for energy-conservation design and establishes a process whereby the designer can systematically match design solutions to climatic conditions. The method permits an identification of "least purchased-energy" design strategies, first by utilizing the natural effects of sun, wind, and nighttime cooling, and, only when these are insufficient, by selecting appropriate mechanical equipment. Rather than the architect presenting the mechanical engineer with a design and the question, "How much mechanical equipment do I need?", the approach implies that architect and engineer first ask, "To what extent can natural energy systems be used?; Can we achieve human comfort conditions with no mechanical equipment?"; and, "If mechanical systems are required, how can they best be integrated into the building design to minimize purchased energy use?"

To present this method of design, the discussion begins in *Defining Human Comfort in Terms of The Building Bioclimatic Chart* with a brief description of human comfort zones on the psychrometric chart or, as we will define it here, the "building bioclimatic" chart, and then details, in *Climate Design Strategies*, the design solutions available to meet comfort requirements under the various climatic conditions. The third section, *Climate-Based Design*, summarizes how these alternatives might be incorporated into a climate-based architectural design method.

For readers who are not fully familiar with the psychrometric chart, a technical note at the end of the chapter reviews basic psychrometrics and includes common engineering definitions of the terms referred to below.

Defining Human Comfort in Terms of the Building Bioclimatic Chart

The parameters of human comfort vary from culture to culture and evidence wide variation between individuals as a function of one's physical condition, activity or lack of it, and psychological expectations. The acceptable comfort range also varies for the same individual throughout the year, so that one might speak of distinct summer and winter limits within the comfort zone. But

1. Victor Olgyay and Alavar Olgyay: *Design with Climate*, Princeton University Press, Princeton, NJ, 1963.

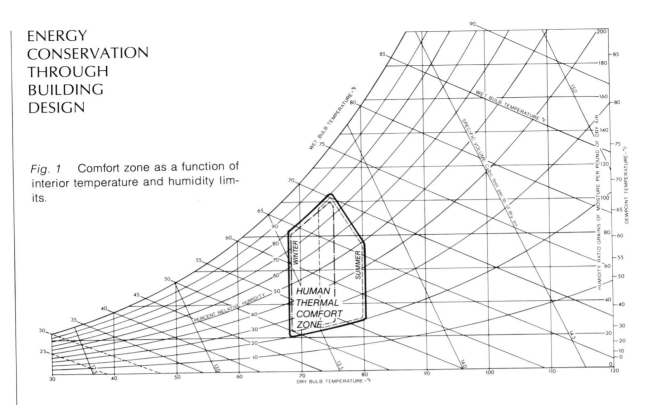

Fig. 1 Comfort zone as a function of interior temperature and humidity limits.

there are obvious limits to the range of temperature, humidity, and ventilation within which human comfort can be maintained and beyond which some physiological stress occurs. Various authors have developed more or less precise definitions of the comfort zone.[2] From them, we can make the approximation that the comfort zone for Americans falls roughly between 68F and 78F, and 20% to 80% relative humidity (RH), excluding the "hot-humid" corner of these coordinates. This range is represented in *Figure 1* as the *comfort zone.* If ambient conditions (outside shade-temperature and humidity) are within this zone, then, in effect, no building is required; that is, one would be comfortable under a shade tree or tent. (Although these zones are shown by distinct lines in this and the following figures, it should be remembered that these are generalized averages and should not be read to mean that a variation of one or two degrees Fahrenheit or of a few percent relative humidity would place one either inside or outside the bounded condition.)

In *Figure 2,* the ambient (outside) temperature and humidity conditions are indicated by the zones wherein human comfort during overheated periods can be attained by properly designing the *building envelope to control interior temperatures.* This can be achieved by time-lag effects through the structure, which then acts as a surface for radiant cooling, with or without nighttime ventilation (discussed in *Climate Design Strategies* below). At higher humidities, still-air conditions within the building would cause undue discomfort due to moist skin, and additional design strategies are needed. *Figure 3* shows ambient climate conditions

2. Givoni: *Man, Climate and Architecture.*

when cooling is required and within which interior comfort can be achieved primarily by *ventilation* (control of interior air movement).

Notice that there is an overlapping zone wherein temperature control either through time-lag or ventilation may be used, time-lag effects being more applicable in warm-dry climates, where

Fig. 2 Ambient conditions during overheated periods controllable through building envelope design.

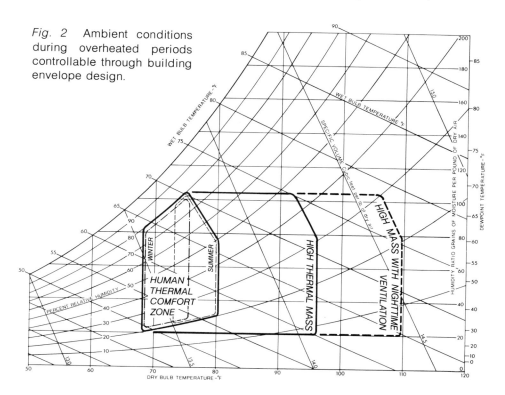

Fig. 3 Ambient conditions during overheated periods controllable through ventilation design.

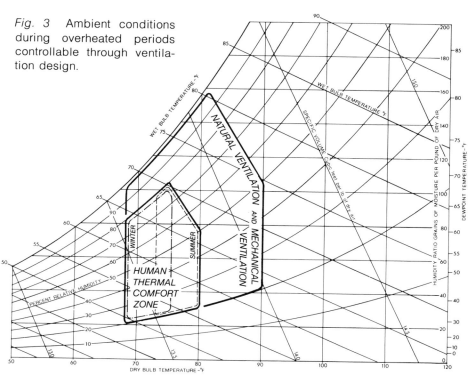

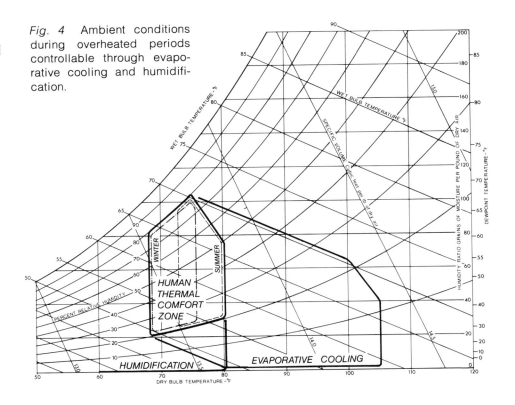

Fig. 4 Ambient conditions during overheated periods controllable through evaporative cooling and humidification.

nighttime temperatures are appreciably lower than day temperatures. These choices and similar overlaps will become more apparent as the discussion proceeds.

Above-comfort ambient temperature and humidity conditions that cannot be suitably met by building envelope design or by ventilation alone, but which can be handled by adding techniques of *evaporative cooling,* or *humidification,* are shown in *Figure 4.* For warm-climate ambient conditions that fall beyond the limits of either building materials, ventilation, or evaporative-cooling strategies, *mechanical cooling* or air conditioning must be used, but with some distinctions in the relative effectiveness of dehumidification mechanisms (discussed in the next section). In extreme hot-dry conditions, as well as in the zone that has comfortable temperatures but is otherwise too dry, humidification is desirable. For cool-climate conditions below the lower limit of temperature comfort, passive solar thermal designs can achieve interior temperatures above the comfort minima, depending upon the structural properties of the building and the availability of sunshine during the cold season. The temperature range from outside ambient to interior comfort can be greater in dry-cold conditions than in a "raw" wet-cold climate, where high humidity causes greater discomfort, given the same temperature reading. Below this, some form of "active" solar heating or other mechanically assisted means of heating is required.

Each of these design strategies is discussed individually in the following section with reference to the Building Bioclimatic Chart.

Climate Design Strategies

In this section, climate design strategies are reviewed, first as used for heating a building (that is, maintaining interior comfort when ambient conditions are below, or to the left of, the comfort zone)—passive solar heating, active solar heating, and humidification—and then as used for cooling (that is, when ambient conditions are above, or to the right of, the comfort zone)—high-mass structures, ventilation, evaporative cooling, and conventional dehumidification and air conditioning.

Heating Design Strategies

Passive Solar Heating of High-Mass Structures   The simplest method of passive solar heating is through large south-facing windows which bring in winter sunlight to directly heat the floors and walls. If the building is built of lightweight materials, then the solar radiation will heat up its "low" thermal mass quickly and soon raise air temperatures above the comfort zone. At night, low-mass structures cool off just as rapidly. A more successful passive building design would be one in which sunlight falls on materials of "high" thermal mass which store the heat and then give it back 12 or more hours later. In indigenous buildings this is often accomplished simply by an earthen floor or adobe walls. In contemporary passive buildings, the heat storage is accomplished either by the use of masonry or by placing water in containers behind a window wall, or in plastic bags on the roof. The storage mass then serves as a radiant heat source. Radiant heat transfer is simply the transfer of energy from warm objects to cold objects, without appreciably changing air temperature. As described in the previous chapter, the passively heated storage elements also create air convection currents that help distribute the heat within a space.

Glass traps solar energy through the "greenhouse effect": glass is transparent to solar radiation, but "opaque" to longer-wave lower-temperature radiation emitted by the interior building materials. Contemporary buildings could be extremely efficient solar collectors, provided that the south-facing glass is properly sized and exposed to sun in winter and shaded against overheating during the summer. Insulating shades are necessary to prevent heat loss at night.

The outer limits of the "passive solar" zone on the Building Bioclimatic Chart are defined by winter outside air temperature and by the amount of available daily radiation, given by the latitude and local sky clearness conditions as a function of altitude, local climate, or pollution. There is also a relationship that might be assumed between the ratio of glass area to the building's floor surface. In contemporary North American homes, the area of the glass usually ranges from 8% (as in the Arkansas energy house) to 20% (the upper limit allowed in the California State Residential

ENERGY
CONSERVATION
THROUGH
BUILDING
DESIGN

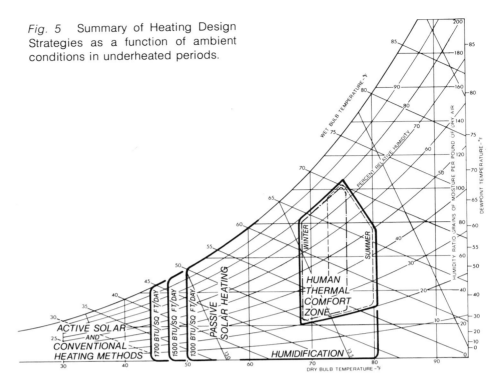

Fig. 5   Summary of Heating Design
Strategies as a function of ambient
conditions in underheated periods.

Energy Standards). Assuming clear sky conditions, the total daily insolation on each square foot of south-facing glass is about 1,700 Btu at 32°N during winter months, 1,500 Btu at 40°N, and 1,300 Btu at 48°N. (For any given latitude, of course, there are further variations of an equal magnitude, due to sky clearness variables.) If this is captured by a small 1,000-ft² building with 200 ft² of south-facing glass, comfortable indoor conditions can theoretically be maintained for one day without supplemental heat if the most severe average daily temperatures range approximately above 43F, 46F, and 49F at 32°N, 40°N, and 48°N, respectively. This assumes an over-all system efficiency of 0.33 for collection, storage, and distribution of the passive solar heating. However, there will be many overcast and stormy days during the winter, when solar radiation will be greatly reduced and, at times, negligible. In *Figure 5,* the outer limits of the passive solar heating zone for a building typical of the foregoing assumptions are shown, to represent the limits of average daily temperatures in areas receiving the indicated amount of insolation. These limits might be extended by a new generation of passive designs that utilize a greater percentage of window or storage than the averages above assume, and more effective window insulation or thermal storage designs than are now currently used in conventional building.

Active Solar Systems or Conventional Heating Methods   The effectiveness of windows as passive solar collectors is limited by the area of glass that can face the sun and by the efficiency of the heat transfer into interior walls and floors or other "high-mass" materials which act as thermal storage. In a passive building, the occupants live, in effect, inside a solar collector, and the most serious problem facing the designer is how to maintain indoor temperatures, without underheating and overheating, throughout the daily temperature cycle. Passive designs are effective, for the most part, only in low-rise structures and in the periphery rooms of any larger structures.

In an "active" solar heating system, the collection and storage components are each separate from the interior volume and are designed for much higher temperatures than can be achieved with passive systems. At higher collection and storage temperatures, heat can be transported effectively by pumps and/or fans through longer distances, as required in large-building heat distribution systems. In large buildings, the entire roof, as well as the south wall in northern latitudes, can be used for collectors.

On the Building Bioclimatic Chart, the active solar heating zone is limited only by the amount of available solar radiation and the area of the building on which collectors can be mounted. However, as a practical matter, the most stringent limit to widespread application of active solar systems is its installation cost, relative to conventional methods of heating. Therefore, when heating needs cannot be met by passive means, the designer must use life-cycle cost analysis to decide between active solar or conventional methods of heating.

Conventional heating methods which consume coal, gas, oil, or wood, introduce their own set of architectural complications because of open-flame combustion, which must somehow be contained inside a building. There is the danger to the occupants of asphyxiation or suffocation by smoke inhalation because the available oxygen supply has been consumed by combustion. There is also an increased fire hazard to buildings, which in turn impacts on building and social welfare costs to prevent and control these fires. It should thus be recognized that conventional methods of providing warmth for human comfort carries with it related costs in the incidence of heating-system–related fires, and resulting injuries, fatalities, and property loss, as well as the pollution that results wherever fossil fuels are burned.

Conventional heating methods which consume electrical energy, while safe and clean at the building, are less economically attractive in many areas of the United States when compared to active solar systems. However, there may be special situations where heat pump or resistance heating is the only feasible alternative. If electric demand is reduced by maximum use of available conservation and passive design measures, then on-site or local power generation might be economically provided by wind or hydroelectric sources.

Humidification In the area immediately below the comfort zone, the dry-bulb temperature range is perfect, but the air is much too dry. Here, humidification is required for comfort during the heating season. The humidification process is similar to evaporative cooling, discussed below, except that, in this case, most of the moistened air is recycled within the space rather than continuously exhausted and replaced. Initially the air being humidified will be cooled (by evaporation), but is soon heated up again by conduction and convection from walls, floors, and ceiling.

In natural environments it is rare to find the need for humidification alone, without also needing heating or cooling as well. On extremely cold crisp days the air is very dry, because the maximum amount of moisture that cold air can hold is very small compared to warm air. In this respect, the polar ice caps are like deserts. In very cold climates, centrally heated buildings that use a great deal of fresh air usually require humidification. *Figure 5* shows that if outside air at 30F and 50% RH is drawn indoors and heated up, moving horizontally across the chart to 80F, its relative humidity will be much less than 10%, which is far too low for comfort. This is especially true if there is a need for a high ventilation rate, as in a gym or locker room, or if there is a large infiltration loss, as in a "leaky," poorly insulated house. From the comfort point of view, low humidity causes dryness in the throat and nose, and elderly persons and children are especially susceptible to resulting coughs and nose bleeds. On a dry, crisp, winter day, so much static electricity will build up on someone walking across a rug that opening a door or shaking hands can be unpleasantly shocking. This happens because there is not enough moisture in the air to drain away these static charges.

In well-insulated buildings, especially residences, normal indoor activities such as cooking, bathing, breathing, and perspiring provide adequate sources of moisture to increase humidity enough to reach the comfort range. The expiration of moisture from plants in greenhouses also might be used for similar results.

Cooling Design Strategies

Passive Cooling of High-Mass Structures If the hottest extremes of outdoor conditions fall within the high-mass zone (Figure 2) and the average daily temperatures fall within the comfort zone, then comfortable indoor conditions can be easily achieved in high thermal-mass buildings. This design strategy is most appropriate in areas with a marked day-night temperature differential, such as warm-dry climates, where the thermal mass serves to "flatten out" the extremes and delay the effect of peak conditions to the interior. Such buildings might use heavy soil or masonry materials in floors, walls, and ceilings. In newer designs, such as roof-pond systems, water is used for thermal mass. When the daily temperature range is as high as 34F, an adobe wall 1 ft thick should result in an indoor temperature variation of about half that amount, as a rough rule of thumb, or 17F, with a time-lag of about 12 hours. This means that the coldest part of the night is felt indoors at mid-afternoon. In this case, the naturally cooled building walls or roof/ceiling provide a cooling effect by absorbing sensible heat from interior partitions, floors, and furniture without appreciably cooling the interior air. The human body can then effortlessly dissipate heat at its normal rate to these objects or directly to the cold wall (or roof).[3] Typically, in buildings designed for radiant cooling, openings are deeply recessed to prevent direct solar penetration, outside surfaces are as reflective as possible, and shaded outdoor living spaces are utilized. These are traditional building design features in the Mediterranean and other temperate to warm-dry climates.

In more arid climates, the cooling effect of high-mass buildings neither adds nor subtracts moisture from the air, so that the limits of this zone simply extend out horizontally to the right of the comfort zone along the lines of constant moisture. Below the lower boundary of this zone, it is too dry for comfort, and high-mass construction will have no effect on this problem. The use of high thermal mass for cooling is most effective as a "thermal flywheel," to absorb overheating effects during the day and to "cool down" at night, when outside temperature, wind, and sky conditions increase the cooling rate by conduction, convection, and radiation. On clear dry nights the radiant temperature of the sky must be low enough to draw heat from roofs or other building surfaces. The upper limit of this zone is established by the fact that in humid climates, high-mass buildings are quite unsatisfactory, firstly because moisture precipitates on cold walls and floors creating serious (and quite unnecessary) mildew problems, and secondly, whatever cooling effect might be achieved by nighttime cooling is offset by the slow rate of cooling of high-mass structures (in contrast to the high rate of cooling of low-mass structures, which is discussed in the next section).

Natural Ventilation for Cooling When the daily temperature/humidity readings fall in the region of "natural ventilation" (Figure 3), it is possible to maintain comfortable indoor conditions simply by designing the building to be exposed to prevailing breezes and to utilize resulting positive and negative air pressures to maintain airflow throughout the interior. Because nighttime temperatures in hot-humid climates are only slightly below those at daytime, such buildings must have a low thermal mass by using lightweight materials, including wood, fibers, and various types of insulation, in order to cool quickly. Indigenous buildings of this type found in tropical climates are the deeply shaded thatched structures, typically raised off the ground for increased exposure to cooling breezes.

It is possible that comfortable indoor conditions can be achieved even at the outer limits of this zone, provided that the building is carefully protected from solar radiation with good thermal

3. Givoni: *Man, Climate, Architecture*, chaps. 2, 3 & 4.

insulation, highly reflective external walls and roofs, deep overhangs, and nonreflective ground cover.

The Bioclimatic Building Chart zone of passive building design using natural ventilation roughly follows the 20% and 90% RH curves. If air velocity is great enough, comfort is achievable during sedentary indoor functions, wearing lightweight summer clothes, even at temperatures at high as 90F. In this case, air motion affects human comfort in two ways: by convecting heat away from the body, and by evaporating perspiration which cools the skin. The upper limit of this zone is the speed at which the wind itself becomes the source of discomfort by blowing away loose papers, messing up coiffures, or creating too much noise. Obviously, the upper limit of comfortable air velocity is very different for an office compared to a factory, so that occupant activity parameters come into consideration in establishing limits of natural ventilation.

When natural ventilation alone is insufficient for air movement, mechanical means must be used. Of all of the conventional design strategies, mechanical ventilation which requires little electric energy if the building and system are properly designed is one of the most efficient from the energy point of view, particularly if used to ventilate non-occupied spaced such as uninsulated attics or double roofs.

High Mass with Programmed Nighttime Ventilation for Cooling When only nighttime temperatures fall within the comfort zone, much more care is required in designing and using the building if only passive means are available. Daytime comfort conditions can be maintained by carefully programmed ventilation: cooling the building's interior mass with nighttime breezes, then closing it up during the heat of the day. In extreme cases, mechanical ventilation may be necessary to move enough nighttime air through the building. Such buildings, like those described in the previous section, will typically have thick walls with a highly reflective outer surface, a well-insulated and sometimes earth-covered roof, and deeply recessed, but *operable,* openings. For practical purposes, the outer limits of the zone are defined only by the maximum day-night temperature range that might occur in a hot-arid climate, usually in the range of 30F to 40F. Indigenous buildings that typify this design strategy are the cylindrical, thatched-roof mud dwellings of the Cameroon.

Evaporative Cooling Indigenous builders have known of the principal of cooling by evaporation, but could seldom afford the luxury of using it to cool an entire building because it is rare in a hot-arid climate to have enough water to "waste" in this way. Nonetheless, in the courtyards of the Alhambra, at Tivoli near Rome, and in Persian gardens, water was sprayed from fountains to evaporatively cool the air.

Because evaporatively cooled air is generally close to 100% saturation, it cannot be recycled, but must be continuously thrown away and replaced with freshly moistened air. The Building Bioclimatic Chart shows (in the scale on the right) exactly how much water must be added to each volume of dry air to produce a given reduction in dry-bulb temperature. For example, 105F air at 10% RH will be cooled to 76F at 60% RH by the addition of about .0065 lb of water or 45.5 grains of moisture per pound of dry air (one lb of water equals 7,000 grains of moisture). Typically, this is done by blowing the dry air through a wet cloth or porous fiber mat or by blowing a fine mist into the air. An alternative is to spray or drip water through a specially designed intake chamber in the ventilation system, the traditional device used in indigenous examples being wet vases at the bottom of air shafts (Chapter 1, Figure 2).

When water is evaporated, cooling takes place because the energy needed to change water from a liquid state to a gas comes from the reduction in temperature of the surrounding air. In a well-designed system, no energy is gained or lost in the process, which means that it must follow one of the lines of constant energy (enthalpy) which run diagonally down to the right (*Figure 6*). This explains why the evaporative cooling zone extends downward at an angle. Its outer boundary is defined only by the cooling capacity of the volume of air that can be comfortably moved through the interior of the building. This also assumes that sufficient amounts of water are available. For all practical purposes, 25F temperature reductions are about the limit of what can be achieved at reasonable indoor air velocities.

Building surfaces too can be cooled by evaporative cooling,

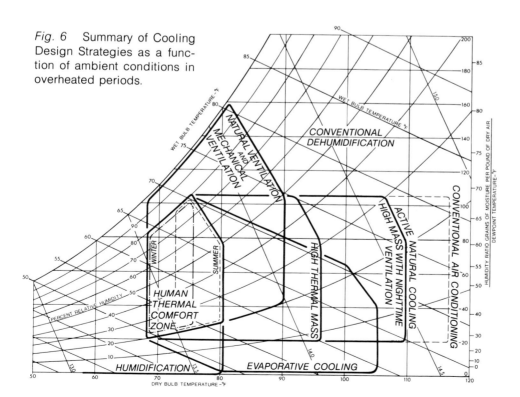

Fig. 6 Summary of Cooling Design Strategies as a function of ambient conditions in overheated periods.

splashing water on a courtyard being a familiar habit in many hot-dry zones. A few decades ago, spraying of roofs was the subject of experimentation to determine its evaporative cooling effect and has been used to supplement radiant cooling systems, such as roof ponds.[4] In all these cases, the availability of water in warm-arid climates appears to be a serious constraint.

Conventional Dehumidification and Air Conditioning   Above the human comfort zone in the chart is a region where there is too much moisture in the air, but which is otherwise within comfortable temperature limits. In the absence of ventilation, there are no simple passive architectural methods for dehumidifying air, beyond devices in the experimental stage which will be mentioned subsequently. This means that the only realistic choice is to use equipment powered by mechanical or electrical energy.

Dehumidification is conventionally accomplished in the same way as air conditioning. Air is passed through a chiller coil which cools it down below its dew point so that the water vapor precipitates out and drains away. The now-dry air can then be warmed up almost to its original temperature by passing it back through a heat exchanger in the inlet loop where it helps to cool down the incoming air.

The Building Bioclimatic Chart shows that if the air was originally at 75F and 100% RH, and if the cooling coil was about 65F, the air would cool down along the saturation line and would fall from 133 to 91 grains of moisture per pound of dry air (in the scale on the right). Thus, for every pound of air passing through the chilling coil, 42 grains of moisture will precipitate and drain away. If this air is passed back through a heat exchanger where its temperature can climb back up to 75F, its relative humidity will be only 70%.

Under ideal conditions, chemical desiccants can take moisture directly out of the air while keeping the temperature nearly constant (there will only be a slight rise in temperature in the drying process). On the chart, this is shown as a drop from one moisture level to another, vertically down the dry-bulb temperature lines.

On the chart beyond the regions where ventilation strategies can be relied upon to create comfortable indoor conditions, air conditioning is the only alternative. Most commonly, these are conventional refrigerant or absorption systems powered by electrical or mechanical energy. However, as the economics of energy conservation change, heat pumps become more cost effective, particularly if also used during the heating season in conjunction with solar heating.

Experimental Cooling Proposals   In addition to the foregoing methods, there are a number of experimental techniques for utilizing natural energies for cooling. Several methods use variations of systems already discussed to cool a thermal storage medium by pumps or fans to achieve a day-to-night heat exchange

4. R. A. Bacon and W. E. Long: "Evaporative Cooling of a Residential Roof," *Heating and Ventilating,* November 1952.

effect (that is, the storage is not used to store heat, but to be cooled at night in order to cool the building the following day). Solar-heated rock storage installations can be used for summer cooling if the rock storage is cooled at night to then be available at a lower temperature to absorb heat from the house airstream the next day. If the air is dry enough, the gravel can be sprinkled to provide additional evaporative cooling.

In the Givoni Roof Radiation Trap System, the air is supplied to an underfloor gravel bed from an attic space that is cooled at night by natural radiant and evaporative cooling.[5] John Yellott is now testing the Energy Roof, a variation of the Skytherm Roof System, whereby water is cooled at night by flowing down a slightly inclined roof surface and then stored for its heat absorption effect in the ceiling of a low-rise structure.[6] Unfortunately, night-sky radiation cooling alone is not effective in the hazy atmosphere of a hot-humid climate. This is one area on the psychrometric chart where there seems to be no alternative except using mechanical or electrical equipment.

In what is often referred to as active "solar cooling," heat from solar collectors is used to vaporize an organic fluid such as lithium bromide to drive an absorption chiller, or, in a low-temperature boiler of a Rankine Cycle engine, to drive the compressor of a conventional air conditioner.

Other methods have been proposed for cooling, but unfortunately, none of them can lay claim to any of the areas of the Building Bioclimatic Chart that are not already covered by the strategies discussed above. At present, most of the experimental approaches are not cost effective when compared to conventional refrigerant or absorption systems, although this situation may change radically as the cost of conventional energy continues to rise.

Climate-Based Design

Having reviewed the way that ambient temperature and humidity data on the psychrometric chart can be related to the inherent capability of various building design strategies, the general design approach should be apparent: determine the ambient climatic data for a given site and then identify the design strategies, alone or in combination, that create human comfort conditions with the most appropriate, available means. In the foregoing discussion, certain strategies are emphasized as passive techniques to make the point that their proper engineering is a function of the building design itself. In practice, electrical controls may be used to operate insulating devices without which passive heating is limited, or to control air flow by fans, without which ventilation, evaporative cooling, and humidification schemes are particularly constrained. But for areas where there is no possibility of mechanical assist, such as parts of the developing world where

5. B. Givoni: "Solar Heating and Night Radiation Cooling by a Roof Radiation Trap," *Energy and Buildings*, vol. 1, no. 2 (October 1977).
6. A. Lincoln Pittinger, William R. White and John I. Yellott: "The Energy Roof, A New Approach to Solar Heating and Cooling," in *Energy Use Management Conference Proceedings*, R. Fazzolare and C. B. Smith, eds., Pergammon Press, New York, October 1977.

ENERGY
CONSERVATION
THROUGH
BUILDING
DESIGN

housing needs are most urgent, passive strategies can, in fact, be used more than is generally appreciated.

As outdoor climatological conditions extend farther from the comfort zone, or as other building design considerations prevent proper passive engineering, mechanically assisted or "active" natural energy techniques must be used. Any mechanical assistance should work with the natural energy flows within the structure, rather than in brute force against it. If properly designed, the amount of purchased energy required is a small fraction of the "free" natural energy that is "harvested." If neither passive nor active natural energy systems are sufficient, the control of comfort conditions must depend on conventional furnaces, boilers, resistance heating, refrigerant or absorptive air conditioning, or chemical dehumidification. Again, given proper building design, these mechanical or electrical systems, in most cases, are needed only in a supplemental capacity, to "top off" the natural energy systems.

As this method of correlating climatological data with building design strategies becomes better appreciated as a basis of energy conservation design, it can be hoped that climatic statistics will be made available in a form directly suited to the designer's information requirements.

Until that time, however, it is nonetheless a simple matter to make a psychrometric profile of any climate in the United States from the annual summaries of local climatological data available for thousands of weather stations throughout the country.[7] For each month, the *Annual Summary* gives the average daily maximum and minimum temperatures as well as the average RH at 4:00 am, 10:00 am, 4:00 pm, and 10:00 pm. For design purposes, a reasonably accurate picture of the local climate can be reconstructed from this data. To meet the preliminary design needs, it is thus possible to map the climate of any building site by plotting the average monthly "loops" from climatological data for the nearest weather station.

There are many systems for categorizing climate types, some of which identify dozens of different climate regions.[8] But, when dealing with building types, most authors generalize all climates into one of four groups (hot-dry, hot-wet, temperate, and cold) and then give specific recommendations for designing buildings for each.[9] However, many locations do not fit neatly into just one of these categories. Almost all areas in the United States have more than one season, each of which may be climatologically quite different from the other. Indigenous or traditional building types have been developed to respond to composite climates in almost every part of the world, with especially interesting examples found in Iraq and in the Himalayan country of Bhutan.[10]

The challenge for the modern architect is to design a single building that responds in an equally appropriate manner to each of the different seasons within a given climate. Even when outdoor

7. *Local Climatological Data, Annual Summary* National Oceanographic and Aeronautic Administration, U.S. Government Printing Office, Washington, DC.
8. Arthur Strahler: *Physical Geography*, John Wiley and Sons, New York, 1968.
9. Givoni: *Man, Climate and Architecture*; Olgyay and Olgyay: *Design with Climate*; O. H. Koenigsberger, T. G. Ingersol, A. Mayhew and S. V. Szokilay: *Manual of Tropical Housing and Building*, Longman Group Ltd., London, 1973.
10. Awni Shaaban: "The Impact of Hot-Dry Climate on Housing in Iraq," masters thesis, School of Architecture and Urban Planning, UCLA, June 1977; also see chap. 1, Refs. 5 and 6.

conditions stay entirely within the human comfort zone, the architect must be careful to design a building envelope which does not destroy otherwise benign climate conditions. When outdoor conditions fall beyond the comfort zone, the designer's task is more difficult, particularly if the climate conditions in different seasons require non-compatible solutions. The cost-effectiveness of various design techniques has to be compared to the particular energy demand profile of the location, as well as to the local differences in the cost of available purchased energy. The solution to a heating requirement could also help cooling needs, such as offered by the roof-pond systems or other dual uses of high thermal mass in the building structure or in a separate storage component.

An insensitively designed building can only be made comfortable by using unnecessary amounts of purchased energy. Well-known examples are glass boxes in warm climates and poorly insulated structures in cool climates. Once the simplicity of passive design strategies is recognized, we could add to this list of examples any building in temperate climates that needs to be unnecessarily heated or air conditioned by mechanical means. As world energy and resource problems become more severe, such a building will be an increasing source of embarrassment to the architect and engineer who designed it.

Technical Note: Basic Psychrometrics

The psychrometric chart is a graphic representation of air temperature, humidity, and other data that are important in climate control design (*Figure 7*). In this chapter, the ''dry-bulb'' temperature (a measure of sensible heat as read on a standard thermometer and shown on the psychrometric chart by vertical lines read along the horizontal axis), and the *relative humidity* (the ratio of vapor pressure in an air-water mixture to saturation vapor pressure, shown by the curved lines that climb from left to right) are used as a basis for determining appropriate climate-design building strategies.

The *dew point temperature* (DP) at which moisture from the air begins to condense, forms the upper curved boundary of the chart, the line of 100% humidity. It represents the fact that as the temperature falls (from right to left on the bottom axis), the maximum amount of moisture that the air can hold falls with it. For example, if summer indoor conditions are 75F and 68% RH, the dew point temperature is 64F (found by moving horizontally along the constant moisture line to the 100% RH curve at the left edge of the chart and then reading the temperature). This means that in these conditions, precipitation will occur on any surface colder than 64F, no matter whether it is a glass of ice water, the coil of an air-conditioning unit, or a foundation wall.

Other quantities that are detailed in standard mechanical

engineering texts and that are shown on the psychrometric chart include:

- *Wet-bulb Temperature* (WB), shown on lines that slope down from left to right and read on the curved line on the upper left edge of the chart, is the temperature indicated by a thermometer whose bulb is covered by a wet wick and exposed to a stream of air moving between 500 and 2000 fpm.
- *Humidity Ratio* (W), also known as specific humidity, is the ratio of the mass of water vapor in each pound of dry air to the mass of air and is shown on the horizontal lines and read along the right-hand vertical axis.
- *Vapor Pressure* (Pw) is the pressure exerted by water vapor in the air. (Vapor Pressure Scale is not included in Figure 7).
- *Sensible Heat Ratio* (SHR) is the ratio of the sensible heat to total heat in a process. Sensible heat is heat which, when added to a substance, changes only its temperature and not its state.
- *Specific Volume* (V) is the volume occupied by one pound of a substance and shown on the psychrometric chart as the cubic feet of the mixture per pound of dry air. The reciprocal of specific volume is density, pounds per cubic foot.
- *Enthalpy* (h) is a mathematical quantity used in thermody-

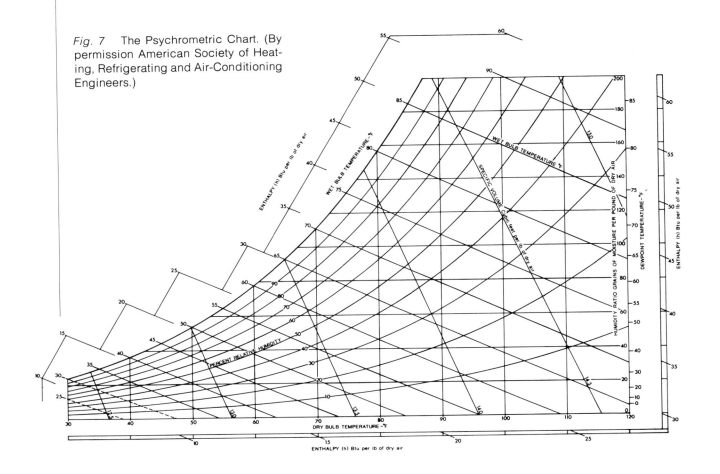

Fig. 7 The Psychrometric Chart. (By permission American Society of Heating, Refrigerating and Air-Conditioning Engineers.)

namic calculations and equal to the internal energy of a substance plus the pressure times the volume ($h = u + pv$).

The psychrometric chart thus contains in one graphical reference the entire range of quantities needed for climate control design as summarized in *Figure 8*.

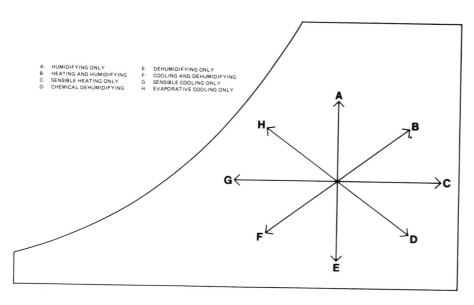

A. HUMIDIFYING ONLY
B. HEATING AND HUMIDIFYING
C. SENSIBLE HEATING ONLY
D. CHEMICAL DEHUMIDIFYING

E. DEHUMIDIFYING ONLY
F. COOLING AND DEHUMIDIFYING
G. SENSIBLE COOLING ONLY
H. EVAPORATIVE COOLING ONLY

Fig. 8   Climate-conditioning processes.

7

FENESTRATION AND HEAT FLOW THROUGH WINDOWS

John I. Yellott

Fenestration, derived from the Latin *fenestra* and the French *fenêtre*, is currently defined as, "the arrangement and proportioning of windows." Windows have long been matters of concern, controversy, and even conflict. They were objects of taxation in eighteenth-century England,[1] and the mere rumor of the possible imposition of similar taxes in colonial America caused a near-insurrection.[2] In England, the "Doctrine of Ancient Lights" has, for centuries, protected property owners from having their share of daylight impaired by the erection of new buildings which would diminish the amount of sunshine falling on long-existing windows. We in the United States do not enjoy such protection,[3] although, with the rapidly increasing importance of solar heating and cooling, several states, led by New Mexico, have begun to enact legislation guaranteeing the "right to light."

Windows have, for at least 40 years, been a subject of particular interest to the members of ASHRAE (the American Society of Heating, Refrigerating and Air-Conditioning Engineers) Technical Committee 4.5 which is concerned with fenestration heat gains and losses. The heat gains which occur in winter when south-facing windows receive solar radiation are the basis for many of today's passive heating systems, while the gains which occur in summer cause much of the cooling load which both conventional and solar air-conditioning systems seek to overcome. All windows, regardless of their orientation, lose heat by *conduction* when the temperature is higher indoors than out, and the situation reverses when the air becomes warmer outdoors than in. When bright sunshine falls on windows, however, they generally admit far more heat than they lose.

The purpose of this chapter is to summarize for architects, designers, and engineers the very large amount of information which is now available on the subject of fenestration heat gains and losses and to show how this can be put to practical use. The principal references cited here are the *ASHRAE Handbook of Fundamentals*[4] and a number of technical papers which have appeared in the monthly *ASHRAE Journal*, in the Society's *Transactions* and in *Solar Energy*, the quarterly scientific journal of the International Solar Energy Society.

Glazing Materials and Their Properties

Glass Most of the fenestration in the world is glazed with clear single glass varying in thickness from less than 1/8 in. for small windows to 1/2 in. or more for large windows on the upper floors of high-rise buildings, where wind velocities can be very high and the consequences of breakage catastrophic. Throughout history, glass has been produced by many processes, and today glass of good quality is available virtually everywhere in the world. "Single-strength" and "double-strength" clear sheet glass, approximately 1/12-in. and 1/8-in. thick respectively, are generally

1. S. H. Steinberg: *A New Dictionary of British History*, 2nd ed., s.v. "Window Tax," St. Martin's Press, New York, 1971.
2. M. Martin and L. Gelber, eds.: *Dictionary of American History*, s.v. "Frie's Rebellion," Scribners, New York, 1976.
3. R. L. Robbins: "Law and Solar Energy Systems," *Solar Energy*, vol. 18, no. 5, pp. 371–379 (1976).
4. American Society of Heating, Refrigerating, and Air-Conditioning Engineers: *Handbook of Fundamentals*, 1977 ed., New York, chap. 26.

used for small residential windows, while ¼-in. glass is used almost universally in larger residential windows and in commercial and institutional applications. The thinner glass is still made by "drawing," while architectural glass is now made almost entirely by the "float" process, developed by England's Pilkington Brothers. Solar collectors generally use double-strength sheet or float glass, and tempering is usually employed to reduce the danger of breakage.

The most important property of glass, as far as solar energy technology is concerned, is its ability to transmit the shortwave radiation that comes from the sun. *Figure 1,* the solar radiation spectrum at sea level on a clear day when the sun is directly overhead (the air mass is 1.0),[5] shows that the invisible ultraviolet portion shorter than 0.4 μm in wavelength contains only about

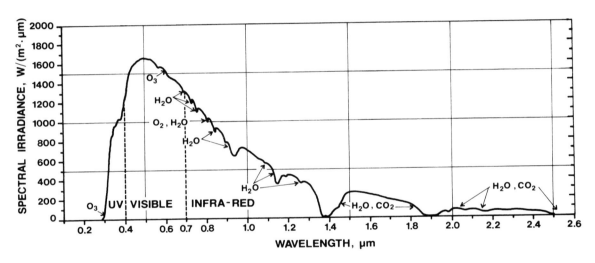

Fig. 1 The solar spectrum at the earth's surface with the sun directly overhead at sea level (air mass = 1.0).

5% of the total solar energy. This small fraction is very important, however, because it is responsible for the fading of fabrics, the deterioration of paints and polymers and, in some cases, skin cancer. The fraction is considerably higher, nearly 9%, in outer space, but a protective layer of ozone (O_3) in the upper atmosphere absorbs most of the shorter and more potent UV radiation. Most clear glass transmits about 50% of the ultraviolet energy and, while the glass itself is not harmed, drapes, rugs, upholstery and other fabrics exposed to this radiation will generally deteriorate rapidly unless some kind of protection is provided.

Only the spectral range between 0.4 and 0.7 μm can be detected by the average human eye, and so it is called "visible." Only the radiation between 0.4 and 0.7 μm is properly termed "light" or "sunlight," and it accounts for about 47% of the total solar energy that reaches the earth. The most intense radiation in the entire solar spectrum is at 0.480 μm, in the blue-green region.

5. M. P. Thekaekara: "Data on Incident Solar Energy," Supplement to *Proceedings of the 20th Annual Meeting,* Institute of Environmental Sciences, Mt. Prospect, IL, 1974. See also NASA Technical Report TRR-351, October 1970, and *Solar Energy,* vol. 14, no. 2, pp. 109–120, (1973).

This happens, perhaps by chance but more probably by design, to be close to the region in which the human eye is most sensitive.

The near-infrared portion of the spectrum, between 0.7 and 3.0 μm, contains the remaining 48% of the terrestrial sunshine. This is quite invisible to the human eye, although it can be detected readily by electronic or thermal means. It provides heat to the earth, and the band between 0.700 and 1.000 μm helps plants grow tall. Most clear glass is relatively transparent to this portion of the spectrum, which can be very helpful for passive heating systems in winter, although it is often quite annoying in summer unless it is blocked out in some manner.

The transmittance values which are reported by glass manufacturers are generally made at near-normal incidence (see *Figure 2a*) with incident angle θ less than 10 deg, using a spectrophotometer which can measure the transmittance as it varies with wavelength. Two values are usually given, the first being for "average daylight," which is the transmittance for the visible

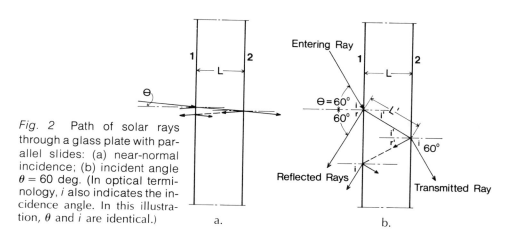

Fig. 2 Path of solar rays through a glass plate with parallel slides: (a) near-normal incidence; (b) incident angle $\theta = 60$ deg. (In optical terminology, *i* also indicates the incidence angle. In this illustration, θ and *i* are identical.)

portion of the spectrum between 0.4 and 0.7 μm. It is generally higher than the second value, often designated as "total solar," which means that it covers the entire solar spectrum from 0.4 to 3.0 μm. As an example, a leading manufacturer quotes 0.89 as the "average daylight" transmittance for his double-strength clear glass, and 0.80 as its "total solar" transmittance; for ¼-in. clear float glass, transmittances are 0.87 and 0.75, respectively.

The transmittance of glass is dependent upon the wavelength of the radiation striking it. Most clear glass (*Figure 3*) transmits nothing below 0.3 μm and, as mentioned above, unless special precautions are taken, about 50% of the UV below 0.4 μm is transmitted for incident angles up to 30 deg. Visible transmittance is quite high, as is transmittance in the near infrared, out to the end of the solar spectrum at 2.8 to 3.0 μm. At that point, for thicknesses of ⅛ in. and above, transmittance falls abruptly to virtually zero and *none* of the longer infrared is transmitted.

The heat-absorbing glasses, also as shown in Figure 3, are

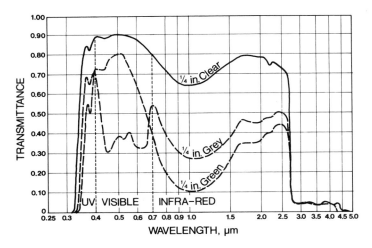

Fig. 3 Spectral transmittances for ¼-in. architectural glass: (a) clear; (b) gray heat-absorbing; (c) green heat-absorbing.

characterized by relatively wide variations in transmittance in the visible portion of the spectrum, but their average transmittance over the entire solar spectrum is about 50% of the transmittance of clear glass of the same thickness. None retains any transmittance beyond 4.5 μm.

This characteristic of glass distinguishes it from most of the plastic glazing materials which generally are transparent to radiation in the infrared spectrum, which raises their transmittance well above the zero value that makes glass so valuable in many solar applications. The temperatures attained by sun-warmed indoor surfaces rarely exceed 130F and so, in accordance with Wien's displacement law, the wavelength of their most intense radiation, λ_{max}, is:

Equation No. 1
$$\lambda_{max} = \frac{5216}{(t_s + 460)} = \frac{5216}{590} = 8.84 \ \mu m$$

Radiation at this wavelength is entirely absorbed by ordinary glass and this gives rise to the "greenhouse effect," by which solar radiation is trapped when it enters an enclosed space through a glass window. The incoming radiation is absorbed and converted to heat by surfaces which then become radiation sources. The radiant energy absorbed by the window raises its temperature until the absorbed energy can be dissipated, primarily to the outdoor environment, and so it is incorrect to say that none of the entering radiation escapes. However, the amount that escapes is much less than if the window were unglazed or if the glazing were transparent to the infrared radiation.

The greenhouse effect has been a subject of debate ever since the eminent physicist R. W. Wood became convinced that the principal advantage of glass in a greenhouse lay in its ability to minimize convection heat loss.[6] Later work has shown that both radiation and convection must be suppressed if a sun-heated surface is to remain warm, and fortunately glass performs both functions.

The transmittance of a particular sample of glass is determined primarily by its thickness and by the iron content of the sand used in its manufacture. The highest transmittance is attained by premium grade "water white" glass, which contains only about 0.035% of iron in the form of Fe_2O_3. Standard architectural glass contains about 0.10% iron oxide, while bronze or gray heat-absorbing glass, with a total solar transmittance of about 0.46, typically contains 0.48% Fe_2O_3. This type of glass is generally called "soda-lime" glass because, in addition to silicon dioxide, which constitutes about 73% of its composition, it contains oxides of calcium, magnesium, sodium, and potassium.

The physical properties of glass also depend largely upon its chemical composition.[7] For soda-lime glass, the density is about 157.27 lb/ft³ (0.091 lb/in.³). A single square foot of double-strength (⅛-in.) window glass weighs about 1.64 lb, while ¼-in. architectural glass weighs 3.28 lb/ft². Thermal conductance of soda-lime glass varies almost linearly with temperature from 7.35 Btu/[hr. ft.² (F/in.)] at 68F, to 7.48 at 100F, and 7.68 at 150F. The coefficient of thermal expansion for ordinary window glass is about 6×10^{-6} in./in. F. The specific heat of soda-lime glass is about 0.19 Btu/lb$_m$ F.

Borosilicate glass, typified by Corning's Pyrex®, has a density of 138 lb/ft³; its thermal conductance is 8.12 Btu in./hr ft² F; its specific heat is 0.18; and its coefficient of thermal expansion at 100F is only 2.0×10^{-6} in./in. F. It is more likely to be used in tubular form than in flat sheets, although the latter can be obtained when low thermal expansion is essential.

Other Glazing Materials There are many other materials that are "diathermanous," which simply means that they are capable of transmitting radiant energy, but only a few have all of the properties required for fenestration. They must be resistant to abrasion, UV deterioration, and other forms of weathering, and they must be transparent to solar radiation but relatively opaque to wavelengths longer than 3.0 μm. There are a number of polymers which possess many of these properties as well as ability to resist dimensional deformation at temperatures up to about 180F. The behavior of most of these materials, as far as solar energy utilization is concerned, is so similar to that of glass that they will not be given special treatment here, other than to mention some of their more valuable properties.

The thermoplastic glazing materials, to use their generic name, are generally shatterproof and several are so tough that they are, in suitable thicknesses, virtually bullet-proof. The polycarbonates, in particular, are frequently used for glazing where breakage and

6. R. W. Wood: "The Greenhouse Effect," *Philosophical Magazine*, London, 1908.
7. E. B. Shand: *Glass Engineering Handbook,* 2nd ed., McGraw-Hill Publishing Company, New York, 1958.

vandalism are serious problems. Some, including the acrylic, polymethyl methacrylate,[8] have demonstrated their ability to withstand aging in the hostile southwestern desert for at least 20 years. Others, generically known as fluorinated hydrocarbons, possess high transmittance, great resistance to UV degradation and, when mounted to prevent frequent flexure, they have long life in outdoor applications.

Their thermal conductance is generally lower than that of glass, but the U-factor (over-all coefficient of heat transmission, Btu/hr ft² F) for single- and double-glazed fenestration is about the same for both glass and plastics. The density of polymers varies widely, ranging from below 60 lb/ft³ for polyethylene to 75 for the acrylics and 140 for polytetrofluorethylene (the completely fluorinated and ultrastable fluorocarbon known by the trade-mark name Teflon®).

Many of these materials can be drawn and extruded, while others can be admixed with glass fibers to give them highly desirable physical properties of strength and durability. For specific applications, advice should be sought from manufacturers, because this art is changing very rapidly and experience is showing that some thermoplastics are suitable for use in glazing applications while others are not. In most cases, the discussion presented below with glass as the principal example will apply equally well to plastics with comparable optical characteristics.

Solar Optical Properties and Their Significance

Definitions and Optical Laws The transmittance, τ, reflectance, ρ, and absorptance, α, for glazing materials in the wavelength band covered by the solar spectrum are known as their solar-optical properties because they obey the laws of physical optics as they apply to this wavelength range. These properties depend upon the composition and thickness of the material, the quality of polish on its surfaces, the wavelength of the incident radiation, and the angle of incidence between the line normal to the surface and the incoming solar rays. *Figure 2b* shows what happens to a beam of shortwave radiation when it strikes a polished, diathermanous material such as glass. A small fraction of the incident radiation, It_θ, striking the glazing at an incident angle θ, is reflected from the front surface at an angle which, for a perfectly polished surface, is exactly equal to the incident angle. The fraction that is reflected varies with the incident angle θ but, for angles less than about 30 deg, the reflectance is about 4% for the interface between air and glass.

The remainder of the ray, containing about 96% of the original energy, enters the glass where the ray is bent *towards* the normal, thus experiencing the phenomenon known as *refraction*. The angles of incidence and refraction, i and i', are related by the *refractive index, n'* where:

8. L. G. Rainhart and W. P. Schimmell: "Effect of Outdoor Aging on Acrylic Sheet," *Solar Energy,* vol. 17, pp. 259–264 (September 1975).

$$n' = \sin i / \sin i' \text{ (Snell's law)} \quad \text{\textit{Equation No. 2}}$$

Typical values of the refractive index are:[9] soda-lime glass, 1.526; Plexiglas® or Lucite® polymethyl methacrylate, 1.48; Tedlar® polyvinylfluoride, 1.45; water, 1.33. For near-normal incidence, there are no complicating effects such as polarization and the first-surface reflectance is found by Fresnel's law:

$$\rho_1 = [(n' - 1)/(n' + 1)]^2 \quad \text{\textit{Equation No. 3}}$$

Thus, the first surface reflectances for the substances listed above are: soda-lime glass, 0.0434; acrylics, 0.0375; Tedlar®, 0.0337; and water, 0.0201.

If the incident angle i is, for example, 60 deg, and the material is soda-lime glass, the angle of refraction will be:

$$i' = \text{arc sin } (\sin 60)/1.526 = 35.58 \text{ deg} \quad \text{\textit{Equation No. 4}}$$

The refracted beam will proceed through the glass, losing some of its energy by absorption within the glass. This absorption, for a homogeneous medium such as glass or water, obeys still another law, which introduces the actual length of path L' ($L' = L/\cos i'$) and the *extinction coefficient K*, which is a property of the glass itself:

$$\tau_{1-2} = \begin{array}{c} \text{Transmittance} \\ \text{from glass surface} = 1.0/e^{KL'} \\ \text{1 to surface 2} \end{array} \quad \text{\textit{Equation No. 5}}$$

The extinction coefficient K varies from about 0.11 for the best "water white" glass to 0.68 for commercial-grade window glass. For ¼-in. thickness, KL' at near-normal incidence will be 0.275 for the "water white" ultraclear glass, and its internal transmittance would be $\tau_{1-2} = 1/e^{0.275} = 0.973$. Allowing for 0.08 total reflectance at the two air-glass surfaces, the transmittance would be close to 0.893. For the commercial-grade glass, $KL' = 0.17$ and $\tau_{1-2} = 1.0/e^{0.17} = 0.844$. Again subtracting the 0.08 reflectance, the actual transmittance would be about 0.764.

The reflection at the second surface will take place at the angle of refraction i', and the reflected beam will undergo both absorption within the glass and reflection at the next glass-air interface, with subsequent multiple reflections until no energy is left to be reflected.

9. A. H. Whillier: *Applications of Solar Energy for Heating and Cooling of Buildings*, ASHRAE, New York, 1977, chap. VIII.

The transmitted beam, surviving after two reflections and partial absorption, emerges with another refraction at surface 2 to resume a path parallel to the original direction, but slightly displaced from it. For ordinary clear glass, the total solar reflectance at near-normal incidence will be close to 0.08 and the transmittance, allowing for both reflectances and absorption, will be about 0.86 for double-strength (⅛-in.) and 0.75 for ¼-in. float. The absorptance can be found by applying the law:

Equation No. 6   **Transmittance τ + Reflectance ρ + Absorptance α = 1.00**

Thus the absorptance for ⅛-in. glass is 0.06, and for ¼-in. glass, it is 0.17.

The reflectance from glass surfaces can be reduced by several processes, but none is in use at this time for window glass. Instead, metallic or organic coatings are often applied to increase the reflectance or the absorptance, and thus to reduce the transmittance of unwanted excess sunshine during the summer. Unfortunately, these processes also reduce winter heat gain, which may be undesirable if the window is to be a source of welcome warmth.

Variation of Solar-Optical Properties with Incident Angle   The solar-optical properties for a given sample of glazing material vary primarily with the incident angle θ between the solar ray and the line normal to the surface. *Figure 4* shows the surface-solar angles which are important in this discussion as they apply to a vertical surface.[10] The solar altitude β and azimuth ϕ locate the sun with respect to a specific point O in the horizontal plane. Values of

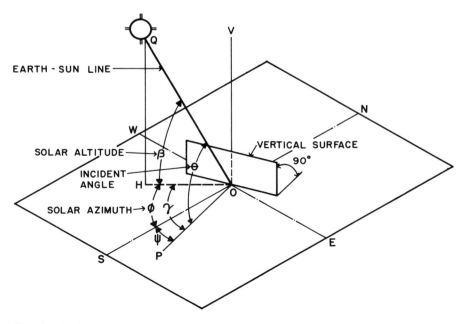

10. *Footnote 4,* p. 26.10, Table 13 and footnotes.

Fig. 4   Surface-solar angles for vertical windows.

β and φ are given in *Reference 4* (Chapter 26, Tables 2–10) for the daylight hours of the 21st day of each month, for latitudes from 0°N to 64°N, by increments of 8 deg. Linear interpolation is adequate to find these angles for other than even hours and the designated latitudes. For programable hand calculators, the equations are:

$$\text{Sin altitude, } \beta = \frac{\text{Cos}}{\text{local latitude}} \times \frac{\text{Cos}}{\text{solar declination}} \times \frac{\text{Cos}}{\text{hour angle}}$$
$$+ \frac{\text{Sin}}{\text{local latitude}} \times \frac{\text{Sin}}{\text{solar declination}}$$

Equation No. 7

After the altitude has been found, the solar azimuth is found by:

$$\frac{\text{Sin}}{\text{solar azimuth}} = \frac{\text{Cos}}{\text{solar declination}} \times \frac{\text{Sin}}{\text{hour angle}} \Big/ \frac{\text{Cos solar}}{\text{altitude, } \beta}$$

Equation No. 8

The local latitude is found from maps or tables, and declination is found from an almanac or, approximately, from the following equation:[11]

$$\text{Solar declination, } \delta = 23.45 \text{ deg} \times \sin\left[360 \times \frac{284 + D}{365}\right]$$

Equation No. 9

where D is the year day, counting from January 1.

As an example, consider Boston, Massachusetts, latitude 42.37°N, on December 6, 1977 at 1:30 pm, apparent solar time, and find the solar altitude and azimuth. The declination δ is − 22.5 deg and the hour angle H is (13.5 − 12.0) × 15 = 22.50 deg. For 40°N, December 21, at 1:00 and 2:00 pm, the nearest tabulated values are: solar altitude β = 25.0 and 20.7 deg; solar azimuth φ (measured from the south) = 15.2 and 29.4 deg. By interpolation, the desired values would be: β = 22.9 deg; φ = 22.3 deg.

By calculation, knowing that for December 6 the year day D = 340, it is found that the solar declination is approximately − 22.7 deg (only 1% away from the exact value) and the solar altitude is actually 21.9 deg. The solar azimuth is calculated to be 22.4 deg, so it is obvious that the interpolated values are sufficiently accurate for all practical purposes.

11. J. A. Duffie and W. A. Beckman: *Solar Energy Thermal Processes*, John Wiley and Sons, New York, 1974, pp. 78–81.

Returning to Figure 4, one can see that the angles which designate the surface orientation are its tilt upward from the horizontal, shown as 90 deg in this illustration; and its azimuth, ∠ SOP, designated by ψ, which is the angular distance in the horizontal plane between the south-north line SON and the normal to the surface, line OP. Azimuths are generally designated in terms of compass notation in the ASHRAE tables. An azimuth designation of SSE, for example, designates a surface facing south-southeast, with an azimuth, measured from the *south*, of 22.5 deg.

The angle HOP in Figure 4 designates the surface-solar azimuth, γ, which is most readily determined by inspection when the solar and surface azimuths are known. If Figure 4 is redrawn, as in *Figure 5*, to show the horizontal plane, it becomes obvious that, in this case, the surface-solar azimuth γ is the *sum* of the surface azimuth and the solar azimuth. In the example used above, the solar azimuth proved to be 22.4, so the surface-solar azimuth would be 22.4 + 22.5 = 44.9 deg. If the surface had been facing

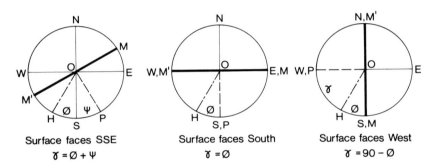

Surface faces SSE
$\gamma = \varnothing + \psi$

Surface faces South
$\gamma = \varnothing$

Surface faces West
$\gamma = 90 - \varnothing$

Fig. 5   Solar angles in the horizontal plane.

due west, its azimuth would have been 90 deg (in these calculations, the azimuth is always positive) and so the surface-solar azimuth would be the angular *difference* between the two azimuths.

The most important angle displayed in Figure 4 is the incident angle, ∠ QOP, between the earth-sun line OQ and the normal to the surface, OP. The incident angle θ determines both the intensity of the direct component of the solar radiation striking the surface and the ability of the glazing to transmit, reflect and absorb the incoming solar energy. For any *vertical* surface, and most windows are vertical, the incident angle can be found from:

Equation No. 10 $\text{Cos } \theta = \text{Cos solar altitude} \times \text{Cos surface-solar azimuth}$

Tabulated values of the incident angles for vertical surfaces are given in the tables cited above for the daylight hours of the 21st day of each month, for latitudes from 0°N to 64°N. For the example given above, the latitude was 42.37°N, the date was December 6, 1977, and the time was 1:30 pm. The exact solar altitude was 21.9 deg and the surface-solar azimuth was 44.9 deg. By the use of Equation 10, it is found that the incident angle is 48.5 deg.

Using the tabulated values for 40°N latitude, for the same date at 1:00 and 2:00 pm, θ is found to be 44 and 55 deg, respectively, and interpolation between these values gives 49.5 deg, indicating that, once again, the tabulated values are quite close enough for most purposes.

The primary reason for finding the incident angle is to estimate values of the solar-optical properties of the glazing material under consideration. Turning back to Figure 2, we recall that the incident radiation, I_t, striking the surface at incident angle θ, undergoes a first reflection at the air-glass interface, then a refraction as the ray enters the glass, and then absorption takes its toll as the ray passes through the glass to the indoor side, designated by the number 2. There it undergoes a second reflection, and the reflected ray returns to the first surface, where a minute fraction is re-reflected, to undergo successive internal reflections until it is all absorbed. Most of the re-reflected ray passes back through the glass-air interface where part of it is refracted to follow a path parallel to the first reflected ray. For clear glass, when the incident angle θ is quite small, the total reflection is about 8% of the original beam.

As it passes through the glass, some of the radiant energy is absorbed, raising the glass temperature enough to enable the absorbed energy to be dissipated by radiation and convection from surface 2 to the indoor environment, and from surface 1 to the outdoor environment. It will be seen subsequently that in summer about 73% of the absorbed energy is dissipated outdoors, while the remaining 27% makes its way indoors to become part of the heat which is *admitted* through the glazing. In winter, these become 80% and 20%, respectively.

As the incident angle is increased, the reflected fraction of the incident radiation also increases, with a major rise occurring after θ passes 35 deg. When θ becomes 90 deg, all of the radiation is reflected and so there is none left to be transmitted or absorbed. An increase in incident angle also lengthens the path length through the glass and so, as predicted by Equation 6, the absorption within the glass will increase until the incident angle reaches about 50 deg. At higher values of θ, the rapidly increasing reflectance will so drastically reduce the energy entering the glass that both the transmitted and absorbed energies will drop off rapidly to zero.

The variation of the solar-optical properties with changing

ENERGY
CONSERVATION
THROUGH
BUILDING
DESIGN

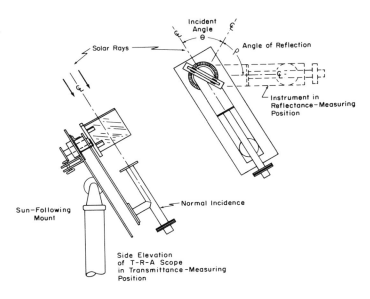

Fig. 6   The TRA-Scope for measuring solar-optical properties of polished plates with parallel sides.

incident angle can be calculated for single, unshaded glass by using the laws of physical optics as explained by Whillier in *Reference 9,* or they may be measured directly. A relatively simple instrument, called the TRA-Scope, shown in *Figure 6,* has been developed for this purpose.[12] It consists of a normal-incidence solar radiometer, preferably of the silicon cell type because of its ultrarapid response, mounted on an arm which can be rotated around a shaft which also carries a sample-holder. The incident angle between the sun's rays and the sample can be adjusted from 0 to about 70 deg, and the transmittance can be measured almost instantaneously by connecting the output of the pyrheliometer through a potentiometer to a strip-chart millivolt (mV) recorder. The instrument is trained on the sun with no glass in the sample-holder and the potentiometer is adjusted to give a 100% reading on the recorder. With the chart drive running, the sample is inserted and adjusted to make the incident angle equal to 0.0 deg. The recorder immediately displays the normal incidence transmittance.

The incident angle is then varied by any desired increment and the recorder will give the transmittance at each angle. To obtain the reflectance at any angle above about 10 deg, the sample is set at the desired angle and the arm carrying the pyrheliometer is then rotated to the angle of reflection. At this point, it picks up the reflected beam and the strip-chart recorder immediately shows the reflectance. When there is bright, steady sunshine, the entire range of incident angles can be covered and repeated in only a few minutes. If the glass possesses unusual spectral properties, a "color-blind" pyrheliometer should be employed, using a thermopile as its sensor. This is somewhat slower in its response than

12. J. I. Yellott: "Selective Reflectance, A New Approach to Solar Heat Control," *ASHRAE Transactions,* vol. 69, p. 418 (1963).

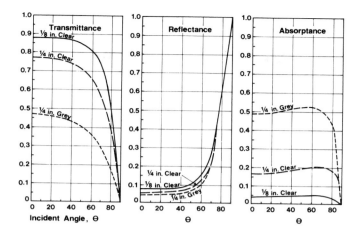

Fig. 7 Variation with incident angle of solar-optical properties for clear and heat-absorbing glass.

is the silicon cell instrument, but the results are then independent of the spectral behavior of the glass.

Figure 7 shows the variation of the solar-optical properties with θ for three different kinds of glass. There is very little change until θ exceeds 30 deg, and then the transmittance falls off towards 0, the reflectance increases towards 1.00, and the absorptance increases until θ reaches 50 to 60 deg, and then it also heads towards 0. The importance of these variations will be seen in the following sections.

Fenestration Heat Losses and Gains, Without Sunshine

Heat Flow Through Sunless Glass   When no radiant energy is involved, heat flow through glass is calculated by the conduction equation:

$$Q = A \times U \times (t_o - t_i)$$ *Equation No. 11*

where Q = rate of heat flow, Btu/hr
   A = area of the glazing, excluding framing, ft²
   t_o and t_i = outdoor and indoor dry-bulb temperatures, F
   U = over-all coefficient of heat transfer, Btu/hr ft² F

When t_o exceeds t_i the heat flow is inward through the glazing to the enclosed space. When t_i exceeds t_o the heat flow is outward.

U, the over-all heat transfer coefficient, accounts for both radiation and convection at the two surfaces of the glass as well as conduction through the glazing material. It is convenient to think in terms of thermal resistances rather than conductances, since, for a series situation such as a window, the resistances are additive. The thermal resistance, generally symbolized by R, is the reciprocal of the thermal conductance, which has the units: Btu/hr ft² F. Thus, R should have as its units: hr ft² F/Btu.

This is an awkward and non-informative collection of symbols and it is helpful to rewrite it in this form: F/(Btu/(ft² hr)). The thermal resistance is thus the number of degrees of temperature difference required to cause heat to flow from the warm surface of a building element to the cool surface at the rate of 1 Btu/(hr ft²). For glass, the resistance is L/k, where L is the thickness in inches and k is the thermal conductivity in (Btu in.)/(hr ft² F).

Since glass used in fenestration is generally quite thin and its thermal conductivity is relatively high, the resistance to heat flow of the glass in a fenestration system is always quite small. The major part of the resistance is offered by the processes needed to bring the heat *to* the warm surface and to remove it *from* the cool surface. Both radiation and convection are involved in these two processes and they are generally combined into a single "surface coefficient," designated as h_i and h_o for the indoor and outdoor surfaces, respectively.

For many years, it has been customary in ASHRAE fenestration calculations to use a single value, 1.46 Btu/(hr ft² F), for the combined inner surface coefficient h_i when natural or free convection prevails at the inner surface of the glazing. Actually, both the convection and the radiation components of h_i are temperature-dependent, as shown by:

Equation No. 12

$$h_i = 0.27(t_g - t_i)^{0.25} + \frac{0.84 \times 0.1713}{(t_g - t_i)} \times [(T_g/100)^4 - T_i/100)^4]$$

where: t_g, t_i = glass and air temperature, F
T_g, T_i = absolute glass and air temperatures, R

The assumption is made here that the room surfaces are perfectly "black," in the radiation sense, and that they are at the same temperature as the indoor air. The accepted value of the hemispheric emittance of uncoated glass, e_g, in the temperature range involved here is now 0.84 (in *Reference 12*, see Figure 6 and Table III).

Using *Equation 12*, it is found that the conventional value of h_i, 1.46 Btu/(hr ft² F), and the corresponding resistance, $R_i = 0.68$ F/(Btu/(hr ft²)), are correct for two quite different conditions. In winter, when $t_g = 20F$ and $t_i = 70F$, and in summer when $t_g = 90F$ and $t_i = 75F$, h_i is very close to the "standard" value. For very hot glass in summer,[13] h_i can rise as high as 1.79; in winter, on mild days when the glass temperature is a relatively warm 65F, h_i can be as low as 1.25. The range in resistance is from 0.56 in summer to 0.80 in winter.

13. *Footnote 4*, p. 26.14, Table 15.

For very tall windows, and for windows with forced circulation over the inner surface, h_i is probably considerably higher than the values given above. The radiation component is unaffected, but the convection component, h_{ci} will be about:

$$h_{ci} = 0.99 + 0.21 \times \text{air velocity, fps} \qquad \textit{Equation No. 13}$$

For moderate differences in temperature between the glass and the indoor air, a simplified form of the radiation coefficient is:

$$h_{Ri} = 0.1713 \times 4 \times e_g \times (T_g)^3 \times 10^{-8}/\Delta t \qquad \textit{Equation No. 14}$$

$$h_{Ri} = 6.85 \times e_g \times (T_g/100)^3 \times 10^{-3}/\Delta t \qquad \textit{Equation No. 14a}$$

The outer surface coefficients which have been in use in ASHRAE computations for at least 40 years are 4.0 Btu/(hr ft² F) for summer, wind speed = 7.5 mph; and 6 Btu/(hr ft² F) for winter, wind speed = 15 mph. The resistances R_o are 0.25F/[(Btu/hr)/ft²] in summer and 0.17 in winter. These values are based on work done at the University of Minnesota in the late 1920s, using relatively small plates in a wind tunnel. The radiation component is based upon the assumption, which is only approximately correct, that the outdoor environment is essentially "black" at the temperature of the ambient air. This assumption may be considerably in error on cold, dry, winter nights, when the effective radiation temperature of the sky is substantially below the actual dry-bulb temperature of the atmosphere.

For all practical purposes, the outer surface coefficient is a linear function of the outdoor wind velocity, with a roughness correction which needs to be considered for surfaces such as stucco.[14] For wind speeds up to 20 mph,

$$h_o = 2.0 + 0.267 \times \text{vel, mph} \qquad \textit{Equation No. 15}$$

U-Values for Single and Multiple Glazing The over-all coefficient of heat transfer, U, for any unshaded single glazing can be found when the three resistances involved—outdoors, glass, and indoors—and the air velocities are known or can be estimated reasonably well. The resistance concept is used, since $U = 1.0/R$ total

14. *Footnote 4, chap. 22, p. 222, Fig. 1.*

and $R_{total} = R_i + R_g + R_o = 1/h_o + L/k + 1/h_i$

where L = thickness of the glazing, in inches
k = thermal conductivity of the glazing, Btu/[hr ft² (F/in.)]

Thermal conductivity is expressed either in consistent American units as Btu/[hr ft² (F/ft)] = Btu/(hr ft F) or in more familiar units as Btu/[hr ft² (F/in.)] = (Btu in.)/(hr ft² F). For glass, the *ASHRAE Handbook* (*Reference 4*) gives several conflicting values, including 7.08 Btu in./hr ft² F in the comprehensive table of the properties of solids (Chapter 37, p. 37.2), and 10.0 in the tabulated values of thermal properties of building materials (Chapter 22, p. 22.17). The latter appears to be considerably too high, while the former is somewhat too low, and a value of 7.5 gives better agreement with the U-values listed in *Table 1*.

For plastic glazing materials, the thermal conductivity is much lower than that of glass. An exact value is difficult to obtain because of the wide variety of formulations used in producing the materials, but a value slightly greater than 1.0 (Btu in.)/(hr ft² F) is consistent with the U-values found in the *ASHRAE Handbook* (*Reference 4*) (p. 26.29, Table 32).

TABLE 1

U-Values for Single Unshaded Glass and Plastic (Acrylic and Polycarbonate) Sheets. Units Are Btu/hr ft² F

Thickness (in.)	Glass		Plastic	
	1/8	1/4	1/8	1/4
Winter	1.10	1.10	1.06	0.96
Summer	1.04	1.04	0.98	0.89

The thermal resistance of the glass is treated inconsistently in this table, but these are the values recommended by the leading glass manufacturers and so they will be used here. For plastic glazing, the treatment is more consistent, and more attention is paid to the thermal resistance of the material.

For multiple glazing, additional thermal resistance is added primarily by the air space or spaces, and their width is a matter of considerable importance. *Figure 8* shows, in very simplified form, the mechanism of heat transfer in a typical double-glazed window. The surfaces are, by ASHRAE convention, designated as shown, with 1 designating the outdoor surface of the outer light, and 4 the inner surface of the inner light. The inner and outer surface coefficients are determined by the same laws which operate for single glazing, but the air space resistance, R_{as}, is much more complex. The air space conductance, h_{as}, the recip-

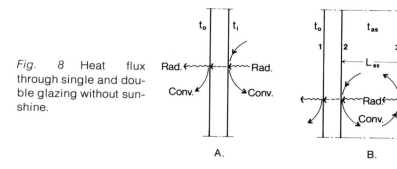

Fig. 8 Heat flux through single and double glazing without sunshine.

rocal of the resistance, is the *sum* of the convective and the radiative effects, since they are operating in parallel.

$$h_{as} = h_{rad} + h_{con} = E \times 0.1713 \times \frac{(T_3^4 - T_2^4)}{(t_3 - t_2)} \times 10^{-8}$$

$$+ C_N \times \frac{k}{L_{as}} \times (Gr)^{0.327}$$

Equation No. 17

where E = effective emittance = $1/(1/e_2 + 1/e_3 - 1)$
e_2, e_3 = hemispherical emittances of surfaces 2 and 3
k = thermal conductance of air, (Btu in.)/(hr ft² F)
L_{as} = width of air space, in.
Gr = Grashof number for the air space
    = $(g \times \Delta t \times L_{as}^3)/(T_{as} \times$ kinematic viscosity²)
$\Delta t = (t_3 - t_2)$ and $T_{as} = (t_3 + t_2)/2 + 459.6$, deg R
g = coefficient of gravity, 32.2 ft/sec²

For uncoated glass on both surfaces, $E = 0.72$. There is some uncertainty about the constant C_N in Equation 21 (see *Reference 11*) and so the *1977 ASHRAE Handbook* gives tabulated values of h_{as} for a wide range of air space widths (0.188 to 0.50 in.), effective emittances (0.05 to 0.82), air space temperatures, and temperature differences. The U-values given in *Table 2* employ 1.3 as the value of h_{as}, and this appears to be appropriate for summer conditions, but too high for cold winter situations.

In order to reduce U-values for "insulating glass," a commercial term for multiple glazing, many manufacturers have developed methods of depositing thin metallic coatings on surfaces 2 or 3 for double glazing. By reducing e_2 or e_3, the effective emittance E can be reduced and thus h_{as} will also be reduced. The reflectance for solar radiation of these coatings varies from 10% to 45%, with corresponding reductions in transmittance, so they are not likely to be used when heat *admission* is desired.

Tabulated values of U-factors for double and triple glazing are given in *Reference 4;* Table 13, p. 26.10, gives data for glass, and Table 32, p. 26.29, gives comparable data for acrylic and polycarbonate sheets. (*Table 2* below summarizes these values.)

TABLE 2

U-Values for Unshaded Multiple Glazing

Double-glazed	Glass ⅛ in. or ¼ in. Winter	Summer	Thermoplastic ⅛ in. Winter	Summer	¼ in. Winter	Summer
³/₁₆-in. space	0.62	0.65	—	—	—	—
¼-in. space	0.58	0.61	0.55	0.56	0.49	0.50
½-in. space	0.49	0.56	0.47	0.50	0.43	0.45
Triple-glazed*						
¼-in. spaces	0.39	0.44	—	—	—	—
½-in. spaces	0.31	0.39	—	—	—	—

*Glass thicknesses are ¼, ⅛, and ¼ in. Winter conditions are 15 mph wind speed, 0F outside and 70F inside air temperatures. Summer conditions are 7.5 mph; 89F outdoors, 75F indoors, with 248.3 Btu/(hr ft²) incident solar radiation.

Glazing Temperatures The temperatures attained by single unshaded glass, when there is no solar irradiation, can be calculated readily if the thermal resistance of the glazing material is considered to be negligible.[15] The basic equation for glass temperature *with* solar irradiation, t_{gs}, is:

Equation No. 18

$$t_{gs} = N_i \times t_i + N_o \times \left[\frac{I \times \alpha}{h_o} + t_o \right]$$

where
t_g = glass temperature, assumed to apply to both inner and outer surfaces, with sunshine
N_i, N_o = inward- and outward-flowing fractions of absorbed solar irradiation
I = irradiation heat flux, Btu/hr ft²
α = absorptance of glazing for solar radiation
t_i, t_o = indoor and outdoor air temperature, F

When there is no sunshine, $I = 0$ and Equation 18 simplifies to:

Equation No. 19

$$t_{gd} = N_i \times t_i + N_o \times t_o$$

where t_{gd} = glass temperature, no sunshine
$N_i = h_i/(h_i + h_o) = 1.46/(1.46 + 6) = 0.20$ winter
$= 1.46/(1.46 + 4) = 0.27$ summer
$N_o = 1.00 - N_i = 0.80$ winter and 0.73 summer.

For the conventional winter conditions, with 0F outdoors and 70F indoors, $t_{gd} = 0.20 \times 70 + 0.80 \times 0 = 14F$.
For a summer night condition, with 89F outdoors and 75F indoors, $t_{gd} = 0.27 \times 75 + 0.73 \times 89 = 85.2F$.

15. J. I. Yellott: "Solar Optical Properties, Heat Transfer Coefficients and Shading Coefficients for Architectual Glass," *ASHRAE Journal*, March 1971, pp. 41–46.

Derivations of N_i and N_o for single glazing are given in *Reference 15*. The error involved in neglecting the thermal resistance of the glazing is small, as is seen from the following alternative means of finding the glass temperature:

$$q = U \times (t_o - t_i) = h_i \times (t_g - t_i) \qquad \text{Equation No. 20}$$

where q = heat flux rate, Btu/hr ft^2
Using summer values for glass, without sun,
$$q = 1.04 \times (89 - 75) = 12.46 = 1.46 \times (t_{gd} - 75)$$
$$t_{gd} = 75 + 12.46/1.46 = 83.2F$$
Using winter values for glass, again without sun:
$$t_{gd} = 1.10 \times (70 - 0) = 77.0 = 1.46 \times (70 - t_{gd})$$
$$t_{gd} = 70 - 77/1.46 = 70 - 52.7 = 17.26F$$

The differences are small enough to be neglected and to justify the use of the simpler form for most purposes. The important point is that single unprotected glass attains very low surface temperatures on cold winter days when the sun is not shining. This brings on problems of condensation of moisture on the inner glass surface and the formation of frost unless the relative humidity indoors is reduced to a very low point.

For double and triple glazing, the temperature of the indoor glass can be found by the use of Equation 20. For winter conditions, using double glazing with ¼-in. glass and ½-in. air space,

$$q = 0.49 \times (70 - 0) = 34.3 \text{ Btu/hr ft}^2$$
$$= 1.46 \times (70 - t_{gi}), \text{ so } t_{gi} = 70 - 34.3/1.46 = 46.5F$$
where t_{gi} = temperature of glass surface No. 4 (indoors)
With triple glazing, with ½-in. air spaces,
$$q = 0.31 \times (70 - 0) = 21.70 \text{ Btu/hr ft}^2$$
$$= 1.46 \times (70 - t_{gi})$$
$$t_{gi} = 70 - 21.7/1.46 = 55.1F$$

These values are significant enough to justify a summary; for winter conditions of 70F indoors, 0F outdoors and no sunshine, indoor glass temperatures will be approximately: single, 17.3F; double, 46.5F; triple, 55.1F.

Heat Admission Through Sunlit Glass

Heat Gains Through Single Unshaded Sunlit Glazing   The title of this section intentionally implies that, when the sun is shining directly on a window, there is almost invariably a net heat *gain* within the room. For single unshaded glazing, the basic equation for heat admission is:

$$q_{Ad} = I_t \times (\tau + N_i \times \alpha) + U(t_o - t_i) \qquad \text{Equation No. 21}$$

The term "admission" is used because heat enters the glazed space both by transmission *through* the glazing and by inward flow (in summer) due to radiation and convection from the indoor glass surface. In winter, t_o is generally lower than t_i and so heat is conducted outward through the glazing.

The net rate of heat gain for sunlit single glass is then:

Equation No. 22
$$q_{Ad} = I_t \times (\tau + 0.20 \times \alpha) - 1.10(t_i - t_o)$$

and the efficiency of collection would be:

Equation No. 23
$$\text{Eff.} = (\tau + 0.20 \times \alpha) - U \times (t_i - t_o)/I_t$$

Efficiencies of conventional collectors are generally measured at near-normal incidence, when the incident angle θ is not more than 30 deg, so introducing the transmittance and absorptance of ¼-in. clear float glass in this range would give:

Equation No. 23a
$$\text{Eff.} = (0.78 + 0.20 \times 0.16) - 1.10 \times (t_i - t_o)/I_t$$

Equation No. 23b
$$= 0.81 - 1.1 \times (t_i - t_o)/I_t$$

To consider south-facing vertical windows at noon on January 21, for latitudes from 24 to 56°N, we would use the data in the 1977 *ASHRAE Handbook,* Chapter 26, as shown here in *Table 3.* Using 40°N latitude as our example, with $I_t = 292$ Btu/hr ft², the efficiency equation becomes:

Equation No. 24
$$\text{Eff.} = 0.81 - 1.1 \times (70 - t_o)/292$$

TABLE 3

Clear Day Total Irradiation and Incident Angles for South-Facing Vertical Surfaces at Solar Noon, 24 to 56°N Latitude

Latitude, °N	24	32	40	48	56
I_t, Btu/(hr ft²)	261	283	292	282	230
θ deg	46	38	30	22	14
SHGF, *Btu/(hr ft²)	227	246	254	245	205

*SHGF denotes the Solar Heat Gain Factor which is explained below.

TABLE 4

FENESTRATION
AND HEAT
FLOW THROUGH
WINDOWS

135

Collection Efficiency for a Single-Glazed (¼-in.) Window at 40°N Latitude, Jan. 21 at Noon Solar Time

t_o, F	70	60	50	40	30	20	10	0	-10	-20
P	0.00	0.034	0.068	0.103	0.137	0.171	0.205	0.240	0.274	0.308
Eff.	0.81	0.77	0.73	0.70	0.66	0.62	0.58	0.55	0.51	0.47

For outdoor temperatures from 70F down to −20F, the following values of the parameter $(t_i - t_o)/I_t$, designated by P, and the collection efficiency are found, as shown in *Table 4*.

As predicted at the beginning of this chapter, there is definitely a net gain, and a quite substantial gain, at noon under the assumed conditions for any outdoor temperature that is likely to occur on a clear January day. The break-even temperature can be found from Equation 27b by setting the efficiency equal to 0.0 and solving for t_o. The resulting value, −145F, might be encountered on the moon, but not at 40°N latitude here on earth!

A new term, SHGF, with dimensions of Btu/hr ft², was introduced in Table 3. This is the designation for the Solar Heat Gain Factor which is defined as the rate of solar heat gain, due to transmission and inward flow of absorbed solar radiation, through ⅛-in. clear, unshaded glass ($\tau = 0.86$; $\rho = 0.08$; $\alpha = 0.06$ at near-normal incidence for solar radiation) under specified clear-day conditions of latitude, date, time of day, AST (*Apparent Solar Time*[4]), and surface orientation. These conditions determine the total solar irradiation on the designated surface as well as the solar-optical properties of the reference glass. The Solar Heat Gain Factor is simply the first term in Equation 21, with transmittance and absorptance for ⅛-in. clear glass:

$$\text{SHGF} = I_t \times (\tau + 0.27 \times \alpha) = 0.87 \times I_t = I_t/1.15 \qquad \textit{Equation No. 25}$$

It is relatively simple to set up a program for computing SHGF for any desired set of conditions (*Reference 4*, Chapter 26) using the clear-day data derived by Jordan, Liu, and Threlkeld of the University of Minnesota. Tables 17–25 in the *ASHRAE Handbook*, Chapter 26, 1977 give these values for the daylight hours of the 21st day of each month, for latitudes from 0 to 64°N, for orientations around the compass from N to NNW, by 22.5-deg intervals.

For fenestrations with more complex glazing than clear single glass, it is possible to determine the rate of solar heat gain by using the Shading Coefficient concept, originally proposed by D. J. Vild of Libbey-Owens-Ford Glass Company. He found that the shading coefficient, SC, as employed in Equation 26, is a unique characteristic of each glazing system and is virtually independent of incident-angle variations. The rate of heat admission through sunlit fenestration in summer is:

Equation No. 26 $q_{Ad} = SC \times 0.87 \times I_t + U \times (t_o - t_i)$

Since, from Equation 25, SHGF = $0.87 \times I_t$, we have, for winter conditions:

Equation No. 27 $q_{Ad} = SC \times 0.87 \times I_t - U \times (t_i - t_o)$

Equation No. 28   and   Eff. $= 0.87 \times SC - U \times (t_i - t_o)/I_t$

Equation No. 28a   or   Eff. $= 0.87 \times SC - U \times (t_i - t_o)/(1.15 \times SHGF)$

Heat Gains Through Unshaded Sunlit Double-Glazing   Double glazing will be seen to offer both an advantage and a disadvantage when its solar heat admission is studied. *Table 5* summarizes the solar transmittance, Shading Coefficient, and *U*-value data for single and double glazing for the two most widely used glass thicknesses, ⅛ in. and ¼ in.

TABLE 5

Total Solar Transmittance, SC and *U*-Value for Clear Single and Double Glazing Using ⅛- and ¼-in.-Thick Glass, with ½-in. Air-Space Width

	GLAZING TYPE			
	Single glass		Double glass	
Thickness (in.)	⅛ in.	¼ in.	⅛ in.	¼ in.
Solar Transmittance	0.86	0.78	0.71	0.61
Shading Coefficient	1.00	0.94	0.88	0.81
U-Value, Btu/(hr ft² F)	1.10	1.10	0.49	0.49

For single ¼-in. heat-absorbing glass, the solar transmittance is about 0.46 and the SC is 0.69. Double glazing, with ¼-in. heat-absorbing float as the outer light and ¼-in. clear glass as the inner light, has a solar transmittance of 0.36, and its SC is 0.55. Obviously, if heat admission is an important consideration, clear glass is superior. There are, of course, other factors to be considered, such as protection against excessive glare or summer heat gain, so the choice must be made with care.

Using Equation 28a, with appropriate values from Table 5, the following equations result:

GLAZING TYPE   EFFICIENCY EQUATION, WINTER

Equation No. 28a   Single ⅛ in. $\eta = 0.87 - (1.10/1.15) \times (t_i - t_o)/SHGF$
Equation No. 28b   Single ¼ in. $\eta = 0.82 - 0.96 \times (t_i - t_o)/SHGF$
Equation No. 28c   Double ⅛ in. $\eta = 0.77 - 0.49 \times (t_i - t_o)/(SHGF \times 1.15)$

$$\text{Double } \tfrac{1}{4} \text{ in. } \eta = 0.70 - 0.43 \times (t_i - t_o)/\text{SHGF} \qquad \textit{Equation No. 28d}$$
$$\text{Single } \tfrac{1}{4} \text{ in. } \eta = 0.60 - 0.96 \times (t_i - t_o)(\text{SHGF} \times 1.15) \qquad \textit{Equation No. 28e}$$
$$\text{heat-absorbing (H-A)}$$
$$\text{Double } \tfrac{1}{4} \text{ in. } \eta = 0.48 - 0.43 \times (t_i - t_o)/\text{SHGF} \qquad \textit{Equation No. 28f}$$
$$\text{H-A plus clear}$$

The equations for these glazing combinations are linear with respect to the parameter $\rho = (t_i - t_o)/I_t$, since changes in U with changing temperature are not considered. The more conventional use of such plots is to show how collector efficiency varies as the fluid inlet temperature is raised. In this case, the indoor temperature is assumed to remain constant despite variations in outdoor temperature, and no stratification or other variation in the indoor air temperature is considered. The entire glass area is assumed to be exposed to essentially still air at temperature t_i, and it is the outdoor temperature that changes. *Figure 9* shows the efficiency for the six glazing systems listed above, for the conditions prevailing in Tables 3 and 4.

Day-Long Performance of South-Facing Windows The collection efficiencies shown in Figure 9 are appropriate for near-noon conditions on clear winter days. For an entire 24-hour day, a different approach may be taken to estimate the heat flux

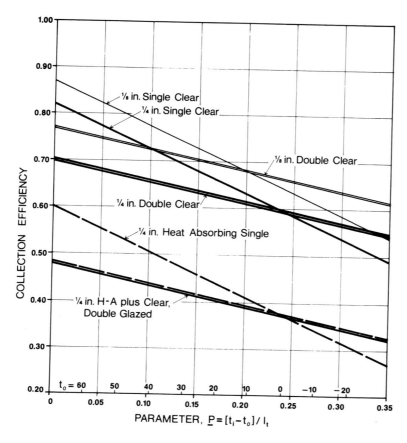

Fig. 9. Collection efficiencies for single and double south-facing windows.

through the window. The day-long conduction heat flow, due only to the indoor-outdoor temperature difference, is:

Equation No. 29

$$Q_{con} = A \times U \times (70 - t_{av}) \times 24 \text{ Btu/day}$$

where A = fenestration glazed area, ft²
t_{av} = day-long average outdoor air temperature, F

Thus for a single square foot of ¼-in. clear unshaded glass on a typical January day in Boston when the average outdoor temperature is 30F, we have as the day-long heat *loss:*

Equation No. 29a
Single glazing: $q_{con} = 1 \times 1.11 \times (70 - 30) \times 24 = 1,056 \text{ Btu}$

Equation No. 29b
Double glazing: $q_{con} = 1 \times 0.49 \times (70 - 30) \times 24 = 470 \text{ Btu}$

This loss would occur regardless of the orientation of the glass, but the sun's contribution to the total heat flux through the glazed area will depend very directly upon the window's azimuth. If the window faces towards the south, from ESE to WSW, the solar contribution during the daylight hours of a clear day will be more than enough to compensate for the conduction loss. If manageable insulation is used to minimize the conduction heat loss when the sun is not shining, there will be very significant heat gains on clear days, and there will be very few days when the windows will not contribute far more than they will lose.

The equation for estimating clear-day *heat gain* is:

Equation No. 30

$$Q_{sol} = A \times (\text{Day-long SHGF}) \times \text{SC}$$

Values of the Day-long SHGF are found in Tables 17–25 of the 1977 *ASHRAE Handbook,* Chapter 26, *(Reference 4,)* for latitudes from 0 to 64°N, by 8-deg increments, for the 21st day of each month. Half-day totals are given, and these must be added together intelligently to obtain the day-long values needed in Equation 30. Since the apparent motion of the sun across the sky is symmetrical about the south-north line, the orientation designators at the top of the ASHRAE Tables apply to the before-noon hours, while the designators along the bottom apply to the afternoon hours. Thus, the day-long total SHGF for a surface facing southeast (SE) is found by adding the morning total, 904 Btu/ft² for 40°N, January 21, to the afternoon total, 273 Btu/ft², to obtain 1,177 Btu for the entire day. The net heat flux for the day is then:

Equation No. 31

$$Q_{net} = A \times [(\text{Day-long SHGF}) \times \text{SC} - 24 \times U \times (70 - t_{av})]$$

Figure 10 summarizes the mid-winter situation for the principal orientations, for 40°N latitude. East-facing windows will gain heat in the morning and lose heat during the rest of the day and the night, while west-facing windows will gain in the afternoon and lose throughout the remaining hours. *Table 6* summarizes the situation for uninsulated single- and double-glazed windows on January 21 in Boston.

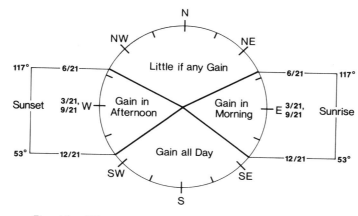

Fig. 10   Effect of window orientation upon their effectiveness as solar collectors.

TABLE 6

Day-long Heat Flux for Boston, Jan. 21, 70F Indoor Temperature, 30F Outdoor Temperatures, Unshaded Single- and Double-Glazed Windows. (Negative sign denotes heat loss; positive sign denotes heat gain.)

Orientation	ENE, WNW	E, W	SE, SW	SSE, SSW	S
Day-long SHGF, $\frac{Btu}{ft^2}$	260	514	1177	1493	1626
Daily Heat Gain					
Single, SC = 0.94	+245	+483	+1106	+1403	+1528
Double, SC = 0.81	+211	+416	+953	+1209	+1317
Day-long Heat Flow					
Single, U = 1.10	−811	−573	+50	+347	+472
Double, U = 0.49	−259	−54	+483	+739	+847

From this simplified analysis, it is evident that, on *clear days*, both single- and double-glazed windows, even without any additional insulation, are heat gainers for orientations from southeast to southwest, with the double-glazed windows making the best showing because of the more than 50% reduction in heat loss during the sunless hours. Addition of such a simple shading device as an internal drape or shade will reduce the U-factors to 0.83 Btu/hr ft² F for the single-glazed windows, and to about 0.38 for winter. If the shades are drawn during the 16 hours per day when there is no sunshine, the losses will be substantially reduced. The weighted average U-factor for single glazing will become 0.91, reducing the heat loss per ft² to 961 Btu/day. For the double-glazed window, the weighted average U will be 0.41, and the heat loss will be about 393 Btu/ft²/day.

If sliding panels of insulating material are used which will reduce the U-factors to approximately 0.10 Btu/hr ft² F when the panels are closed, the weighted average U-values will be 0.43 for the single- and 0.23 for the double-glazed windows, and the daily loss will drop to 454 and 108 Btu/ft², respectively. With assurance that the movable insulation will actually be moved whenever the outdoor temperature falls drastically, even east-facing and west-facing windows will be heat gainers instead of heat losers.

Experience with double-glazed south-facing windows of large area has been gained in a number of installations, particularly those in mountainous New Mexico, and in many cases it has been found that the movable insulation has not required "management" until outdoor air temperatures in the 0F range have been encountered.

Windows as Heat Sources It is apparent that southerly-oriented windows, particularly those of the clear, double-glazed variety, can be very effective heat sources on sunny days. "Window management," in the form of controllable insulation of such a simple form as roller shades, preferably with positive closure at the edges, or tightly woven drapes, can reduce to acceptable levels the heat losses which occur at night or on sunless days. A major problem which remains is to provide heat storage in the surfaces which are struck by the sun's rays. Thermal mass in the form of masonry or containers of water is the best answer currently available to this requirement, although "heat-of-fusion" construction materials and finishes, such as floor or ceiling tiles, are now being proposed to solve this problem.

Conclusions

Vertical windows on the southerly exposures of buildings can become very valuable sources of heat in winter because of the favorable solar angles and irradiation intensities which prevail from October to April. Fortunately, the excessive input of solar heat which might be anticipated during the summer months is relatively easy to control because of the high solar altitudes during the midday hours. The interior shading which is needed to provide insulation during the winter can also provide very desirable sun control during the summer. Double clear glass admits light as well as heat, but excessive solar radiant energy can be deflected back outdoors by the use of highly reflective shades or drapes.

The chapter on fenestration in *Reference 4* provides a wealth of information on relatively simple methods of calculating solar heat gains and conduction heat losses. Other references are cited therein that are readily available in other ASHRAE publications for those who need to study fenestration heat gains and losses in greater detail.

8

COMPUTER-AIDED ENERGY DESIGN FOR BUILDINGS

Francisco N. Arumi

ENERGY
CONSERVATION
THROUGH
BUILDING
DESIGN

1. The Numerical Simulation Laboratory has been funded in part through grants from the National Science Foundation, the Energy Research and Development Administration, the City of Austin Energy Conservation Commission, and the University Research Institute of the University of Texas. The efforts of the following people who have made valuable contributions to the development of the Numerical Simulation Laboratory and to the work reported in this chapter are gratefully acknowledged: Gustavo Behr, Ron Davis, Mosen Hourmanesh, Stephen Jaeger, Don Johnston, Stephen Kubenka, C. E. Laird, Thelma Longoria, Bernardete McGinty and Robert Swaffar.
2. W. J. Mitchell: *Computer-Aided Architectural Design*, Petrocelli/Charter, New York, 1977; G. P. Mitalas: "An Assessment of Common Assumptions in Estimating Cooling Loads and Space Temperatures," *ASHRAE Transactions*, 1965; T. Kusuda: "NBSLD, Computer Program for Heating and Cooling Loads in Buildings," *NBS Report*, NBSIR 74-514, November 1974; A. Rosenfeld: Cal-ERDA Project Phase II Proposal, November 1976.

Energy exchange within buildings and with the external environment is a complex and time-dynamic phenomenon, much more so than can be accurately depicted by long-hand calculation methods. Computer analysis of energy flows in buildings has offered new understanding of the interaction of building materials exposed to daily and seasonal climatic variation and to changing conditions of use. Computer-aided energy design now offers the building designer new methods by which to develop a solution for the specific environmental control requirements given by each site, orientation, and internal building program. As a result, computer-aided techniques could become an essential part of energy conservation in building design. These new techniques have an obvious impact on the way that architects and mechanical engineers coordinate their work during the design process, as well as on the way that the designer organizes the conceptual design process so that it interacts with computer programs. Given the increasing availability, flexibility, and lower cost of computers, we are near the point where lack of familiarity by the professional with computational and graphic display possibilities may be a significant barrier to improved energy design practice.

There are innumerable points during the design process—some very early in the conceptual phase—where computer-aided methods are of great value. The number of computer programs that are applicable is increasing so rapidly that the design professional unfamiliar with computer language and use might be easily overwhelmed. To show their applicability to energy design questions, this chapter describes some computer-based design programs that have been developed by the author and students at the Numerical Simulation Laboratory (NSL) of the School of Architecture, University of Texas at Austin.[1]

While the examples are not intended to represent the wide range of computer-aided energy design methods, they do offer examples of their applicability to actual design problems. Additional examples of current work are given in the references.

The original purpose in developing the programs at NSL was to teach energy considerations in architecture. But some have obvious application to design practice. The ultimate energy demand of a building is a function of time-dynamic interactions of outside climate, the building envelope, and internal loads. The software necessary to analyze each of these variables is either already operational or is in its final stages of development.[2] NSL Computer programs that address these variables are described below under the following topic headings: *Dynamic Thermal Behavior of Wall Systems; Insolation Analysis; Solar Control Design and Testing;* and *Integrated Energy Analysis.*

Dynamic Thermal Behavior of Wall Systems

Depending upon their composition and the location of air

spaces or insulation, building materials in wall systems have different abilities to "hold heat," manifested through effects such as time-lag, dynamic attenuation of heat flux, and modulation of internal temperatures. These effects can be used to design the energy cycles of a room to match the activities for which the room is designed. When these effects are taken into account the calculation is called dynamic, and when they are ignored the calculation is called static.[3]

The magnitude of these effects depends on the properties of the materials (heat conductivity, specific heat, and density); the properties of wall surfaces (visible and infrared emissivities; texture); the weather conditions (cloudiness, wind, temperature); wall orientation; time of year; and latitude. In short, they depend on a large number of variables, many of which are continuously varying and are described by the laws of classical thermal physics.

The equations involved in a numerical description of dynamic energy flows can be solved through appropriate matching of boundary conditions, and the algorithm for the solutions can be programed in the computer and made accessible to the user in a number of modes. The laboratory mode can be used for instructional purposes while an interactive mode can be used for design-aid purposes.[4] *Figures 1* through *4* show the heat flow characteristics of walls as different properties are varied in numerically simulated controlled experiments. Figure 1 shows the behavior of the heat flux in Btu/ft² hr through a wall when the heat conductivity is allowed to change. Note the time shift of the local maximum and minimum as the heat conductivity changes. Note also that the amplitude of the heat flow does not increase linearly with increasing heat conductivity. *Figure 2* shows three different wall sections. One-third of the thickness of each section is filled with insulation and the other two-thirds with masonry. The relative position of the insulation is different in each case. Figure 2 also shows the temperature distribution within the walls for each arrangement of the insulation for the same time of the day. *Figure 3* shows the instantaneous heat flux through each of the three walls for a 24-hour period, illustrating the "inside-out" effect: the location of the insulation in the wall does have an effect on the heat flux through the wall. None of these effects is accounted for by standard *U*-value calculations. Figure 4 shows the diurnal cycle of external surface temperatures of six identical walls when each one is oriented along the different cardinal directions, illustrating the potential value of matching the plan location and orientation of a room with the activities for which it is designed.

Sensitivity analysis can be made with computer programs to determine the importance of specific design variables as they might affect the energy demand for heating and cooling of a building. Such an analysis was made at NSL to determine the importance of thermal inertia in the seasonal energy performance

3. T. Kusuda, ed.: Proceedings of the Symposium, *Use of Computers For Environmental Engineering Related to Buildings*, National Bureau of Standards, Building Science Service 39, 1971.
4. F. N. Arumi: "Energy Considerations: Quantitative Methods in Teaching Architecture," *Journal of Architectural Research*, vol. 9, no. 3 (July 1975); F. N. Arumi and R. L. Dodge: "Energy Considerations: Quantitative Methods in Teaching Architecture," Design Methods Group *DMG-DRS Journal*, vol. 9, no. 3 (July 1975); D. H. Mall et al.: "Interactive Graphics Input Methods for Residential Building Load Calculations," *ASHRAE Journal*, August 1977.

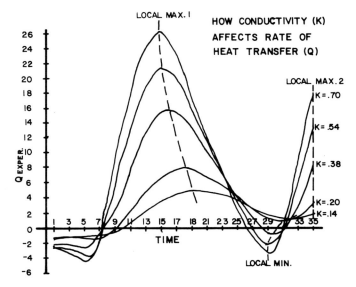

How Conductivity (K) Affects Rate of Heat Transfer (Q)

Fig. 1 Instantaneous heat flux through a wall over a 24-hour period. The heat capacity and the thickness are held constant while the heat conductivity is varied.

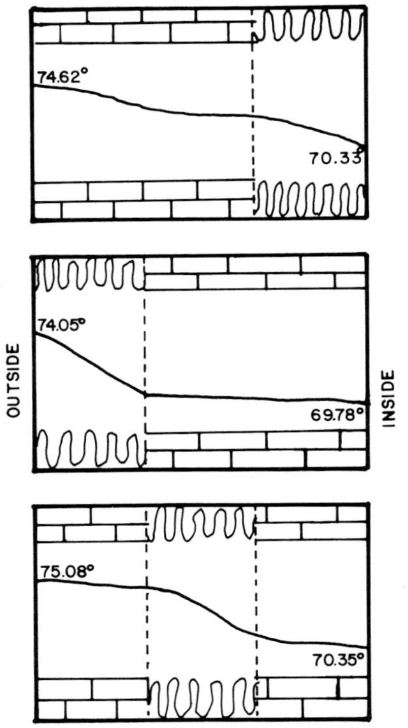

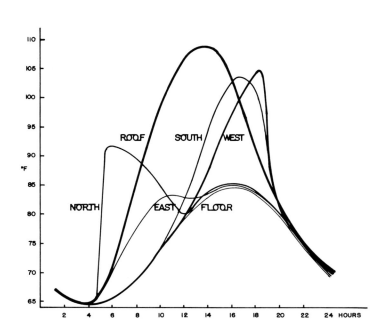

Fig. 2 Instantaneous temperature profiles for three different arrangements of insulation in a masonry wall.

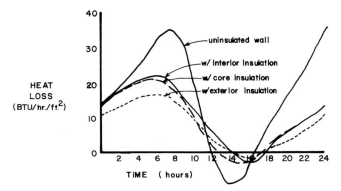

Fig. 3 The importance of the relative position of insulation within a wall. The result shows that the most important step is to insulate the wall. Refinements can be achieved by the location of the insulation. The closer the insulation is placed to the outside, the more effective the insulation becomes.

Fig. 4 Impact of orientation on the external surface temperature of identical walls during a clear day in June, in Austin, TX.

of walls.[5] The results of the calculations show that thermal inertia effects become relatively less important in determining the total energy demand as the severity of the weather increases and as the thermal inertia value of the wall decreases. These conclusions are confirmed by researchers who have developed the M-factor method.[6]

The Thermal Inertia Index used in the NSL analysis is a dimensionless quantity that represents the ratio of the wall thickness to the thermal penetration depth for diurnal frequencies, and which is given by the equation:

$$\gamma = \sqrt{\frac{\omega \rho c}{2k}} \times L \qquad \text{\textit{Equation No. 1}}$$

where ρ = mass density
c = specific heat capacity
k = heat conductivity
L = wall thickness
ω = diurnal frequency in radius/time

The gamma (γ) values for composite walls depend on the sequence of the layers as well as on the thermal properties of these layers. While the precise calculation of the γ-value of composite walls is too difficult to be reasonably done by hand, it can be done very easily with the use of a computer.

The Energy Demand Surfaces The result of parametric or sensitivity analysis to determine the trade-off between insulation and mass in the seasonal energy performance of walls can be summarized through a three-dimensional graph that shows the energy demand for a given site as a function of wall conductance and thermal inertia. A function of two variables when plotted in a three-dimensional graph generates a "surface." *Figure 5* shows one such surface for the energy demand over a cooling season in Austin, Texas. In general, the shape of the energy demand surface depends on many variables. All else being the same, the surface will be different for the heating cost than for the cooling cost. The shape depends on which energy cost is being displayed; among other variables, it depends on the climate of the region, on the rate of heat generation in the occupied space, and on the geometry of the room. The performance of three commonly used walls are contrasted explicitly in the Figure 5 example. These walls were chosen to contrast the benefits of insulation against those of thermal inertia: the wall with the greatest insulation value was chosen for its low inertia, and the wall with poorest insulation value because of its relatively high inertia. The third wall was chosen to have intermediate values.

The results of the static calculation (when thermal inertia effects are ignored) are represented by the $\gamma = 0$ curve. As expected, the walls with better insulating properties (lower conductance) place

5. F. N. Arumi: "Thermal Inertia in Architectural Walls," Report to the Energy Research and Development Administration (ERDA) and the National Concrete Masonry Association (NCMA). Published by NCMA, McLean, VA, 1977.
6. S. E. Goodwin and M. J. Catani: "Simplified Thermal Design of Building Envelopes for Use With ASHRAE Standard 90-75," Portland Cement Association Engineering Bulletin EB089.01B, 1976.

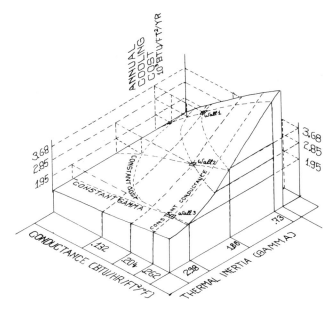

Fig. 5 Energy demand surface. Seasonal cooling energy demand for Austin, TX as a function of the two thermal parameters of conductance and thermal inertia. The results of the static calculations are obtained by setting the thermal inertia index (γ) to zero.

Description	Conductance (Btu/hr ft² F)	Gamma (γ)
1. Aluminum/Steel (insulated)	.132	.73
2. Concrete/Insulation/Concrete	.204	1.88
3. Concrete block (uninsulated)	.262	2.98

less demand on the mechanical equipment, resulting in lower annual cooling energy demand. However, the results of the dynamic calculation for these particular walls and climatic conditions are precisely opposite to the static results. The wall with higher conductance (poorer insulating properties) places less demand on the mechanical equipment and is, therefore, less expensive to operate. The reduced energy cost for the more poorly insulated concrete-block wall arises because the beneficial aspects of its thermal inertia more than compensate for the disadvantages of its lack of insulation.

The Curves of Constant Gamma (γ) show how walls perform with the same γ and different conductance values. When the γ value is zero, the resulting curve represents the static approximation. *The Curves of Constant Conductance* show how walls with the same conductance and different γ values perform. For a given wall, a comparison of the height of the surface at the point of the wall and at the point where the γ value is zero results in an evaluation of the discrepancy in the calculation when the static approximation is used. *The Curves of Constant Energy Demand* show the γ-conductance combinations the energy performance of which are identical. Any wall, therefore, in which thermal parameters are such that they fall on this curve are thermally equivalent for the conditions described by the surface. These curves can also be called contours of constant energy costs.

This concept of "equivalent walls" is not available in the static approximation.

Internal Heat Generation Artificial lighting, office equipment, people, and all other sources of heat that make up the internal activity of a space contribute to the internal heat generation of the space. The internal heat generation can have a significant impact on the relative thermal performance of walls. When there is no internal heat generation, a "good wall" tends to keep the warm air inside the space during the winter and the cool air inside during the summer. However, when there is internal heat being generated, this good wall will also tend to keep this extra heat inside. In small enough quantities this extra heat can be beneficial during the heating season without being too adverse during the cooling season. In larger quantities, however, this extra heat becomes undesirable and must be dissipated. The good wall can become a liability precisely because it tends to hold this extra heat inside. *Figure 6* illustrates the transformation of an energy surface as the rate of internal heat generation increases. The calculations were carried out for Austin, Texas for a large space (surface/volume = .05 ft^{-1}). The energy demand is the total annual demand for heating and cooling. For this size room, an internal heat generation of 5 Btu/hr ft^2 is already large enough to reverse the desirability of insulation, while an internal heat generation of 10 Btu/hr ft^2 represents a transitional value between the two extremes. This last case, which is represented by the

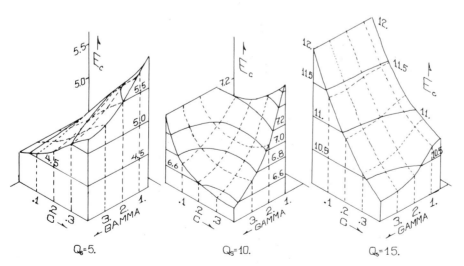

Fig. 6 Transformation of the energy demand surface as the annual climatic characteristics change. C = heat conductance (Btu/hr F) per ft^2 of wall; Qs = rate of internal heat generation (Btu/hr) per ft^2 of wall; Ec = annual energy cost (10^4 Btu/year) per ft^2 of wall. Constants of the calculation: s/v = .05 ft^{-1}, force ventilation rate of 2 volumes/hour; thermostat 68F to 78F; brown color; west orientation at 31°N; 9-year climate average for Austin, TX.

middle surface in Figure 6, illustrates the trade-off between the desirability to dissipate excess heat and the desirability to isolate the internal space from the external elements. Observe, for instance, the curve of constant γ equals 3; the energy cost decreases, at first, with increasing conductance. In this range the wall is not able to dissipate the internally generated heat fast enough. The energy demand bottoms out at a conductance of about .25, and it increases from there as the conductance increases. This happens because, beyond this point, it has become more desirable to isolate the inside from the external elements.

The Role of Thermal Inertia Notice that in all three cases depicted in Figure 6, the energy demand decreases with increasing γ. This means that, independent of the internal heat generation, the walls with greater thermal inertia always yield a lower total energy demand on a conditioned space.

Climatic Effects The same rate of internal heat generation in identical rooms will have different impacts on the shape of the energy surface in different climates. In colder climates, the additional internal heat will reduce the heating cost significantly more than it will increase the concomitant cooling cost. In warmer climates, the same rate of internal heat generation will increase the cooling cost significantly more than it will reduce the concomitant heating cost. Consider, for example, an east-facing room with a surface-to-volume ratio of .3 ft^{-1} and an internal heat generation of 5 Btu/hr ft^2 of surface. The energy surfaces associated with the east wall for three different climates are shown in *Figure 7*.

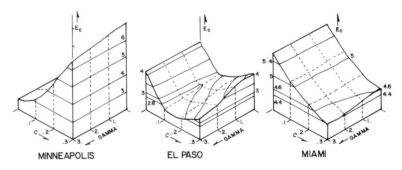

Fig. 7 Transformation of the energy demand surface as the annual climatic characteristics change. Internal heat generation = 5 Btu/hr per ft^2 of wall; s/v = .3 ft^{-1}.

Minneapolis was chosen for its severe heating season; the energy cost increases with increasing conductance. However, the rate of increase accelerates substantially for conductances greater than 1 Btu/hr ft^2 F. This change in the rate of increase reflects the fact that cooling problems may begin to be apparent even in Minneapolis, when at low conductance (high insulation) the wall is not able to dissipate the internal heat sufficiently fast. But, for the conditions of the calculation, the benefits of the reduced heat loss during the cold of winter make additional insulation still desirable. Miami was chosen to represent the other extreme because of its prolonged cooling season. In this case, reduced insulation results in reduced energy costs because the need to dissipate the internal heat is substantially greater than the need to isolate the internal space from the external climate. El Paso was chosen because it provides a climate of intermediate severity on both extremes. The results of the calculations show the existence of an optimum "valley." For conductances greater than the optimum values, the need to isolate the inside space from the external climate is more important than the need to dissipate the internal heat, whereas the opposite is true for conductances less than the optimum values. Although in these three cases the γ dependence is not as pronounced as the conductance dependence, the earlier observation still holds, that increased γ results in reduced energy consumption.

From these and other similar sensitivity analyses, the following rules of thumb can be deduced to help the designer decide whether or not the dynamic effects are important in calculating the energy demands associated with a wall. If the γ-value of the wall is less than 1, then the dynamic effect can be ignored. If the γ-value of the wall is greater than 1, then the importance of dynamic effects in calculating the annual energy demand can be classified on a scale ranging from "not important" to "critically important," according to the climatic characteristics of the site and on the design thermostat setting. "Not important" means that the overestimate associated with the static approximation is 5% or less; while "critically important" means that the overestimate is 95% or greater. Both percentages are measured relative to the static calculation.

A. For the heating season:
1. Dynamic effects are "not important"
   if $T_h > T_M + \Delta T$

   Equation No. 2

2. Dynamic effects are "critically important"
   if $T_h < T_M - T_x$

   Equation No. 3

B. For the cooling season:
1. Dynamic effects are "not important"
   if $T_c < T_M - \Delta T$

   Equation No. 4

2. Dynamic effects are "critically important"
   if $T_c > T_M + T_x$

   Equation No. 5

where T_h = design thermostat setting for heating, and T_c = design thermostat setting for cooling; T_M = mean annual temperature; ΔT = annual average of the diurnal temperature amplitude; T_x = annual temperature amplitude of the average daily temperature.

Example: For El Paso, Texas
$T_M = 62F; \Delta T = 14F; T_x = 20F$

which means that, for a day during the hottest part of the year, the temperature, on the average, oscillates between: $T_M + T_x - \Delta T = 68F$, and $T_M + T_x - \Delta T = 96F$, and the average temperature is $T_M + T_x = 82F$. For a day during the coldest part of the year, the temperature oscillates between: $T_M - T_x - \Delta T = 28F$ and $T_M - T_x + \Delta T = 56F$, and the average temperature is $T_M - T_x = 42F$.

Thus, if the design thermostat setting for heating is $T_h = 68F$, then $T_h = 68F < T_M + \Delta T = 76$, and $T_h = 68F > T_M - T_x = 42$. The dynamic effects in calculating the energy demand for heating is neither critically important nor can it be ignored. And if the design thermostat setting for cooling is $T_c = 78F$, $T_c = 78 < T_M - \Delta T = 48$, and $T_c = 78 > T_M + T_x = 82$.

The dynamic effect in calculating the energy demand for cooling is "almost" critically important. In conclusion, for El Paso weather, the dynamic effects of a wall should be taken into account in the design and calculation for both heating and cooling. On the other hand, for Minneapolis, Minnesota, $T_M = 46F$, $\Delta T = 10F$, $T_x = 30F$. For the heating season we have $T_h = 68F > T_M + \Delta T = 56F$. Therefore, the dynamic effects are definitely not important. During the cooling season $T_c = 78 > T_M + T_x = 76$; therefore, the dynamic effects are critically important.

Insolation Analysis

During the preliminary stages of design, major decisions about building shape and orientation can be made by taking into account total solar exposure (insolation values).

For shapes that have no sides casting shadows onto adjacent sides of the same shape, the calculation is straightforward and it can be done by hand. *Figure 8* illustrates the results of such calculations for a fixed number of blocks arranged in various ways. The total internal volume remains constant for all arrangements. The relative solar exposure, however, is different for each arrangement throughout the year. Based on this analysis, one can rank various arrangements according to their insolation behavior during the winter, the summer, or the entire year. The value of the computer for such problems becomes particularly apparent when shadows are cast by one surface of the object into another. Insolation calculations by hand, in this case, become highly impractical.

The introduction of a new structure among existing buildings can have a number of effects. It can obstruct the sun; in the case of new buildings with reflective glass, it can magnify the thermal irradiation on neighboring buildings. Both of these effects can be deduced qualitatively by inspection, but a quantitative analysis of the effects of solar obstruction and magnification require extensive computation. Foreknowledge of these effects is desirable from the standpoint of ethical or legal responsibility.

Shadows   The results of analysis can be graphic or numerical. *Figure 9* is a composite of shadow and shade interactions of three geometric shapes at different times of the day. These halftone pictures were produced with a high-speed printer on regular output paper, illustrating that it is not necessary to have sophisticated color graphics if the reduced resolution is acceptable.

Reflections   To illustrate the use of the computer in dealing with solar magnification, take the example of determining the impact that a tall building with reflecting glass skin will have on adjacent buildings. *Figure 10* illustrates the analysis of one such case, where a hypothetical building site is shown in an urban context. The tall building has external walls made of reflecting glass. The problem is to determine the pattern of shadows and reflections impacted upon the empty site at various times. (The number of sections can be increased to match the sensitivity

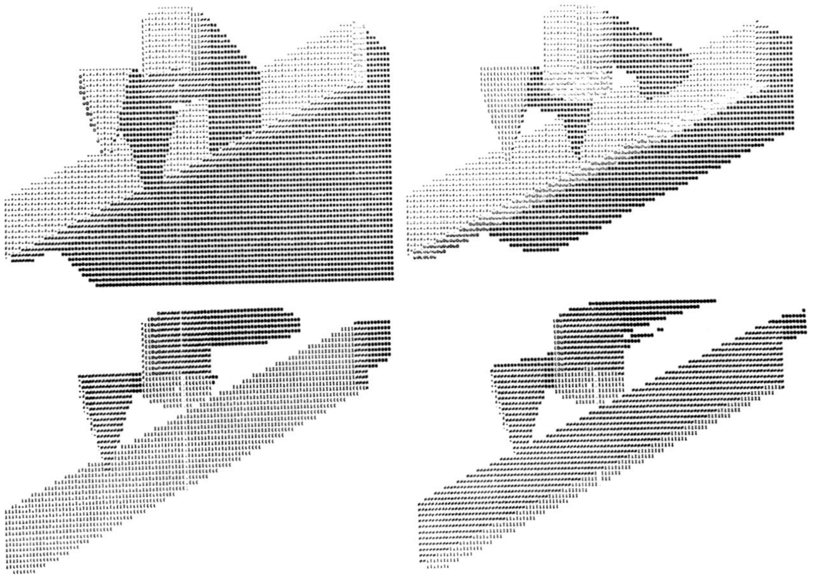

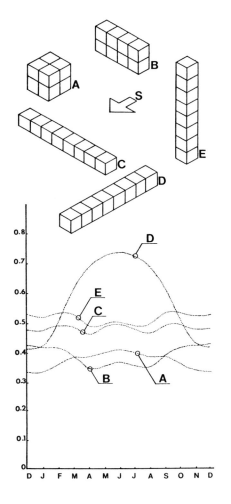

Fig. 9   Shadow and shade interaction of three shapes at four times of the day.

Fig. 8   Daily relative insolation on five arrangements of eight building blocks.

152

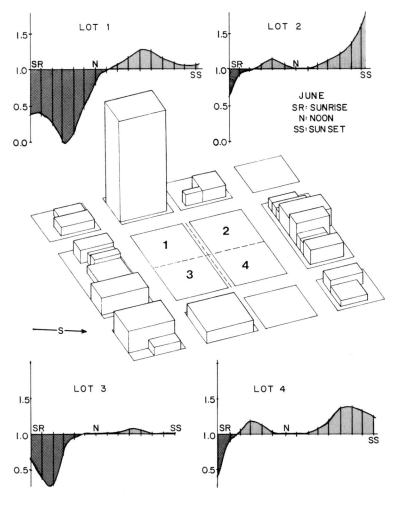

LOT 1

LOT 2

JUNE
SR: SUNRISE
N: NOON
SS: SUNSET

Fig. 10 Instantaneous reflection and shadow analysis on an urban site due to the presence of a tall building with reflective glass exterior.

LOT 3

LOT 4

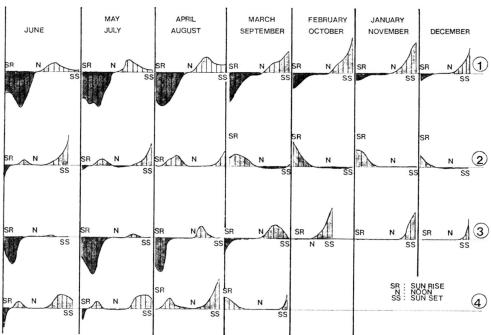

Fig. 11. Instantaneous reflection and shadow analysis for each site section for the design day of every month of the year.

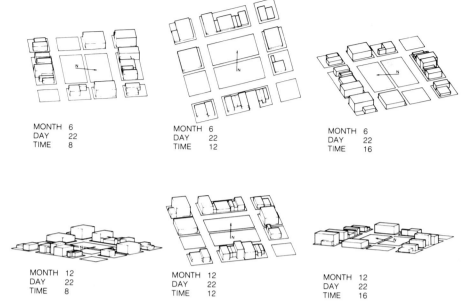

MONTH 6
DAY 22
TIME 8

MONTH 6
DAY 22
TIME 12

MONTH 6
DAY 22
TIME 16

MONTH 12
DAY 22
TIME 8

MONTH 12
DAY 22
TIME 12

MONTH 12
DAY 22
TIME 16

Fig. 12 Six different solar views as generated by the computer that are used to determine visually the design hours that will be used to establish the vertical property lines in the site. These property lines are determined by the requirement that the solar rights of the existing structures are respected. The top three views are for 8:00 am, 12:00 noon, and 4:00 pm in June; and the bottom three for the same hours in December.

requirements of the problem.) There are four graphs, one for each section of the site, inserted in Figure 10, to show the results of the analysis for the design day in June (summer solstice). They show the instantaneous insolation received by the section relative to the insolation that would otherwise be received by an unobstructed horizontal surface. Thus, a value 1 means that the section is neither in shade, nor does it receive reflected radiation; a value less than 1 means that the section is in shadow, e.g., if it is equal to .5, 50% of the section is in shadow; and a value greater than 1 means that the section is receiving additional irradiation due to reflection. *Figure 11* shows corresponding graphs for the design days for other months of the year. These results show, for instance, that Section 3 is in shade during the summer months while receiving very little reflected radiation. As the seasons change into the winter months, the shading disappears while the reflected radiation grows stronger. These conditions may prove advantageous for the design of a building or a park. On the other hand, Section 2 exhibits the opposite behavior, thus making it a potentially unattractive building site.

Solar Rights The computer can also be used to aid in the design of structures that must respect the solar rights of its neighbors. *Figure 12* shows a hypothetical site in its immediate urban context. This figure includes six different solar views to

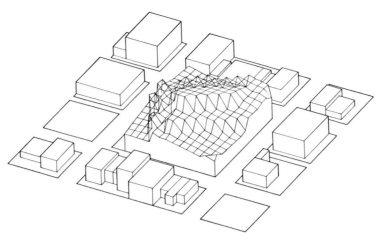

Fig. 13 Visual representation of the vertical property lines generated by the requirement that the solar rights of existing buildings be
respected.

help in the visual identification of the critical design times. The
hypothetical solar rights statement in this example requires that
any new structure in the given site must never shade the roof of
any existing building. The solution to the problem is stated in the
form of "vertical" property limits that can be shown in tabular
form for numerical analysis, or in graphic form (*Figure 13*) for
visual evaluation of the results.

Solar Control Design and Testing

Solar control devices, such as overhangs, louvers, and vertical
fins, can be used to control the amount of direct solar irradiation
that windows and other openings receive.

The form and dimensions of solar controls are determined by
the shape, size, and orientation of these openings as well as by
the criteria chosen for their performance. For most places within
the United States, for instance, one may want to have all windows
totally shaded from the direct sun in the summer, and totally
exposed to the available direct winter sun. The actual design of
the controls, especially for south-facing windows, can be done
by hand. For complex applications, however, the procedure can
be computerized and put in an interactive mode. The testing of
the design can best be done with the computer.

The test can be carried out by generating solar views of the
building being designed. Views are obtained for critical hours of
days required by the performance criteria. Shown in *Figure 14* are
pen drawings generated by the program ALKAZAM of a student-
designed house. The figures are, respectively, a winter and
summer view. By visual inspection one can thus determine that
the windows are indeed exposed to the winter sun and shaded
from the summer sun.

The test of the solar control device can also be carried out by

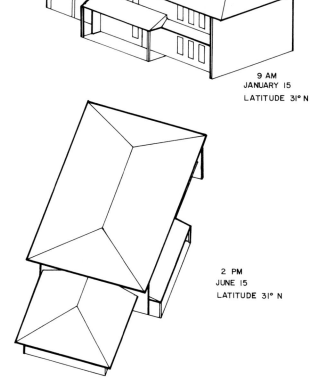

9 AM
JANUARY 15
LATITUDE 31° N

2 PM
JUNE 15
LATITUDE 31° N

Fig. 14   Winter and summer solar views of a house.

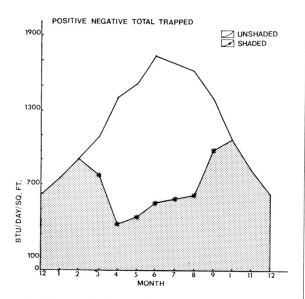

Fig. 15   Daily heat gain through an east-facing window, with and without a fixed shading device.

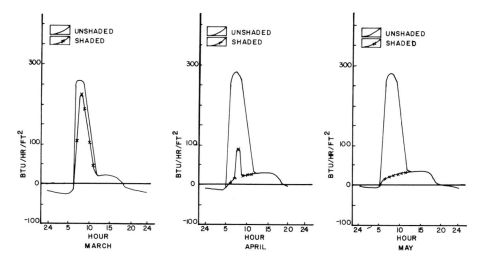

Fig. 16   Instantaneous rates of heat gain or loss through an east-facing window comparing the values when the shading device is in place with values when the shading device is not in place.

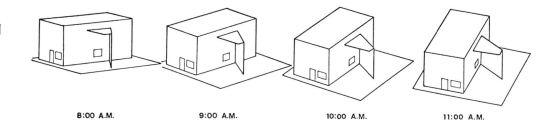

8:00 A.M.   9:00 A.M.   10:00 A.M.   11:00 A.M.

LATITUDE: 31
MONTH : 12
DAY   : 15

Fig. 17 Visual evaluation of the December performance of the shading device through an hourly sequence of solar views.

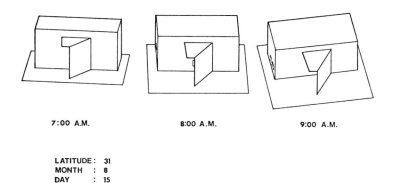

7:00 A.M.   8:00 A.M.   9:00 A.M.

LATITUDE: 31
MONTH : 8
DAY   : 15

Fig. 18 Visual evaluation of the August (April) performance of the shading device through an hourly sequence of solar views.

calculating the energy gained and lost through the window. *Figure 15* is a graphic representation of the daily heat gained and lost by an east-facing window throughout an entire year. The heat gain is compared with the performance of the window when a shading device is constructed so that it shades the window from April through August. Instantaneous rates of heat gain or loss can also be displayed, as in *Figure 16* for March, April, and May. These figures show that the window is shaded in May, while only partially shaded in March, a result to be expected since March was used as the transition month between total shade and total exposure. What is surprising is that in April the window appears to be partially exposed to the sun at 8:00 am, when by design, it was supposed to be totally shaded.

When such failures in the design occur, one can again use the graphic output to evaluate the design. *Figure 17* shows a sequence of solar views of the window and its shading device during December from 8:00 am to 11:00 am and with the window 100% exposed to the sun. *Figure 18* shows a corresponding sequence for the month of August (symmetrical to April in terms of the sun's position with respect to the summer solstice), and it shows the window to be totally shaded at 7:00 am and 9:00 am as it is supposed to be. However, at 8:00 am, the time for which trouble was detected in Figure 16, the solar view shows the window to be partially exposed, and by reinspection, the design error can be corrected.

Integrated Energy Analysis

The considerations outlined in the above three sections deal with isolated effects. In order to complete the energy analysis of a building, however, all of these effects must be analyzed in an integrated form.[7] Integrated analysis is needed because some of the results of isolated analysis may be altered significantly when specific variables are considered in context of the total design.

Peak Loading vs. Energy Consumption *Figure 19* illustrates, through a simple example, the trade-off between initial cost of cooling equipment (maximum power demand) and operating cost (total energy consumed in a day). Two cubic rooms, 10 ft on each side, are placed next to one another. One room faces east, the other west. All the walls are concrete, 1 ft thick. They thus have relatively high "heat-holding" properties. The east room has no openings; the west room has a west-facing window. The thermostat in each room is set for cooling at 80F, and each room has its separate air-conditioning system. It is summertime in Austin, Texas. As expected, the west room gains heat very rapidly in the late afternoon when the sun directly hits the west window. This same window, however, permits rapid cool-off in the late evening,

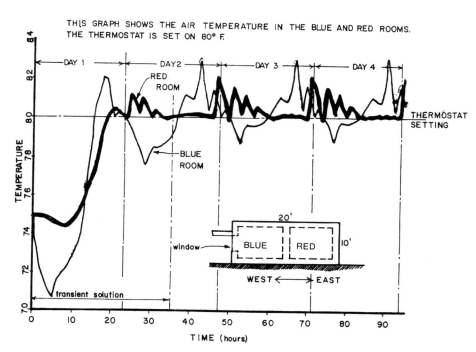

Fig. 19   A four-day temperature history of two adjacent rooms.

7. J. E. Hill and T. Kusuda:
"Manchester's New Federal
Building," *ASHRAE Journal,*
August 1975.

allowing the air-conditioning system to be turned off for several hours at a time. The east room, on the other hand, never gains heat as dramatically as the west room, but because of the heat holding properties of the walls, it demands that the air conditioning be on at a more steady rate. The maximum load on this room is about half that of the other, but the total energy consumed in a 24-hour period is larger.

Passive Systems A second example of the value of integrated analysis comes from the simulation of a "passive design."[8] *Figure 20* shows the schematic configuration of an experimental space attached to a Trombe wall (described in Chapter 5). The purpose of the experiment was to identify the design parameters that would make a Trombe wall economical as a supplement to the heating demands during the Central Texas winter without adding

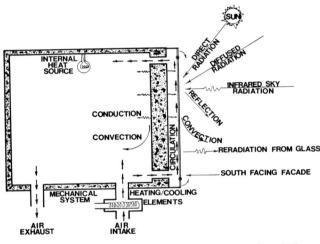

Fig. 20 Schematic diagram of a Trombe wall.

to the cooling demand during the severe summer months. The results of the experiment show that for a statistically typical January day, most of the needed heat can be provided by a Trombe wall with open vents that allow the circulation of the room air through the front space of the wall and back into the room. The wall area must be about equal to the floor area of the space to be heated. The summary of these results is shown in *Figure 21*. For summer operation, the Trombe wall can be designed so that, not only does it not add to the cooling load, but in fact may help reduce it, providing the wall surface is totally shaded and the front space of the wall is externally vented. These results, summarized in *Figure 22*, show that in this location any additional insulating panels would offer no outstanding advantage. From these experiments it was also deduced that the optimum wall thickness is about 1 ft, a result also reported by others.[9]

Daylighting Another example of integrated energy analysis comes from daylighting and its impact on total energy demand, to include energy consumed for lighting as well as for space heating and cooling, and in particular, the impact that heat

8. F. Arumi and M. Hourmanesh: "Energy Performance of Solar Walls, A Computer Analysis," *Energy and Buildings*, vol. 1, no. 2 (1977).

9. See Chapter 5; also J. E. Perry: "Mathematical Modeling of the Performance of Passive Solar Heating Systems," Mediterranean Working Group, NATO Committee on the Challenges of Modern Society, October 1977, Nice, France.

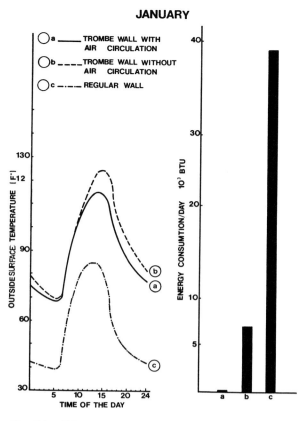

JANUARY

Fig. 21 Winter operation of Trombe wall in Austin, TX. Best results are obtained with vents to the interior space open.

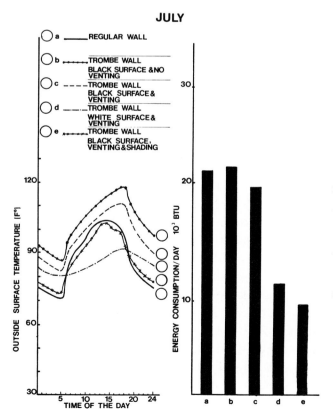

JULY

Fig. 22 Summer operation of Trombe wall in Austin, TX. Best results are obtained when Trombe wall is externally vented and shaded.

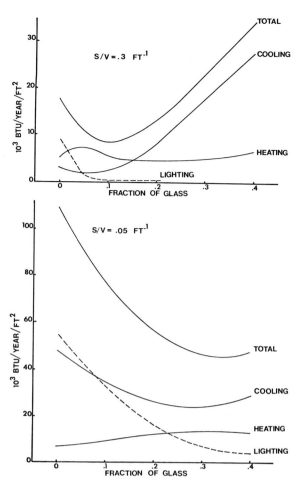

Fig. 23 Total energy demand for heating, cooling, and lighting for two different south-facing rooms in Austin, TX, as a function of window area.

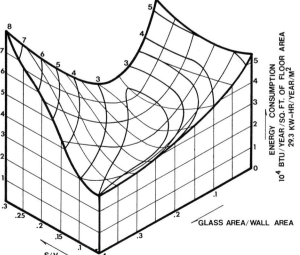

Fig. 24 Three-dimensional graph of the total energy demand for heating, cooling, and lighting as a function of window area and surface-to-volume ratio. Notice the trade-off possibilities between these two variables.

generated by artificial lighting has on the space heating and cooling demands. *Figure 23* shows the annual energy consumption for lighting, heating, and cooling for two spaces as a function of window area.[10] Both rooms shown have only a south-facing external surface (as if they were part of a larger building mass). The more shallow room has an external surface-to-volume ratio of .3 ft^{-1} and the deeper one a ratio of .05 ft^{-1}. The annual energy consumption is measured in Btu per year per unit of floor area. The independent variable is the glass area measured as a fraction of external wall area. The glass is shaded from direct solar rays from March through September. The spaces are occupied only from 8:00 am to 5:00 pm. The lighting intensity is required to remain at a fixed value on the floor surface. Whenever energy is consumed to provide the required illumination level, it means that daylighting through the windows is not sufficient. Both cases shown in Figure 23 exhibit a well-pronounced minimum total energy consumption for finite amounts of glass. For the shallow room (s/v = .3 ft^{-1}), the optimum window area is 10% of the wall area, while for the deeper room (s/v = .05 ft^{-1}) the optimum window area is about 30%. These calculations were done for Austin, Texas, and the quantitative results are expected to be different for other sites, although the qualitative conclusions are expected to be similar; namely, that daylighting, when properly integrated with artificial lighting, can result in significant energy savings for the periphery zones of buildings. *Figure 24* is a three-dimensional graph showing the total annual energy consumption for heating, cooling, and lighting as a function of window area and surface-to-volume ratio. The basis for these daylighting calculations is referenced in *Footnote 11*.

Conclusion

This chapter has outlined a variety of computer-aided design tools used at NSL in an effort to develop effective pedagogical methods to train future architects for the energy exigencies that society is about to place on them. These examples can hardly be fully representative of the wide range of energy design problems to which computer methods can be applied. However, they do show that, with the aid of increasingly available and lower-cost computer methods, we are offered vastly improved techniques for analysis of energy expenditure in buildings. As the methodology for this analysis is refined, its application to the conceptual design process in interactive ways can also be developed, and herein lies the greatest challenge to practicing design professionals. Without intelligent questions, even computer-generated answers are not going to be helpful. Emerging computer-aided methods make possible building designs suited quite specifically to their particular climatic and programatic needs in ways that would not otherwise be perceived. These techniques only await the direction of the creative designer.

10. F. N. Arumi: "Daylighting as a Factor in Optimizing the Energy Performance of Buildings," *Energy and Buildings,* vol. 1, no. 2 (1977).
11. R. G.: Hopkinson: *Architectural Physics: Lighting,* Her Majesty's Stationary Office, London, 1963; S. Selkowitz and A. Rosenfeld: "Beam and Diffuse Daylighting and Peak Power Proceedings," *Effective Management of Lighting Energy Symposium,* D. K. Ross, ed., FEA, 1975.

9

LIFE-CYCLE COSTING GUIDE FOR ENERGY CONSERVATION IN BUILDINGS

Harold E. Marshall and
Rosalie T. Ruegg

This chapter is revised and extended from "Energy Conservation Through Life-Cycle Costing," *Journal of Architectural Education*, February 1977, and is a contribution of the National Bureau of Standards; not subject to copyright. The authors thank their colleagues Stephen R. Petersen for suggestions and data contributions and Stephen F. Weber for critical evaluation of the manuscript, and to many others at the National Bureau of Standards who participated in preparation. Any remaining errors are solely the authors' responsibility.

ENERGY
CONSERVATION
THROUGH
BUILDING
DESIGN

The purpose of this chapter is to provide practicing architects, mechanical engineers, building financiers, and others interested in the design process with a guide to life-cycle cost techniques for evaluating building designs for energy conservation.

The first section is an overview of the state of the art of life-cycle costing (LCC) of energy conservation design in buildings, provided in the format of a primer. The second section describes selected case examples and applications of LCC; and the concluding section a discussion of potential impediments to the immediate application of LCC techniques and the benefits to the building community that can be expected as LCC analysis gains wider acceptance.

Primer on Life-Cycle Costing

What is life-cycle costing? Life-cycle cost analysis is a variation of benefit-cost analysis, a technique for evaluating programs or investments by comparing all present and future expected benefits with all present and future costs.[1] To be worthwhile economically, the long-run benefits or cost savings produced by an investment must exceed the long-run costs. As one would expect from its name, the focus of LCC analysis is on costs. However, this does not preclude the treatment of benefits in an LCC analysis if the benefits can be conveniently stated as negative costs, as is the case with fuel cost savings.

LCC analysis, as applied to energy conservation features in buildings, is the evaluation of the net effect over time of reducing fuel costs by purchasing, installing, maintaining, operating, repairing, and replacing energy-conserving features. The results of LCC analysis may be expressed as (1) the total of conservation investment and energy consumption costs, (2) the net savings from the investment in energy conservation, or (3) the ratio of savings to costs. The choice will depend in part on the preference of the analyst and in part on the nature of the investment problem.[1] The net savings from energy conservation are computed as shown in Equation 1:

1. More extensive treatments of benefit-cost and LCC analysis are provided in A. K. Dasgupta and D. W. Pearce: *Cost-Benefit Analysis: Theory and Practice,* Barnes and Noble, New York, 1972; Reynolds, Smith and Hills, Architects - Engineers - Planners, Inc.: *Life-Cycle Costing Emphasizing Energy Conservation: Guidelines for Investment Analysis,* rev. ed., Energy Research and Development Administration Manual 76/130, May 1977 (hereafter cited as *Life-Cycle Costing*) and R. T. Ruegg, J. S. McConnaughey et al. *Life-Cycle Costing, A Guide for Selecting Energy Conservation Projects for Public Buildings,* National Bureau of Standards Building Science Series 113, May 1978.

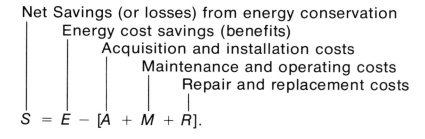

Net Savings (or losses) from energy conservation
Energy cost savings (benefits)
Acquisition and installation costs
Maintenance and operating costs
Repair and replacement costs

$$S = E - [A + M + R].$$

A positive value for S indicates that the energy-conserving feature results in net savings and is, therefore, economically efficient; a negative value indicates that it results in net losses and is, therefore, uneconomical.

LCC analysis may be used to address two types of economic efficiency choices: first, how much of a single energy conservation feature to use (if at all), and second, how much of each of several energy conservation features to use in combination. By comparing the net life-cycle effects of successively increasing amounts of a given energy conservation feature, it is possible to determine which level of investment in this feature is most economical. The optimal combination of energy conservation features can be determined by substituting among alternatives until each is being used to the level at which its additional contribution to energy cost reduction per extra dollar spent is just equal to that for all the other alternatives.[2]

Discounting, Taxes, and Inflation The results obtained by LCC analysis and benefit-cost analysis are usually expressed in either present value terms or in uniform annual value terms. "Present value" means that all past, present, and future dollars of expenditures, receipts, or savings—that is, all cash flows—are converted to an equivalent value in today's dollars. "Uniform annual value" means that all past, present, and future cash flows are converted to an equivalent level amount recurring yearly.

It is important to note that the present value of net costs and cost savings from an investment is not found by merely summing the cash flows over the expected life. Nor is the uniform annual value found by dividing cumulative net cash flows by the number of years of expected life (that is, the uniform annual value is not the same as the average yearly value). This is because the value one places on money is time dependent. The time dependency of value reflects not only inflation, which may erode the buying power of the dollar, but also the fact that money can be invested to yield a return over time that is separate from inflation. Hence, to evaluate the profitability of investing in energy conservation—either to determine the desirability of a single investment or to compare alternative investments—it is necessary to adjust for the differences in the timing of expenditures and cost savings.

The conversion of differently timed cash flows to a common time equivalent may be done by a technique called discounting. This technique relies on the application of interest (discount) formulas or, to simplify the calculation, discount factors already calculated from the formulas, to adjust the cash flows.[3]

To apply the discount formulas or factors, it is necessary to select a discount rate. The discount rate should indicate one's time preference for money. For example, if a person had an annual discount rate of 10% (for example, he or she could earn 10% interest in a risk-free savings account at the bank), a given amount of money this year would be worth 10% more than that same amount next year. This person should therefore be indifferent to a choice between a given amount of money now and 10% more than that amount a year from now.

A discount rate may be either "nominal" or "real." A "nominal"

2. For a discussion of the determination of the optimal input combinations to minimize the cost of producing a given output or to maximize the output for a given cost, see E. Mansfield: *Microeconomics: Theory and Applications*, W. W. Norton, New York, 1970, pp. 148–156.

3. A familiar application of an interest, or discounting, formula is the use of the Uniform Capital Recovery (UCR) Formula to amortize the principal of a mortgage loan over a specified number of years at a given interest rate. This formula, together with the following five additional interest formulas, are those most frequently used in investment analysis: a) Single Compound Amount Formula (SCA), used to find the future value of a present amount, b) the Single Present Worth Formula (SPW), used to find the present value of a future amount, c) the Uniform Compound Amount Formula (UCA), used to find the future value of a series of uniform annual amounts, d) the Uniform Sinking Fund Formula (USF), used to find the annual amount which will result in a given total value at a future time, and e) the Uniform Present Worth Formula (UPW) used to find the present value of a series of uniform annual amounts. An in-depth explanation of discounting formulas and tables of discount factors calculated from the discount formulas for a range of years and discount rates are available in most engineering economics textbooks. See, for example, G. W. Smith: *Engineering Economy: Analysis of Capital Expenditures*, 2nd ed., Iowa State University Press, Ames, Iowa, 1977 (hereafter cited as *Capital Expenditures*); and E. L. Grant and W. Grant Ireson: *Principals of Engineering Economy*, The Ronald Press, New York, 1970 (hereafter cited as *Engineering Economy*).

TABLE 1

Discounting Cash Flows from an Energy Conservation Investment[a]

Type of cost or saving (1)	Cash-flow diagram (2)
Purchase and installation of an Energy-Conserving Feature	S, 1, 2, 10 time; $10,000
Repair and Replacement of Parts	S, 1, 5, 10 time; $500
Annual Fuel Savings[b]	S, $1,200, $1,200, $1,200, $1,200; 1, 2, 3, 10 time
Net Total Savings (Fuel Savings Less Costs)	

discount rate reflects both the effects of inflation and the real earning power of money invested over time. A lower, "real" rate, reflecting only the real earning power of money, is appropriate for evaluating investments if inflation is removed from the cash flows prior to discounting, that is, if they are stated in constant dollars.

The discount rate may be based on any of several different measures, such as the rate of return which could be realized from the next best available investment, the interest rate on savings accounts, or the cost of borrowing. There may be a strong subjective element in the specification of the discount rate. The choice of a rate will likely vary depending on the investor's financial position and concern for the timing of expenditures and receipts (time preference).[4] The approach generally taken is to base the rate on a consideration of the factors at hand, and to test the outcome for sensitivity to the use of alternative discount rates where there is great uncertainty as to the correct choice.[5]

Table 1 provides several simple illustrations of the discounting of costs and savings typically associated with investments in energy conservation. The illustrations are based on a discount rate of 10% and a period of 10 years. The first column describes the type of costs or savings. The second column uses a cash-flow diagram to describe the timing of the cash outflows and inflows. The horizontal line with arrows represents a time scale progressing from left to right, on which S (for "start") indicates the present, the number on the scale indicates the number of years, each downward arrow represents an expenditure, and each upward arrow represents a cost saving. The third column shows the present value equivalent, and the fourth column, the annual value equivalent of each cost or saving.

4. For a discussion of subjectivity in selecting discount rates, see James J. Mutch: *Residential Water Heating, Fuel Conservation, Economics, and Public Policy,* prepared by the Rand Corporation for the National Science Foundation, Th 7512, M18, Appendix B, pp. 69–71.

5. When there is uncertainty as to the correct value of one or more important input parameters in an evaluation, such as the discount rate, it is useful to determine whether the outcome would change significantly if alternative values were used for the input parameters. Sensitivity analysis can be used to provide additional information for making economic choices. For a description and illustration of sensitivity analysis and the mathematics of probability in economic studies, see, Grant and Ireson, *Engineering Economy,* pp. 251–301.

LIFE-CYCLE
COSTING GUIDE
FOR ENERGY
CONSERVATION
IN BUILDINGS

165

Present value equivalent (P) (3)	Annual value equivalent (A) (4)
$P_f = \$10,000$	$A_f = \$10,000 \cdot (UCR, i = 10\%, N = 10)$ $= \$10,000 \cdot 0.1628$ $= \$1,628$
$P_r = \$500 \cdot (SPW, i = 10\%, N = 5)$ $= \$500 \cdot 0.6209$ $= \$310$	$A = \$500 \cdot (SPW, i = 10\%, N = 5)$ $\cdot (UCR, i = 10\%, N = 10)$ $= \$500 \cdot 0.6209 \cdot 0.1628$ $= \$51$
$P_s = \$1,200 \cdot (UPW, i = 10\%, N = 10)$ $= \$1,200 \cdot 6.144$ $= \$7,373$	$A_s = \$1,200$
$P_n = P_s - (P_f + P_r)$ $= -\$2,937$	$A_n = A_s - (A_f + A_r)$ $= -\$479$

[a]Nomenclature:
S = Starting time (the present)
P = Present value equivalent
A = Annual value equivalent
F = Future value equivalent

Subscripts: f = first costs
r = repair and replacement costs
s = fuel savings
n = net of total costs and savings

UCR = Uniform Capital Recovery Formula, $A = P \dfrac{i(1 + i)^N}{(1 + i)^N - 1}$.

SPW = Single Present Worth Formula, $P = F \dfrac{1}{(1 + i)^N}$.

UPW = Uniform Present Worth Formula, $P = A \dfrac{(1 + i)^N - 1}{i(1 + i)^N}$.

i = Discount rate per period
N = Number of interest periods

[b]Assumes no change in fuel prices. To include fuel price escalation, the formula becomes

$$P = C \times \sum_{j=1}^{N} \left(\frac{1 + e}{1 + i} \right)^j$$

where C = Fuel cost savings at outset, and e = fuel price escalation rate

Once the various cash flows have been discounted to a present value or to an annual value, they may then be combined to provide a net measure of the economic impact of an investment. In column 3 of Table 1, for example, the present value cost of $10,000 for purchasing and installing the energy conservation feature, plus the present value cost of $310 for repair and replacement, total $10,310. The present value cost savings total $7,373. Net savings of −$2,937 result. This is equivalent to a net loss of $479 per year in terms of annual value. Hence, this investment is not worthwhile even though net savings in undiscounted terms amount to $1,500 (i.e., a total of $10,500 for purchase, installation, repair, and replacement subtracted from $12,000 in aggregate fuel savings equals $1,500.)

Depending upon the degree of accuracy desired in an evaluation, it may be important to consider the impact of taxes. By

ENERGY
CONSERVATION
THROUGH
BUILDING
DESIGN

affecting revenues and costs, taxes can dramatically alter the profitability of an investment.[6] Potentially important tax effects include deductions from taxable income of depreciation allowances on capital expenditures; investment tax credits which directly offset tax liabilities; property taxes on capital investments; and the loss of deductions from taxable income when current operating expenses are reduced by fuel savings.

It is usually not necessary to increase the estimates of cash flows to include inflation in each item of cost or savings. Inflation can often be handled in an LCC analysis by making the simplifying assumption that all costs and revenues, except fuel costs, inflate at the same general rate, and that they therefore remain constant in real terms.[7] Because fuel prices are a dominant factor in the analysis of energy conservation investments, and because they are widely expected to increase at a rate faster than over-all prices in the economy, it is important to adjust estimates of future fuel cost savings to reflect their expected differential rate of price increase, i.e., the rate of increase over and above the general rate of inflation.[8] With these assumptions, all future cash flows can be evaluated with a "real" discount rate. (It should be noted that the treatment of inflation in economic analysis is different from the treatment of inflation for budgeting. To develop reliable budgets, it is essential to take into account the inflation that can occur in planned costs during the lag between the time of the preparation of the economic analysis and the time of actual spending or obligating funds.)

It is not always necessary to go through an elaborate LCC analysis before investing in energy conservation. In some cases, where first costs are low and the potential for energy conservation is high, it will not be necessary to make an explicit evaluation. Weatherstripping around poorly fitting (or leaking) windows and doors is an example of an inexpensive approach to energy conservation which can generally be undertaken with little doubt as to its favorable impact on life-cycle costs.

In cases where first costs are high and/or significant costs and savings are unevenly distributed over time, it is often advisable to do an LCC analysis. Not all energy-conserving features will be economical to use. Their cost effectiveness will depend particularly upon climatic conditions, their purchase and installation costs, their durability and maintainability, their ability to save energy, and the present and future prices of fuel. As is illustrated in specific applications later in this chapter, LCC analysis appropriately used can result in substantial savings both in energy conservation investments and in building costs in general.

Related Methods of Evaluation   There are several other methods of evaluating the economic efficiency of investment in energy conservation which are closely related to LCC analysis. Popular among these are the payback method and the internal rate-of-return method.

6. For a discussion of estimating the impact of taxes on investment decisions, see Grant and Ireson, *Engineering Economy*, pp. 337–382.
7. For a discussion of the conditions under which this assumption of evenly inflating costs and revenues is *not* appropriate, see Smith: *Capital Expenditures*, appen. G, pp. 542–552.
8. Reynolds, Smith and Hills, *Life-Cycle Costing. Guidelines for using differential rates of fuel price increases have been adopted by the Energy Research and Development Administration*, pp. II/10–II/11.

The *payback method* measures the elapsed time between the point of the initial investment and the point at which accumulated savings, net of other accumulated costs, are sufficient to offset the initial investment. (Although costs and savings should be discounted in calculating the payback period, in actual practice they are frequently left undiscounted.) Shorter payback periods are generally preferred to longer payback periods.

The popularity of the payback method probably reflects the fact that it is an easily understood concept and that it emphasizes the rapid recovery of the initial investment at a time when many organizations appear to place great emphasis on flexibility in investment strategy. However, the payback method has the weakness of failing to measure cash flows that occur beyond the point at which the initial investment costs are recovered. It is possible for a project with a longer payback period to yield higher net savings than a project with a shorter payback period. Hence, use of the payback method may lead to uneconomic conservation investments.

The algebraic formulation for determining discounted payback is the following:

$$C - \sum_{j=1}^{Y} \frac{B_j - K_j}{(1 + i)^j} = 0 \qquad \textit{Equation No. 2}$$

where C = the initial investment cost
Y = the number of years elapsed until the present value of cumulative net yearly savings just off-sets the initial investment
B_j = cost savings or benefits in year j
K_j = costs in year j
i = discount rate

The objective is to find the number of years, Y, which solves the equation, given values of the other variables. This may be done by trial and error. Alternatively, for the special case in which the net yearly savings, $B_j - K_j$, is equal to a constant, A, the following expression of the payback equation can be used:

$$Y = \frac{-n(1 - iC/A)}{n(1 + i)} \qquad \textit{Equation No. 3}$$

The *internal rate-of-return method* finds the rate of return that an investment is expected to yield. The rate of return is expressed as that compound interest rate for which the total discounted benefits become just equal to total discounted costs. The rate of return is generally calculated by a process of trial and error in which various interest rates are used to discount costs and benefits to present values. These discounted costs and benefits are compared with each other until that interest rate is found for which costs and benefits are equal and net benefits are, therefore, zero.

As an illustration, let us find the internal rate of return on an investment which requires an initial, one-time cost of $10,000, and yields a yearly recurring savings of $3,000 for 10 years. The initial investment of $10,000 is already in present value terms. We need now to calculate the net present value, *P,* of the $3,000 in yearly savings for various interest rates. First, let us calculate the value of *P* for, say, a compound interest rate of 25%. At this interest rate, the present value equivalent of the $3,000 for 10 years is equal to $10,713. Substracting the present value cost of $10,000 from the present value savings yields a net present value savings of $713. The fact that $713 exceeds zero means that 25% is less than the internal rate of return on this investment. Trying now a higher compound interest rate of 30%, the present value savings over the 10-year period equals $9,276. Net present value savings are now equal to $–724, an amount $724 less than the $10,000 cost. Since an interest rate of 30% results in net losses, this rate must be greater than the internal rate of return on this investment. Thus, we can conclude that the rate of return is bracketed by 25% and 30%. By interpolation, we can now estimate that the investment yields an internal rate of return of a little over 27%. The investment would be considered worthwhile if the 27% rate exceeds the rate of return which the investor could get from alternative investments.

This method of evaluation usually results in a measure consistent with an LCC approach, and somewhat more reliable than the payback method. However, the internal rate-of-return method does have the disadvantage of giving either no solution or multiple solutions under certain conditions.

The payback method, internal rate-of-return method, and LCC method all have particular advantages and disadvantages. Each will serve as a useful tool for investment decisions in certain cases.[9] For most problems of making economically efficient decisions in energy conservation, the LCC method will provide an adequate measure.

Case Applications of LCC to Energy Conservation

Let us examine four applications of LCC to energy conservation. The first deals with insulating an existing building to lower the undesirable heat loss and gain. The second deals with selecting window size, design, and orientation to reduce energy and lifetime building costs. The third deals with determining whether a solar heating system will be cost effective in reducing the consumption of nonrenewable energy resources. The fourth describes the use of LCC in developing energy conservation performance standards for buildings.

Retrofitting Existing Buildings[10] Promoting energy conservation in existing buildings is important for two reasons. First, the existing housing and commercial building stock is very large

9. For a discussion of the suitability of different evaluation methods for treating different kinds of investment decisions, see R. T. Ruegg: "Economics of Waste Heat Recovery," *Waste Heat Guidebook,* K. G. Kreider and M. B. McNeil, eds., National Bureau of Standards Handbook 121, February 1974, pp. 99–105.
10. Retrofitting an existing building for energy conservation means to add insulation, weatherstripping, storm windows, or replacement windows with insulated glass, or to do any other remodeling that contributes to the prevention of unwanted heat loss or gain.

relative to the number of new buildings added to that stock each year. Thus, the greatest potential for energy conservation in terms of numbers is in existing buildings. Second, older existing buildings generally have less insulation than do newer buildings. One cause of this is the historically low cost of fuel relative to other costs for operating buildings, and the consequent emphasis on a low first cost in weatherizing buildings. Furthermore, there had been no government controls to require insulation in buildings until the FHA Minimum Property Standards in 1960 called for increased insulation in FHA-insured residential construction.

A comprehensive handbook for determining the economically efficient amounts of insulation, weatherstripping, storm windows, and insulating glass to add to an existing home is *Making the Most of Your Energy Dollars,* by Madeleine Jacobs and Stephen R. Petersen,[11] based on a technical economics report prepared for analysts.[12] The handbook provides the homeowner with a method of determining how much to buy of any single technique for retrofitting buildings for energy conservation, and what combination of techniques to buy.

The approach and findings of *Making the Most of Your Energy Dollars* serve well as a case illustration of LCC analysis. The illustration is intended to show how the LCC application provides useful information, rather than to present the model in any detail.

To find the most economically efficient investments in energy conservation, a model was developed to compare the value of energy savings over time with costs for each selected alternative type of conservation. An LCC model was written in BASIC programing language to enable an analyst to calculate, at a time-sharing terminal, the optimal package for retrofitting a house. The LCC model is sensitive to the house location (i.e., the climate as measured in heating degree days and cooling hours)[13] and the price of fuel. Both heating and cooling loads are taken into account.

Tables 2, 3, and *4* illustrate the format used in *Making the Most of Your Energy Dollars,* to provide data for making an efficient decision on insulating attic floors and ducts in a heated and air-conditioned residence. The information that would be needed to plan the retrofitting of a given house is the heating and cooling zones (readily available in map form), the fuel type and price, and the level of insulation currently in the house. Tables of index values which combine the climate and fuel information are provided to simplify the computation. For example, Tables 2 and 3 show that a house in heating zone III and cooling zone B, with heating oil at $.34/gal and electricity for air conditioning at $.04/kWh, has an index of 20 for heating and 5 for cooling. These add up to a combined index of 25. For a range of combined heating and cooling index values, Table 4 gives the economically efficient level of resistance to heat flow in the attic and duct insulation of the building, as well as the corresponding thickness of different

11. National Bureau of Standards, CIS-8, June 1975 (hereafter cited as *Energy Dollars*).

12. S. R. Petersen: *Retrofitting Existing Housing for Energy Conservation: An Economic Analysis,* National Bureau of Standards, Building Science Series 64, December 1974 (hereafter cited as *Retrofitting*).

13. "Heating degree days" is a measure of the temperature differences (design conditions) between the interior and exterior of a building that are used to establish the heating load of a building. Annual heating degree days are computed by adding the number of degrees that the daily mean temperature is below 65F, for all days of the year. "Cooling hours" are the number of hours annually in which air conditioning is required. (*ASHRAE Handbook of Fundamentals,* ASHRAE, New York, 1972.)

TABLE 2

Heating Index to Relate Climate and Fuel Price to Cost Savings in Heating Energy

Type of fuel		Cost per unit[a]									
Gas (therm)		9¢	12¢	15¢	18¢	24¢	30¢	36¢	54¢	72¢	90¢
Oil (gal)		13¢	17¢	21¢	25¢	34¢	42¢	50¢	75¢	$1.00	$1.25
Electric (kWh)					1¢	1.3¢	1.6¢	2¢	3¢	4¢	5¢
Heat pump (kWh)		0.9¢	1.1¢	1.5¢	1.8¢	2.3¢	2.9¢	3.5¢	5.3¢	7.0¢	8.8¢
H		I	2	2	3	3	4	5	6	9	12	15
E		II	5	6	8	9	12	15	18	27	36	45
A	Z	III	8	10	13	15	20	25	30	45	60	75
T	O	IV	11	14	18	21	28	35	42	63	84	105
I	N	V	14	18	23	27	36	45	54	81	108	135
N	E	VI	22	28	36	42	56	70	84	126	168	210
G												

[a]Cost of last unit for heating and cooling purposes, including all taxes, surcharges, and fuel adjustments.

TABLE 3

Cooling Index to Relate Climate and Fuel Price to Cost Savings in Cooling Energy

Type of air conditioner			Cost per unit[a]						
Gas (therm)			9¢	12¢	15¢	18¢	24¢	30¢	36¢
Electric (kWh)			1.5¢	2¢	2.5¢	3¢	4¢	5¢	6¢
C		A	0	0	0	0	0	0	0
O	Z	B	2	2	3	4	5	6	7
O	O	C	3	5	6	7	9	11	13
L	N	D	5	6	8	9	12	15	18
I	E	E	7	9	11	14	18	23	27
N									
G									

[a]Cost of last unit for heating and cooling purposes, including all taxes, surcharges, and fuel adjustments.

TABLE 4

Attic Floor Insulation and Attic Duct Insulation

INDEX Heating index plus cooling index for attics	R-Value	Attic insulation Approximate thickness Mineral-fiber blanket	Mineral-fiber loose-fill[b]	Cellulose loose-fill[b]	Duct insulation[a] R-Value	Approximate thickness
1–3	R-0	0"	0"	0"	R-8	2"
4–9	R-11	4"	4–6"	2–4"	R-8	2"
10–15	R-19	6"	8–10"	4–6"	R-8	2"
16–27	R-30	10"	13–15"	7–9"	R-16	4"
28–35	R-33	11"	14–16"	8–10"	R-16	4"
36–45	R-38	12"	17–19"	9–11"	R-24	6"
46–50	R-44	14"	19–21"	11–13"	R-24	6"
61–85	R-49	16"	22–24"	12–14"	R-32	8"
86–105	R-57	18"	25–27"	14–16"	R-32	8"
106–130	R-60	19"	27–29"	15–17"	R-32	8"
131–	R-66	21"	29–31"	17–19"	R-40	10"

[a]Use Heating Index only if ducts are not used for air conditioning.
[b]High levels of loose-fill insulation may not be feasible in many attics.

TABLE 5

LIFE-CYCLE
COSTING GUIDE
FOR ENERGY
CONSERVATION
IN BUILDINGS

171

Costs and Savings for a Range of Attic Insulation Levels Given an Index Value of 25[a]

	Dollar cost			
Insulation resistance (1)	Insulation (acquisition & installation costs) (2)	Energy consumption (present value of future costs) (3)	Total life-cycle costs (4) = (3) + (2)	Marginal life-cycle savings (5)
R-11	300	1878	2178	N.A.[b]
R-19	500	1126	1626	552
R-22	580	986	1566	60
R-30	780	739	1519	47
R-33	860	676	1536	−17
R-38	990	592	1582	−46
R-44	1140	514	1654	−72
R-49	1280	483	1763	−109

[a]Assumptions are the following:
Degree days = 5,000; cooling hours = 750 (New York City)
Oil = 34¢/gal; efficiency = .6
Electricity = 4¢/kWh; COP = 2.0
Insulation prices are based on typical 1976 installed costs.
Present Worth Factor = 20 (based on the assumption of a 20-year life and a rate of fuel price escalation equal to the discount rate).
[b]N.A. means not applicable. The value of energy consumed when no insulation is installed was not computed.

types of insulation which would be required to achieve the indicated resistance, or "R" value. For example, the combined index of 25 calls for R-30 insulation in the attic and R-16 around attic ducts. The recommended resistance value, R-30, is shown to be provided alternatively by 10 in. of mineral-fiber batt blanket, 13–15 in. of mineral-fiber loose-fill, or 7–9 in. of cellulose loose-fill insulation. The retrofit requirements for the attic and ducts are then calculated as the difference between the amount indicated by the tables and the amount of insulation already in place in the house.

The economic significance of failing to install R-30 insulation in the attic under the described conditions is illustrated in *Table 5.* For each "R" value of insulation (column 1), the table shows the total life-cycle costs (column 4), as well as the marginal life-cycle savings (column 5). Note that the minimum total life-cycle cost (column 4) is $1,519, and that the corresponding resistance level is R-30. That is, the sum of insulation costs (column 2) and energy consumption costs (column 3) are at a minimum for R-30 insulation. Another way of establishing R-30 as the optimal level is to examine marginal life-cycle savings. Note that marginal savings (column 5) from each additional amount of insulation is positive as "R" increases up to R-30, but beyond that point marginal savings become increasingly negative (i.e., life-cycle costs begin to increase). The increment from R-22 to R-30 brings a marginal savings of $47 ($1,566 − $1,519), but the next increment, R-30 to R-33, brings a loss of $17 ($1,519 − $1,536). Thus, a quantity of insulation that provides a resistance value of R-30 is the economically efficient level of insulation among those shown in Table 5; it is the level for which the building owner will maximize net savings from energy conservation. Installing more insulation would not raise savings sufficiently to offset the additional cost of the insulation; installing less would mean foregoing fuel savings in excess of the required cost.[14]

Selecting Windows for Energy Conservation and Economic Efficiency Another recent application of life-cycle cost analysis to energy conservation in buildings pertains to window selection and use. Although it is estimated that about one-fourth of the total energy used for heating and cooling buildings in the United States each year is lost through windows, a recent study at the National Bureau of Standards has shown that it is possible to alter considerably the impact of windows on energy consumption and total lifetime building costs. Depending upon critical design and use decisions, it was shown that windows can increase, decrease, or have little impact on energy and building costs.[15]

The NBS research first identified specific window systems with potential for saving energy. A computer model was developed for estimating the impact of selected window systems on energy conservation. Life-cycle costing techniques were then used to combine the costs of acquisition, maintenance, repair, and energy, in order to determine the over-all impact of alternative window systems on the cost of the building.[16]

NBS conducted 18 case studies of window use—nine for residential buildings and nine for commercial buildings. The following nine geographical locations, covering five major heating zones and four major cooling zones in the United States, were treated: Washington, DC; Miami, Florida; Atlanta, Georgia; Portland, Maine; Indianapolis, Indiana; San Antonio, Texas; Los Angeles, California; Bismark, North Dakota; and Seattle, Washington.

Life-cycle costs were estimated for (1) a range of window sizes, (2) alternative orientations, (3) choices of single, double, and triple glazing, (4) the use of two interior accessories—venetian blinds and insulating shutters; and (5) the use of windows for daylighting. Costs were estimated for gas heating and electric cooling, and for electric heating and cooling, as well as for a range of energy escalation values.

The study is relevant to the design of new buildings in that it identifies the least-cost window system from among alternatives, and to the retrofit of existing buildings in that it indicates how existing windows may be accessorized and used more efficiently.

Following is an example of results taken from the Washington, DC case study for windows in a detached, single-family residence. *Figures 1* and *2* show graphically the behavior of net life-cycle costs associated with single- and double-glazed windows as the area of the window is increased relative to the wall area. The costs are based on using varying sizes of double-hung wooden windows in a "typical" family-room–kitchen of a brick rambler.

14. In *Footnotes 12* and *13* (Jacobs and Petersen: *Energy Dollars;* Petersen: *Retrofitting*), additional alternatives for retrofitting, such as weatherstripping, storm doors and windows, and caulking are evaluated, and alternative measures of economic desirability, such as the years required for an investment to pay back its costs, are also evaluated.

15. R. T. Ruegg and R. E. Chapman: *Economic Evaluation of Windows in Buildings,* vols. 1 and 3, National Bureau of Standards Building Science Series, in press.

16. R. Hastings and R. W. Crenshaw: *Window Design Strategies to Conserve Energy,* National Bureau of Standards Building Science Series, June 1977; T. Kusuda and B. L. Collins: *Simplified Analysis of Thermal and Lighting Characteristics of Windows: Two Case Studies,* National Bureau of Standards Building Science Series, November 1977. Only those costs and benefits which could be measured in dollars with a relatively high degree of confidence were included in the analysis; the benefits of natural ventilation and psychological, safety, and aesthetic effects were not included.

LIFE-CYCLE
COSTING GUIDE
FOR ENERGY
CONSERVATION
IN BUILDINGS

173

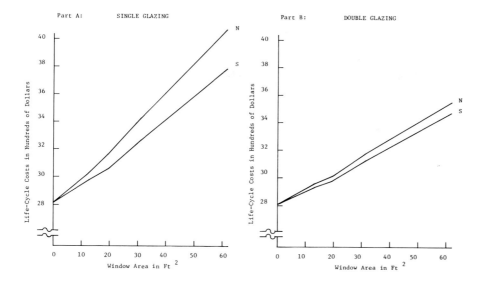

Fig. 1 Washington, DC Case Study: Life-cycle costs for a room with a north (N) or south (S) window area without energy conservation accessories and without daylight utilization.

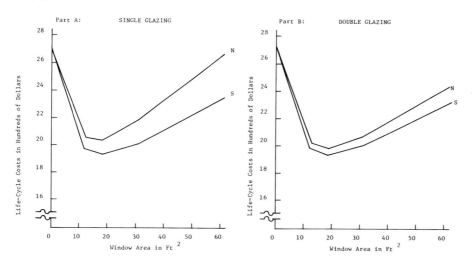

Fig. 2 Washington, DC Case Study: Life-cycle costs for a room with a north (N) or south (S) window area with energy conservation accessories and daylighting utilization.

In each figure, Part A is for single glazing, and Part B is for double glazing. Two situations of window use are described by these figures. Figure 1 shows the costs based on the assumption that the window is bare and is not used for daylighting. Figure 2, in contrast, shows the costs based on the assumption that the window is accessorized with insulating shutters which are closed at night during the winter, and venetian blinds which reduce undesirable solar radiation in summer. It is further assumed in Figure 2 that the window is used for daylighting, thereby reducing the reliance on electric lighting. It is also assumed that the thermostat is adjusted at night for energy conservation.

For simplicity, only two orientations, north and south, are shown. Costs are shown for gas heating at $.30/therm and electric cooling at $.03/kWh. A 12% annual rate of escalation in energy prices is assumed, and future cash flows are discounted to present value with a discount rate of 8%. The vertical axis of each figure measures the life-cycle costs in present value dollars. The horizontal axis measures the window area in square feet, beginning with zero (no window) at the origin and going to 60 ft^2. When the room is windowless, the figures show only the costs for heating and cooling the room. When a window area is added to the room, the figures show the combination of the room's energy costs and costs of purchasing, installing, maintaining, and repairing the window area over and above the costs which would be incurred for an equal area of opaque wall.

From Figure 1 we can draw the following conclusions about a bare window area, unutilized for daylighting, in a house in a moderate climate like Washington, DC: (1) the larger the window, the larger the life-cycle costs of the building; (2) the life-cycle costs of windows are lower on the south side than on the north side of the building; and (3) if there is a relatively high rate of escalation in energy prices, double glazing is economical for all window sizes examined, both on the north and south sides of the building.

From Figure 2, we can draw the following conclusions about windows that are equipped with energy-conserving accessories and used for daylighting in a house in a moderate climate like Washington, DC: (1) over-all cost of the building can be lowered by adding a window area, provided steps are taken to reduce its undesirable heat gains and losses, and if it is used during the day to eliminate electric lighting; (2) the greatest savings result from adding a small-to-medium, single-glazed window area on the south side; and (3) with rapid escalation in energy prices, double glazing tends to be cost effective for all window sizes examined, except for small-to-medium windows on the south side.

Apart from the consideration of psychological or other factors, these conclusions suggest that a homeowner, builder, or designer of a house in the Washington, DC area could reduce the house's life-cycle costs by keeping window areas as small as possible in those rooms which are not used much during the day or which, for some other reason, cannot be used effectively to reduce electric lighting requirements. Where daylighting can be used effectively, it appears better from a life-cycle cost standpoint to have a window area—even a relatively large one—than to have a windowless exterior wall. In either case, however, small- to medium-sized window areas tend to be more economical than large areas. With rapidly rising energy prices, it will generally pay to use either insulating and shading accessories like those described, or double glazing, or in most cases both accessories and double glazing. The use of accessories and double glazing is

LIFE-CYCLE
COSTING GUIDE
FOR ENERGY
CONSERVATION
IN BUILDINGS

175

particularly important for large window areas and north-facing areas.

LCC Evaluation of Solar Energy Systems   Another application of LCC to energy conservation investments in buildings is in the evaluation of solar energy systems. This investment is similar to many other approaches to energy conservation in that it requires a relatively large initial expenditure to achieve fuel cost savings over time. It works, however, by replacing nonrenewable energy sources with renewable energy, rather than by reducing the building's energy requirements.

LCC analysis may be applied both to the evaluation of the cost effectiveness of a given solar energy system in a specific application, and to the optimal sizing and design of a solar energy system for a specific application. The primary difference is in the complexity of the number of analyses to be performed.[17]

In the case of evaluating the cost effectiveness of a particular system for a given building, the analysis consists of using a model like that described in the first section of this chapter to compare life-cycle investment costs against life-cycle fuel cost savings. In the case of optimally designing and sizing a solar energy system, the approach is to evaluate the costs and cost savings associated with marginal changes in the various design and size alternatives. One tries to identify that design and size which maximizes net savings, or, when said another way, minimizes the life-cycle costs of providing a given comfort level in a building.[18]

To calculate the life-cycle costs to the owner for a heating and/or cooling system, the following items are relevant: (1) acquisition costs, which consist of the costs of "identifying" and/or designing the system, as well as purchasing, delivering, installing, and modifying the building to receive it; (2) system repair and replacement costs, including damage losses and insurance premiums, net of reimbursements; (3) routine maintenance costs; (4) operating costs, comprised mainly of fuel costs; and (5) salvage values in excess of removal and disposal costs, or alternatively, resale value if the building is to be sold during the time frame of the analysis. In assessing costs, it is also important to take into account the impact of property and income tax effects, as well as the impact of any available incentive programs provided by the state or federal government.

A computerized model to assess the life-cycle costs of solar heating systems has been developed at the National Bureau of Standards, and is referred to in *Footnote 19*. The following example is based on this report.

The solar energy LCC model allows the user to specify the values of key parameters, such as the cost per unit of the collector, the present price of fuel, its anticipated rate of escalation, and the discount rate. It was developed to assess the impact on owner costs of seven different types of financial incentives which could be provided to homeowners and to businesses. The inclusion of

17. For a description of the major steps in LCC analysis as applied to solar energy systems, see R. T. Ruegg: "Life-Cycle Costs and Solar Energy," *ASHRAE Journal,* November 1976.
18. For a more comprehensive discussion of the necessary conditions for the economic optimization of solar HVAC systems and the building envelope, see R. T. Ruegg: *Solar Heating and Cooling in Buildings: Methods of Economic Analysis,* National Bureau of Standards Interagency Report 75-712, July 1975, pp. 35–40.
19. R. T. Ruegg: *Evaluating Incentives for Solar Heating,* National Bureau of Standards Interagency Report 76-1127, September 1976.

incentives in the model was in recognition of the considerable legislative activity at both the state and federal levels to enact financial programs to encourage the widespread use of solar energy systems.[20]

Table 6 presents the results of eight hypothetical case studies described in the National Bureau of Standards publication. The case studies are for climate regions typical of Madison, Wisconsin, and of Albuquerque, New Mexico. They assume solar equipment costs, fuel prices, and tax rates typical of those found in many parts of the country, but not necessarily specific to Madison and Albuquerque. Costs are based on 500 ft² of a "standard" liquid collector at $10.50/ft² installed, plus $1,700 of non-collector components, or a total of $6,950. The solar heating system is assumed to supply 75% of the 65×10^6 Btu heating load of a

20. National Conference of State Legislatures Energy Task Force, *Turning Towards the Sun*, vol. 1 (Abstracts of State Legislative Enactments of 1974 and 1975 Regarding Solar Energy), n.d.; Robert M. Eisenhard: *A Survey of State Legislation Relating to Solar Energy*, National Bureau of Standards Interagency Report 76-1082, April 1976; and J. Glen Moore, "Solar Energy Legislation in the 94th Congress: A Compilation of Bills through June 30, 1976," the Library of Congress, Congressional Research Service, unpublished abstracts of bills.

TABLE 6

Annual Savings to the Owner of a Solar-Equipped Building with and without Incentives: Case Studies[a]

Building type	Selected locations	Fuel cost/ therm output
Residential	Albuquerque, NM	$.45
		$.90
	Madison, WI	$.45
Commercial		$.90
	Madison, WI	$.45
		$.90

LIFE-CYCLE
COSTING GUIDE
FOR ENERGY
CONSERVATION
IN BUILDINGS

177

1,500 ft² house in Albuquerque, and 47% of the 118 × 10⁶ Btu heating load of a 1,500 ft² house in Madison, Wisconsin. The assumed system life is 25 years. Tax effects are computed with a composite state and federal rate of 32% for systems used on owner-occupied residences, and 50% for systems used on commercial buildings. Future cash flows are discounted with a real rate of 3% for residential systems, and 10% for commercial systems. For each location and building type, life-cycle costs are evaluated first for a fuel cost of $.45/therm of heat output, and second for a cost of $.90/therm of heat output. The $.45/therm fuel cost is equivalent to a price of $.015/kWh of electricity, $.38/gal of fuel oil, and $.27/therm for natural gas. The $.90/therm fuel cost is equivalent to a price of $.03/kWh, $.76/gal, and $.54/therm. The fuel costs per therm of heat output are based on the

Annual net savings in dollars

(1) Before taxes No incentives	(2) With taxes No incentives	(3) Grant or tax credit $1,000	(4) 3% prop. tax exempt.	(5) 5-yr. depr. allow.	(6) 4% sales tax exempt.	(7) Interest subsidy 2%	(8) Fuel tax 20%
−110	−190	−110	−50	−80	−180	−160	−140
300	230	310	370	350	240	260	340
−60	−140	−60	10 — −20 130ᶜ		−130	−100	−70
410	340	420	480 — 460 600ᶜ		350	370	470
−200	−350ᵇ	−300	−250 — −190 −90ᶜ		−330	−300	−310
180	−150	−70	−40 — 10 110ᶜ		−130	−100	−70

ᵃNote that this compilation of annual savings is based on a specific set of assumptions regarding input variables such as cost and performance of the system, the heating load of the building, the future escalation of energy prices, and discount rates and tax rates. A different set of assumptions would produce different results.

ᵇUse of a double-declining balance method of depreciation and a 10-year life instead of a straight-line method and a 25-year life would reduce annual losses with existing taxes from $350 to $204.

ᶜThe annual savings or losses are based on a combination of the two incentives bracketed.

following system efficiencies: electric resistance system, 100%; oil furnace, 60%; natural gas system, 60%. Energy prices are assumed to escalate at a rate 5% faster than general price inflation.

The results of the case studies are given for a homeowner and a business in terms of the annual net savings (or annual net losses where a minus sign precedes the number) to be realized by the building owner under eight different conditions: (1) before any taxes and without incentives; (2) with existing "typical" taxes and without incentives; (3) with taxes and a grant or a tax credit of $1,000; (4) with taxes and an exemption of the assumed 3% property tax; (5) with taxes and a five-year depreciation tax write-off of the investment cost of the solar energy system; (6) with taxes and an exemption of the assumed 4% sales tax on purchase of the solar equipment; (7) with taxes and an interest subsidy of 2% on the loan for the purchase of the solar energy system; and (8) with taxes and a special tax on fuel of 20%. From Table 6, we can see that the cost effectiveness of this particular solar heating system is quite sensitive to the cost of fuel, as well as to the applicable tax rules and special governmental incentive programs. With a fuel cost of $.45/therm of heat output, for example, this particular system appears not to be cost effective, except for a residential structure in Madison under conditions (4) and (5) combined. However, with a fuel cost of $.90/therm of heat output, this particular system appears generally cost effective to home-owners under all eight conditions described. For the same system installed in a commercial building with an equal heating load (i.e., only the tax provisions are different), the outcome appears less favorable to the use of the solar heating system. That is, it is cost effective on an after-tax basis only under condition (5).

It should be stressed that the results presented in Table 6 are based on specific conditions and are not measures of the cost effectiveness of solar energy systems in general. The point is that it is possible to apply an LCC model for the particular circumstances of an individual building owner and thereby gain a clearer idea of the economic desirability of fitting the building with a solar energy system.

Energy Conservation Standards for New Buildings A promising new application of LCC analysis in energy conservation is in the development of energy conservation performance standards for new residential and commercial buildings. Title III of Public Law 94-385, The Energy Conservation Standards for New Buildings Act of 1976, requires the Secretary of Housing and Urban Development (HUD) to develop and promulgate building performance standards that achieve the "maximum practicable improvement in energy efficiency" while meeting minimum habitability criteria.

Several questions have to be answered about these standards. First, should one standard be used for all types of buildings in the United States, regardless of building type and fuel price? Second,

TABLE 7

LIFE-CYCLE
COSTING GUIDE
FOR ENERGY
CONSERVATION
IN BUILDINGS

179

Present Value of Life-Cycle Costs of Alternative Energy Budget Standards for a Small Office Building[a]

Annual energy budget (1,000 Btu)	Present value of energy costs	Mild climate		Cold climate	
		First cost	Total life-cycle cost	First cost	Total life-cycle cost
(1)	(2)	(3)	(4) = (2) + (3)	(5)	(6) = (2) + (5)
40	$18,000	$25,000	$43,000	$50,000	$68,000
50	22,500	20,000	42,500	40,000	62,500
60	27,000	16,667	43,667	33,333	60,333
70	31,500	14,286	45,786	28,572	60,072
80	36,000	12,500	48,500	25,000	61,000
90	40,500	11,111	51,611	22,222	62,722

[a] Assumptions are the following:
Heating and Cooling Only: cold climate has twice the kWh requirements of the mild climate for the same design.
Life = 30 years
Discount Rate = 10%
Fuel Price Escalation Rate = 6%
kWh used annually for HVAC = 40,000
Present Cost per kWh = $.025
Energy requirements are inversely proportional to conservation investment.

on what factors should the development of a standard depend? Should we base it on potential LCC savings of energy and investment costs, or on a selected percentage reduction in building energy consumption?

The National Bureau of Standards is conducting research on the development of building standards for energy conservation. An LCC approach is being studied which bases the standard for a given climate/fuel price/building type on the expected savings in energy over the life cycle of that building and the costs of the energy-conserving technique. The economically efficient standard will require that level of energy conservation beyond which an additional investment would not be covered by extra dollar energy savings, and below which potential net dollar savings would be lost.

An example of the dollar losses that could result from a standard that does not take into account life-cycle costs and savings is illustrated in *Table 7*. Assume that a performance standard in the form of a maximum "energy budget" (i.e., a maximum allowable energy consumption for specific uses, such as heating and cooling) is to be assigned to an office building. A set figure, such as GSA's budget of 55,000 Btu/gross ft²/year for new buildings, could be established, or a variable budget could be selected as a function of climate and fuel price.

Table 7 shows, in dollar terms, how the same annual energy budget required of two identical office buildings, one located in a mild climate (e.g., Atlanta) and the other in a cold climate (e.g., Chicago), could result in economic losses to building owners in both regions. (Although building type and fuel price are fixed in

Table 7, these variables too affect the optimum energy budget.) Looking at columns 4 and 6 in comparison with column 1, we see that the annual energy budget that minimizes total life-cycle costs for the building in a mild climate is 50,000 Btu, for a cost of $42,500. In a cold climate, it is 70,000 Btu, for a cost of $60,072. Picking an energy budget that is efficient for either one of the climate regions would be inefficient for the building in the other region. For example, establishing 50,000 Btu as the budget would result in a loss of $2,428 (i.e., $62,500 − $60,072) for the building in the cold climate, for which the efficient budget is 70,000 Btu. Picking a budget below or above the range bounded by the efficient levels (50,000 to 70,000 Btu) would also result in losses. For example, establishing a budget of 80,000 Btu would result in a loss of $6,000 to the building owner in the mild climate and $928 in the cold climate. An efficiency loss occurs even when a budget between the optimal levels is chosen. Taking 60,000 Btu in this case, for example, will result in a loss to the building owner in the mild climate of $1,167, and in the cold climate of $261.

The examples of dollar losses described above show clearly the life-cycle savings to be gained by having an economically efficient energy budget for each climate. What is less obvious, however, is that building owners as a group may gain not only in energy cost savings, but in savings of initial investment costs as well. For example, looking again at Table 7, and taking 60,000 Btu as the standard for both climates, the combined first cost will be $50,000. But if we take the efficient budgets of 50,000 Btu for the mild climate and 70,000 Btu for the cold climate, the combined first cost is $48,572. In this case, a combined first-cost savings of $1,428 results from selecting efficient budgets for each climatic region. Note further that these energy and first-cost savings are achieved at the same level of 120,000 Btu of energy consumption (i.e., 60,000 Btu + 60,000 Btu = 50,000 + 70,000 Btu).

Promulgators of a single uniform standard might defend it on the basis that it is easier to determine, explain, and enforce. However, tables like Table 7 can be provided to local code authorities with the energy budgets appropriate for their region, not only in terms of climate factors, but in terms of fuel prices and building types as well. The potential national resource savings from setting energy budgets which are sensitive to climate and life-cycle costs may outweigh considerably the inconvenience and cost of administering a variable standard.

Where Do We Go From Here?

This chapter has described state-of-the-art techniques for measuring life-cycle savings of energy-conserving approaches to building design.

One might conclude from this chapter that architects and engineers have only to apply LCC analysis to all design decisions to determine the most cost-efficient allocation of resources for energy conservation in buildings. Theoretically this is true; certainly a broader awareness of LCC techniques in the design professions will, in fact, lead to greater economic efficiency in the use of energy conservation designs for buildings. Impediments to widespread application of these techniques do exist, however, and it will be helpful to know what they are.

One impediment is that the calculation of life-cycle costs and savings require life-cycle data on performance, durability, dependability, present and future operation and maintenance costs, and knowledge of the appropriate discount rate. Thus, although LCC analysis is relatively straightforward, the results are generally sensitive to a number of data assumptions, some of which may be quite uncertain. A second deterrent to the application of LCC analysis is that the analyses of complex systems may be expensive. At present, it is generally advisable to undertake an LCC analysis for individual projects only when large expenditures are involved and the economic feasibility of various design alternatives is not apparent. Advances in computer technology and access to better data may change this in the future. Third, and probably most significant, the building owner or developer may have objectives that are in conflict with the selection of the energy conservation techniques that are the most economically efficient. For example, speculative builders producing units for quick turn-over generally have a very short time horizon and are interested in minimizing total building costs for only that short possession period prior to the first sale. Thus, many builders are likely to aim at minimizing only those costs they themselves incur and may not take into account the life-cycle costs that accrue to subsequent building owners. Hopefully, building purchasers will become more informed about the potential savings from energy conservation design and consequently will be willing to pay more for energy-conserving buildings, which in turn will make it profitable for builders and developers to extend their investment time horizon beyond their actual period of ownership and to seek the architect's assistance in choosing building designs with cost-effective, energy-conserving features.

In conclusion, we envision wider use of LCC analysis in evaluating energy-conserving designs and a better understanding and use of the LCC analysis at all levels in the building community, including builders, owners, architect/designers, mechanical engineers, and mortgage lenders. A wider use of LCC analysis will thus enable more efficient allocation of energy resources for use in buildings, lower total life-cycle costs for buildings than would otherwise result, and more energy conserved per dollar invested in conservation techniques.

10

ENERGY REQUIRED FOR BUILDING CONSTRUCTION

Richard G. Stein and
Diane Serber

In the past, the study of buildings and energy use has been almost entirely devoted to energy required to operate buildings. This is understandable and important since it represents approximately 33% of all national energy use. There has been an underestimation, however, of the energy required to build, alter, and maintain the buildings that will be required in the future. These, according to a study conducted by the authors with the University of Illinois Center for Advanced Computation, require 6.25 % of all energy use for all purposes in the United States.[1] Together with non-building construction, it totals over 10%. There is enormous variation in what is required to build buildings, what is required to produce the materials for buildings, what the relationship is between capital energy—that is, the energy to build the buildings—and the operational energy, the energy to permit them to serve their intended purposes throughout their useful lifetimes. In order to understand these variations and to go to the next step, which is to improve the efficiency of energy use throughout the entire building sector, the nature of the building process and the way in which energy is embodied in fabrication and erection of components of the building must be given quantitative value.

Building construction is properly considered as an industry; that is, its statistics are reported to government agencies in recognized categories of the Standard Industrial Classification, and its cohesiveness as an industry can be confirmed by looking at the precision of trade union jurisdictions on a construction job.

However, the building industry is also a complex amalgam of material producers, manufacturers, designers, and assemblers. It includes the mining and lumbering sectors as well as the steel mills, sawmills, aluminum smelters, and cement factories. It includes glass factories, curtain-wall manufacturers, and millwork plants. It includes the electrical and plumbing jobbers, contractors, architects and engineers, building tradesmen, and subcontractors. Its product is an assembly of thousands of parts produced by a wide range of industries and brought to the job-site or to the assembly plant, shaped to fit compatibly with all of its neighboring products, and finally assembled into a building, no two of which are identical. The number of different skills and procedures that are called into play is enormous. As a result, it is a difficult process to understand; and after one understands it, it can be seen that it is a formidable one to change.

And yet, there are factors that impel us to do exactly that, probably the most important of which is the enormous impact of the building industry. It is responsible for about 10% of the Gross National Product (GNP) with an end value of over 100 billion dollars annually. The proportion of energy it requires, moreover, is considerably greater than its proportionate share of GNP, primarily because it is a user of large quantities of materials such as steel, aluminum, cement, bricks, and glass, all of which are

1. B. M. Hannon, R. G. Stein, B. Z. Segal, D. Serber and C. Stein: "Energy Use for Building Construction—Final Report," ERDA COO-2791-3, Center for Advanced Computation, University of Illinois at Urbana-Champaign, December 1976. (Available from NTIS, Springfield, VA, 22151.)

bulk materials whose manufacture requires large amounts of energy per unit of product. In addition, buildings require more bulk material per dollar of product than almost any other sector of our economy. There may be 10 times the weight of material per dollar in a building than there is in an automobile, and 100 times the weight of material per dollar that there is in an office machine. As a result of this high energy use per unit of product and the large number of units produced annually, even what appears to be a small fraction of the entire industry may be, in itself, an important user of energy.

At the moment, the most carefully documented summary available of energy use has been developed through the Energy Input-Output model at the Center for Advanced Computation of the University of Illinois, using 1967 as the data base.[2] This is the last year for which sufficiently detailed information has been assembled to determine energy use by the construction industry on a yearly basis. The information originally recorded in dollar terms has been translated into British Thermal Units (Btu) per building type, per building component, and per unit of material. There have not been sufficiently significant changes in the building industry's construction methods since then to invalidate the units derived from this study, although there would be modifications in the totals. Where we have a figure of 702,000 Btu/ft² of single-family residences applied to 844,000 single-family residences in 1967 (Statistical Abstract of the United States, 1971, p. 668), the Btu per unit would be applied to 896,000 single-family residences in 1975 (Statistical Abstract of the United States, 1976, p. 737). The figure reported to the F. W. Dodge Co. for total square feet of single-family residential construction was 1.051 billion ft² in 1967. Dividing this figure by 844,000 units, gives us a per-unit size of just under 1,200 ft², which is a reasonable figure to use today. In other words, the general information derived from the Energy Input-Output Model using the 1967 benchmark gives us information which is sufficiently accurate to make policy decisions based on a determination of what their impact will be on the whole construction industry.

Improvements in the energy efficiency of major industries would naturally have their effect on the energy embodied in products incorporated in buildings. In fact, there has been a general improvement in the energy used for producing certain basic materials in the last few years (concrete for example), but not of sufficient magnitude to distort the general picture presented by the study. The direct energy use for the industrial process is only a part of the entire embodied energy in a product, which also includes energy in all previous processes and transportation of materials, as well as prorated accounting for plant, equipment, and energy used for administration, management, and sales.

Our model divides the economy into 399 sectors, 49 of which represent construction activity. Numbered in accordance with

2. R. A. Heredeen and C. W. Bullard: *Energy Cost of Goods and Services, 1963 and 1967*, CAC 140, Center for Advanced Computation, University of Illinois at Urbana-Champaign, November 1974.

TABLE 1

Construction Industry Sectors

Sector	399-Order index
New Construction	
Residential Single-Family Housing, Non-Farm	23
Residential Two- to Four-Family Housing	24
Residential Garden Apartments	25
Residential High-Rise Apartments	26
Residential Alterations & Additions	27
Hotels & Motels	28
Dormitories	29
Industrial Buildings	30
Office Buildings	31
Warehouses	32
Garages & Service Stations	33
Stores & Restaurants	34
Religious Buildings	35
Education Buildings	36
Hospital Buildings	37
Other Non-Farm Buildings	38
Telephone & Telegraph Facilities	39
Railroads	40
Electric Utility Facilities	41
Gas Utility Facilities	42
Petroleum Pipelines	43
Water Supply Facilities	44
Sewer Facilities	45
Local Transit Facilities	46
Highways	47
Farm Residential Buildings	48
Farm Service Facilities	49
Oil & Gas Wells	50
Oil & Gas Exploration	51
Military Facilities	52
Conservation & Development Facilities	53
Other New Non-Building Facilities	54
Maintenance & Repair Construction	
Residential	55
Other Non-Farm Buildings	56
Farm Residential	57
Farm Service Facilities	58
Telephone & Telegraph Facilities	59
Railroads	60
Electric Utility Facilities	61
Gas Utility Facilities	62
Petroleum Pipelines	63
Water Supply Facilities	64
Sewer Facilities	65
Local Transit Facilities	66
Military Facilities	67
Conservation & Development Facilities	68
Highways	69
Oil & Gas Wells	70
Other Non-Building Facilities	71

their position in the 399-sector matrix, they are listed in *Table 1*. These 49 sectors can be arranged in four basic groups: New Building Construction (18 sectors), New Non-Building Construction (14 sectors), Building Maintenance and Repair (4 sectors), and Non-Building Maintenance and Repair (13 sectors). *Figure 1* outlines the gross energy consumption statistics of these basic groups. Each column is subdivided into individual sectors, the largest of which are identified.

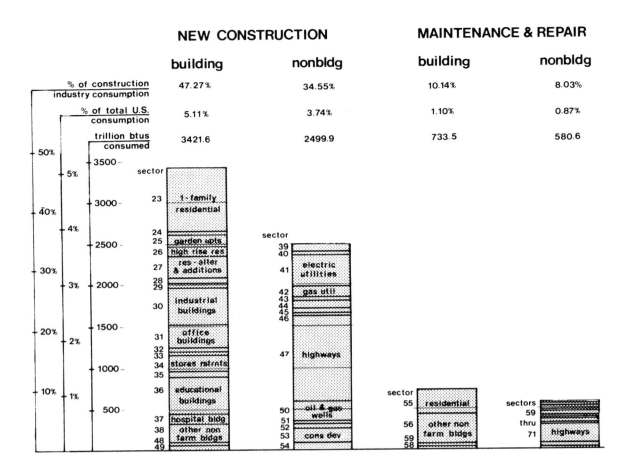

NEW CONSTRUCTION

MAINTENANCE & REPAIR

	building	nonbldg	building	nonbldg
% of construction industry consumption	47.27%	34.55%	10.14%	8.03%
% of total U.S. consumption	5.11%	3.74%	1.10%	0.87%
trillion btus consumed	3421.6	2499.9	733.5	580.6

49 CONSTRUCTION SECTORS - breakdown by major sector groupings - 1967

TOTAL % OF U.S. CONSUMPTION = 10.82%

TOTAL BTUS CONSUMED = 7235.6 TRILLION

Fig. 1. Energy used in construction in 1967.

Further investigation shows varying patterns of material- and service-energy use typical of individual sectors and groups of sectors. These are discovered through the breakdown of the energy embodied in each construction sector into its immediate contributors. These include: the energy embodied in the direct energy (refined petroleum, natural gas, and electricity) purchased by the contractor and used in his office and at the job-site; energy embodied indirectly in the materials required from all other sectors of the economy which supply products to the construction industry; and the energy embodied in the transport of materials from the supplier to the job-site, and in other services necessary to the transactions of the construction industry. It is interesting to note that less than half of the 399 sectors makes a direct contribution to any of the construction sectors.

There is a major difference between building and non-building categories. In general, a much greater percentage of energy embodiment is direct in the non-building sectors; also, there is a much greater degree of specialization in the non-building categories and, hence, a greater amount of variation from one non-building sector to another. (For example, in New Telephone & Telegraph Construction, 45.9% of the embodied energy comes from Non-ferrous Wire; in New Sewer Construction, 30% of the embodied energy comes from Clay Products or Concrete Products. By comparison, Non-ferrous Wire provides only 2.2% of the energy embodied in all New Building Construction; Clay or Concrete Products provide only 1.8% collectively.)

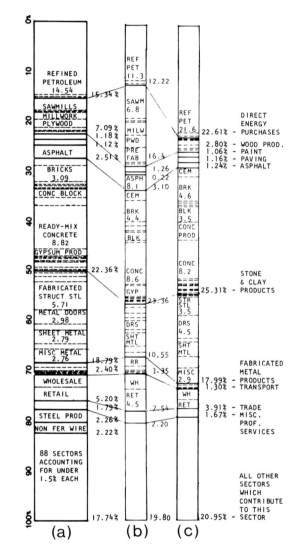

Fig. 2. Energy profiles for (a) All New Building Construction; (b) New One-Family Residences; and (c) New Dormitories.

Although we have considered all areas of the industry, our main emphasis has been on new building construction. *Figure 2* shows the basic profile for an aggregation of the 18 sectors which comprise all new building construction, broken down by percentages of energy embodiment contributed by all other sectors at the 399-sector level. The four largest contributors—Refined Petroleum Products, Ready-Mix Concrete, Fabricated Structural Steel, and Bricks—by themselves account for nearly a third of the total energy embodied.

Direct energy use on the job-site is the largest single energy user in the building industry, accounting for 15% of the 6.25% total, or almost 1% of all national energy. It is almost entirely made up of refined petroleum products—gasoline, diesel fuel, kerosene, heating fuels, and asphalt and road oils. The asphalt and road oils, even though they are reported as representing the energy that would be released if they were burned, are actually used for road surfacing, parking lots, and driveways. In our automobile-oriented culture, the asphalt, separated from the other direct energy uses, is second only to ready-mix concrete in the ranked list of high-energy users.[3]

While there is a great similarity among the various building sectors, there are important differences which must be noted as well. For example, New One-Family Residential Construction, which was the largest energy consumer among the New Building sectors, is less than half as energy intensive in terms of Btu embodied per square foot of construction (Btu/ft²) as New Dormitory Construction, which accounted for a smaller total embodiment. (One-Family Residental = 702,000 Btu/ft² vs. 1,431,000 Btu/ft² for Dormitories.) Examination of the embodiment profiles for the two sectors (Figure 2) shows a greater emphasis on the use of low-energy-intensive materials, such as those found in various wood products sectors in one-family residential construction; and conversely, a greater emphasis on high-intensity materials, such as those found in the fabricated metals sectors in dormitory construction.

An examination of similar profiles for all building types gives an indication of which areas will be fruitful for application of conservation strategies, whether these are the substitution of less energy-intensive materials in place of energy-expensive ones; use of less material through more precise structural design and construction techniques; or application of conservation procedures to the production of key materials.

Substitution of Materials

The key tool for any effort to conserve energy through substitution of materials is an energy estimating handbook. Similar in format to a standard cost estimating manual, such a listing will give values for the energy embodied in building components, rather than for their dollar cost.

By application of dollar per unit ($/unit) figures derived from data in the Census of Manufactures[4] to the energy intensities (in Btu/$) available from the Energy Input-Output matrix, we have established the methodology and reporting format for such a handbook and have begun to compile a series of usable energy values. A sample listing is given in *Table 2* which follows on pages 190 and 191.

It is not possible to derive the energy embodiments of all

3. Beyond the apparent straightforwardness of an energy conservation proposal, any of these items related to buildings, such as pavings, leads directly to social and economic considerations. Questioning our dependence on automobiles has a bearing on whether the crossroads shopping center is the most desirable way to secure necessary merchandise, whether the sprawling suburb is our ultimate form of habitation, whether the individual automobile is the desirable successor to mass transportation, whether as a result, cities can continue as the historic reservoirs of culture.

4. Department of Commerce: *1967 Census of Manufactures*, vols. I and II, U.S. Government Printing Office, Washington, DC, 1971.

materials and components in this simple manner. In the case of sectors such as Ready-Mix Concrete, where the entire output of the sector is expressed basically in one product, this method is valid. Similarly, in sectors such as Primary Iron and Steel, where the price differential among a multitude of products appears to be directly related to the amount of energy needed for their production, the respective costs per unit of product, multiplied by an average Btu/$ for the entire sector, produces a series of energy embodiments which we feel are valid. In other cases, however, a sector includes many disparate products, which are produced by very different processes, and which are reported in incompatible units. Also, in some cases, there is no definition of the average unit.

An example of this occurs in the Millwork sector, which includes prefabricated wood windows and doors of various types and sizes. Census of Manufactures data list total number of units without differentiating as to size or construction. In cases of this type, it is necessary to perform a *hybrid analysis* to arrive at an energy embodiment for a given unit and also to estimate the nature of the "average" unit to which average costs and energy embodiments can refer.

We performed a sample hybrid analysis for wood casement windows, breaking up the window into its major component parts: wood molding and double-strength window glass, and assigning to these components their proper energy embodiments. To the total embodiment of the components we added factors for assembly of the unit; for transport of the components to the factory; for the overhead operations of the window manufacturer; and for transport of the finished window to the job-site. Our sample window unit was 3 ft wide by 4 ft high—a dimension which, in our experience, is an average unit. The result of analysis was a total embodiment of 1 million Btu for the window with single glazing and 1.24 million Btu for the same unit double-glazed. These totals exclude hardware, caulking, and plastic components (themselves subjects suitable for hybrid analyses on their own) and are generally in accord with the somewhat higher figure of 1.19 million Btu which may be derived directly from Census of Manufactures average data. Similar analyses developed values for other sizes.

Sample Building Components

An informed choice in materials selection can reduce building energy use appreciably. A sample analysis of interchangeable floor systems based on similar loading conditions and fire-safety ratings demonstrates that the production of a reinforced-concrete structure will use less than 60% of the energy needed to produce a comparable standard steel structure. As an example, we computed the energy embodied in a section of floor slab, 30 feet

TABLE 2

Energy Embodied in Typical Building Materials

Material	Unit	Embodied energy (Btu/unit) Before delivery to job-site	After delivery to job-site
Wood Products			
Softwood —Rough Lumber	Bd Ft	5,229	7,661
—Dressed Lumber	Bd Ft	5,399	7,859
Hardwood—Rough Lumber	Bd Ft	6,744	9,816[1]
—Dressed Lumber	Bd Ft	6,633	9,655[1]
Wood Shingles & Shakes	Ft²	4,682	7,315
Wood Window Units			
Double-Hung	Each	845,671	1,127,234[2]
Awning & Casement	Each	893,021	1,190,349[2]
Other	Each	1,373,150	1,830,335[2]
Wood Doors			
Panel Type—Int. & Ext.	Each	654,851	872,881[2]
Flush Type Hollow Core	Each	259,952	346,502[2]
Flush Type Solid Core	Each	893,696	1,191,182[2]
Veneer & Plywood			
Hardwood	Ft²	12,942	17,025[3]
Softwood—Interior	Ft²	3,790	4,986[3]
Softwood—Exterior	Ft²	4,393	5,779[3]
Prefabricated Structural Wood Members			
Glued & Laminated	Bd Ft	14,673	16,733
Paper Products			
Construction Paper	Lb	8,841	10,479[4]
Paint Products			
Exterior Oil Paints & Enamel	Gal	413,066	488,523[5]
Exterior Water Base Paints	Gal	413,519	489,063[5]
Interior Oil Base Paints	Gal	429,932	508,475[5]
Interior Water Base Paints	Gal	369,519	437,025[5]
Asphalt Products			
Roofing Asphalt	Lb	6,701	6,914
Roll Roofing—Smooth Surface	Ft²	7,514	7,753
Roll Roofing—Mineral Surface	Ft²	10,673	11,012
Standard Strip Shingles	Ft²	24,553	25,334
Asphalt Saturated Felts	Lb	13,210	13,630
Tar Saturated Felts	Lb	16,416	16,938
Glass Products			
Window Glass—Single Strength	Ft²	11,895	13,659
Window Glass—Double Strength	Ft²	13,437	15,430
Plate Glass—Average (3/16″)	Ft²	41,828	48,031
Laminated Plate—Average	Ft²	185,058	212,504
Stone & Clay Products			
Portland Cement	Bbl (376 lb)	1,526,498	1,582,126
Brick—2¼″ × 3⅝″ × 7⅝″			
Common & Face	Each	13,570	14,283
Other Unglazed	Each	24,306	25,582
Facing Tile and Ceramic			
Glazed Brick	Each	31,749	33,416
Quarry Tile	Ft²	46,589	51,031
Ceramic Mosaic Tile—Glazed	Ft²	62,682	68,660
Ceramic Mosaic Tile—Unglazed	Ft²	58,081	63,619
Concrete Block 8″ × 5″ × 16″	Each	29,018	31,821
Ready-Mix Concrete	Cu Yd	2,584,938	2,594,338
Quick Lime	Ton	6,394,720	6,867,465
Hydrated Lime	Ton	8,812,374	9,463,852
Dead Burned Dolomite	Ton	9,077,302	9,748,365
Gypsum Building Materials	Ton	6,189,370	6,970,088
Mineral Wool Insulation			
Loose Fiber	Ton	11,426,830	12,826,171
Batts, Blankets & Rolls 3½″ Thick	Ft²	6,112	6,860

(Continued on next page)

TABLE 2 (Continued from preceding page).

Energy Embodied in Typical Building Materials

Material	Unit	Embodied energy (Btu/unit) Before delivery to job-site	After delivery to job-site
Primary Iron & Steel[6]			
Pig Iron	Lb	7,075	7,444
Carbon Steel Sheet—Hot Rolled & Enameled	Lb	15,965	16,803
Carbon Steel Sheet—Galvanized	Lb	26,458	27,836
Hot Rolled Bars & Shapes, Carbon Steel	Lb	17,808	18,736
Carbon Steel Reinforcing Bars	Lb	14,888	15,664
Alloy Steel—Plates & Structural Shapes	Lb	25,577	26,910
Wire for Prestressed Concrete	Lb	42,423	44,633
Carbon Steel Nails & Staples	Lb	32,331	34,016
Steel Wire—Plain	Lb	29,635	31,179
Steel Wire—Galvanized	Lb	32,683	34,385
Concrete Reinforcing Mesh— (Welded Wire)	Lb	22,989	24,187
Carbon Steel Pipe	Lb	24,535	25,813
Stainless Steel—			
Sheets—Hot Rolled	Lb	76,814	80,816
Sheets—Cold Rolled	Lb	131,449	138,298
Bars—Hot Rolled	Lb	149,454	157,241
Bars—Cold Finished	Lb	183,579	193,144
Wire	Lb	228,046	239,927
Fabricated Metal Products			
Fabricated Structural Steel	Lb	21,711	22,707
Primary Non-ferrous Metals			
Aluminum[7]			
Plate	Lb	113,049	115,567
Sheet	Lb	94,596	95,943
Rolled Bars & Structural Shapes	Lb	90,852	92,146
Screw Machine Products			
Hex Nuts, Lag Screws & Bolts, Studs & Threaded Rods	Lb	22,474	26,625
Rivets ½″ & over	Lb	14,640	17,344

Since all embodiments were derived by multiplying average dollars per unit (from the Census of Manufacturers) by an average Btu/$ of product (from CAC matrix), special market considerations can affect recorded embodiments.

[1]Negligible differences in energy embodiment of rough versus dressed lumber are assumed to be a function of market conditions rather than difference in industrial process. The average has been assumed to be accurate.

[2]These figures relate to "average" units. A general investigation of prefabricated wood doors and windows indicates that an average window is approximately 3′0″ wide by 4′0″ high, and an average door is 3′0″ wide by 6′8″ high. An average garage door is 8′0″ wide by 7′0″ high.

[3]Hardwood plywood has face veneers shipped long distances, while softwood plywoods are manufactured close to the softwood forests. The price differential is often dependent on market conditions rather than process.

[4]Construction paper is sold in rolls by the square (100 ft²) at an average weight of 5 lb/square for 1-ply paper and 10 lb/square for 2-ply paper.

[5]On an average, 1 gal of paint will supply 1 coat of paint for 300–350 ft² of exterior wood or masonry wall; 475 ft² of interior wood or masonry wall; 475 ft² of interior wall or trim; and 525 ft² of exterior trim.

[6]Energy in steel products is average nationwide and includes differences in blast furnace or other furnace methods, differences in ore quality, not differences in location of facilities.

[7]These are average energy values and do not include differences in bauxite quality and use of recycled metal.

ENERGY
CONSERVATION
THROUGH
BUILDING
DESIGN

square, typical of contemporary high-rise office buildings. Two interchangeable structural systems—steel and reinforced concrete—were investigated (*Figure 3*).

In spite of their names, each uses both steel and concrete in varying proportions. In standard steel construction the floor deck is typically concrete, designed to be strong enough to span between the beams on which it rests. It is shown poured over a corrugated metal deck, which acts as formwork for the concrete. In concrete construction a great deal of steel (in the form of reinforcing bars) is used to take care of tensile stress. Over-all, however, there is less steel (by weight) in a concrete structure, and the steel which is used here is all in reinforcing bars, which have a lower energy embodiment per pound than does fabricated structural steel (15,664 vs. 22,698 Btu). Even so, 55.5% of the energy embodied in the concrete system is due to reinforcing steel. Although columns have not been considered in this analysis, a preliminary investigation indicates that the proportional differ-

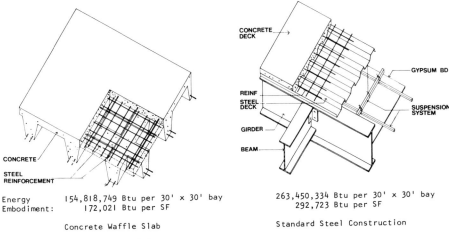

CONCRETE
STEEL
REINFORCEMENT

Energy   154,818,749 Btu per 30' x 30' bay
Embodiment: 172,021 Btu per SF

Concrete Waffle Slab

CONCRETE DECK
GYPSUM BD
REINF STEEL DECK
SUSPENSION SYSTEM
GIRDER
BEAM

263,450,334 Btu per 30' x 30' bay
292,723 Btu per SF

Standard Steel Construction

Fig. 3. Alternate floor slabs.

5. Structural analysis and computations by Robert Silman, P.E. and Ding Carbonelle, P.E., of Robert Silman Associates, New York City.
6. The steel system, using a total of 0.49 man-hours of labor per square foot has 68% of its labor embodied in the material brought to the job-site. This drops to 37% in the concrete system, which uses only 0.36 man-hours per square foot, total. Direct on-site labor, however, is less than a quarter of total labor in the steel system, but over half (56%) in the reinforced concrete system. The balance in each case is margin labor which amounts to about 10%. B. M. Hannon, R. G. Stein, P. Deibert, M. Buckley, D. Nathan: "Energy Use for Building Construction Supplement," Center for Advanced Computation, University of Illinois at Urbana-Champaign, October 1977.

ence in embodied energy between steel and concrete systems carries through the entire structure in spite of the fact that the concrete slab is approximately twice as heavy as the steel one. This is a conservative estimate, not taking into consideration lateral loads on tall buildings or certain aspects of the building code which would penalize steel structures to a greater extent than concrete ones and which would pertain to the design of any specific building.[5]

It is interesting to note that although the costs of the two systems will fluctuate with market conditions, labor conditions, and location, in general, on large projects the two systems will cost approximately the same. While, to the contractor, the cost of the materials which make up the steel system is very much higher than the cost of materials of the concrete one, concrete construction uses a great deal more labor on-site than does steel.[6] The higher materials cost, on the one hand, may balance the higher labor cost on the other, and the choice of one system over the other is made for reasons other than first cost. Conditions vary sufficiently from one project to another, from one location to another, and from one time to another, to invalidate generalizations. If energy embodiment is to be the primary criterion, concrete will obviously be the system of choice. Although the difference in embodiment appears to be negligible in our example (120,000 Btu/ft²), it takes on significance when applied to an entire building category. We have estimated that a total of 157.5 million ft² of new office building construction was built in 1967. Assuming that half of this area had been constructed originally using concrete framing and the other half had been steel (a conservative estimate), a shift to concrete construction for all office buildings in that year would have resulted in a reduction of 9.5 trillion Btu *from floor slabs alone.* At 6.3 million Btu/barrel, this reduction is equivalent to the saving of 1.5 million barrels of No. 6 fuel oil.

Comparative Wall Sections

Another set of comparisons was made with regard to two wall systems typical of one-family residential construction. In 1967, a representative year, a total of about 1.1 billion ft² of one-family residences was constructed. In that year, this sector accounted for 30% of the square footage of all buildings constructed, and 23% of the energy embodied in all new building construction. These are significant percentages of the building industry, and a change in the way the buildings in this sector are built can have an important effect on all energy use.

In this building sector, and in other small residential building, 2- by 4-in. wood stud construction is typical. The examples we chose to study are typical variations of this construction which have a similar thermal performance.

As shown in *Figures 4* and *5*, both examples have a basic framework of 2- by 4-in. studs on 16-in. centers, gypsum wallboard inside, and plywood sheathing plus building paper outside. They differ only in their exterior finish: one wall has wood shingles, and the other has brick veneer with a 1-in. air space between the brick and sheathing. Thermal performance, that is, the rate at which heat will flow through a given assembly, is expressed in terms of the U-factor. The U-factors for the shingled and brick walls are .25 and .24 respectively. Adding up the energy embodied in the components of 1 ft² of each wall yields total embodiments of 25,426 Btu/ft² of shingled wall and 119,566 Btu/ft² of stud wall with brick veneer. The addition of 3½ inches of mineral wool batt insulation (at 6,860 Btu/ft²) will raise the total embodiments to 32,286 Btu/ft² (shingle) and 126,426 Btu/ft² (brick) and will lower the U-factor for both alternatives to .085.

The wide gap between the energy embodiments of these two

walls is a function of the low energy intensity of wood and the high energy intensity of brick. Brick veneer is a common material in this building type, and in other low-rise construction as well. Figure 2 shows brick contributing 4% of the energy embodied in one-family residential construction. All told, one-family residences alone accounted for 78 trillion Btu in 1967 (see Figure 1) of which the energy embodied in bricks (4.4%) is equal to 34.32 trillion Btu. At 85,698 Btu/ft² (six bricks per ft² of wall at 14,283 Btu/brick) this represents 400 million ft² of brickwork. If the comparison between the brick veneer and the wood shingle construction assemblies shows a difference of 94,140 Btu/ft² (119,566 − 25,426), it accounts for a differential of a total of 37.66 trillion Btu for the entire square footage above. At 150,000 Btu/gal, this amounts to 251 million gal of No. 6 oil (or nearly 6 million barrels). It is apparent that a significant saving in energy con-

Fig. 4. Wood-frame walls.

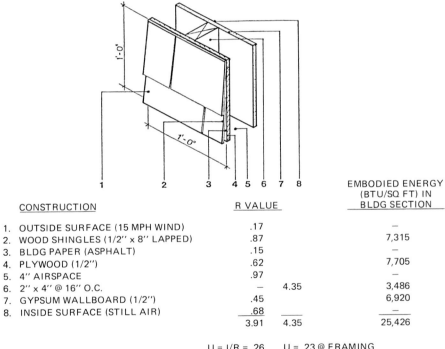

CONSTRUCTION	R VALUE		EMBODIED ENERGY (BTU/SQ FT) IN BLDG SECTION
1. OUTSIDE SURFACE (15 MPH WIND)	.17		—
2. WOOD SHINGLES (1/2″ x 8″ LAPPED)	.87		7,315
3. BLDG PAPER (ASPHALT)	.15		—
4. PLYWOOD (1/2″)	.62		7,705
5. 4″ AIRSPACE	.97		—
6. 2″ x 4″ @ 16″ O.C.	—	4.35	3,486
7. GYPSUM WALLBOARD (1/2″)	.45		6,920
8. INSIDE SURFACE (STILL AIR)	.68		—
	3.91	4.35	25,426

$U = 1/R = .26$ $U = .23$ @ FRAMING

ADJUSTED U (TO ACCOUNT FOR FRAMING) = .25

ADDITION OF INSULATION	R VALUE	EMBODIED ENERGY (BTU/SQ FT) IN BLDG SECTION
ADD 3 1/2″ BATT INSULATION	11.00	ADD 6,860
DEDUCT R VALUE OF AIR SPACE	.97	
	10.03	
ADD TO ABOVE R VALUE	3.91	
	13.79	32,286

$U = 1/R = .07$ $U = .23$ @ FRAMING

ADJUSTED U (TO ACCOUNT FOR FRAMING) = .085

sumption could be achieved if brick and other energy-intensive materials were limited to those uses where their inherent qualities made them most desirable.

In this part of our study we compared only two facing materials. A complete study, which would be necessary for a truly informed choice of materials to be made, would also include other alternatives, such as asbestos shingles, asphalt shingles, aluminum siding, and cement-asbestos board.

Energy Life-Cycle

The figures quantifying the energy embodied in various materials and assemblies are placed in better perspective when they are considered together with the energy needed to operate buildings.

Fig. 5. Brick on wood-frame walls.

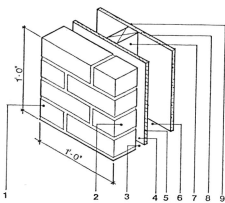

CONSTRUCTION	R VALUE		EMBODIED ENERGY (BTU/SQ FT) IN BLDG SECTION
1. OUTSIDE SURFACE (15 MPH WIND)	.17		—
2. BRICK & MASONRY (4″)	.44		105,004
3. 1″ AIRSPACE	.97		—
4. BUILDING PAPER (ASPHALT)	.15		—
5. PLYWOOD (3/8″)	.47		5,779
6. 4″ AIRSPACE	.97		—
7. 2″ x 4″ @ 16 O.C.	—	4.35	3,486
8. GYPSUM WALLBOARD (3/8″)	.32		5,297
9. INSIDE SURFACE	.68		—
	3.98	4.35	119,566

U = 1/R = .25   U = .23 @ FRAMING
ADJUSTED U (TO ACCOUNT FOR FRAMING) = .24

ADDITION OF INSULATION	R VALUE	EMBODIED ENERGY (BTU/SQ FT) IN BLDG SECTION
ADD 3 1/2″ BATT INSULATION	11.00	ADD 6,860
DEDUCT R VALUE OF AIR SPACE	.97	
	10.03	
ADD TO ABOVE R VALUE	3.98	
	14.01	126,426

U = 1/R = .07   U = .23 @ FRAMING
ADJUSTED U (TO ACCOUNT FOR FRAMING) = .085

ENERGY
CONSERVATION
THROUGH
BUILDING
DESIGN

To extend an example described in Chapter 3, two government office buildings in Albany, New York, were analyzed for the purpose of reducing the energy needed to operate them. As designed in the mid-1960s, the buildings, with a combined gross area of 1.19 million ft², required a total of 28 million kWh of electricity and 626 thousand gal of No. 6 oil annually. At 3,412 Btu/kWh and 150,000 Btu/gal of oil, this is equal to 190 billion Btu/year for building operation measured on site. Dividing by the gross area, this is equal to 159,664 Btu/ft².

If the energy consumed by the two buildings is measured at source, the value for electricity will be raised from 3,412 to 11,380 Btu/kWh (based on Niagara Mohawk Power Corporation's heat rate of 10,803 Btu/kWh + 5% transmission losses.) Using these figures, the annual energy consumption of the two buildings will be 350,115 Btu/ft² for the buildings as designed. According to information derived from the Energy Input-Output matrix in 1967 (a comparable construction year), the energy embodied in office buildings averaged 1.6 million Btu/ft², that is, the source energy needed for 4.6 years of operation in this case. As building owners become more energy conscious, and as buildings begin to be built and operated in energy conservative modes, this ratio can be expected to change. The Albany Study is a good example of this. At the time the study was initiated, New York State had been operating the buildings in accordance with its own conservation program, consisting, in the main, of selective delamping. The result was a 12% reduction in energy consumption and an equivalent annual energy demand on site of 183 billion Btu, or 153,781 Btu/ft². As a result of the study, further conservation measures, including more delamping and adjustment and rebalancing of the HVAC systems in the two buildings, resulted in a projected lowering of the annual operating energy by 81.9 billion Btu, or 68,824 Btu/ft² on site, or 164,745 Btu/ft² at source. Since no material was to be added, the embodied energy would remain the same. At this point, the energy embodiment would equal the source energy necessary for 10 years of building operation.

This figure approaches a recent GSA Standard for new federal government office buildings: 55,000 Btu/ft²/year as maximum on-site energy to operate all services in new buildings, roughly equivalent to 110,000 Btu of source energy.[7] (The two existing Albany office buildings could be brought into conformance with this standard by replacing the existing 120,000 ft² of single glass with double glazing.)

As a result of such a concerted effort to conserve operational energy, the energy embodied in construction itself would now be about 30% of the source energy needed to maintain the building throughout its lifetime.

It is thus evident that life-cycle costing is as important in embodied energy cost estimating as it is in operating energy cost estimating. The above example, examined in terms of net energy

7. *Energy Conservation Guidelines for New Office Buildings,* General Services Administration, Washington, DC, February 1975.

life-cycle, projects annual savings of about 18,000 Btu/ft² at source, at an energy embodiment cost of 4,800 Btu/ft². "Energy payback," that is, when operational energy saved equals added embodied energy, will occur in three to four months.

The building shell is of particular importance in life-cycle costing because its components affect not only the total embodiment of the building, but also the amount of energy the building will require in its operation. We therefore extended our study of typical residential wall assemblies as previously described to see what the life-cycle energy consequences might be when the thermal transfer characteristics of the residential building shell (walls, roof, and windows) were improved and the demand for heating was consequently reduced.

The amount of energy demanded by a given construction is a function of the rate at which heat will flow through it (expressed in terms of its *U*-factor) and the average temperature pattern of the location of the building (expressed in terms of degree days). While the addition of insulation to an existing building will be restricted by the amount of interior space which the building occupant is willing to give up, a new building can be designed to accommodate whatever wall thickness is considered to perform best. It need not be restricted in depth as is the case within an existing wall.

Table 3 tabulates the characteristics of different types of woodstud walls with wood-shingle exterior and gypsum wallboard interior. The walls vary in nominal thickness and in amount of mineral wood insulation they contain. For walls over 8 in. thick, rather than continue to increase the depth of the studs, we have assumed a double 2- by 4-in. stud wall. The annual demand is based on the national average of 4,734 degree days.[8]

It is evident that while each additional increment of insulation provides an additional savings, the amount of savings is progressively smaller. Increasing insulation from 3½ in. to 5½ in. will increase the embodied energy of the wall by 2,384 Btu/ft² and will save nearly 4,000 Btu/ft² each year. Energy payback will

TABLE 3

Comparison of Energy Embodiment and Annual Operational Energy Demand for Heating Imposed by 1 Ft² of Shingled Wood Frame Wall with Varying Thicknesses of Insulation. (National Average, 4,734 Degree Days.)

Nominal wall thickness	Type of framing	Insulation	U-Factor	Embodied energy (Btu)	Annual demand (Btu)
4″	2 × 4 @ 16″	0″	.250	25,426	28,404
4″	2 × 4 @ 16″	3½″	.085	32,286	9,657
6″	2 × 6 @ 24″	5½″	.051	34,670	5,794
8″	2 × 8 @ 24″	7½″	.043	38,074	4,885
10″	(2) 2 × 4 @ 24″	9½″	.032	40,174	3,636
12″	(2) 2 × 4 @ 24″	11½″	.025	42,274	2,840
14″	(2) 2 × 4 @ 24″	13½″	.022	44,374	2,500

8. Data from the National Climatic Center, Asheville, NC. Average regional weather data (for period of July 1931 through June 1976) weighted in accordance with the regional population characteristics.

occur in a little over half a heating season. Increasing insulation from 11½ in. to 13½ in. which will increase the embodied energy of the wall by 2,100 Btu/ft² will save only 340 Btu/ft² each year. Energy payback would take six to seven years.

However, the decision to build a wall of a given thickness is not made in progressive stages but, rather, once and for all. To increase insulation from 3½ in., which is now typical, to 9½ in. would increase the embodied energy of the wall by 7,888 Btu/ft² and would save 6,021 Btu/ft² each year. Energy payback in this case would be in 1.31 years. These figures are not inconsequential: 6,021 Btu multiplied by the total number of square feet of one-family residential walls constructed in a given year would result in a substantial cumulative effect. According to the 1971 Statistical Abstracts, there were 844,000 one-family residential housing starts in 1967. Assuming that 1,280 ft² of exterior wall (as used in the example which follows) is average, this amounts to a total of 1.08 billion ft² of walls built in one year. The total annual energy savings represented by adding 10 in. of insulation to these surfaces would be 6.50 trillion Btu—equivalent to 1.1 million barrels of fuel oil saved per year as a result of a simple structural modification of one year's new housing stock. Energy payback for the additional embodiment—8.52 trillion Btu—would be in less than two heating seasons.

Extensions of this analysis to a similar consideration of single versus double glazing and flat roofs with 5½ in. or 11½ in. of mineral wool insulation has allowed us to make a general comparison between the outer shells of two typical 1,500 ft² one-family residences. *Table 4* outlines the general structural and energy characteristics of both building shells: House A which has 3½ in. of insulation in the wall, 5½ in. in the roof, and single glazing, would have an embodied energy value of 171.8 million Btu. Operational energy demand by the shell would be 59.1 million Btu/year for heat lost through thermal transmission. House B, which has 5½ in. of insulation in the walls, 11½ in. in the roof, and double glazing, would have an embodied energy value of 188.2 million Btu (9.5% more than House A), and an operational energy demand, due to thermal transmission losses, of 31.8 million Btu/year (46% lower than the first example).

In addition, both buildings would require a further input of operational energy to counteract heat lost through infiltration and the opening of doors and windows. We have estimated this increment of demand to be 40.8 million Btu/year. Total energy demanded for heating, therefore, would be 99.9 million Btu/year for House A and 72.6 million Btu/year for House B.

Thus, an extra energy embodiment of approximately 16.5 million Btu would net over 27 million Btu saved annually, and energy payback time would be about one-half a heating season. Twenty-seven million Btu is equivalent to over 4.5 barrels of No. 6 fuel oil saved per year. Multiplied by 844,000 private one-

TABLE 4

ENERGY
REQUIRED FOR
BUILDING
CONSTRUCTION

199

Comparison of Embodied vs. Annual Operational Energy for Two Alternate One-Family Residence Shells (4,734 Degree Days)

	House A	House B
Dimensions	30' × 50'	
Floor Area	1,500 Ft²	Same
Roof Area	1,500 Ft²	Same
Wall Area	10' × 160' **perim.** = 1,600 Ft²	Same
Windows	23 @ 3' × 4' = 276 ft²	Same
Doors (Exterior)	2 @ 3' × 6'8" = 40 Ft²	Same
Walls	1,600 − 316 Ft² = 1,384 Ft²	Same
Studs	2" × 4" @ 16" o.c.	2" × 6" @ 24" o.c.
Ext. Finish	Wood shingle	Same
Int. Finish	½" gypsum board	Same
Insulation	3½" rock wool	5½" rock wool
Window Glazing	Single glazed	Double-glazed
Roof		
Rafters	2" × 12" @ 16" o.c.	Same
Roofing	Built-up (on plywood)	Same
Ceiling	½" gypsum board	Same
Insulation	5½" rock wool	11½" rock wool

	Energy embodied		Annual energy demand	Energy embodied		Annual energy demand
	Btu	**Unit**	**Btu/ft²**	**Btu**	**Unit**	**Btu/ft²**
Walls	32,286	Ft²	9,657	34,670	Ft²	5,794
Roof	70,003	Ft²	4,090	76,303	Ft²	2,363
Windows	1,070,652	Each	128,386	1,242,852	Each	65,897
Doors	346,502	Each	128,386	346,502	Each	65,897
Total (Embodied)	171,777,724			188,249,380		
Conducted			59,104,564			31,807,448
Infiltration			40,817,968			40,817,968
Total (Btu)	171,777,724		99,922,532	188,249,380		72,625,416

family housing starts recorded for 1967, the potential savings inherent in a relatively simple set of structural adjustments applied to one year's new housing would amount to 3.8 million barrels—about 0.1% of our 1975 refinery output.[9]

It is evident that, although in both houses the energy embodied in the outer shell is a small percentage of the energy which either house will demand over its lifetime, the choice of materials of construction will have a significant effect.

Examination and Modeling of Energy Flow

Another approach to conservation of energy within a large area of the economy, such as construction, is to apply conservation practices to its major contributing industries.

From the Energy Input-Output matrix, it is possible to establish immediately:

a. The total amounts of each primary energy resource (coal, crude petroleum, non-fossil electricity, and imports) required due to the direct or indirect demand from New Building Construction.

9. U.S. Bureau of the Census: *Statistical Abstract of the United States, 1976*, Washington, DC, 1976.

b. The amounts of energy embodied directly or indirectly in the materials and services provided to New Building Construction directly for incorporation into the completed buildings.

Connecting these two poles are a yet-to-be determined number of inter-industry transactions which, when quantified and graphically represented, will complete the flow diagram. The diagram will show: the transactions between primary energy resources and those sectors which consume primary energy resources directly (e.g. the steel industry, which purchases coal, or the oil refining industry, which purchases crude petroleum); transactions between the energy industries which use energy resources directly and the energy industries which sell the energy product to some non-energy industry (e.g., that portion of the electrical industry which uses refined petroleum for generation); and, finally, the flow of energy embodied in materials, machinery, and administrative and service functions, through interindustry transactions, leading finally to the products which are sold directly to the building contractor (*Fig. 6*).

The purpose for establishing this network is not only to assess the impact on energy embodied in construction of conservation strategies within contributing industries, but also to permit the identification of nodes in the flow which may become control or limiting points for alternative materials strategies. Some nodes, such as machine tool production, may not appear in industries selling to final demand, but may nevertheless be large energy users, with their energy appearing as embodied energy in Fabricated Structural Steel, Ready-Mix Concrete, and other products depending on plants and sophisticated equipment.

Developed as a dynamic computer model, the flow diagram would permit changes at any point in the eventual delivery of goods and services to New Building Construction, to be evaluated with respect to the impact which they will have at any other critical point. From a policy-making point of view, the limitation in using the information developed by the Input-Output method is that the figures are average figures, reported industry-wide across the entire United States, and with average intensities for what are called the margins in the Input-Output terminology. These margins represent the transportation, the prorated energy costs for plant and equipment, for overhead and office use, and for doing business (e.g. advertising and administration). Since all of these are average energy costs, in order to determine how susceptible they are to change, one would have to know what the upper and lower limits are and what kind of performance standards each of these limits provides. On that basis, knowing what constitutes a satisfactory lower limit of expenditure, one could assume that this would become the average. Or, allowing for human fallibility and using a somewhat higher figure as the new

Fig. 10-6 Summary of Energy Flow in the Building Construction Industry based upon 1967 data (Reference in Footnote 1). Each column represents energy use *within* specific industrial sectors related to building construction. The paths between columns indicate energy transactions *between* industries. All sectors progressively shift from useful energy to increasing percentages of embodied energy—moving from left to right—as the materials become increasingly refined.

Columns 1 through *4* indicate increasingly refined energy resources from the point of recovery of pre-industry purchase and use. Column 1 represents the total energy resource input which would be required if all products for new building construction were produced domestically. The reductions at the bottom of Column 2, 3 and 4, shown as Sector C, represent the energy that would have been required by those products that were in fact imported.

Columns N-3 through *N-1* represent the transactions in which the energy resources are purchased and consumed by manufacture, transportation and construction. Column N-1 represents the energy sectors (B-1, B-2 and B-3) amd non-energy sectors (A-1 and A-2) that end up as products sold directly to new building construction built in place *(Column N).*

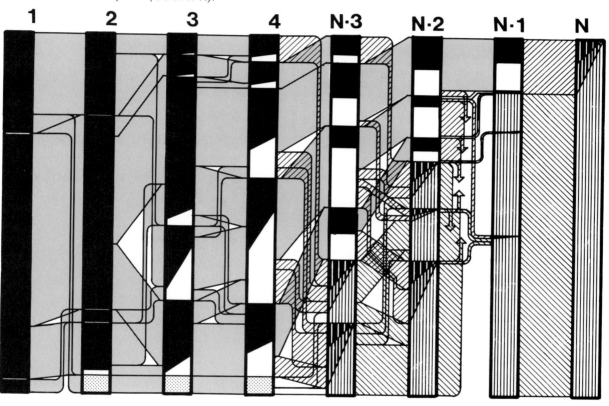

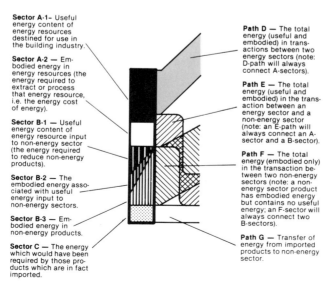

Sector A-1– Useful energy content of energy resources destined for use in the building industry.

Sector A-2 — Embodied energy in energy resources (the energy required to extract or process that energy resource, i.e. the energy cost of energy).

Sector B-1 — Useful energy content of energy resource input to non-energy sector (the energy required to reduce non-energy products).

Sector B-2 — The embodied energy associated with useful energy input to non-energy sectors.

Sector B-3 — Embodied energy in non-energy products.

Sector C — The energy which would have been required by those products which are in fact imported.

Path D — The total energy (useful and embodied) in transactions between two energy sectors (note: D-path will always connect A-sectors).

Path E — The total energy (useful and embodied) in the transaction between an energy sector and a non-energy sector (note: an E-path will always connect an A-sector and a B-sector).

Path F — The total energy (embodied only) in the transaction between two non-energy sectors (note: a non-energy sector product has embodied energy but contains no useful energy; an F-sector will always connect two B-sectors).

Path G — Transfer of energy from imported products to non-energy sector.

average, one could make a projection of the savings that might be achievable in the construction industry. Going beyond this and instituting more efficient methods of energy estimating, of planning, and of construction, one could then begin to lower the average to reflect a new level of efficient material and energy use for the building sector.

Parallel investigations can be made in improving the energy efficiency in the manufacturing process. For example, reports comparing energy use in Sweden and West Germany with American industry indicate surprisingly large margins, suggesting that we can anticipate reducing energy use here. In comparison with Sweden, our steel industry uses 1.293 times as much.[10] In comparison with West Germany's steel industry, it uses 1.558 times as much.[11] After materials have been efficiently produced, there is also a margin of reduction that can be achieved by using these efficiently produced materials closer to their strength capability. The difference in wood use, for example, in the wood hull of a sailboat in comparison with the wood shell of a vacation house is striking, even though the boat hull is subject to much greater stresses and strains in movement than is its landbound counterpart. Where spaces have been designed for mobility, as in ships, trains, and trailers, both material use and space standards are subject to a more rigorous analysis. One can compare a stairway in an early New England house built by a ship's carpenter with the more extravagant space allocations of a house builder today. One can also compare the intensive, and often very efficient, space use in a trailer home designed for mobile vacations with the less efficient space use in tract houses. Or the efficient arrangement for washrooms developed for the Pullman car and air transport in comparison with the space allotments in standard construction. By a selective borrowing from and cross-referencing of decisions among these various space builders, we can expect that there will be a further reduction in the amount of energy necessary to construct the space needs for various activities.

Conclusions

The energy required by the construction industry, which has been referred to speculatively up to now, can be analyzed against a sound data base. While the building of new buildings requires about one-fifth as much energy as is expended in operating buildings on an annual national basis—that is, the energy to operate our entire stock of buildings for a year is five times greater than the energy to build one year's worth of new buildings—the picture is quite different when one looks at the constructional and operational energy of individual buildings. As operational energy becomes more efficient, the ratio of operating energy to capital energy changes. Based on the federal General Services Administration energy budget of 55,000 Btu/ft²/year for on-site energy use

10. Lee Shipper and Allan J. Lichtenberg: "Efficient Energy Use and Well-Being: The Swedish Example," *Science*, vol. 194, p. 1001, (December 3, 1976).

11. R. K. White and R. Goen: *Comparison of Energy Consumption Between West Germany and the United States*, Stanford Research Institute, Menlo Park, CA, June 1975. (It should be borne in mind that there are difficulties in making comparisons since process and reporting techniques differ. For example, there is a greater use of scrap metal by the West German steel industry. While this results in a lower per-ton energy requirement, it is also a reflection of an economy that still characterizes American industrial methods. There are the beginnings of greater economy in energy use on an industry-wide basis, with reports of savings of 5% and more in steel and other industries.)

(the equivalent of about 110,000 Btu of source energy) and an average figure of 1.65 million Btu to build a square foot of high-rise office building, it will take 15 years of operation to equal the amount of capital energy required to build the building. While the proportion varies from building type to building type and from one individual case to the next, nevertheless, as the effort toward efficient energy use in all areas of the nation's activities becomes more necessary, the opportunities for reduced energy use in construction will constitute a worthwhile target. The degree of success in achieving it will result from a complex series of apparently small actions including: selection of the least energy-intensive materials or assemblies to achieve predetermined performance levels; improved methods of construction to reduce on-site energy use; more accurate engineering to determine precise amounts of required material; extended use of worthwhile existing structures to avoid unnecessary new building; improved production methods to reduce embodied energy per unit of material; and greater use of regionally available materials to reduce unnecessary transportation. It is evident that there is a need to develop additional information and detail in order to achieve maximum savings. Among the important areas for further research are:

- An amplification of the energy per unit of building material accounting and the incorporation of the complete list in an energy estimating handbook and/or computer-based program.
- Completion of the intermediate steps in the energy flow diagram and translation of the static graphic diagram into a dynamic computer model.
- Expansion of the basic research into other conservation paths which appear potentially fruitful.

A target reduction of 20% seems feasible. Twenty percent of the 5.11% of national energy consumption represented by new building construction in 1967 is equal to 1% of the national energy consumption in that year, or 669 trillion Btu. Assuming an average heat rate of 10,500 Btu/kWh/kW capacity,[12] this represents the fuel needed annually to run 10 or 11, 1,000-MW generating plants. Or, to use another comparison, at 5.8 million Btu/barrel, 669 trillion Btu is also equivalent to 115.3 million barrels of crude oil, an amount equal to nearly half of the oil we imported from Saudi Arabia (and greater than our total imports from Iran) in 1975.

12. Battelle Research Report: *An Input-Output Analysis of Energy Use Changes from 1947–1958 and from 1958–1963,* Battelle Institute, Columbus, OH, June 1972.

11

ENERGY MANAGEMENT FOR COMMERCIAL BUILDINGS: A PRIMER

Fred S. Dubin

This chapter is adapted from several research reports by the author: Dubin-Bloome Associates: "Energy Conservation Program and Report for the Chemistry Building No 555, Brookhaven National Laboratory, Upton, NY," June 1976; and Fred S. Dubin: "Energy Management for Commercial Buildings," Workshop Presentation, Lawrence Berkeley Laboratory, Berkeley, CA, July 1976.

Too frequently the role of energy conservation is addressed out of context of broader social issues. Often, the immediate interest of one individual building owner or one sector of society is in conflict with others, and trade-offs must be made. With sufficient knowledge, a building owner can evaluate the trade-offs between the objectives most appealing to him: (1) minimize initial costs, (2) minimize operating costs, (3) minimize life-cycle costs, (4) maintain continuity of operation, or (5) minimize noise and on-site pollution. In some cases, all or most of these objectives can be attained simultaneously. For society, some of the objectives include: (1) limit oil and gas imports, (2) minimize environmental degradation, or, hopefully, improve environmental quality, (3) conserve natural resources for future generations and for other essential purposes—fertilizer, drugs, foodstuffs, and so forth, (4) reduce capital investments and site requirements for central utility plants, and (5) increase employment.

In the long run, the interests of the individual and of the greater society may coincide; if they conflict in the short term, legislation is needed to protect society and compensate those individuals who may be harmed in the process. But in any case, decisions can be made wisely and justly only when the facts are identified, quantified, and disseminated.

Commercial buildings include public and private office buildings, retail stores, hotels and motels, hospitals and nursing homes, warehouses, schools and colleges, and recreational, cultural, and other institutions. These are the facilities that the utility companies include in the "commercial customer" class. The operating energy requirements of these diverse facilities are directly responsible for about 16% of the energy used nationally. When off-site utility systems to support the buildings are included, they account for about 16×10^{15} Btu/year, equivalent to more than 7 million barrels of oil per day. They also account for a major portion of peak electric consumption and demand in many utility company service areas. A study for the State of New Jersey Department of Public Advocate revealed that the electrical energy consumption in the eight counties served by the Public Service Electric & Gas Company for the commercial customer rate class for 1975 was $9,000 \times 10^6$ kWh, while the residential and industrial rate classifications used $7,673 \times 10^6$ kWh and 10,014 kWh respectively.[1] From 1980 on, the consumption for the commercial rate class is forecast to exceed all other customer rate classes. However, with a vigorous energy conservation and solar energy program applicable to all buildings, it was forecast that by 1990 the commercial customer class would consume only $8,813 \times 10^6$ kWh annually, compared to $9,203 \times 10^6$ kWh and $10,498 \times 10^6$ kWh for the residential and industrial rate classes respectively. Peak electric demand also fell into the same pattern; with energy conservation management, the commercial customer peak demand could fall below both residential and industrial peak loads.

1. Dubin-Bloome Associates: "A Study of Electric Energy Usage in the Public Service Electric and Gas Company Service Territory," State of New Jersey, June 30, 1976.

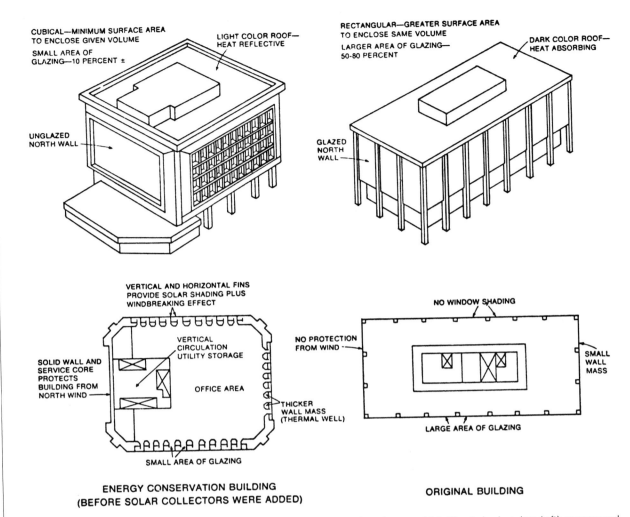

CUBICAL—MINIMUM SURFACE AREA TO ENCLOSE GIVEN VOLUME

SMALL AREA OF GLAZING—10 PERCENT ±

LIGHT COLOR ROOF— HEAT REFLECTIVE

UNGLAZED NORTH WALL

RECTANGULAR—GREATER SURFACE AREA TO ENCLOSE SAME VOLUME

LARGER AREA OF GLAZING— 50-80 PERCENT

DARK COLOR ROOF— HEAT ABSORBING

GLAZED NORTH WALL

VERTICAL AND HORIZONTAL FINS PROVIDE SOLAR SHADING PLUS WINDBREAKING EFFECT

VERTICAL CIRCULATION UTILITY STORAGE

SOLID WALL AND SERVICE CORE PROTECTS BUILDING FROM NORTH WIND

OFFICE AREA

THICKER WALL MASS (THERMAL WELL)

SMALL AREA OF GLAZING

NO WINDOW SHADING

NO PROTECTION FROM WIND

SMALL WALL MASS

LARGE AREA OF GLAZING

ENERGY CONSERVATION BUILDING (BEFORE SOLAR COLLECTORS WERE ADDED)

ORIGINAL BUILDING

Fig. 1 Federal Office Building, Manchester, NH. Final design (on left) compared to early scheme (on right). Isaak and Isaak, Architects (Mori Mitsui, Project Architect); Dubin-Mindell-Bloome Associates, Engineering Consultants.

Fig. 2 Carey Arboretum, Millbrook, NY. A partly underground building with a complete solar heating system. Malcomb Wells, Architect; Dubin-Mindell-Bloome, Associates Engineering Consultants. (Courtesy of Malcomb Wells)

As the shift in our economy moves from manufacturing to services, the commercial sector will account for an even greater portion of the national energy use and peak electric demand, assuming the same degree of conservation applied equally to all customer classes. However, opportunities for energy conservation and peak electric demand control are more immediate in the commercial sector with available hardware, building materials, mechanical and electrical equipment and systems, and building operational practices, than in the residential and industrial sectors, although many of the same energy conservation measures and energy management programs are effective in all building types.

In this chapter, the energy conservation design and management opportunities available for commercial buildings are discussed, first in terms of a general approach to analysis, and then, by reference to a recent case study, specific "technical-fix" measures applicable to existing buildings, and other equally promising developments in view for existing or new buildings.

The Process of Analysis: The Energy Conservation Potential

In order to reduce energy consumption in existing commercial buildings, it is essential to analyze seven key variables:

1. The specific factors which cause energy to be used in a building.

2. The extent to which excess energy is being used to provide environmental control (heating, ventilating, cooling, illumination, hot water, and essential services).

3. The opportunities to change the level of environmental control and/or functional use of the building and its operating and maintenance practices to reduce energy consumption.

4. The performance of the mechanical and electrical systems and the potential to reduce energy consumption by modifications to the hardware and controls, or their replacement, as the case may be, with the potential reduction in energy use by doing so.

5. The materials, configuration, and condition of the building envelope (roof, walls, windows, doors), and their influence on energy consumption, and the potential for reducing the building load by modifying the envelopes.

6. The load profile during each 24-hour period to determine the causes and extent of peak electric loads.

7. The options available to use alternative energy sources to reduce both the consumption of fossil fuels and their resulting operating costs.

Before energy can be conserved, the ways in which it is used must be understood. The building structure—walls, windows, roof—and the passive components of the mechanical and electrical systems—ducts, pipes, filters, or lighting fixture louvers—do not directly consume energy, but they do influence the amount that is finally consumed. The primary energy-conversion equipment such as coal, oil or gas burners and boilers/furnaces, refrigeration chillers and compressors, motors, and electric lighting fixtures consume energy to supply the *building load* and to compensate for the *distribution load*.

The term "building load" refers to the amount of energy in Btu or kilowatts that would be required to maintain desired indoor space conditions and to operate building equipment if the distribution system and energy-conversion equipment were 100% efficient. The "distribution load," or "parasitic" load, is a measure of the energy required to deliver energy from the primary conversion equipment to supply the building load. The efficiency of this energy-conversion equipment ultimately determines the actual amount of energy consumed to supply both loads. (The term "energy-conversion equipment" here is applicable to the means used to convert fuel to heat and/or electricity to power or light.)

Energy usage, then, depends upon two main factors: the magnitude and duration of the loads, and the seasonal efficiency of the primary energy-conversion equipment. Building loads will be reduced if the temperature and relative humidity are changed to levels that are lower in the winter and higher in the summer than previously maintained (except with certain systems which include terminal reheat systems); if heat loss, heat gain, and infiltration through the building envelope are decreased; if ventilation rates are reduced; if domestic hot-water temperature and quantity are reduced; if the level of illumination by electric heating is lowered; and if the number of hours of operation are reduced for such elements as elevators, business machines, and cooking equipment.

The building load must be considered on a seasonal basis rather than for peak conditions only. Although two buildings may have the same heating load for the peak hours, one of them may have a considerably higher load on a seasonal basis than the other, due to the duration of peak or near-peak conditions. The distribution loads will be decreased by reducing the amount of power required for pumps and fans, reducing heat loss or gain from ducts and pipes, and by eliminating steam, water, and air leaks. Distribution loads are often excessive because systems are designed to operate continuously at the maximum capacity required to meet peak building loads, even though these peaks occur for relatively short periods of time (usually less than 5% of the year).

Peak efficiency is usually based on a one-hour performance. A better measure which reflects the average for the entire season is the *seasonal efficiency,* the ratio of useful work in Btu performed by the equipment over a period of time, to the Btu value of the fuel or electricity consumed by the equipment over the same period.

Reducing building load, then distribution load, and then improving primary conversion-equipment efficiency are most effective when done sequentially, since the latter ones depend upon the magnitude of the preceding ones. The potential for reducing distribution loads depends upon the operating conditions and characteristics of distribution systems.

Changes implemented for a particular purpose often induce secondary effects which also reduce energy usage. For instance, reducing lighting levels and increasing the effectiveness of the lighting system also reduces the cooling load. On the other hand, it increases the heating load (by reducing the numbers of lighting fixtures that contribute heat to the building). Additional heat usually can be supplied more efficiently, and at lower energy cost, by the heating system rather than the lighting system. In large offices, schools, and stores, where the heat from lighting is responsible for a large percentage of the energy which is used for cooling, measures to reduce energy for lighting are doubly important.

Nationwide, the systems that consume the most energy in order of magnitude are: heating and ventilating; lighting; air conditioning (cooling) and ventilating; equipment and processes; and domestic hot water. However, depending upon climate, building construction, use and mode of operation, and type, control, and efficiency of mechanical and electrical equipment, the relative order of energy use between the first three systems will change.

The amount of energy required for domestic hot water is significant in hospitals, housing, and athletic or cooking facilities in schools and colleges. In many areas of the country, the amount of energy to heat water is second only to space heating in the north, and air conditioning in the south. In hospitals, the amount of energy to heat hot water may exceed the amount of energy required for lighting. In retail stores with high levels of general illumination and display lighting and/or a large number of commercial refrigeration units, electricity consumes the greatest amount of energy.

In climatic zones with mild winters (below 2,500 degree days), the seasonal cooling load may be larger than the seasonal heating load and may consume more energy, depending upon the respective efficiencies of each system. In office buildings, schools, and retail stores in this zone, the electrical load for lighting, which is relatively independent of climate, may exceed either heating

ENERGY
CONSERVATION
THROUGH
BUILDING
DESIGN

or cooling. Buildings used for only a few hours per week, however, may consume more energy for heating, unless indoor temperatures are set back during unoccupied periods, and boiler or furnace efficiencies are high.

In cold climates (6,000 degree days and above), heating usually consumes the most energy per year in office buildings and schools, followed by lighting, and then cooling. For retail stores in that zone, the most likely order of energy use is lighting-heating-cooling, or lighting-cooling-heating. Generally, heating consumes the most energy for buildings used for only a few hours per week in most climatic zones above 3,000 degree days, with lighting and cooling following in that order.

In mid-climates (2,500 to 6,000 degree days), the order of magnitude of energy use by systems largely depends upon the type of mechanical and electrical systems and the characteristics of the building structure in which they are installed. In all zones, the energy required for industrial buildings exclusive of process loads is generally similar to commercial office buildings. *Table 1* lists the systems by buildings and climates in the general order of annual energy usage with "1" the greatest energy demand in each case and "5" the least. However, within any building type, each building must be analyzed individually to determine its actual annual usage.

TABLE 1

Comparative Energy Use by System and Building Type

	Zone	Heating & ventilation	Cooling & ventilation	Lighting	Power & process	Domestic hot water
Schools	A	4	3	1	5	2
	B	1	4	2	5	3
	C	1	4	2	5	3
Colleges	A	5	2	1	4	3
	B	1	3	2	5	4
	C	1	5	2	4	3
Office Bldgs.	A	3	1	2	4	5
	B	1	3	2	4	5
	C	1	3	2	4	5
Commercial Stores	A	3	1	2	4	5
	B	2	3	1	4	5
	C	1	3	2	4	5
Auditoriums	A	3	2	1	4	5
	B	1	3	2	4	5
	C	1	3	2	4	5
Hospitals	A	4	1	2	5	3
	B	1	3	4	5	2
	C	1	5	3	4	2

Climatic Zone A: Fewer than 2,500 degree days
Climatic Zone B: 2,500–5,500 degree days
Climatic Zone C: 5,500–9,500 degree days

There is no general rule to determine which part of a particular system accounts for the most energy use of that system. The burner/boiler seasonal efficiency can vary from 78% down to 30%; for buildings in climatic zones above 2,500 degree days, improving the efficiency of the combustion device may be the single most effective measure. However, lighting accounts for a tangible percentage of energy used in all climates, and the potential for conservation is high. Savings of 25% to 50% of the energy required for lighting are possible with little initial cost. HVAC systems, such as dual-duct, terminal reheat, and multizone, which mix hot and cold air together, or simultaneously heat and cool a space, are particularly wasteful and offer a high potential for energy conservation. In all cases, reducing the building load will conserve energy, but for some particular buildings, the savings in energy by decreasing the distribution loads and increasing the seasonal efficiency of the primary energy-conversion equipment are even greater.

While it is important to quantify the amount of energy used in buildings throughout the United States in order of priority and by system to establish national policy objectives, the dependence upon national "averages" as a basis for individual building energy conservation programs leads us into the same trap of "generality" which has been a major factor in constructing and operating energy-intensive and energy-wasteful structures in the first place. Energy to provide environmental control has been indiscriminately expended by over-heating and over-cooling, or over-lighting areas which have less critical requirements by treating them in the same manner as the most critical areas—often because the mechanical and electrical system design does not have the capability for proper zoning.

An energy conservation program must thus begin with a careful analysis of building use patterns, climatic conditions, an understanding of the thermal characteristics of the building structure, and the performance and specific characteristics of all the mechanical and electrical systems. Hotels, motels, auditoriums, and school buildings are typical of building types that consume and waste energy during the long periods when they are not occupied.

A Case History

A chemistry building in the Brookhaven National Laboratory Complex in Upton, Long Island, New York is illustrative of many existing buildings, designed and constructed before the current energy era, which are using excessive energy due to underutilization of the building and due to the design and operation of the mechanical and electrical systems. A proposed conservation program, in this case, is able to promise a reduction of annual energy consumption by 57%.

A brief description of the existing conditions of the building

TABLE 2

Breakdown of Present Energy Consumption in Case Study Example. All Figures Are at the Building Boundary, Based on 1975 Energy Audit.

	kWh × 10³		Btu × 10⁶		Dollars		
	Occup.	Unocc.	Occup.	Unocc.	Occup.	Unocc.	Total
1. Lighting	275	131			7,370	3,511	$ 10,881
2. Supply Fans	385	587			10,318	15,732	26,050
3. Lab. & Rm. Exh. Fans	287	453			7,692	12,140	19,832
4. Propeller Exh. Fans	26	—			697	—	697
5. Chillers	790	1,025			21,172	27,470	48,642
6. Chilled-Water Pumps	42	42			1,126	1,126	2,252
7. Condenser Water Pumps	84	84			2,252	2,252	4,504
8. Cooling Tower Fans	50	42			1,340	1,126	2,466
9. Condensate Ret. Pumps	18	26			482	697	1,179
10. Hot-Water Circ. Pumps	29	71			777	1,903	2,680
11. Misc. Equipment	112	—			3,002	—	3,002
12. Lab. Equipment	1,271	—			34,063	—	34,063
13. Preheat Load— Winter			3,008	9,222	8,362	25,637	33,999
14. Terminal Heating Load			6,962	17,140	19,354	47,649	67,003
15. Transmission— Winter			1,336	4,309	3,714	11,979	15,693
16. Solar Gains— Winter			−725	−308	−2,015	−856	−2,871
17. Internal Gains— Winter			−1,588	−1,829	−4,415	−5,085	−9,500
18. Humidification— Winter			2,543	6,263	7,070	17,411	24,481
19. Reheat Load— Summer			4,013	7,765	11,156	21,587	32,743
20. Solar Gains— Summer			−547	−262	−1521	−728	−2,249
21. Internal Gains— Summer			−1,249	−1,371	−3,472	−3,811	−7,283
22. Domestic Hot Water			208	—	578	—	578
23. Piping Losses			690	1,628	1,918	4,526	6,444
Total	3,369	2,461	14,651	42,557	131,020	184,266	$315,286

and the proposed conservation measures that were recommended should be helpful in demonstrating the potential for energy management when confronted with a building which was designed without a concern for energy and which, in many other respects, is typical of the commercial building type. *Table 2* shows the results of a complete energy audit of the chemistry building for each subsystem in 1975. It included annual energy use and peak electrical demand as follows:

- 5,830,000 kWh electricity
- Total cost for electric power—$156,000 at $2.68/kWh
- Peak power electrical demand—1,800 kWh
- Electricity cost attributable to peak demand—11%

- 57.2 billion Btu thermal energy, requiring 48.0 million lb of steam at 125 psi (1,191 Btu/lb).
- Total cost for steam—$159,000 at $2.78/million Btu.
- Total cost of energy $156,000 + $159,000 = $315,000.
- Equivalent Btu per gross square foot including thermal and electrical energy—558,000 at building boundary, or 847,000 raw source energy.

ENERGY
MANAGEMENT
FOR
COMMERCIAL
BUILDINGS:
A PRIMER

213

Factors Contributing to Excessive Energy Consumption

A combination of major factors contribute to excessive energy consumption in the chemistry building. The basic functions performed in the building require that exhaust hoods operate for a considerable number of hours per year to expel noxious fumes and other contaminants from the building. The quantity of air which is expelled through laboratory hoods and room exhaust grilles must be replaced with an equal volume of outdoor make-up air, requiring thermal energy to heat and humidify the air in the winter to maintain room conditions. Humidification is required for occupant comfort and health (when outside air is heated, the relative humidity becomes very low if no moisture is added) and for quality control of paper products in computer rooms. In the summertime, outdoor make-up air must be cooled, dehumidified, and reheated, thus imposing a heavy power demand upon chillers and their auxiliaries. Due to the basic system design—a terminal reheat system—the outdoor air must first be over-cooled for spaces which have relatively low internal and solar heat gains, and then reheated again using thermal energy for that purpose. In addition, considerable power is consumed by supply and exhaust fans and, to a lesser extent, by pumps to move the air and water. All of these related mechanical design solutions are representative of an entire class of similar commercial building types, built without energy efficiency criteria.

The following items summarize the foremost problem areas that were identified in the case study of the chemistry building:

1. The quantity of exhaust air and corresponding make-up air is greater than that required to meet the building's functional program. All laboratory spaces were designed to accommodate fume hoods, and the exhaust system for each laboratory, whether equipped with exhaust hoods or not, is operated in the same manner and capacity, even though the exhaust requirements for a laboratory without hoods is considerably lower.

2. The basic design of the HVAC distribution system and space plan contribute to excessive energy use. In most of the

zones, a common duct supplies conditioned air at the same temperature and humidity conditions to laboratories which are in the interior of the building and have no outside wall exposure, as to perimeter offices; in some cases, the same supply duct serves north-facing offices as well as south-facing offices.

3. In each of the air handling zones, except two, there are scattered computer facilities in one, two, or three rooms within the zone, with the result that to maintain environmental controls in the rooms in which computers are located, these conditions have to be met for the entire zone.

4. Excessive energy is used for cooling since the system is designed and operated to provide chilled water at a constant temperature of 43F to the coils of each air handling unit.

5. Chiller efficiency is penalized due to the low chilled-water temperature which is maintained at all times, even though ambient outdoor air conditions would permit operation for long periods of time at higher chilled-water temperatures when cooling loads are light (about 1.75% of the power requirements for chillers can be saved for every degree rise in chilled-water temperature).

6. While there are light switches in most individual rooms (as compared to some buildings where there is only one switch per floor) a single switch does not permit turning off selected fixtures in rooms, laboratories, and corridors which are unused or where daylight is adequate.

7. The current space utilization and low occupancy density contribute to excessive energy usage. (While the building was originally planned for about 160 scientific personnel, an average of 80 use the building at any one time, and at night and weekends only 5 or 10 are scattered throughout the entire building.)

By analyzing the basic causes of excess energy consumption and then quantifying the energy usage, it became quite clear that a great range of energy conservation options were cost-justified separately or in different combinations, within various payback periods. The conceptual aspects of each opportunity to conserve energy were derived, and the engineering and economic feasibility of 40 or more specific measures were analyzed.

The measures, summarized in the following 10 categories, are listed here because they have general application as a checklist for similar commercial building types.

ENERGY
MANAGEMENT
FOR
COMMERCIAL
BUILDINGS:
A PRIMER

215

1. Reduce Volume of Outdoor Make-up Air to Reduce Energy for Heating, Humidification, Cooling, and Dehumidification This measure included, among many others, the following steps: install a separate multi-speed fan switch for each exhaust air fan to reduce capacity when hood functions permit; provide a new automatic damper in the air supply duct to each laboratory and interlock it with exhaust fan operation to reduce room air supply when exhaust requirements permit; interlock exhaust fans with inlet volume control dampers on each air handling unit to reduce total quantity of air supplied to the zone; shut off unneeded exhaust fans serving rooms without exhaust hoods, and rebalance air supply accordingly.

2. Lower Thermostat Settings in Winter to Reduce Heating Energy Lower the thermostat setting to 68F during occupied periods and install an automatic night set-back system to lower indoor temperatures to 55F during unoccupied periods in laboratories, shops, and rooms.

3. Reduce the Humidification Load in the Winter Deactivate winter dew-point control of each air handling unit. Install room humidistat in corridors to control steam humidifiers in each air handling unit. Set to maintain 30% RH. Install room humidifiers in computer rooms where higher relative humidity is required.

4. Reduce Energy for Reheat in the Summer In addition to reducing air flow, install automatic controls to raise summer supply air temperatures and to turn off reheat in non-critical rooms during unoccupied periods. A reset switch in the room thermostat can override in special areas requiring closer temperature control. Use rejected heat from chiller condensers for reheat.

5. Reduce the Energy Required for Chillers and Auxiliaries In addition to reducing air flow and changing thermostat settings, do the following: adjust the repair chillers to improve efficiency; provide enthalpy controller to raise chilled-water temperature for periods when outdoor enthalphy is lower; provide control valves on all chilled-water coils to permit individual zone control as needed; provide separate packaged air conditioner for rooms with computers and/or high internal heat gain so that the existing air handling system can be operated in a more energy-conserving manner to serve the other spaces within the zone; add reflective coatings to south-facade glazing.

6. Recover the Energy Lost through Exhaust Air to Reduce Heating and Cooling Loads In addition to reducing air volume and changing thermostat settings, provide a run-around coil system to recover energy from the exhaust system and transfer it to the make-up air supply.

7. Reduce Energy Required to Offset Building Conductive Heat Loss and Heat Gain, and Solar Heat Gain Add another pane of glass to single-glazed windows. Add new insulation during reroofing. (These had longer payback periods than other recommended measures.) Add reflective coating to reduce heat gain

TABLE 3

Case Study Example: Consumption after All Energy Conservation Measures Are
Implemented

	kWh × 10³		Btu × 10⁶		Dollars		
	Occup.	Unocc.	Occup.	Unocc.	Occup.	Unocc.	Total
1. Lighting	180	71			4,824	1,903	$ 6,727
2. Supply Fans	358	491			9,594	13,159	22,753
3. Lab. & Rm. Exh. Fans	193	294			5,172	7,879	13,051
4. Propeller Exh. Fans	26	—			697	—	697
5. Chillers	308	258			8,254	6,914	15,168
6. Chilled-Water Pumps	39	39			1,045	1,045	2,090
7. Condenser Water Pumps	78	78			2,090	2,090	4,180
8. Cooling Tower Fans	46	37			1,233	992	2,225
9. Condensate Ret. Pumps	18	26			482	697	1,179
10. Hot-Water Circ. Pumps	27	66			724	1,769	2,493
11. Misc. Equipment	104	—			2,787	—	2,787
12. Lab. Equipment	1,271	—			34,063	—	34,063
13. Preheat Load— Winter			8	1,505	22	4,184	4,206
14. Terminal Heating Load			3,512	4,476	9,763	12,443	22,206
15. Transmission— Winter			826	1,444	2,296	4,014	6,310
16. Solar Gains— Winter			−725	−308	−2,015	−856	−2871
17. Internal Gains— Winter			−1,588	−1,829	−4,415	−5,085	−9,500
18. Humidification— Winter	13	28	892	1,147	2,480	3,189	5,699
19. Reheat Load— Summer			—	—	—	—	—
20. Solar Gains— Summer			—	—	—	—	—
21. Internal Gains— Summer			—	—	—	—	—
22. Domestic Hot Water			—	—	—	—	—
23. Piping Losses			310	712	862	1,979	2,841
Total	2,661	1,388	3,235	7,147	79,958	56,316	136,274

through south-, east- and west-facing windows. (This measure will be effective if reheat system controls are changed according to earlier recommendations.)

8. Reduce Energy Consumption for Domestic Water Heating In the case study example, the amount of energy to generate hot water used for domestic and process purposes is small compared to energy used for heating and cooling. However, the measures to reduce hot-water energy consumption are also relatively inexpensive. They include reinsulating storage tanks, condensate receivers, and piping (for heating as well); and using condensate to preheat hot water.

9. Reduce Heat Losses from Piping and Ducts The distribution system losses are small compared to energy used to meet

ENERGY
MANAGEMENT
FOR
COMMERCIAL
BUILDINGS:
A PRIMER

217

heating and cooling loads, but not insignificant. Reduce these loads by adding insulation to steam and hot-water piping where they run through the basement or service chases.

10. Reduce Energy Consumption for Lighting and Power Although lighting levels had already been reduced and power saved by removing some lamps and disconnecting ballasts, additional opportunities to reduce energy consumption existed in the case study example.

Within these 10 conceptual approaches, specific energy conservation measures were analyzed in detail, taking into account initial costs, energy savings, operating costs, space requirements, noise during construction, and other influences in the continuity of the building program. *Table 3* is a tabulation of the resulting energy requirements for each system in the case study, based on full implementation of the measures outlined above.

The study demonstrated that more than 80% of the annual thermal energy and 30% of the annual electrical energy presently consumed can be saved by a comprehensive energy conservation program. At current energy prices, this would amount to $180,000 annual savings for an initial investment of approximately $600,000 including engineering fees, providing an over-all payback of slightly over three years.

Other Energy-Conservation and Use-Management Proposals

The potential savings in annual energy usage and peak load reduction for the Brookhaven Chemistry Building is by no means unique. Many buildings have already been retrofitted for energy conservation (though too few so far to make a major impact on national energy use) with reductions in energy usage from 25% to 50%. For new buildings, energy savings of the operating costs associated with standard design and construction are even more dramatic. Frequently, the extra insulation, multiple glazing, heat recovery equipment, and other load-reducing measures result in sufficient savings in smaller mechanical system installation costs to offset their own initial cost. In many cases, especially in task lighting systems and variable-air-volume systems, the installation costs are lower than more energy-intensive systems.

It is also important to realize that these savings in energy in new and existing buildings can be done with readily available hardware, equipment, and systems, and with thoughtful, discriminating, innovative design. There is also a need to develop improved technologies, new equipment, and systems to reduce initial costs and improve performance. If we develop hardware and systems which move energy from one level to another, rather than simply input new energy, the potential for additional conservation can be doubled again. Today we have designed our building control systems, for the most part, with the "first-law" (of thermodynamics) principle. We must start to design systems which are based on "second-law" principles, which match the energy requirement to the energy source in order to reduce conversion waste and can thus double the efficiency of current equipment energy usage.

Like the measures discussed in the previous section by reference to the case study, many effective ideas involve little or no cost investment to better design and manage energy use with existing technical options. Other concepts require research, development, and marketing, which ought to be accelerated in a nationwide energy program. By way of a summary checklist of energy conservation and management measures, various technical-fix options are listed below, followed by more innovative ideas that require development and the legislative and programatic proposals that might therefore be anticipated and encouraged.

Increase the Seasonal Efficiency of Oil-Fired Boiler Plants (By as Much as 20%)

- Use an oil additive to provide better combustion.
- Introduce water vapor into the oil before combustion. The water particles explode when heated and help break up the oil molecules, resulting in more complete combustion.
- Use automatic viscosity controllers on fuel oil systems to attain the best combustion atomization. This also permits a flexibility of mixing and using any grade of fuel oil, either distillate or residual.
- Recover heat from stack gases with an economizer or use an air-to-air heat exchanger or heat pipe to preheat combustion air and make-up feed.
- Use a solar energy collector to preheat heavy oil. The oil storage tank serves as the energy storage system.
- Use sealed combustion chambers.
- Investigate fluidized-bed combustion boilers.
- Provide maximum burner turndown ratio for light loads.

Increase the Efficiency of Refrigeration Systems

- Provide an automatic control to "follow the load" and permit operation at higher chilled-water temperature. Most systems need chilled water at its minimum-low temperatures less than 5% of the time. Most of the time, the average chilled-water temperature can be 4F to 8F higher than that needed for peak requirements. Raising the cooling thermostat setting from 72F to 78F permits raising chilled-water temperatures and could result in a 30% energy savings in a 750 cooling degree-hour zone.

ENERGY
MANAGEMENT
FOR
COMMERCIAL
BUILDINGS:
A PRIMER

219

- Reduce condenser-water temperature with flow control or use variable-pitch blades on the cooling tower, or both. Automatic control that senses condensing temperatures, outside wet-bulb temperatures, and load, provides immediate control adjustment without delay.
- Pipe two or more chillers in series rather than in parallel, with properly designed evaporators to reduce frictional losses. The average suction temperature of the compressors will be higher.
- Use blow-through built-up air handling units, field-assembled if necessary, to permit chiller operation at higher suction temperatures.
- Use chilled-water storage and operate the chillers at night, storing chilled water for use during the day, whenever outdoor wet-bulb conditions are low enough to reduce energy requirements by operating refrigeration units at lower condensing temperatures. Chilled-water storage also reduces peak loads during the day and can result in substantial cost savings through lower demand.
- Consider using solar energy for absorption cooling or for regenerating a desiccant in a dehumidifying system, or both. In some areas, conventional flat-plate collectors with selective surface and reflectors can provide water hot enough to operate absorption units. Evacuated-glass tubular collectors can be used in place of the conventional flat-plate collector to provide fluid temperatures from 240F to 300F at a collector efficiency close to 50%, and they are suited to operate absorption refrigeration units or Rankine Cycle cooling.
- Evaporative cooling is used in arid areas of the country, primarily for residences. But a much wider range of application is possible. Some air handling units have both cooling coils and sprays, which permit operation of evaporative cooling without refrigeration for a substantial number of hours (savings in horsepower), or for refrigeration alone (for fewer hours) when outdoor wet-bulb temperature is excessive. In many cases, by installing a desiccant to lower the relative humidity, it will be economical to operate the evaporative cooling unit for the entire cooling season. Solar heat or waste heat from the building or processes can be used to regenerate the desiccant to operate newer-style absorption units (180F generator temperature).
- Consider the installation of enthalpy controllers, as well as an economizer cycle control, to reduce the energy required for air conditioning 20% to 80%, depending on ambient outdoor seasonal wet-bulb conditions. Each installation must be evaluated individually to determine the cost/benefits relationship using wet-bulb cooling degree hours rather than cooling degree days.
- For large installations, consider ''piggyback'' steam-driven

centrifugal refrigeration units working in combination with absorption refrigeration units, instead of direct electric-drive units. The steam-driven chiller, in combination with a double-effect absorption chiller using extracted steam for the heat source, can provide a ton of refrigeration with less than 9 lb of steam under some conditions. A single-effect standard absorption unit alone requires about 18 lb of steam per ton of refrigeration, and the newer double-effect high-pressure absorption units need about 13 lb. The piggyback system uses no more raw source energy than electric-drive units, and can reduce electricity demand charges significantly.

Recover Low-Grade Waste Heat

- Heating and/or cooling and dehumidifying outdoor air, introduced into a building for ventilation or as make-up air for exhaust systems, accounts for 20% to 80% of the heating or cooling load in nonresidential structures. After reducing the volume of make-up air, consider measures to recover energy from exhaust air, or from other processes, and transfer it to the outdoor-air intake stream.
- Consider all opportunities to recover waste heat (or cooling) by using run-around coil systems, thermal wheels for sensible and/or latent heat recovery, heat pipes, or even heat pumps. Just 1,000 cfm of outdoor air requires the equivalent of 200 gal of oil a year for heating every 1,000 degree days, or up to 1,600 gal of oil a year in an 8,000 degree-day zone. Heat recovery units are 50% to 80% efficient, and their use has the effect of reducing the heat required for tempering outdoor air by the same percentages.
- The heat pump, similar to the latent heat-transfer wheel, should be considered because it transfers latent heat as well as sensible heat. It is often feasible to provide uncooled or slightly tempered air to direct-supply hoods (auxiliary-air hoods) and save energy for both heating and cooling. To be effective and protect workers from fumes, hoods must be carefully designed, with supply air entering from top and sides. Direct-air make-up hoods are available and should be considered for new installations. For existing installations, an attachment is available which can be fitted to hoods to convert them for auxiliary direct make-up air. There are opportunities to recover waste heat or, in the case of refrigeration units, heat from hot gas. A hot-gas heat exchanger in a 3-ton heat-pump circuit provides virtually all the domestic hot water the year round, saving some 4,250 kWh and 50 million Btu of raw energy a year. Prime candidates for such systems are hotels, hospitals, laundries, and industrial plants with large service or domestic hot-water requirements, coupled with large air-conditioning or heat-pump systems.

Consider Heat Pipes

ENERGY
MANAGEMENT
FOR
COMMERCIAL
BUILDINGS:
A PRIMER

221

- A novel system uses a heat pipe to provide evaporative cooling without raising indoor humidity. Extending the heat pipe through the roof, wetting the surface of the pipe, and blowing exhaust air from the building over it causes a cooling effect at the end of the pipe, which protrudes into the building. Air circulated over the heat pipe in the building is then cooled.
- Heat pipes can also be used to transfer heat from a boiler stack to a space to be heated or to make-up combustion air. A sound boiler, though old and inefficient, can be kept in service without penalty as long as the stack heat is recovered.

Consider Heat Pumps   The heat pump is becoming the workhorse of energy conservation. Using heat pumps instead of electric resistance heating requires only one-half to one-third the amount of electric power. In some cases, they reduce electric consumption by 80%, depending on the coefficient of performance (COP) of the heat pump. COP increases as evaporator temperatures rise and condensing temperatures are reduced. In small heat pumps, the refrigeration circuit flows are reversed when the operating mode changes from cooling to heating (a recently developed unit does not require a reversing valve). But in larger heat pumps, the condenser and chilled-water flow circuits are reversed, and the COP is considerably higher. Double-bundle condensers, and in some cases double-bundle evaporators, are of the latter type; COPs of 5, or slightly better, have been attained in some installations. Some ways to increase the COP of various heat pump systems include:

- Use well or ground water, if available, as a heat source for water-to-water heat pumps, instead of ambient air for air-to-air heat pumps.
- Raise the temperature of an air-source heat pump by using exhaust air from the building or processes as a heat source. Heat source candidates include waste heat from engines, hot-water drains, flashed steam, condensate, exhaust hoods, kitchen equipment, and incinerators. When the waste heat is either warm air or warm gas, it can be mixed with colder outdoor air to raise the COP of air-to-air or air-to-water heat pumps. When the waste heat is liquid, it can be circulated through coils in the airstream of air-source heat pumps, or water-to-water heat pumps can use the warm liquid as a direct heat source.
- In larger sizes, the double-bundle condensers and evaporators arranged in series with a basic chiller (the cascade system) can be used to transfer energy from interior areas of a building, which may require cooling all year, to the perimeter

222

ENERGY
CONSERVATION
THROUGH
BUILDING
DESIGN

of the building, where heat is required simultaneously. If the perimeter does not require all the available heat, excess heat can be stored in hot-water tanks. Heat from storage can be used for heating at night, during warm-up periods in the morning, or for reheat for humidity of zone temperature control. Heat pumps can be engine-driven as well as electrically powered. Direct engine-driven refrigeration systems must be carefully installed to keep vibration to a minimum.

- Engine or turbine prime movers can be used in other ways. For example, in the General Services Administration's energy conservation demonstration building in Manchester, New Hampshire, the emergency diesel-engine generator drives a centrifugal heat pump. The waste heat from the engine is recovered and used as a heat source for additional absorption cooling. The combined cycle is efficient. Since the emergency generator serves a dual function, capital costs for the entire system were reduced. Solar energy will be used to supplement the heat from the engine to power the absorption unit. In case of engine breakdown, utility power will supply the heat pump.[2]

- Solar-assisted heat pumps can supply as much as 85% of the yearly energy requirements for space heating and domestic hot water if the building is designed (or retrofitted) to reduce heat loss. In all solar heating and cooling installations, it is essential that heating and cooling loads first be reduced through building design. By reducing heat loss, smaller collectors (the most expensive item in the system) as well as smaller heat pumps, can be used. Also, the building can be heated with water or air at lower supply temperatures without requiring excessively large heating coils or air quantity. Lower temperatures result in higher heat-pump COP and higher systems efficiency, since the supplementary heat required is less at extremely low outdoor temperatures. The collectors are also more efficient at lower fluid temperatures.

Reduce Lighting Energy   Design methods have been developed and equipment is available to reduce the amount of energy used for lighting in buildings by 50% or more, without sacrificing visual performance or the quality of illumination. Methods and equipment include:

- Selective lighting systems designed to provide the correct amount of light for each task without over-lighting adjacent areas where tasks are less demanding.
- Multilevel ballasts with integral switches are available to vary luminaire output from 100% to 200%. Individual lamps in the luminaire can be turned on or off at will to meet specific task requirements. When tasks are less critical, lower illumination levels can be provided from the same luminaire.

2. Fred S. Dubin: "GSA's Energy Conservation Lab Grows in Manchester," *Actual Specifying Engineer,* August 1975; J. E. Hill and T. Kusuda: "Manchester's New Federal Building," *ASH-RAE Journal,* August 1975.

- Krypton-filled incandescent lamps provide 8% more lumens/watt than standard lamps.
- Low-pressure sodium lamps provide four times more lumens than fluorescent tubes for the same wattage input. Other high-efficiency HID lamps are available in smaller lamp sizes for indoor applications.
- Photocells can be used to turn off selected lamps to take maximum advantage of natural illumination and to save power needed for lighting and air conditioning. Circuiting and switches must be designed to accommodate the system.
- Compared to 60-Hz systems, high-frequency lighting—3,000 Hz or more—requires about 10% less power for the same lumen output and extends ballast life.
- Lighting built into, and made integral with, office furniture can provide sufficient non-glare illumination directly on the task. At the same time, sufficient background lighting is provided to meet acceptable contrast limits. Using task lighting and other selective lighting arrangements means that only 1½ to 2 watts/ft² will be needed, compared to the usual 3 to 5 watts/ft².

Avoid Systems that Simultaneously Heat and Cool the Same Space

- When designed in the conventional manner, dual-duct systems, induction units, and even variable-air-volume (VAV) systems are forms of terminal reheating. VAV systems, generally more efficient than other types of reheat systems, can be designed to optimize energy conservation in new buildings by using separate air handling units for each perimeter zone, and one for the interior zone. Each unit is equipped with a heating and cooling coil, and the VAV boxes are arranged to modulate in both the heating and cooling modes. Fan speed is reduced in accordance with static pressure or an inlet restriction with vaned inlet control which reflects variable air quantities.
- Where dual-duct systems are required, separate air handling units for each exposure can virtually eliminate the reheat effect. This is accomplished by providing the highest cold-duct temperature and the lowest hot-duct temperature required by any zone rather than the extreme temperatures that might be required if one unit serves all five zones (east, west, north, south, interior).
- For new buildings, the HVAC system can be designed for optimum energy conservation, e.g., VAV with zone air handling units. In existing buildings, reheat-type systems can be modified and provided with operating controls to approach the standard of systems selected for new buildings.

ENERGY
MANAGEMENT
FOR
COMMERCIAL
BUILDINGS:
A PRIMER

223

Consider Thermal Barriers that Block Windows at Night Insulating barriers are one of the cost-saving measures that can be employed to reduce building heat loss in cold climates, even down to 3,000 degree-day zones. Thermal barriers used in combination with a double glazing can easily reduce the U-factor of that portion of the external wall to as low as .1, which is better than most opaque walls today.

Consider Central Controls to Monitor and Control System Used with or without computers, these controls optimize energy conservation in HVAC, lighting, and power systems. For all buildings or groups of buildings of at least 50,000 ft², computer control is particularly effective.

Consider Total Energy Systems These systems are not new, but there are very few large installations (10,000 kW or more) in operation. Escalating prices for electricity and fuel, coupled with diminishing supplies, require that a renewed investigation of these systems be made.

- If all combustion turbines now used for base loads in New York City's central electric generating plants were installed in housing projects, industrial plants, or commercial complexes, as total energy systems with waste heat recovered for heating, hot water, and air conditioning, approximately 220 million gal of oil would be saved every year.
- As new communities are built and existing cities redeveloped, planning for total energy by locating facilities that have major year-round thermal needs adjacent to the generating plant will be cost-effective as well as energy conserving (low-grade heat can be distributed long distances without losing its potential through piping losses).
- Some combustion turbines now require only 11,000 Btu/kWh, equivalent in heat rate to some of the best central generator plants. The required waste heat is a bonus. With proper load balance, attainable through design, system efficiencies of 60% to 80% could be attained. Topping cycles, bottoming cycles, and cogeneration are concepts to be considered for large complexes and new communities.

Consider Wind Energy Many areas of the country have enough potential energy in the winds to supply most electric energy requirements for a region. There is technology available for building wind generators ranging from 40 to 1,500 kW. Using wind generators to generate electricity that in turn produces hot water for heating is more economically feasible than using them to generate electricity for end-use because of the prohibitive cost of storing electric energy, as compared to storing thermal energy. The development of wind systems along with hydrogen and fuel cells, however, should be pursued, because the potential success in developing these technologies is very high. At the same time, the costs appear to be competitive with other new electric generating processes.[3]

Consider Seasonal Storage The ACES, or seasonal storage system concept using heat pumps to provide heating in winter and to manufacture ice at the same time for use in summertime for air conditioning, can utilize existing equipment and produce a high seasonal COP with or without solar collectors as a supplement. There is one such residence in Tennessee and a proposed VA hospital installation in Delaware. The system moves towards the design principle inherent in the second law of thermodynamics.

Other Innovative Concepts Some other proposals that should be considered are mentioned here, so as to identify those that need professional interest to secure a more rapid entry into conventional building practice and to encourage their development. The following ideas are representative of technologies and equipment that are not fully developed, but which promise energy conservation advances:

- More efficient fractional-hp motors.
- Multispeed heat pumps in 10-hp sizes and smaller.
- More efficient heat exchangers to provide closer approach temperatures for low-cost applications.
- Packaged blow-through air handling units.
- Packaged desiccant air dryers to reduce relative humidity and refrigeration loads. The desiccant must be rechargeable by solar heat or other sources of low-grade heat (180F or lower).
- Direct-submerge gas- and oil-fired combustion units to permit transfer of heat from fuel directly into water without stack losses.
- Turndown-ratio capabilities for small oil burners under 2-gph firing rate.
- Safe combustion-control systems to permit complete close-off of smokepipe breaching to reduce stack losses between firing cycles.
- Packaged heat exchangers to recover energy from hot-water drains for schools, hospitals, industrial facilities, and hotels.
- Fluidized-bed boilers.
- Heat-recovery incinerators for large buildings.
- Packaged coal-fired boilers.
- Packaged heating and cooling equipment with better-insulated casings for outdoor installations to save building space and cost.
- Low-cost systems to provide zone control in each room of a building to allow selective temperature control for heating and cooling.
- High-temperature solar collectors.

3. Dubin-Mindell-Bloome Associates: "A Study of Existing Energy Usage on Long Island and the Impact of Energy Conservation, Solar Energy, Total Energy and Wind Systems on Future Requirements," Department of Environmental Control, County of Suffolk, New York, 1975.

- Small Rankine Cycle and Stirling Cycle engines for commercial use.
- Combination solar collectors/heat-storage units in one package for a single room or a building.
- Heat-actuated absorption refrigeration units that operate at full capacity at 160F generator temperatures for cooling applications, using low-grade waste heat or solar energy.
- A control to monitor air quality and operate outside-air dampers or air-regenerative devices, as needed.
- Thermal storage units with phase-changing materials to increase capacity and to reduce the volume of the storage system.
- Lower-cost solar cells for direct conversion of sunlight to electricity, and means for capturing the heat generated for heating purposes.
- Electricity storage systems to enhance wind generator and photo-voltaic cell applications for generating electricity.
- Multiperformance materials for walls and roofs of buildings, incorporating sensible and phase-change heat storage, and absorptive, reflective, and emissivity properties, as required under changing ambient temperature, humidity, wind, and solar radiation conditions.
- Insulation material of thin laminations that could be used as shades to draw over building windows, greenhouses, or display windows, to reduce heat loss at night in winter.
- High-frequency lighting systems with static converters at each light fixture to eliminate double distribution systems.
- Multilevel ballasts operable by wall switches to permit changing room illumination levels as tasks change.
- High-output lamps, such as high-pressure sodium, in small sizes for indoor installations.
- Light tubes that introduce daylight into interior space.
- Less costly Btu meters for monitoring energy use in subsystems or multioccupancy facilities.
- Test procedures for determining part-load characteristics of mechanical and electrical equipment.
- Methods for making cheaper and faster energy use and economic analyses. Current methods impose a heavy cash-flow burden on the designer or owner who must pay these costs.
- Lower-cost time-of-day metering equipment to provide the basis for utility company load management.
- A total-systems manual for load management for utility companies to improve the effectiveness of existing electrical generating and distribution systems, and to eliminate the need for additional generating stations that would otherwise be necessary as economic activity increases.
- Lower-cost fuel cells for electricity generation with waste-heat recovery.

- Low-cost, large, wind generators, 1,500 kW and larger, for direct electrical power generation.

Innovative Program Incentives New legislation, additional incentives, and the development of the concept of "economic and resources cost/benefits" (energy accounting) are essential to encourage the use of off-the-shelf hardware, to say nothing of providing incentives to develop, produce, and manufacture new products, and to induce consumers to utilize them. The following program needs may thus be essential to realizing the full potential for energy conservation:

- Establish an institute of energy conservation. The institute should carry the same weight as the Atomic Energy Commission, the Coal Resources Board, and other agencies devoted to energy supply. Its function would be to gather and disseminate information on conservation; promulgate conservation guidelines and performance standards; sponsor a computer program for the public to analyze energy conservation measures with costs and benefits quantified (and continually updated); store computer analyses performed for specific projects to provide a base for practitioners; and other functions that its governing body (composed of practicing engineers, architects, and university, industrial, federal, state, and municipal personnel) might deem productive.
- There are too few trained personnel to design innovative or even "standard" energy conservation systems, or to analyze existing buildings in terms of energy management. Legislation should provide grants to universities for students in the design profession and for continuing education.
- Totally integrated system design is not sufficiently developed. The development of simple methods of cost/benefits analyses is important to serve as a base for promulgating and obtaining acceptance for energy conservation measures. For example, a current investment in equipment that could conserve energy in operation and reduce operating costs must generally show a payback in three years or less to be accepted by industry— and then the benefits must be definitive and assured before industry will make the investment. It will become increasingly necessary, however, to conserve much more energy than the amount accomplished by an investment with a three-year payback period. Incentives are necessary to induce industry to devote its resources to energy conservation with longer payback periods, rather than to competitive investments for production machinery, land, or activities unrelated to the company's main business.
- At present, institutional practices do not reward conservation efforts nor penalize wasteful practices. There is little, if any, legislation that encourages energy conservation. Obviously,

price and the marketplace are not enough incentive. Legislation is needed to enable the government to subsidize and guarantee low-cost (2% to 3%) and long-life (40-year) loans by financial institutions for energy conservation designs and systems that entail initial costs which cannot be financed.

- Promote legislation establishing energy budgets for all buildings so that the end-goal of saving natural non-replaceable resources can be established. Such legislation requires the necessary appropriations to develop the proper energy budgets. This can be done by analyses of current energy usage in buildings, of building materials and configurations in separate climatic zones, and of alternative mechanical and electrical system combinations.

- Legislation should be passed granting industry tax credits and write-offs for using energy conservation systems and equipment, rather than for energy consumption (as is the present 100% write-off for operating expenses). These credits could start after any company shows a 15% reduction in energy use. A precedent for such a measure is the 7.5% tax credit for industrial expansion.

- Funding is needed to help identify physiological needs in relation to indoor climate so that design standards and conditions relevant to building occupants can be established. Funds are also needed to promulgate a set of energy conservation design manuals similar to those developed by the government years ago for fall-out shelters, and to support industry research and product development where there is now only a long-term payback in sight.

- A meaningful national energy policy must be delineated so that all sectors will understand the framework within which efforts are to be made to reduce the gap between domestic supply and demand.

- A large-scale energy audit is needed to determine exactly what systems and subsystems in building, industry, and transportation now use energy. There is no common reporting form to monitor and process the data to be collected. Energy-use forms with sufficient building data should be considered for the next United States census. It appears that this would be the most efficient way to collect data needed to build a conservation program from the existing base. A questionnaire with each utility bill monthly would be effective.

- There must be a wide dissemination of design techniques, hardware, equipment, and materials that are now available for energy conservation in buildings.

- A government-sponsored insurance program to back up manufacturers' warranties is needed.

- A rigorous research and development program with joint participation by government and industry should be developed. It should aim at furthering cost-effective, energy-conserving equipment and systems that take full advantage of the scientific principles that are well known, but not yet infused into engineering and commercial practice.

- An extensive research and development program (including large-scale demonstration projects in all regions of the country) is needed to gather and disseminate information about the generation of electricity with solar and wind energy. These technologies can be brought on-line within the next 10 years in sufficient strength to significantly reduce the drain on our natural resources.
- The federal government should undertake a massive retrofit program on all buildings in every department—military and non-military—to reduce energy consumption and create a ready market for existing and new products, which will enhance and accelerate energy conservation design products, systems, and knowledge. A similar program to utilize solar energy for process heating, space heating, and cooling in government buildings—new and existing, where appropriate—would move our fledgling solar energy industry by a giant step.

The purpose here has been to show that we have only begun to explore the possible range of energy conservation measures for existing and new commercial buildings. The combined effect of existing technical-fix options and of innovative concepts and systems would have a dramatic impact on stabilizing national energy needs. But, the effort now requires a national energy conservation program, including government support and legislated incentives.

Additional sources of detailed conservation guidelines for commercial buildings are listed in *Footnote 4* below. Beyond these, it will be important to continue to collate and update case histories and design and performance data as we move forward with the practice of energy conservation and management.

4. Energy conservation references for commercial buildings include: *Energy Conservation in Building Design*, American Institute of Architects, Washington, DC, May 1974; *Design and Evaluation Criteria for Energy Conservation in New Buildings*, American Society of Heating, Refrigerating and Air-Conditioning Engineers, New York, 1976; Robert R. Gatts, Robert G. Massey and John C. Robertson (U.S. Department of Commerce, National Bureau of Standards): *Energy Conservation Program Guide for Industry and Commerce*, U.S. Government Printing Office, Washington, DC, 1974; Dubin-Mindell-Bloome Associates: "Guidelines for Saving Energy in Existing Buildings: ECM-1 and 2," Federal Energy Administration, Washington, DC, June 1975; Dubin-Mindell-Bloome Associates: "Total Energy," Education Facilities Laboratories, New York, May 1970.

12

SOLAR ENERGY, BUILDING, AND THE LAW

Ralph L. Knowles

An earlier version of this chapter appeared under the same title in the *Journal of Architectural Education,* February 1977, and has been expanded to include recent work of the author under a grant from the National Endowment for the Arts.

Where their paths cross today, architects and lawyers can often be heard discussing solar energy. The popularity of this topic lies in a complex background of recent and historical events. The emerging fact is that anybody seriously concerned with future policies and designs governing building must consider solar energy as a way to temper the constructed environment.

The policy implications of this emerging fact have been seriously discussed in legal terms by a growing number of experts who agree that two basic questions must be answered: first, who will make allocations of sunlight between competing users; second, on what legal principles will this apportionment be made.

There is a related set of design implications that we are studying in a multidisciplinary research program at the University of Southern California (USC). This work is concentrating on two basic design questions that, in my view, must be answered in the modern context of both new and existing development: first, can location (including project orientation and siting) be an effective design adaptation to solar energy; second, can form (including project size and potential complexity) be used as an interrelated design tool. While our major emphasis is on design, we have recognized the need to consider public policy and private development feasibility as well as design concepts.

Starting in the fall of 1976, our first step was to request material on solar allocation policy from cities in this country and abroad. Early answers were disappointing, but told of staff work underway in city planning departments. This has subsequently proved to be the case, and we have received additional material from a number of American cities.[1] Before these very impressive staff working papers began to arrive, we proceeded on our own to examine what kinds of laws might be needed for solar allocation and how they might best be administered. The 12 students involved in the discussions raised what they considered to be a prior question that distinguishes between rules or laws, on the one hand, and "basic rights," on the other. Their question centered on the order of concern: before a legal question can be posed, would it not be useful to consider what basic condition is to be protected, so that we do not lose our way in the machinery of law? Shouldn't we be concerned with what is moral before we are concerned with what is legal?

The question is profoundly innocent and needs to be pursued along ethical lines if the problem is to be freshly defined, and not assumed. As a consequence, we began to examine ethical precedents for solar allocation. We tried to think of examples from our own experience where values and obligations evidently predominated over rules and enforcement. A contemporary example can be found on the sunny beaches of Southern California.

Imagine yourself comfortably ensconced on the warm sand. Your eyes are closed against the sun that heats your lids to a rusty glow. The surf and the pleading gulls echo each other and gently

1. The two most impressive staff working papers we received came from the city planning departments of Los Angeles and Davis, CA. (The cities of Santa Clara, CA and Osaka and Tokyo, Japan are also reported to be well advanced in the area of solar zoning.)

meter your thoughts. Suddenly the rusty glow fades to dark grey and the ocean breeze turns chill. Your eyes open to discover a generous and brightly colored beach umbrella between you and the sun. A lovely umbrella perhaps, but how dare they?! How could they?! Don't they understand why people come to the beach? They are obviously barbarians without a developed sense of obligation in a sophisticated world.

The likelihood of this scenario taking place is, in fact, not very great on California's beaches or anywhere, for that matter. Sunbathers tend to recognize and respect one another's access to the sun and will go out of their way to avoid interference. The beach is one place where your "right to the sun" is recognized and respected without benefit of rules and enforcement. Only when the setting sun drops near to the horizon do conflicts appear. Even then people can often be seen systematically and obligingly shifting their positions, thus evoking a time-honored mode of adaptation to natural variation—migration.

The example of sunbathers is interesting because it contains some of the vital ingredients of a more complex situation involving solar allocation among buildings. Few contemporary examples of this can be found because modern development generally occurs independently of the sun. One must look back in time to find an arrangement built by people who valued the sun as an energy source. Adaptation might be read in the location and form of their buildings.

A good historical example of this sort of solar adaptation can

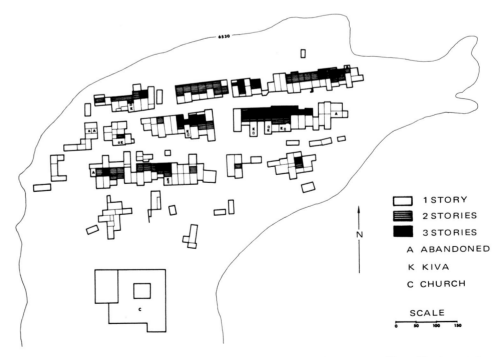

Fig. 1 Acoma Pueblo, NM. Plan shows east-west rows with critical spacing between the two northern-most rows based on story height. (From Ralph L. Knowles, *Energy and Form.*)

be seen at Acoma Pueblo, fifty miles west of Albuquerque, New Mexico (*Figure 1*).

Imagine yourself flying east from Los Angeles to Albuquerque at a low enough altitude to see the rows of pueblo buildings and their shadows, at about 10:00 am on December 21, the winter solstice. What you would see is an apparent example of a solar value system or ethic at work. Useful energy-receiving building forms are virtually shadow-free during the winter months, when they are used to store and transmit energy to the living spaces (*Figure 2*). Where buildings are taller, spacing increases to avoid shading. The most obvious manifestation of this occurs between the two northern-most rows of buildings.

As the buildings increase in height from two to three stories, the road or space between the rows increases in dimension, thus ensuring that shadowing buildings to the south will not interfere with energy-receiving surfaces to the north. Whether this condition

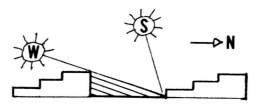

Fig. 2a   Three-story section shows winter solstice shadow at base of northern row.

Fig. 2   Acoma Pueblo, NM. Typical sections show the critical spacing between rows of houses to ensure solar access.

Fig. 2b   Two-story section shows narrower spacing between rows. Vertical surfaces of masonry with a high-heat transmission coefficient and high-heat storage capacity receive solar energy most directly in winter. Horizontals of timber, reeds or cactus fiber, grasses, and clay with insulating properties receive solar energy most directly in summer. The combination of location (building spacing and orientation) and form (shape and materials) mitigates the effects of natural thermal variation.

results from behavior based on regard for one's neighbor, or upon laws and their effective enforcement, the point could certainly be argued that there is great advantage to a generally accepted solar ethic in regulating such adaptive behavior. If the ethic is strong enough, laws and their enforcement are of secondary importance and may not be required at all. There is strong evidence that this was the case at Acoma.

Following our discussions of ethical behavior at the beach and at Acoma, my directed research students at USC turned their attention briefly to the modern potential of educating young children. Their point was idealistic: if children could be taught to value the sun, would they not, as adults, feel obligated to respect their neighbor's "rights"; further, wouldn't this feeling of obligation make the framing of laws and their administration secondary or, at the very least, an easier task?

I followed their lead by posing a problem for the group: they were to speak spontaneously, as if they were explaining to first graders about the ethical implications of solar allocation. The results were later refined and written down by each student. The results can best be summed up in one stanza from a poem written for the occasion by Kenneth Downes. He called his poem "The Shadow Monster."

> 'The sneaky monster came out at dawn leaving his footprints upon the lawn.
> And when the children came out to play, they played in the shade, the shade all day.'

The message is that the next-door neighbor is an enemy whose building casts harmful shadows that come with the rising sun. The same message with variations appeared in most of the presentations. Such an ominous picture can perhaps be understood as an expediency useful in getting an idea across to six year olds, but our investigations of current efforts by legal experts indicate that this view of the neighbor as victimizer permeates much discussion of solar allocation. Their point is that solar energy for heating and cooling buildings is most likely to generate disputes between private parties (*Figure 3*). Surely this is true; but just as surely, in matters of the sun, every property owner is potentially a victim as well as victimizer. What can cast a shadow, can as well be cast upon.

Is it not proper then for us to seek solutions that avoid future

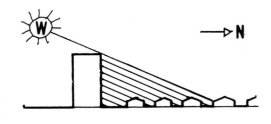

Fig. 3 Shadow impact. The example is from a typical situation in Los Angeles where high-rise buildings shade houses to their north. Lawyers cite such conditions to prove that the use of solar energy to heat and cool buildings is most likely to generate disputes between private parties.

problems as far as possible? Can't we design a legal and physical framework for urban growth and change where neighbors are not in constant conflict over their basic rights?

Certainly a beginning point is with the clear definition of rights themselves, and in this regard I am encouraged by the efforts of research lawyers like Grant Thompson, Gail Hayes, and Alan Miller at the Environmental Law Institute in Washington, who discuss the "right to receive solar energy," thus implying something about how the world should work. I think this value set is correct and useful in a new field where no clear legal precedents exist, where there is no accumulation of time and events, but where there is a growing need for a *solar ethic*. It would seem to be critical to keep before us a clear picture of where we want to go, of what condition we want to attain and maintain, lest in seeking to establish laws, we are confounded by the world as it is, instead of polishing the image of what it ought to be.[2]

If, for example, we can agree that some sort of access to solar energy ought to be guaranteed, we must face the fact that, as the law is, property owners in the United States have no right to receive solar energy across another's land. They are guaranteed what comes vertically down on them, but this does not always answer their needs for solar collectors; not to mention trees, plants, people, and buildings themselves which can, like Acoma, act directly as energy converters for environmental control.

If solar access is to be guaranteed, the legal questions raised earlier (who will apportion and on what principle) may require a clarification or change of existing laws, or even new laws. This raises an interesting question of legal precedents.

Laws protecting rights are generally the result of collected experience. Hastily drawn laws can, in some instances, be unfair and may defy proper administration. Since there is no solar law in the United States, legal experts have sought helpful precedents both here and abroad. The most commonly cited law outside of the United States is the English doctrine of "ancient lights."

William Thomas of the American Bar Foundation has written extensively about this doctrine.[3] It provides that if a land owner has received light from across his neighbor's land for a certain time, he has a right to continue enjoying it. The length of time necessary to establish this right in England is now 27 years. Thomas and others point out some difficulties with applying this law to protect solar users in the United States.

First, the law only deals with the luminous, not the thermal component of solar energy. Second, the right is not to all the available light, but only to a reasonable amount, generally enough to read a book in the middle of the room. Third, the prescriptive period is far too long to offer any protection to the purchaser presently thinking of converting his house to solar heating.

In spite of these drawbacks, Thomas points out that the chief reason for securing a right to light several centuries ago was the

2. Herbert A. Simon: *Sciences of the Artificial*, The MIT Press, Cambridge, MA, 1969. (I have particularized on the general distinction Simon makes between science, that deals with the world as it is, and design, that deals with the world as it ought to be.)

3. William Thomas: "Access to Sunlight," *Solar Radiation Considerations in Building Planning and Design*, Proceedings of a Working Conference, National Academy of Sciences, Washington, DC, 1976, pp. 14–18.

lack of interior lighting. In the face of energy shortages, this concern for natural light is returning, and with it has come an interest in solar energy as a heat source. If energy shortages persist, we may return to the doctrine of ancient lights out of necessity.

Other legal experts, pointing to the fact that this doctrine has been repeatedly disavowed in the United States, prefer to consider alternative laws in their search for precedents. Oil and gas law, for example, has been considered because both oil and gas possess certain physical characteristics analogous to sunlight. Each must be captured by mechanical means in order to develop its energy potential, but the fundamental difference in available quantities in each resource creates distinctions which seem to make oil and gas law an inappropriate precedent. Oil and gas are nonrenewable resources, while energy from the sun can, for all practical purposes, be considered completely renewable.

A more useful precedent in the United States, discussed here more to define the architectural problems than to outline legal solutions, is water law. Mary D. White, writing in the *Colorado Law Review* suggests that, like sunlight, water is used rather than captured and sold.[4] Both may be consumed, but both are renewable. In addition, and I would stress here, of particular interest to the architect, there is an equivalence between upstream and downstream in water law and the geometry of solar shadowing. To clarify this last point, it is useful to consider in more detail, the two basic approaches states use to water laws; first, the *prior appropriation* doctrine used in the arid West, then the *riparian doctrine,* derived from English common law, and used in humid states with ample supplies of water.

The doctrine of prior appropriation is a formalization of the general practice among early western settlers of apportioning available water according to who first put it to beneficial use. The doctrine can be more simply put: "He who gets there first gets the most." It was the frontier's answer to the exigencies of pioneer settlement. A rough example of how the law worked can be described as follows: Settler A establishes his residence along a river and puts the water to beneficial use by diverting some of it for irrigation (*Figure 4a*). Subsequently, Settler B takes up residence downstream, while Settler C locates upstream from A. Under the prior appropriation doctrine, both B and C, who presumably settle with foreknowledge of A's prior claims to the river, do so acknowledging those claims and agreeing to endure, without protest, A's continued use of the river. On the other hand, A has some responsibilities in the matter and cannot significantly change the conditions accepted by B and C when they first settled. There the matter lies, unless, through some prior agreement among the three, or through subsequent court action taken by one of the parties, a change in the balance of use may result.

The second water law discussed by Mary White is the riparian

4. Mary R. White: "The Allocation of Sunlight: Solar Rights and the Prior Appropriation Doctrine," *Colorado Law Review,* vol. 47, pp. 421–427 (1976).

Fig. 4   Water law. The examples are of two different kinds of water law used in the United States.

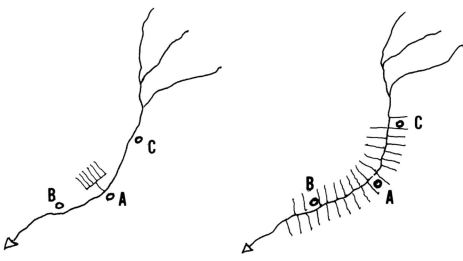

Fig. 4a Prior-appropriation doctrine is used in the arid states. If A first puts the river to beneficial use by diverting it for irrigation, B downstream and C upstream must agree to endure his continued use of the river water without protest.

Fig. 4b   Riparian doctrine used in the humid states gives A, B, and C equal access to river water independent of their location or time of ownership.

doctrine. In humid states with a lot of water, the first settlers brought with them the law of England where the abundance of water made the right-of-use seem to belong appropriately to ownership of land along a stream. Again the doctrine can be simply put: "Everybody has an equal share." Each riparian owner had a right to use the plentiful water that flowed past his property. It made no difference where or when A, B, and C acquired ownership along the river (*Figure 4b*). Of course, an emphasis on "plentiful" must be understood. This doctrine makes little sense where a resource is scarce or modified by pollution from prior usage.

In comparing these two doctrines for application to solar allocation, Mary White makes these additional legal points. First, under conditions where the flow of water is cyclic and generally scarce, there is bound to be more litigation, so that laws have tended to be more developed in prior-appropriation states. The result is a more consistent pattern of law than in the riparian states, and consequently a more useful precedent for application to solar access. Second, in riparian states there is presently a trend toward the adoption of some sort of permit system that would replace the riparian doctrine. This fact would suggest serious legal difficulties in pressing the analogy for solar allocation. While both of these legal points would seem to favor the prior appropriation doctrine as a precedent for solar allocation, I would like to point out a somewhat different conclusion we are testing as a working hypothesis at USC.

Neither prior appropriation nor riparian doctrines are likely to be applied to solar allocation in any pure terms. However, each may have an approximate, but different, analogy. Consider first an analogy of solar law in terms of prior appropriation (*Figure 5a*). Developer A sites a building that casts shadows to the north. Some time later, Developer B locates his building to the north (downstream). Developer B, like Settler B in our frontier example, must contend in some way with a prior appropriation of a resource. Under present law, B would have no right to receive solar energy that crossed A's air space. His only right would have been to sunlight falling perpendicularly onto his land. If the doctrine of prior appropriation were applied, this condition would not change. Consequently, if direct access to solar energy on building surfaces is an essential condition for development, if solar energy is the building's *raison d'etre*, the envelope of buildable volume meeting that condition may have a top and no bottom. On the other hand, A cannot change B's condition in the future by building higher.

To continue the analogy, there is a somewhat different situation to the south (upstream). If A's prior appropriation of the sun is guaranteed by law, Developer C who comes along later would have to accept the limitations of a building envelope with a bottom and no top.

Fig. 5.   Solar analogy to water law.

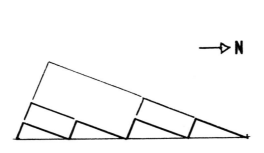

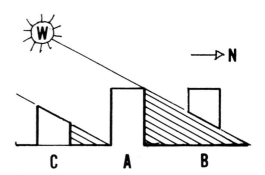

Fig. 5a Prior-appropriation doctrine is applied here where Developer A has previously sited a building. This existing building then limits what B can do to the north (downstream) and C can do to the south (upstream). Developer B has a potentially developable envelope with solar exposure only on the top; because C cannot shade A, his envelope only has a bottom. (This case assumes a constant height restriction for all three parcels.)

Fig. 5b Where riparian doctrine is applied, the result would generally be a pyramidal envelope of developable volume that derives its specific size and shape from the size, shape, slope, and orientation of the property. Small, repetitive lots would produce many small pyramids. Successively larger land assemblages would produce larger envelopes to accomodate an array of community needs.

Obviously this is a limited example and does not consider what goes on in the world beyond the sites of A, B, and C. What is made clear is that existing buildings impact on the surroundings in a way somewhat analogous to the settlement along a river, covered by the doctrine of prior appropriation. If that doctrine were to be applied, it would probably find greatest use where there is existing settlement and where the exigencies of shadowing from existing buildings must somehow be responded to favorably by reducing uncertainty in an obviously complex situation. People need to know where they stand. They may have to settle for less than total exposure to sunlight, but where buildings exist, there may be no choice.

The concept of "first come, first served" permeates many areas of our law. Where it seems too unfair, one possible remedy, for which there may be no analogies in water law, is energy sharing. For example, if Developer A is in a position to make the first beneficial use of the sun, and in so doing denies B and C, he may reasonably be expected to provide energy to B and C by virtue of his superior capacity. They, in turn, would be expected to pay a fair price to A.

While the resource is different, this concept suggests itself in such cases as the Sears Tower in Chicago. The courts held that the tallest building in the world could be erected even though it would block the reception of thousands of television sets. How much better if the biggest member of the community had collected and redistributed the signal to its neighbors. Of course this sharing principle has limits based on the supplier's ultimate capacity, and also on the increasing susceptibility of a more centralized supply system.[5] The principle appears sound, however, and is being further pursued in our studies.

I have suggested an apparent suitability of prior appropriation where uncertain circumstances accompany existing development. I would take another step now, and suggest that there may be some benefits from applying riparian doctrine to new development, if not in actuality, then in spirit. Under circumstances of raw land settlement or where rather large segments of existing cities have been cleared for construction, the complexities described earlier do not exist. Shadowing can either be avoided altogether or can be controlled by the designer.

Under such raw land conditions, the spirit of riparian doctrine could be developed in a three-dimensional approach to zoning that does not now exist. Each land parcel could be guaranteed equal access under the law. The mechanism for this guarantee would be a *solar envelope* of developable volume that would derive its size and shape from both spatial and temporal constraints (*Figure 5b*).

Under such circumstances of equal access, if larger buildings were required to fulfill community needs, larger land parcels would have to be developed through some process of land

5. Ralph L. Knowles: *Energy and Form: An Ecological Approach to Urban Growth*, The MIT Press, Cambridge, MA, 1974. (I have treated the subject of centralized energy supply in Chapter 8 from the viewpoint of sequence or phasing and the need for variety and equitability in community development. A subject for further study is the susceptibility of centralized power supply. The legal problems of solar allocation are so difficult that an easy answer is to supply energy from a central source, including a central solar source, thereby causing minimal impact on existing buildings. The danger of this approach lies in the susceptible nature of any highly centralized, and therefore specialized, system.

assemblage. Since all relationships in such a geometric progression are proportional, each larger building would require an appropriately larger assemblage of land (*Figure 6*). Where the uncertainties of existing development don't interfere, and where new buildings are being arranged in completely new combinations to form new communities, the riparian doctrine seems to hold some promise.

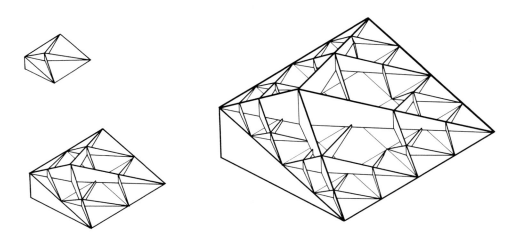

Fig. 6   Planned unit development. Planes represent the upper limit of pyramids of developable volume that respects the solar access of surrounding hillside property sloping to the east. As land parcels are assembled into progressively larger planned units, the potential for greater diversity as well as energy self-sufficiency increases. (From Ralph L. Knowles, *Energy and Form.*)

My point in describing these two analogies in some detail is that different kinds of users will probably require different kinds of laws to govern solar allocation. This discussion can be extended to describe other analogies we have made in our work at USC, under the separate headings of new and existing development.

While legal experts struggle with the troublesome problems of precedents for a new issue, architects around the country are seeking to explore the design implications of energy conservation as a new governing criterion. As a legal framework for these efforts, they seem to prefer building codes and zoning laws that determine how their projects will act rather than how they will look. For example, they would rather have a law that limits the amount of energy that can be converted per unit of constructed volume, than one that tries to achieve the same purpose of conserving energy by limiting the amount of glass on the west wall. While this preference to work within statements of performance over prescriptions of means is generally understandable, specific conditions may require different laws. This point may be illustrated by expanding on my earlier hypothesis covering first, existing, and second, new development.

The correlation between existing development and prior-appropriation doctrine may be expanded to include prescriptions of means for solar allocation that are locally administered. This would seem to be appropriate for three related reasons. First, the size of any project would very likely be small, often involving the renovation of a single building with small capital outlays and unsophisticated contractors who would not have the ability to satisfy a performance requirement with any great imagination. Under circumstances of small-scale and simple processes, there is a second fairly direct correlation with local administration of the law. The local building official, operating in a one-to-one relationship with the contractor, can more easily deal with the problems of solar allocation if the means are clearly prescribed.

New development, for which the correlation with riparian doctrine has already been described, presents a quite different set of circumstances that may allow for the application of performance laws that are more remotely administered. Such laws may be administered at the state or federal level, rather than the city or county level. They may describe the performance for a unit of planned development that could vary in its size and complexity up to quite large, interrelated groups of buildings, among which there are designed energy transactions.

Recently at USC, working under a grant from the National Endowment for the Arts to study the design implications of solar access, we have developed the computer capacity to generate solar envelopes based on general spatial and temporal constraints (*Figure 7*). The underlying premises for the envelopes are: (1) guaranteed solar access; and (2) the largest volume within time constraints. Up to now, most of our design work on this project has followed the geometry of the Jeffersonian grid (oriented on the cardinal points of the compass at 34°N). The period of useful reception has been taken from 7:00 am to 5:00 pm in the summer and from 9:00 am to 3:00 pm in the winter. The setting of these time constraints is a critical issue. As our work progresses, we expect the time constraints to change and become more sensitive indicators of land use and climate.

Our initial studies have parceled the land into 50-ft increments (the average detached single-family lot), and then multiplied that increment to make assemblages up to one city block in size. (Larger solar envelopes are not considered likely unless public rights-of-way are eliminated.) The envelope shape varies with assemblage and with block orientation (*Figure 8*).

The location and form of what is built within an envelope becomes, in some part, a function of society's perceived uses of the sun that have now been guaranteed by the envelope. The most important point is that the owner's options have been preserved; choices have not been pre-empted. The owner might opt for a sunny pool or some degree of energy sufficiency or might choose to transfer energy from buildings with large con-

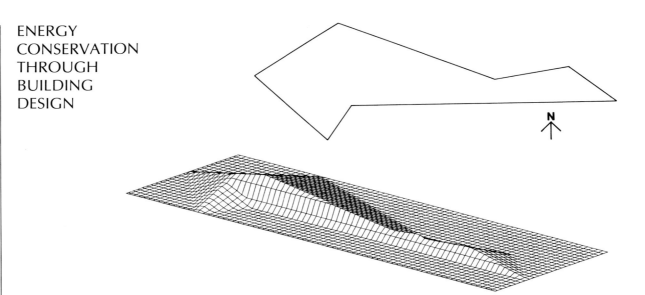

Fig. 7 Solar envelope for irregular site. Sun's view at 9:00 am winter solstice; plan orientation is with North up. Generated Fall 1977 at USC; solar envelopes can be economically generated at USC for any land parcel size and shape, slope, orientation, and latitude, and for any time constraints that are considered useful and desirable. (From Ralph Knowles, "The Design Implications of Solar Access," manuscript in preparation.)

version capacities to those with less, in order to satisfy over-all energy needs.

Regarding the useful conversion of solar energy, one dominant fact of orientation has already emerged from this work. The advantage of southern exposure with small land parcels in blocks that run long in the N-S direction, and with large land parcels in blocks that run in the E-W direction, is shown in Figure 8. In other words, the solar envelope provides a desirable south exposure for small land parcels in the first case, making land assemblage less advantageous for solar exposure than in the second case, where great advantage can be gained through assemblage. This puts a somewhat different view on the generally held notion that land assemblage is always a good thing because it increases developer options.

The inescapable extension of this three-dimensional approach to zoning for planned units of the community has implications beyond energy sufficiency. View, fresh air, sound levels, access to transportation, and other basic community services can all be thought of more usefully in three-dimensional terms. Certainly zoning aimed at optimizing life conditions, rather than prescribing land use, raises problems of policy, design, and development. But considering the state of most of our cities in combination with the general energy picture, perhaps we don't have too much to lose and quite a lot to gain.

Finally, I would like to return to my original policy and design

Block orientation E-W. *Block orientation N-S.*

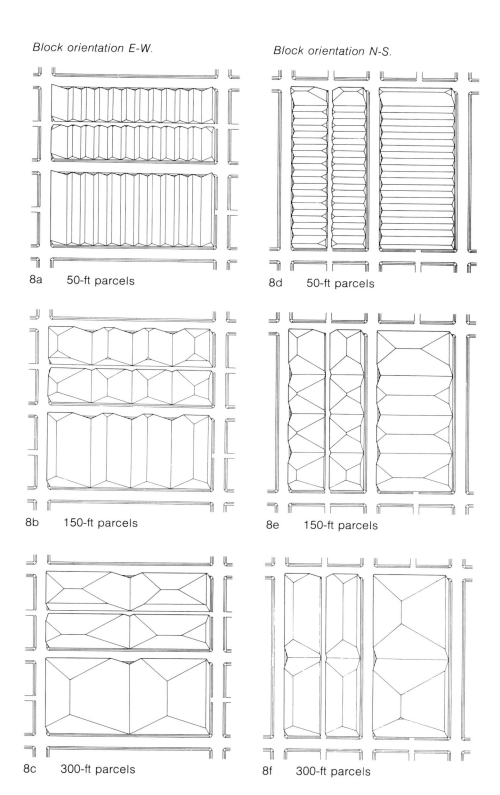

8a 50-ft parcels

8d 50-ft parcels

8b 150-ft parcels

8e 150-ft parcels

8c 300-ft parcels

8f 300-ft parcels

Fig. 8 Solar envelopes within the Jeffersonian grid. Blocks are shown in two orientations: long in the E-W direction (a, b, c); and long in the N-S direction (d, e, f). The blocks are shown with and without alleys; true north is up. Because the streets can be shadowed in these studies, solar envelopes on corners are larger than those inside the block, with some urban design implications. South orientation of the major volume varies with land assemblage and with block orientation. The South advantage occurs where the ridge of the solar envelope runs E-W. This condition occurs for large land parcels where the block runs E-W (8c), and for small parcels where the block runs N-S (8d).

issues. The legal questions—who will allocate solar energy and on what principle—seem to rest on the user. Existing development may require some sort of principle similar to the well-defined doctrine of prior appropriation, with prescribed applications closely monitored by local building officials. New development may allow application of the less well-defined, but theoretically more equitable riparian doctrine, where every planned development can have equal access to the sun.

In either case, solar access to a land parcel can be guaranteed by a simply prescribed envelope that, over time, can have applications even within the existing urban fabric. As cities age, changes of land use probably go hand-in-hand with land assemblage, thus providing greater options for solar design. Also, we can expect pressure for solar access to occur first in the realm of housing where "rights" are more keenly felt and defended.

The design questions, can location and form be effective adaptations to solar energy, would also seem to rest on the user. Existing development may be too locked in to allow much more than conservation measures already prescribed by such states as California, plus limited use of roof-top collectors where there is sufficient sun. However, over time, as transformational growth takes place in neighborhoods of decaying single-family houses and low-density commercial development, solar access can be introduced by straightforward zoning, thus making the application of design principles of location and form a real possibility. New development, in which community units may even be planned for energy self-sufficiency, can employ the design tools of location and form as adaptations, not only to solar energy, but to an array of other performance criteria that can make for a richer and healthier built environment.

13

ENERGY AND PATTERNS OF LAND USE

Philip Steadman

There has not been very much attention devoted to the energy implications of urban development on the larger scale. This is a very broad topic, and at this point it is possible only to review the issues in the most general way. Nonetheless, there are opportunities for energy economy in the pattern of urban development as significant as those achievable through the design of individual structures.

In this chapter, I will refer to theoretical work which has been carried out over the last 10 years on the use of land and the geometrical characteristics of different building layouts.[1] This work has not, up to now, been very much concerned with the question of energy. But there is no doubt that energy is a factor of increasing importance in locational matters and in its effects on land use.

Consider the well-known diagram from *Tomorrow: A Peaceful Path to Real Reform* by Ebenezer Howard, founder of the garden cities movement in England in 1898.[2] Howard's diagram, called "The Three Magnets," was intended to show the relative attractions and disadvantages of living in town and in the country (*Figure 1*). Bear in mind that magnets are capable of repulsion as well as attraction. For instance, under the town "magnet" are listed the various attractive forces bringing people into the city—

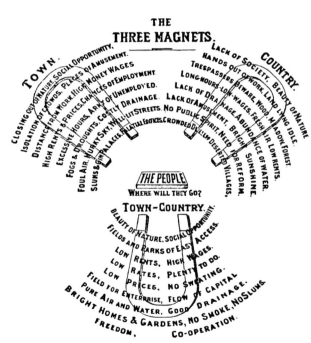

Fig. 1 Ebenezer Howard's diagram of The Three Magnets. (From Ebenezer Howard, *Tomorrow: A Peaceful Path to Real Reform*.)

1. Leslie Martin and Lionel March: *Urban Space and Structures,* Cambridge University Press, 1972.
2. Republished as *Garden Cities of Tomorrow,* Faber, London, 1945.

opportunities for employment and specialized services, entertainment, and social contact. There is also mention of the discomforts and problems of urban life—the loss of contact with nature, problems of pollution ("Fogs, droughts, foul air and murky sky") and the social ills of the city, its "slums and gin palaces." Despite

Fig. 2 "The Dream ×
2 Million." (Le Corbusier,
1937.)

the concentration and density of the city, Howard mentions the
"distance from work," which, he argues, is greater than that in
the countryside where agricultural laborers live in close proximity
to their work. On the disadvantages of country living, Howard
refers to the lack of opportunity for recreation and social life, and
the declining demand for agricultural labor, which in its turn, was
reflected in low salaries and in (the benefits of) low rents.

Howard's solution took the form of a proposed synthesis of
town and country, the garden city, in which the benefits of both
could be enjoyed while the ills of both were banished . . . "All
the advantages of the most energetic and active town life,"
combined with "all the beauty and delight of the country."

Howard's garden city scheme acknowledged forces of economic attraction which were already evident in the growth of the
suburban fringes of British cities, London in particular. With the
decline in agricultural employment and its substitution by industrial jobs, a large number of the working population had made
the move, during the nineteenth century, from country to city.
Most of the working-class population had been at first housed at
high densities within walking distance of their work. Meanwhile,
more mobile members of the wealthier classes had sought to
avoid the worsening unhealthiness and ugliness of the dense
central city by moving to the expanding suburbs, where they
could enjoy open space and access to the country—but pay for
it with longer hours spent traveling. As travel became easier and
cheaper with train travel and the motor car, the opportunity of
living in the suburbs became more available. Thus the 1920s and
1930s in Britain saw the very rapid growth of suburban housing
out along the main roads leading from the principal cities—so-
called "ribbon development"—just as earlier phases of urban
growth in the nineteenth century had followed the railway routes.
The same patterns of suburban growth were, of course, to be

ENERGY
CONSERVATION
THROUGH
BUILDING
DESIGN

found in most industrialized countries in this period, especially in the United States. There was considerable alarm in Britain at the way in which this uncontrolled development was spreading during the war years, consuming large amounts of agricultural land, having a destructive effect on the appearance of the countryside—and also alarm at the house building along the edges of what were intended to be high-speed arterial roads.

One of the principal intentions of immediate postwar planning legislation in Britain was to control the spread of suburban ribbon development by placing green belts around cities and channeling growth into either controlled expansion of existing small towns and villages, or into self-contained new towns, very much according to Howard's original garden city model.

The move to the suburbs did represent, in many ways, a striving for the same conditions which Howard had aimed at: the synthesis of town with country amenities. The disadvantages of the suburbs as they actually developed were twofold. First, it was largely residential development which was decentralized, while employment and many specialized activities remained in the central city. Thus the suburbs were culturally isolated and the suburbanites were involved in journeys of considerable length to work and services. Secondly, the particular pleasures of the countryside, which made urban fringes so attractive for housing in the first place, were lost as the suburbs themselves leap-frogged ever farther. The dilemma is expressed in a sketch, "The Dream × 2 Million," from Le Corbusier's *When the Cathedrals Were White,* in which he describes his reactions to American cities and suburbs (*Figure 2*).[3]

Howard's garden city idea, by limiting the size of the town, was intended both to preserve access to nature and the countryside, and to shorten distances traveled to services and workplaces. Howard's plan presupposed low densities (about 30 persons per acre, including all urban uses) but the over-all size of his town, with a population of only 30,000, was very small. (Of course, Howard's book predates the introduction of the automobile, and he is imagining travel in the garden city to be by streetcar, bus, walking, and cycling.) It may be questioned whether this was sufficiently large to support the range of employment, recreation, and social opportunities which might make it a satisfactory self-contained entity; or conversely, whether, if it were to be expanded in size but kept at the same low density, it would not then lose the very qualities of compactness and access to open country which were the basis of its original rationale. Howard's answer to this possible objection was that several of his towns might be grouped together in a "city federation," housing between 200,000 and 250,000 people, all linked together by rapid transport routes, which in his terms meant railways.

To leave the subjects of Howard, garden cities, and the development of suburbia until later, consider now the question

3. Charles Édouard Jean-neret-Gris (Le Corbusier): *Quand les Cathédrales Étaient Blanches,* Plon, Paris, 1937.

of energy consumption in contemporary cities and the factors by which it might be affected. Taking energy consumption by total end-uses in the United States, we find that roughly one-quarter is used in transport, and that this is very largely—almost wholly—accounted for by fuel, i.e., petroleum. Residential uses account for 19%, and commercial uses for another 14% or 15%. The commercial uses are principally connected with the servicing of commercial buildings; and so we can say that at least one-third of national energy consumption in the United States is related to buildings. Of energy uses in buildings, space heating is the major item, amounting to 18% of the national energy consumption, followed by water heating and air conditioning as the next most significant users. Air conditioning is a major part of commercial energy consumption and has been growing rapidly in recent years.

In Britain, the figures are comparable, with the differences being that less energy is used for transport, presumably because of lower levels of income and car ownership, and possibly because of the relative compactness of the country in relation to its population. A higher proportion of the energy budget in Britain goes to space heating, especially in the residential sector, perhaps due to poor climate and to the fact that the houses are badly insulated and inefficiently heated.

In both countries, the uses of energy in industry account for the balance of around 40% of the total. We can assume that these uses in industry are not going to be very directly affected by patterns of urban development as such (although there are indirect connections). So we can concentrate here on questions of energy consumption in transport and in buildings.

Taking transport first, it frequently has been observed how inefficient the private car is in energy terms as a means of travel. There are a number of reasons: its poor load factor; the fact that every car must have its own small power unit and cannot achieve the efficiencies of the larger engines used in public transport vehicles; and the fact that it is designed for a great range of road conditions and runs on high-friction surfaces and steep gradients, by comparison with the shallow-gradient, shallow-curved, low-friction tracks of railways. The combination of all these factors results in the extraordinary fact that of the chemical energy in the fuel, only some 5% is converted ultimately into energy for the car's kinetic motion.

Much effort is going into the study of technical developments which might increase the efficiency of vehicle propulsion units in themselves. But much more significant in energy conservation terms would be policies, particularly at the level of urban planning, which would reduce the total amount of traveling going on and which would encourage modes of public transport, or better still, bicycling and walking. Besides passenger trips, there would also be energy conservation benefits in the transfer of freight traffic from trucks to more efficient modes, such as trains, or, for some commodities, to pipelines or waterways.

One of the main reasons it is difficult to transfer private passenger transport to public transport is the extraordinary convenience and flexibility of car travel—door-to-door at any time of the day or night. The failure of public transport systems to retain their passengers can be attributed to their inability to compete with this convenience. It is especially difficult for public transport to operate successfully in low-density or suburban districts, where the traveling population is spread out over large areas and where there are relatively few high-volume routes which justify large vehicles and frequent service.

Some authors have suggested that a greater over-all energy efficiency in transport might be achieved by the construction of very compact, high-density cities, in which distances between places of residence, work, and services would be shorter, and the traffic volumes would make high-frequency public transport a workable proposition. The shorter distances would, in themselves, encourage the substitution of car trips by cycling and walking.

We might take, as representative of this argument, the design for a "Compact City" proposed in the recent book of that title by two operations researchers, George Dantzig and Thomas Saaty.[4] Dantzig and Saaty's plans involve the construction of a multilevel city in the form of a shallow tapering cylinder, or frustum of a cone. It has eight separate levels or platforms which act as artificial "land" on which freestanding buildings may be constructed. For a city of 250,000 inhabitants, they propose a cylinder about 9,000 ft—nearly two miles—across, and, allowing 30 ft between the levels, the total height is 240 ft (*Figure 3*).

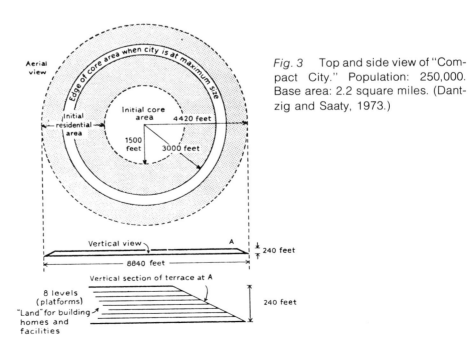

Fig. 3 Top and side view of "Compact City." Population: 250,000. Base area: 2.2 square miles. (Dantzig and Saaty, 1973.)

4. George Dantzig and Thomas Saaty: *Compact City: A Plan for a Livable Urban Environment,* Freeman, San Francisco, 1973.

If the density of development is measured in the normal way—in terms of the surface of artificial "ground" on a single level—then what Dantzig and Saaty are suggesting is a rather low average density. Over the residential areas of the city, the net density (excluding roads, etc.) is approximately seven houses to the acre. The compactness is gained by stacking the eight levels of floor surface vertically, rather than laying the equivalent total area out over an eight-times-greater area on the ground.

There is no doubt that average distances between any two points in the city are thus radically reduced. Vertical travel is provided by elevators, horizontal travel by electric cars or by frequent electric-driven vehicles running radially. The authors argue convincingly that many trips may now be made by bicycle or on foot; and since the city is entirely enclosed, there is no problem with rain or cold, which normally deters people from cycling or walking. Freight traffic, the distribution of goods, and the removal of garbage can be made more energy-efficient than in conventional cities, again because of the shorter distances and the opportunity for using conveyor belts or pneumatic tubes.

Although the city is entirely enclosed, has its own artificial climate, and can have no plants or vegetable life in its interior, its designers argue that the compactness of the design makes it possible for inhabitants to reach the outside quickly and easily. Either they may go up to the roof level which, it is proposed, should be treated as an artificial land surface with planting and parks; or they may travel out to the surrounding countryside. It is one of the arguments in favor of their plan. Dantzig and Saaty say that the construction of cities in this way allows the preservation of natural landscape and reduces the areas of land that would otherwise be consumed in urban sprawl in conventional developments.

Without becoming involved in any of the very important psychological, sociological, aesthetic, or political implications of this kind of proposal, let us simply concentrate on its consequences for energy use. Dantzig and Saaty claim that their design would result in a net over-all energy saving of 15% over present conventional cities, achieved almost entirely through savings in transport of passengers and goods. Set against this, as Dantzig and Saaty themselves allow, there is likely to be a considerable *increase* in energy consumption because of the fact that the whole space of the city is entirely enclosed. It must be lit artificially throughout 24 hours and completely air conditioned. This is not just a question of air conditioning what in conventional cities would be the interior spaces of buildings, but the entire volume of space around buildings, above roads, and so on. The total volume to be air conditioned in "Compact City" can be estimated to be roughly one-third of a cubic mile.

On the face of it, I am thus extremely skeptical that these energy savings are real ones, or that all factors have been taken into

ENERGY CONSERVATION THROUGH BUILDING DESIGN

account. It has been argued by some, notably Buckminster Fuller, that since the principal use of energy in buildings is for space heating, any measure which would reduce the surface area of buildings in relation to their volume would reduce the use of energy. In particular, of course, Fuller has argued this as a virtue of geodesic domes; his proposal to put a one-mile-diameter dome over Manhattan is conceived partly in terms of thus reducing heat losses from the city.

But, depending on the climate and the absolute size of the structure involved, there comes a point with very large structures when the main problem is quite the opposite: how to prevent waste heat from accumulating and the internal temperature rising undesirably high. Already, in very dense concentrations of conventional urban development, this is a problem. In Greater London, for example, the man-made heat output is nearly one-fifth of the solar heat input, and the center of London, as a result, is between 3°C and 7°C warmer than its surroundings. Even in the low densities of the 4,000 square miles covered by Los Angeles and surrounding cities, the ratio of man-made heat output to solar input is around 5% and rising fast. In Dantzig and Saaty's "Compact City" or under Fuller's Manhattan dome, the problem of excessive heat buildup would be extremely serious, and the cooling load in a temperate region—as distinct from the use of such forms for cities in the Artic or in Siberia—could be enormous. One could suppose that compact cities would have to be sited on the seacoast—like nuclear power stations in Britain—to have access to sufficient cooling water for their needs.

There are other observations to be made about the "compact city" type of proposal and its use of energy. I use Dantzig and Saaty's scheme here simply as representative of a whole group of similar proposals, the virtue of their plan for discussion purposes being that they are highly specific about details of their design and the sizes and mechanisms of its various features. There is a lot in common, for example, with a number of Soleri's "Arcology" cities whose designs are motivated by a similar concern to utilize the vertical dimension and to conserve virgin land.

There are also very striking, almost uncanny similarities, incidentally, between "Compact City" and the Goodman brothers' scheme for a "City of Efficient Consumption," presented half sardonically in their book, *Communitas.*[5] The Goodmans were talking about consumption of goods, not energy, and their city is offered jokingly as a kind of ultimate embodiment of the ideals of the consumer society. But, it carries the suggestion that economy in the production, distribution, and consumption of goods would require efficiency in transport both of people and of the goods—hence the multilevel, high-density city form and a consequent efficiency in energy use in transport. Like Dantzig and Saaty's scheme, the "City of Efficient Consumption" is an air-conditioned cylinder on many floors. Passengers are moved about in public

5. Paul Goodman and Percival Goodman: *Communitas: Means of Livelihood and Ways of Life,* University of Chicago Press, Chicago, 1947.

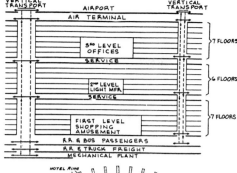

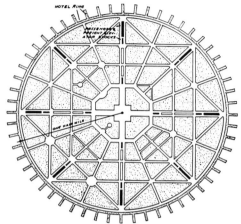

Fig. 4 "The City of Efficient Consumption" (Goodman and Goodman, 1947).

vehicles and elevators, and goods by pneumatic tubes, in the same way. Surrounding the city is open country, as the Goodmans say, "for full flight."

In all cases, the implications of these very dense multilevel city schemes must be that, in order to minimize air pollution, the principal power source is electricity, including the energy supply for space heating and cooling. Dantzig and Saaty are quite explicit about this, and about the further implication that, in all probability, electric power means nuclear-generated electricity. Furthermore, the opportunities for using ambient energy sources, such as solar heat, for meeting domestic needs directly on a small scale are negligible in such schemes as "Compact City."

There is also the question of the considerable energy input into the infrastructure—into actually building the artificial "ground" surfaces—of such a multilevel city, which Dantzig and Saaty do not allow for. And there are other questions that I shall come back to shortly: of inter-city transport and the tranport of foodstuffs into the city, the implication being that the city is supported by a system of industrialized agriculture employing rather few workers situated some distance away; and the removal of urban garbage and the transport of sewage somehow out of the city again for treatment and disposal.

In the light of these arguments, we might seem to be faced with an insoluble dilemma. In order to make economies in energy use in transport, and to encourage a transfer from private to public transport, it would seem necessary to increase residential and central urban densities to very high levels. But these increases in density would appear to carry the penalties of increased energy consumption within buildings, probably the necessity for widespread use of electrical power, and certainly very limited opportunities for the use of direct solar and other ambient energy sources. On the other hand, if we go for dispersed, low-density development, then it will be possible to make effective energy conservation measures in the design of buildings and to make use, particularly, of direct solar energy. But this in turn seems to imply a very inefficient use of land and of energy in transport.

In the long-range future, one could predict the decline of the large central city altogether, combined with a return to a much more dispersed pattern of small, self-contained settlements, a return to the decentralized employment of large sections of the population in agriculture and the local supply of goods and services—a return, in effect, to the seventeenth or eighteenth centuries—in which these energy difficulties would largely disappear (to be replaced by other problems). But that is a distant and perhaps completely utopian prospect and presupposes enormous changes in the structure of society. In the short term, we must face problems of the existing investment in centralized cities, in centralized manufacturing industries and services, and see how future patterns of development might move, or be directed progressively and gradually away from present energy-wasteful conditions.

In this connection, I am skeptical of some claims made by proponents of energy-autonomous or self-sufficient houses, particularly in relation to these broader planning considerations. The argument has been made, specifically, that because such houses are independent of utilities servicing, it is possible to use rural sites, small plots of presently unserviced and marginal land, and the increased capital cost of making the house self-sufficient in energy terms can be compensated for by the opportunity to buy these marginal sites rather cheaply.

My criticism of this argument is that the fact that such sites have no utilities services supplied is only one out of several reasons why the price of this land is low, and probably not the most important. Other more significant factors are that, at present, there are no legal sanctions for the use of this land for housing, and if such permissions were given, its price would increase very appreciably. Furthermore, these marginal areas have very poor access to job opportunities, to places of employment, to shops, schools, and services. This is why their value is low. The corollary is, of course, that if houses are to be sited in these locations, their occupants would have to be involved in considerable travel back and forth to work and on other journeys; and this will almost certainly mean the use of private transport and its inefficient consumption of fossil fuels. Better opportunities exist for conservation and the use of ambient energy sources at the intermediate scale of groups of dwellings, or the neighborhood, than where every house is equipped with its own self-contained stand-alone system.

I have presented, so far, a rather simplified caricature of the contrast between the highly centralized type of "compact city," where efficiencies in transport are paid for by inefficiencies and drawbacks in other respects, and the highly dispersed, decentralized suburban development, which may be suitable for some economies in energy use in buildings, but is energy-inefficient in transport terms. To some extent, this apparent opposition may be resolved by being more precise about the concept of density; the remainder of this article will be devoted to a third possibility for urban form, which is based upon work mentioned earlier, done by my colleague Lionel March, on land use patterns that, from the standpoint of energy, reveal some rather interesting properties. What follows is not presented as a finished *design* in any sense, but rather as an exploration of theoretical geometrical principles according to which urban form might be investigated.

In a paper entitled "Homes Beyond the Fringe," published in 1968, March contrasted two opposite ways of thinking about the *pattern* of urban land use, which he characterized as "think-blob" and "think-line."[6] The point that he wished to emphasize is that, besides thinking about density—the usual quantitative term adopted by planners to describe land use, and in many ways, a rather crude sort of measure—it is very important to consider the geometric pattern or spatial disposition of land use. Development at precisely the same density can be laid out in many kinds of patterns geometrically, and these patterns can have very different functional properties.

In order to illustrate the different geometrical characteristics of certain types of forms, March introduced a simple diagram (*Figure 7*) that shows a principle named after the French physicist Fresnel—used in the construction of certain optical lenses—and which is hence known as the Fresnel square or squares. The geometrical property of this diagram is that every successive ring has the same area as the central square. March applies the principle of the Fresnel diagram to the way in which—very theoretically—urban land use might be arranged in different spatial patterns.

He supposes, for instance, that 10% of the area of land within some given district or region is covered by urban development (10% is in fact just about the proportion of land in England and Wales presently covered by all urban uses, including urban parks). Conceptually, one might imagine that this 10% could be arranged in one large single city (*Figure 8a*), in a moderate number of medium-sized towns (16 in *Figure 8b*), or in a great number of very small concentrations, perhaps villages (256 in *Figure 8c*). The *density* measured over-all is exactly the same in all cases, but clearly the consequences for the functional organization and

6. Lionel March: "Homes Beyond the Fringe," *RIBA Journal,* August 1967 (hereafter cited as *Homes*).

Fig. 5   Street Scene in "The City of Efficient Consumption" (Goodman and Goodman, 1947).

Fig. 6   The Core Exchange in "Compact City" (Dantzig and Saaty, 1973).

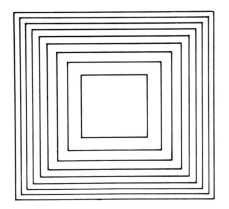

Fig. 7   Fresnel squares. Each successive ring has the same area as the central square. (L. March, 1972.)

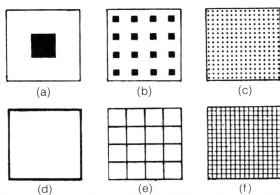

Fig. 8   Theoretical patterns of land use. In every case, 10% of the total area is covered. See text for explanation. (L. March, 1967.)

visual character of each are very different. March refers to these types of nucleated arrangements as "think-blobs"; and depending on the *scale* considered, one may have a dispersed pattern of many blobs or a concentrated pattern of a few blobs.

Suppose now that we invert the whole way of looking at the pattern and think of the rural land, the agricultural uses, as forming the blobs, with the urban land spread out in a linear or grid-like pattern surrounding these agricultural agglomerations. This is what March is talking about when he refers to a "think-line" urban pattern. Illustrated in the figure are three examples (*Figures 8d, e, f*) of, again, exactly the same 10% coverage: a concentrated linear pattern or coarse mesh and two progressively finer mesh patterns.

Remember that the property of the Fresnel diagram is that the very thin square ring around the extreme edge is of exactly the same area as the apparently quite large-sized square at the center. A similar principle applies to these patterns of land use. If we spread the 10% coverage represented by the single concentrated blob into the coarse mesh of the equivalent "think-line" pattern, it actually works out as an arrangement of rather thin, long, linear strips in grid formation. The important point, it should be reiterated, is that the areas of urban and agricultural land are precisely the same throughout all these examples. As March says," . . . these notions of concentrated or dispersed developments have no relationship to population density. It is as possible to have a high density dispersed pattern as a low density concentrated pattern."[7]

The square grid is used only for the purpose of illustration. Very similar geometrical principles would apply to hexagonal, triangular, or informal and irregularly shaped patterns; the important point, in general, being the relationship of the "blobs" to the linear grid and whether the "blobs" are constituted by urban development or by agricultural and other undeveloped land.

For instance, March illustrates (*Figure 9*) a "think-line" equivalent to Ebenezer Howard's city federation.[8] It is a kind of inverse or "anti-form" of Howard's plan. Exactly the same areas of land are covered by the different uses in both cases. The average distance from any point within the urban area of the "think-line" pattern to open countryside is clearly very small. Nevertheless, the accessibility to social activities which are evenly distributed with the population, such as schools or jobs, can be high—higher in fact, as March demonstrates, than in the "think-blob" equivalent. If the "think-line" pattern of urban land is supplemented by a grid of rural main roads, as illustrated in the diagram, then

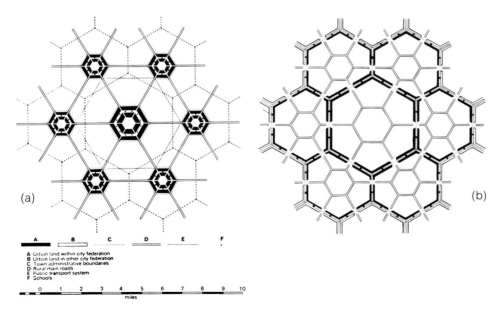

A Urban land within city federation
B Urban land in other city federation
C Town administrative boundaries
D Rural main roads
E Public transport system
F Schools

Fig. 9 (a) Ebenezer Howard's Cluster of Garden Cities; and (b) linear antiform of Howard's City Federation. (L. March, 1967.))

7. March, *Homes*, p. 334.
8. March, *Homes*, fig. 1b, p. 335.

it would be possible to travel through the system on cross-country routes which would pass through built-up areas only infrequently.

What then, are the implications of such a linear pattern of development in terms of the use of energy? Consider the difference between the same amount of urban land uses disposed in the single blob, and in the equal area linear grid, in terms of the problems of transport. The concentrated development will have to be crisscrossed by a fine mesh or web of small roads in order to give access to every point. On the other hand, the linear development can be served with a much shorter total length of higher-capacity road. This fact is capable of mathematical demonstration; indeed, it follows from the same Fresnel square principles which we have just been examining. Along this coarse grid of roads there can be a very high *linear* density of development—a great number of persons or houses per mile of road—and these are precisely the conditions under which public transport becomes an economical proposition.

The same kinds of observation which apply to passenger transport and accessibility are also true for the distribution of goods and for the supply of network services such as piped water or sewage. In a high-density linear grid, the same number of points can be served with a considerably reduced total length of service runs. In the case of piped services, the savings might be very dramatic; since if we assume an equivalent total *volume* of pipework, but in a much-reduced total length of greater diameter, the flow capacities will be disproportionately much greater. (So for equal flows the volume of pipework and the corresponding cost could be much reduced.) The doubling of the diameter of a pipe, for instance, increases its capacity roughly 32-fold.

It has been shown statistically that, in existing cities, the costs of centralized network services and the energy losses in transmission increase greatly with decreasing population densities. This is only to be expected. The whole point of "think-line" is that it is possible to maintain *high* densities along the linear routes, but as a part of an over-all pattern which is still, so to speak, full of holes.

Imagine a built-up section of this linear strip which is devoted to housing. March shows a plan for a development of two-story semi-detached houses with separate garages which, with a small flower bed at front and a field at the back, could still be built at residential densities of from 40 to 80 persons per acre. Every back garden looks out directly onto an enormous area of open country; and yet the houses are not remote from work and services because they front onto the transport routes, and the accessibility is related to a high linear density, not necessarily to a high over-all surface density. Such a form of housing can not only be built simply, but ideally lends itself to the exploitation of ambient energy sources, such as solar heating and natural ventilation. And the high linear density may also allow for communal sharing of services at an intermediate scale which, as was suggested earlier, might bring optimal energy efficiencies.

March says that housing on this kind of pattern might be accomodated "on field borders, in copses and woods . . . with little loss of productive agricultural land and with using the fertile central areas of fields."[9] Quite apart from the attractiveness of this vision, the gardens of the houses and the fringes of the agricultural land enclosed by the linear grid lend themselves to intensive horticulture and the production of vegetables in allotments. This direct proximity of residential population to food production could contribute to some reduction of the enormous energy consumption which now goes into preparing, packaging, and transporting foodstuffs. What is more, organic garbage and sewage might be locally processed and returned to the adjacent land, thus cutting out the expenditure of energy presently devoted to pumping or trucking these materials away from the city centers.

If we worry about the problems which arose in the ribbon development of the '30s—houses set directly alongside the edges of high-speed arterial roads with all the consequent disadvantages of noise pollution and danger—then we may imagine several kinds of design solutions by which those problems might be avoided without destroying the basic geometrical principles of the arrangement. The houses might be set back or placed along a short cul-de-sac within walking distance of the main route, but all still directly in contact with open country. There might be two or more parallel routes in the linear strip: one high-speed limited-access road with service roads for slow traffic and access to the houses. Or, perhaps best of all, as in March's inverted "think-line" version of the Howard city federation, there could be fast cross-country routes which would be quite independent of the strips of developed land and would run through open country, much in the style of the American parkway.

The crucial difference between the "think-line" pattern and the conventional suburb lies in the fact that a high density is maintained along a narrow strip, as distinct from a low density spread across a wide area. Thus, in "think-line," both adjacency to the countryside and accessibility to work and services—the two things which the suburbs wanted and lost—are still maintained.

As March points out, the strategy of "thinking line" rather than "thinking blob" involves taking a much more positive attitude towards agricultural land and the natural landscape. In this concept, the open space is conceived of as the important and integral entity, and urban uses occupy the remaining fringe land, rather than vice versa. Where we now attempt to restrain growth of our existing cities by putting green belts around them, in a "think-line" philosophy of planning we would instead conceive of setting "black belts" around the areas of green. What is more, the linear pattern allows the urban development to be of high

9. March, Homes, p. 337.

density, without bringing the usual penalties, and allows the agricultural and open land to be conserved.

I have dwelt on the energy implications of "think-line" or linear high-density networks of development, since that is the subject of specific interest here. Without embarking on a long discussion, I think it will be clear, nevertheless, that such a proposal for urban form also suggests possibilities for political devolution, democratic local planning policies, and a rather relaxed system of planning controls, by contrast with the totalitarian character of schemes such as "Compact City."

Finally, there is the most important question which any radical proposals about urban form must raise: "How do we get there from here?" Any kind of megastructure design which is not capable of functioning until large sections of it are complete poses fantastic difficulties of political, technical, and social coordination. Meanwhile, present directions of urban change suggest—at least in England—a rapid and accelerating process of decentralization from the cities.

The linear network is not a design so much as a *principle* or an image which could be applied in many situations—towards which continuing development might be channeled and directed gradually, rather in the way in which Ebenezer Howard's garden city image and principles have served to guide urban policies in many parts of the world over the 70 years since *A Peaceful Path to Real Reform* first appeared.

14

APPROPRIATE TECHNOLOGY

Eugene Eccli

This chapter summarizes the results of a study undertaken by the author for the National Science Foundation as reported in Integrative Design Associates: *Appropriate Technology in the United States—An Exploratory Study,* Superintendent of Documents, U.S. Government Printing Office, Washington, DC, 1977.

| ENERGY
CONSERVATION
THROUGH
BUILDING
DESIGN

Our society faces immense problems related to resource short-ages, the environment, and unemployment. The energy crisis alone has, in the last four years, brought with it the worst recession-inflation cycle the United States economy has seen in 40 years. With the increase in cost of imported oil and the growing pressures by the countries we depend on for importation of trace metals, these resource problems will continue and perhaps worsen.[1]

One immediate result of emerging energy and resource prob-lems has become apparent: deficit payments for oil create capital shortages in importing countries, causing high unemployment as well.

The effects of inflation and unemployment are felt most severely by low-income people. The number of poor people in the United States increased by over 10% between 1974 and 1976, so that one of eight Americans now lives within these confined circum-stances (defined as a family of four with a total yearly income of less than $5,000). Moreover, everyone feels the increase in costs for housing, utilities, food, and other essentials. Under these constrained circumstances, many citizens interested in doing something to help themselves have begun efforts to stabilize their level of income. This action-oriented trend is reinforced by increasing public sensitivity about environmental issues and the social impact of technology. Many individuals and small groups in the United States have begun to see opportunities for solving energy, resource, environmental, and income-stabilization prob-lems simultaneously. To that end, they have begun local exper-iments and new business ventures.

Appropriate technology offers a response to multiple problems inside and outside the United States. The term "appropriate technology" refers to efforts to develop innovative solutions scaled to local social and environmental requirements, a matching of resources to need, and maximum democratic participation in problem solving by the affected individuals and communities.

Two kinds of groups are currently involved in appropriate technology. The first—small appropriate-technology-oriented businesses—includes small design, research, and development firms, small farms, and small publishing ventures which distribute information about appropriate technology. The second involves self-help or community-oriented groups—in design and building, agriculture and food distribution, and medical help, as well as information exchange—which are somewhat more socially and environmentally oriented than the businesses. Nevertheless, both groups are working toward the same goals.

Several major conclusions become apparent from the experience of both small businesses and self-help groups in appropriate technology endeavors. Appropriate technology involves a process of establishing social and environmental goals, devising a goal-oriented process or product to meet such goals, and then at-

1. David L. Roper: *Where Have All the Metals Gone,* University Publications, Blacksburg, VA, 1976.

tempting to introduce and sustain a concerted development program in order to fulfill the original criteria. Examples include experiments with energy conservation; renewable energy sources at the household level and lower cost methods for construction and waste disposal; research and experiments in less energy-intensive and lower-cost methods of agriculture in both rural and urban areas; and experiments in the cooperative development of skills and community organizing efforts.

Major problems exist for individuals and groups thus involved in appropriate technology. Self-help groups often are constricted in their efforts, not only for obvious economic reasons, but also for lack of technical information and expertise. Opportunities to share experiences and learn new skills from others do not now exist because extension services, effective means of communication, and funds for demonstrations are largely absent. Small business groups also face serious problems. Although appropriate technology programs involving energy conservation, solar heating of domestic hot water, and organic agriculture are both competitive and are preferred by increasingly large segments of the public, innovative small business firms face complex and time-consuming regulatory problems. Venture capital is difficult to obtain, and the patent system ties up capital and sales for several years. Furthermore, existing economic factors, such as tax subsidies for use of conventional fuels, put small renewable-energy companies at a disadvantage in the marketplace.

The response by both the universities and federal agencies to problems of self-help and small business groups is inadequate. In the university system, both funds and an incentive structure that would encourage research and community outreach efforts are lacking in most instances. At the federal level, there is no policy directed to the needs of these constituencies, and a strict emphasis on "national needs" obscures local problems and reduces funds which could support local solutions, even though the effect of many such efforts would help solve critical national problems, such as the need for energy. In fact, there may be no other effective way to do so.

The continued absence of an over-all innovation policy in the area of appropriate technology has a detrimental impact on this otherwise promising national resource of grass-roots programs. On the other hand, federal programs and policies of research and development still have a unique opportunity to address these needs in the following ways: by exploring areas where obstacles inhibit local technology development and assessment; by creating research and development agendas in appropriate technology; by providing support for developments in priority areas; and by evolving an experimental program of incentives and matching funds that will stimulate inter-agency, state government, and university outreach programs.

A number of questions must be resolved in order to call

attention to appropriate technology developed by small, independent groups as an alternative within an economic environment now limited by large-scale institutional constraints. The most obvious question has to do with the need, in the first place, for appropriate technology. Are research and demonstration efforts of individuals and small groups able to solve critical problems important to an advanced industrial society? During the past century, the organization of scientific work has evolved into large institutional patterns in government and industrial laboratories. Participants have largely been drawn from the ranks of career professionals. Little attention has been given to the local innovator who may be trying to work through the self-help and small business avenues of research and technology utilization. However, both the early history of science and the success of the industrial revolution were based on the efforts of dispersed innovators. The practical aspects of the sixteenth- and seventeenth-century English industrialization movement, which first brought the benefits of scientific thinking to the general public, were introduced by self-help community organizers and small entrepreneurs. In the nineteenth and twentieth centuries, even to our own day, a large percentage of major industrial inventions have been developed by individuals or small research teams.[2]

Today, local innovators have an equally important role in nationwide attempts to adjust to an environmentally and resource-constrained economy. However, questions remain. Given our past experience with efforts to accelerate innovation and to properly utilize technology for social needs, what policies and institutional responses would best enhance the appropriate technology efforts in the United States and elsewhere? What economic policies and current trends in technology development either positively or negatively affect developments in appropriate technology?

To investigate these questions, a survey concerned with activities, goals, obstacles, and possible government involvement was sent to 649 individuals and groups active in local efforts in appropriate technology. Of this group, 45% (294) responded. These are individuals and groups who are experimenting with skills and innovations which could address environmental and resource issues by attempting to solve food, housing, energy, and income-stabilization problems on a household or community level. Their experiments with energy conservation, solar and wind energy sources, recycling, and food production all reflect an attempt to use skills and opportunities that already exist within the reach of an increasingly large group of people, either through self-help or small business technology, who otherwise would not be able to afford, or to learn about, such ways to improve their situation[3] (*Figures 1–5*).

If one might characterize the responses, a goal of "more for less" is often stated and, in this context, means a commitment to

2. John Jewkes, *et al.*: *The Sources of Invention*, W. W. Norton, New York, 1969.
3. Eugene Eccli, ed.: *Low-Cost Energy Efficient Shelter for the Owner and the Builder*, Rodale Press, Emmaus, PA, 1976.

doing as little damage as possible to one's surroundings by living as *efficiently* as possible. Because of this, one wastes fewer resources. Were one to live more efficiently, the quality of life and the possibilities for an equitable distribution of goods and services would improve relative to what they would otherwise be. Hence, "conservation" is taken to be the modern paradigm of "productivity," or other canons of industrialization. Another environmental theme emerges from the approach that respondents generally take to the design process. The goals of creating an "integrated" and "self-renewing life support" system in the home, in the local community, or in agricultural and over-all land use is a dominant thrust of these efforts. This attitude goes beyond the commitment of avoiding waste, wherever possible, to personally embracing environmental and social "affirmative action" by attempting solutions that meet basic needs in the simplest manner possible.

Just as we formerly made technical evaluations based on profitability and efficiency and have begun, in the last 10 years, to consider environmental impacts, now the *social* impact of new technologies has begun to enter our assessments. As with environmental issues, some of the respondents want to go beyond avoiding past excesses to fostering certain values, especially cooperation and democratic participation. Thus, appropriate technology is seen by the key actors as an attempt to integrate social and technical processes of innovation, to marry traditional concerns of technology development with concerns for community, economy, cultural style, and environment. Questions about the way technology is used and the cultural ends it serves become as important as questions of technical feasibility. In this sense, we are witnessing the process of how our society enlarges upon the criteria it uses to assess technology, as well as to create its own self-image.

Using local opportunities then, respondents have tried to create small experiments that reflect integrated systems of economy, environment, and culture. An example is the use of anaerobic waste-treatment techniques that require little capital in comparison to conventional tertiary treatment systems, to produce fertilizer and methane gas (methane is the active component in natural gas). Current experiments include waste disposal methods used in greenhouses to recycle animal and agricultural wastes; the greenhouse acts to heat the methane digestor, the resultant fertilizer is applied to grow food, and the multipurpose methane fuel can be used in household and farming applications.

In the world of science, the concept of "second law" (of thermodynamics) efficiency opens up a new avenue of creative thinking once an energy system is seen, not purely in terms of input and output, but in terms of how each component can be integrated with others to produce the most desirable result with the least expenditure of resources.[4]

4. K. W. Ford, *et al.*: *Technical Aspects of the More Efficient Use of Energy*, American Institute of Physics, New York, 1975.

This sense of utility derived from a systemic approach to organization is also reflected in what our respondents express about their social goals. The emphasis by some respondents on shared ownership and self-management represent a trend that has affected many sectors of society. The value given to the quality of work or services by most of our respondents, and to cooperation with others by many of them, points to a definite social goal—the enhancement of participatory democracy. Their phrase "less is more" emphasizes a situation in which the material output of the system is stabilized or reduced in order to create conditions (a healthy relation with the environment and the time to foster democratic processes) in which social dynamics and human potential can be fully explored.

Problems for the Innovator

Experience in Small Business   Many of the respondents were men and women involved in small business. Given what, in a real sense, is an obstacle course presented by barriers to appropriate technology approaches, why have so many local innovators gone ahead to develop new techniques, products, and services? Part of the answer lies with the drive of the innovator/entrepreneur and the support structure which small business seems to offer in our society. However, there is a larger story here because this group of respondents has not only business, but also environmental and social, goals in mind. The survey respondents involved in business ventures were as concerned with the larger issues as they were with purely financial success. Why has this group chosen perhaps the most difficult path possible? Given the educational level, business and other professional experience, enthusiasm and drive of many of these people, why do they bother?

The answer appears to be that they are highly committed to what they are doing; equally important, their own enthusiasm has been echoed by a range of constituencies: environmentalists, those concerned with the social impact of technology, and those anxious to find solutions to energy, resource, and employment problems. These goals express several themes related to the environment. In the agricultural area, the ecology of the soil, human health and nutrition, and the maintenance of productive land which can sustain its population are all fundamental concerns. The high cost of food and unemployment resulting from farm mechanization are issues which impact on the cities as well as on rural America.[5] An overriding goal of small farmers experimenting with appropriate technology is to bring recognition to agriculture as a process of integrating biological, ecological, economic, and social concerns. In the area of energy, anxieties about safety, health, security, and the availability and cost of fossil

5. Larry R. Whiting, ed.: *Communities Left Behind: Alternatives for Development,* Iowa State University Press, Ames, Iowa, 1974.

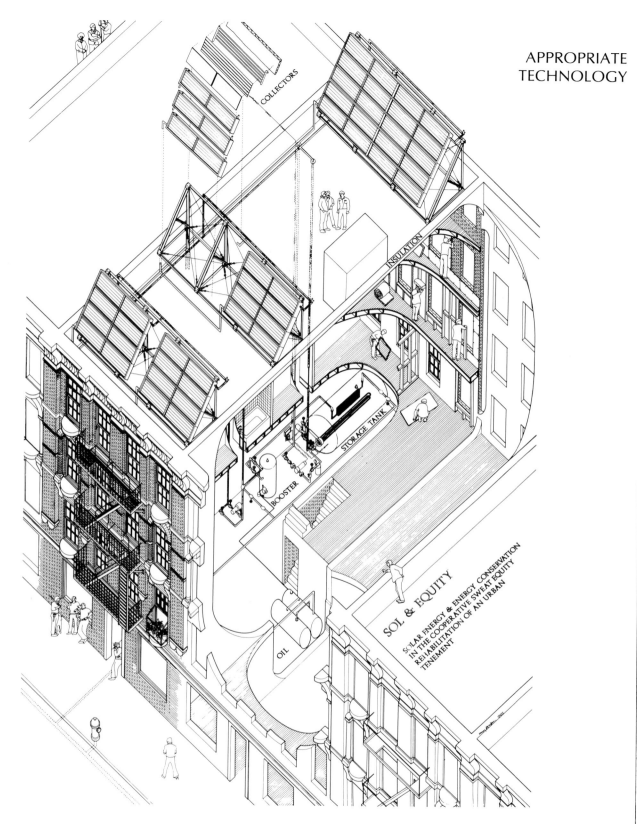

COLLECTORS

INSULATION

STORAGE TANK

BOOSTER

OIL

SOL & EQUITY

SOLAR ENERGY & ENERGY CONSERVATION
IN THE COOPERATIVE SWEAT EQUITY
REHABILITATION OF AN URBAN
TENEMENT

Fig. 1 Energy Task Force, New York City is a nonprofit organization of community-oriented appropriate technology consultants, including architects and engineers, who are currently providing design services for low-income groups related to energy conservation, solar and wind energy systems, and building rehabilitation. The drawing shows their first project on East 11 Street, New York, now completed on a sweat-equity construction basis by a tenant-formed association. (Drawing: Henry Dearborn)

Fig. 2 Insulating Shade Company, Guilford, CT. Tom Hopper is an architect and inventor of the High R® Insulating Shade, a roll-shade which can be used to insulate new or existing windows. After trying unsuccessfully to interest window-shade companies in his invention, Hopper is currently undertaking his own testing and market development program, aided by the U.S. Department of Energy, Office of Energy-Related Inventions. (Photo: Robert Perron)

Fig. 3 Self-Help Enterprises, Visalia, CA is a nonprofit corporation that provides technical and organizational assistance to self-help groups and has aided in the construction of over 1,000 homes. Under a grant from the U.S. Department of Housing and Urban Development, five homes are under construction using the Skytherm® roof-pond system of natural heating and cooling.

6. "Venture Capital for Small Firms," *Nation's Business,* November 1976.
7. Source: Mitchell Kobelinski, Administrator, Small Business Administration.

and nuclear power sources have stimulated interest in conservation and renewable energy sources.

Why do these innovators experience so much difficulty in creating new business ventures? First, a considerable amount of initial effort is required to establish any new business. Five years is a common length of time and, even under normal circumstances, only about one new business in 10 survives this long. Furthermore, the problem of obtaining capital for a new venture is currently a general one in our society. For small technology-related firms, the difficulty is even greater. These groups do not offer the investor enough of an added return to make them very attractive.[6]

Regulations are a serious problem for the innovator/entrepreneur. As with capital investment, this is related to the structure of our society today. In any new area of development in a complex society, many people and user groups are affected. Before consumers can accept an innovation, they must be certain that mechanisms work as they should. This places a great strain on the innovator, regardless of the level of sophistication of the person or group involved. For example, there are currently 256 different regulatory committees at the federal and state levels which have an effect on small business.[7] Further, with the public

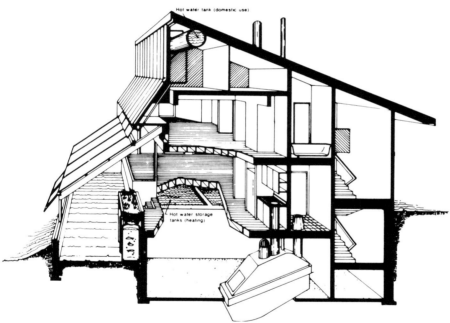

Fig. 4   New Alchemy Institute is a nonprofit organization headquartered on Cape Cod, MA, with an experimental agricultural substation, or "Ark," in Prince Edward Island, Canada (shown above). It combines aquaculture and other greenhouse gardening methods and solar and wind energy systems for a research and visitors facility. (Architects: Solsearch)

8. Earl Finkler and David Peterson: *Non-Growth Planning Strategies: The Developing Power of Towns and Regions,* Praeger Publishers, New York, 1974.

9. A sense of how the contractor/builder feels about increases in housing costs was given in talks by Robert Brennan, President of Columbia Homes, Chevy Chase, MD and by Robert DiAiso, Associate Partner, Dewberry, Nealson and Davis, Severna Park, MD at the National Building and Construction Exposition and Conference in Chicago, November 17–19, 1976. Mr. Brennan estimated that of the 50% rise in construction costs since 1972, fully 40% was due to time delays of two years or more (and hence increased interest on money borrowed) and legal overhead to stay abreast of regulations in the residential housing market. Mr. DiAiso stated that his company now spends an average of 30 months from proposal to ground-breaking in an effort to meet 250 regulations and codes enforced by 50 different federal, state, and local agencies. For information about code difficulties for the owner/builder, see Ken Kern, *et al.*: *The Owner-Builder and the Code: Politics of Building Your Home,* Owner-Builder Publications, Oakhurst, CA, 1976.

concerned about issues like "non-growth" planning policies on a local level, small business feels even more constrained and locked into rapid price escalations.[8] This is particularly true in vital areas like housing.[9]

For the business novice, these problems are very severe, as he or she must learn a host of business and legal skills simultaneously, and frequently with a minimum of investor support, precisely

Fig. 5   Farallones Institute, Occidental, CA is a nonprofit appropriate technology training and research group with major emphasis on household-scaled waste recycling, food processing, and energy conservation. Currently, a series of cabins (see photo) are being tested that compare passive solar heating alternatives under a grant from the State of California. (Peter Calthorpe, Project Director.)

because of inexperience and the "unknown quantity" of a new technology. There is as yet no mechanism designed to help resolve this conflict between the innovator and an increasingly demanding and quality-conscious consumer. While further regulation is seen by many groups as helpful to the public, it places an almost impossible strain on a small business which cannot dilute the impact of increased development costs through traditional business mechanisms, such as a nationwide distribution system. To this extent, society, in being protected from its former worst excesses, is being rigidified at the same time that it would benefit from experimental small-scale innovation.

Appropriate technology-related businesses have to face market problems even more severe than the already difficult capital squeeze and regulatory problems on other small businesses. The *crucial* point is that, for environmentally oriented small businesses, markets are slow to develop, and appropriate technology innovations are thus at a competitive disadvantage. To solve an environmental problem, the new technology must absorb the social costs that the preceding technology avoided, having evolved in a way that enabled it to pass these problems and costs on to society. This was accomplished, for example, by using once inexpensive and now scarce resources, or by conducting manufacturing in an inexpensive, but highly polluting, plant.

Many respondents have, nonetheless, moved into business and managed to survive because there is a growing number of areas which required new services that are just becoming cost-effective and/or attractive enough to the public: energy conservation, solar water heating, low-cost housing, and organic farming.

In general, market constrictions due to environmental and renewable resource factors force small businesses in appropriate technology to provide a diverse range of services simultaneously in order to survive; e.g. design, manufacturing, installation, and often educational services, such as seminars and publications. Furthermore, there is an overwhelming interest on the part of renewable-energy-related business respondents in tax incentives to foster the greater use of energy conservation measures (motivated by the recent development in economic theory of the concept of charging the "replacement cost" of a resource). This is entirely logical if the momentum of existing subsidies to conventional fossil fuels and the resistance to change by society is to be overcome.[10]

The Self-Help Challenge   The emergence of appropriate technology-related business leads to what can be considered the potential bridge between those who are more business-minded and those whose motivation stems from a desire to make a social contribution. Educational services have begun as a way to make a living for small business enterprises that are struggling with a new product for a still undeveloped market. This can be seen as the democratization of knowledge, nurturing the "do-it-yourself" aspect of what some see as the main theme of appropriate technology; namely, the growth of an individually and socially responsible program formed with the intention of solving human, rather than purely technical, problems. Low-income people are the first to feel the devastating consequences of the inflationary crisis. With an interest in self-help strategies, attempts are being made to link the needs of those with the least income with the sensibilities of those who want to create solutions to environmental and resource problems.

At first sight, the problem of providing energy for poor people via costly technology seems almost impossible to solve. However, the possibilities of cost reduction through "sweat equity" presents new options for assisting the poor to stabilize their incomes and meet their needs for energy, housing, and food. The experience of individuals and local groups with self-help methods at the household level could ultimately expand into community-wide cooperative efforts. This may require state and federal funds so that community-managed self-help clinics would be able to initiate such programs. Further, seed money will be necessary to encourage pilot projects which help communities to evolve a horizontally integrated economic system using low-capital technology. In the context of increasing expenditures for welfare, helping families and communities to launch themselves into at least partial self-sufficiency is obviously essential.

Interest in the self-help aspects of appropriate technology is not confined to low-income citizens. In housing, for example, a significant shift from new construction to owner-assisted renovation is occurring. Between 1970 and 1976, renovations moved

10. To give some idea of the magnitude of resistance to change by the public for energy-related matters, Dr. Robert C. Seamans reported that it took 60 years for our society to change from wood and coal energy systems to a substantial use of oil. However, he estimated that we will now have to make a transition to a largely non-oil–dependent energy economy within the next 30 years. Thus, the rate of change will have to accelerate substantially. Remarks by Dr. Robert Seamans, former Administrator, Energy Research and Development Administration, at the National Building and Construction Exposition, 1976.

from 35% of the total construction market to nearly 50% of the total. The projection for 1980 is that renovations will account for over 65% of the total.[11] As another example, high food costs, caused in part by resource shortages, are a major reason why so many have recently become involved in community gardening. Of all the new gardeners surveyed in 1974, 46% said that they began primarily to save money and help the family budget.[12]

Participation in self-help efforts thus has a pragmatic basis. It helps to stabilize income and to address the high initial cost of energy-conserving investments. However, while energy-saving and other environmental-quality-related technologies will become competitive as the price of conventional fuels increases, escalations in energy costs bring other economic problems, such as high unemployment, inflation, and a lack of capital for investment. Thus, the energy-conserving innovations have to be planned for well in advance as a society-wide policy, in conjunction with the self-help strategy. Reducing the initial cost will be of paramount importance in assisting many people to make these investments at precisely the time they otherwise can least afford them. Note that this points to the reason why past societies were slow to grow economically until sources of energy became available at low cost, and why developing countries are becoming interested in labor-intensive development strategies now that the "age of cheap energy" is drawing to a close.

Appropriate Technology in Relation to Policy Trends

Of what value are the efforts of appropriate technology innovators to an advanced industrial society as it grapples with the problems of an environmentally and resource-constrained economy? Will these problems bring with them living standard constraints as some now fear? What lessons, useful to ourselves and possibly to other countries, can be gained from the experiences of these innovators? To address these issues we must now consider current economic policy, and social and technological trends.

Current Economic Policy In response to high unemployment, a policy to increase the rate of industrial innovation is being developed. Attempts are underway to better understand the innovation process so that new enterprises and jobs can be initiated more easily. The Joint Economic Committee of Congress has begun to explore these issues.[13]

A current concern of corporate America, on the other hand, is to maintain the competitive edge currently enjoyed by United States export industries in the face of accelerating foreign competition. This has resulted in policy recommendations which seek to reduce costs by substituting mechanization and automation for human labor. Little attention, however, has been given to whether maintenance of the export market will offset unemployment

11. Source: Morris R. Robinson, Director, Bureau of Building Marketing Research, Chicago, IL, National Building and Construction Exposition and Conference, 1976.
12. Hunger Action Center, *Community Garden Handbook*, Evergreen State College, Olympia, WA, 1976.
13. U.S. Congress, Subcommittee on Economic Growth of the Joint Economic Committee, *Technology, Economic Growth, and International Competitiveness*, U.S. Government Printing Office, Washington, DC, July 9, 1975.

created by automation. Conflicting studies on these issues are reported by business and labor.[14]

Some aspects of automation may be very valuable. Energy-related functions in an industrial society, like the operation of utility systems in large buildings, can be adjusted with controls, to provide substantial savings. Capital that would have been exported to pay for oil can instead be used to develop new businesses at home. A significant portion of the labor displaced by automation could be retrained and absorbed into other economic activities. The picture for certain sectors of the economy, however, may not be as optimistic.

In agriculture, for example, automation and advanced mechanization have had a drastic impact on the labor force. Here the intensity of energy use has reached such levels that a further substitution of machines for labor may no longer promote capital and new enterprise flexibility. Given the escalating cost of welfare programs, the continuation of such policies would be counterproductive as well as callous.

What is currently true for parts of the agricultural sector may become more widespread in other energy- and resource-intensive industries as depletion trends force up the price of raw materials. Capital expenditures to expand such industries would not only then constrain the very growth they were intended to promote, but would leave the social service sectors of our society in an anemic condition. The magnitude of these expenditures has led to the fear that the free market cannot handle the fiscal and public responsibility. Government action to amass capital has been called for, a further move toward nationalization and rigidification of the economy.

Within this context of the problems of a resource-constrained economy and responses by corporate and governmental America, appropriate technology represents a transition strategy that addresses several needs. For increasing numbers of our citizens (those unemployed, marginally employed, or on welfare), it offers the opportunity of income stabilization and of greater self-reliance. However, policymakers must guard against using appropriate technology for a bread-and-circuses welfare system that would only further isolate these groups.

Technological and Institutional Opportunities Appropriate technology could be a valuable tool in the hands of local decision makers because of its simultaneous emphasis on environmental renewal, small business developments, and low-capital technologies which would be accessible to families and communities whether in inner-city or rural locations. However, these communities will want to go beyond a minimal subsistence technology to create an environmentally and socially affirmative economic system. Given the struggle over the last two centuries to improve the material conditions of life in industrial societies, fears exist that a "simple" technology based on a self-sustaining relationship

14. R.J. Barnet and R.E. Muller: *Global Reach: The Power of the Multinational Corporation,* Simon and Schuster Company, New York, 1974, chaps. 10, 11.

with the environment will mean a step backward. Is this actually the case? Several technical and institutional developments indicate that there are opportunities to harmonize environmental, material, and employment needs without losing cultural advantages, and, in fact, positively contributing to the quality of life.

Innovations that positively add to the energy and industrial efficiency of smaller aggregates of residential and commercial social units are on the horizon. For individual homes, solar heating and cooling systems have already been demonstrated which reduce energy consumption by half, even after energy conservation techniques have first reduced the energy demand by perhaps an equal amount. New microcomputer applications are being developed that allow control of the internal environment of a home with a flexibility that was formerly possible only in large buildings. This miniaturization and integration of controls allows not only for greater physical efficiency; but, the quality and physical healthfulness of the environment can be improved because both the radiant "comfort" equilibrium and air pollution standards can be more efficiently controlled. Finally, this could effectively be done using low-cost construction materials and techniques, along with renewable sources of energy, like sunshine and wind.

Appropriate technology thus far has involved experiments which attempt to integrate food, energy, and recycling systems at the household level. This has provided a starting point for those who wish to implement the skills and economic resources most immediately available. This same sense of efficiency and environmental balance could be used to assist communities to draw together human and physical resources into a horizontally integrated local economic system. The technical foundation for such a system would consist of renewable energy and resource recycling techniques to form a self-sustaining balance with bio-regional conditions. The social foundation would consist of community-wide cooperative self-help programs and small business efforts which allow initiative and creativity full play at the local level. The community, visualized as a system, would thus become the interface for microeconomic considerations (e.g., recycling of physical resources and full use of human resources) and macroeconomic considerations (e.g., concerns with resource depletion, pollution, health, unemployment, and net energy costs). In this fashion, the environmentally affirmative design goals and experience of appropriate technology initiators could open a new dimension to problem-solving in a constrained economy.

Will the call for participation—whether via individual, small business, or citizen planning efforts—be an exorbitant expense for our society? Can we maintain the efficiency we need in the face of environmental and resource constraints without moving to an increased reliance on decisions by fewer and fewer highly trained specialists? Some decision makers feel technocratic trends are inevitable. However, changes in the system of mass distribution may offer a different result.

Older patterns of mass distribution were created in an era of industrial centralization and mass production. The cost-effective aspects of national distribution systems are dependent on a low-unit overhead for maintenance and other customer services, based in part on the "once-through" nonrecycling aspect of goods and the resulting high volume of traffic and transfer. The *crucial* point here is that this distribution efficiency will significantly decrease in a resource-constrained economy. Resources will necessarily be recycled, and a high-quality, low-maintenace, long-lived system (hence, low turnover rate) is essential. Thus, a fundamental change will occur in a recycling and renewable resource-based economy: volume of goods will decline, paralleled by an enhanced information flow which will enable people to maintain cultural opportunities and a decent standard of living via self-help efforts and an expansion of the economy into conservation-related business services.

What innovative processes of information transfer can address these new requirements? The experience of survey respondents may be invaluable here. Their efforts to demonstrate and disseminate innovations via self-help and small business groups and the diffusion of information provide a participatory and quality-service ethic that can be more widely adopted. This process would involve a series of interactive local and regional networks. Several recent technical developments and a number of institutional experiments that are underway indicate that these networks could operate on a low-cost basis.

In terms of technical innovations, several new processes using computers and television for continuing education purposes may soon be widely available. Remote teaching systems, such as those being developed by the Goldmark Communications Corporation, allow a person to store training materials in a home television terminal. Home viewers will be able to choose from an enormous variety of programs at their own viewing schedule. A worldwide computer access program for new technology developments is being set up by the Control Data Corporation, which will enable small-business people to gain access to specific problem-solving technology packages on a user-demand basis. These innovations could reduce the cost and complexity of adult training programs as well as provide consulting services for small businesses.

On the institutional side, programs initiated by the National Bureau of Standards and the State of Montana, among others, have begun to evaluate and support work by local innovators and small businesses. The flexible administrative systems set up for review, evaluation, and advisory functions work well and provide a basis for small grants and contracts.

Foreign Policy Does appropriate technology bear any relationship to the difficulties of the developing world in relation to economic policy, social trends, and technical opportunities, within the context of an environmentally and resource-constrained economy? The answer is plainly "yes," because several problems and policy issues in less-developed countries have emerged that affect these relationships.

Problems of fuel costs and capital shortages are more severe in developing countries than in our society. At the same time, high energy costs siphon off capital that could have been used for industrial expansion and rural development programs. Thus, the rate of industrialization is slowed, and it is increasingly difficult to gain stable, long-term support for development-type investments. Finally, these problems have created enormous rural and urban unemployment, forcing less-developed countries to seek alternatives.

Appropriate technology may offer a more immediate opportunity to improve rural conditions, and local people can participate on a self-help basis in creating these. Hence, in the developing world, appropriate technology is receiving increasing attention.[15]

Thus, the analog of a policy in the United States that balances automation with employment is, in developing countries, a policy that attempts to meet immediate, basic, life-support needs with labor-intensive strategies. Further, while the United States addresses the income-stabilization problems of its inner-city and rural citizens via economic revitalization strategies, the developing countries will need to address natural resource and capital constraints via small-scale industrial development. And a critical similarity is the need, in both cases, for a dynamic process of information transfer so that local groups can act knowledgeably.

Appropriate technology may offer United States policymakers several opportunities. The emphasis in appropriate technology on the development of an efficient life style could ultimately reduce the demand by advanced industrial countries for scarce resources, thus easing mounting tensions over this issue. Moreover, this conservation ethic would reduce the rate of use of finite resources, and thus, could provide all parties further time to address the needs of their people during a transition to conservation-based economics. In addition, the emphasis on participation through local development centers, working within a context of communication with similar groups, may provide a cost-effective method both to gain safety and to draw out vitality in the research process. Local failures can be accepted more easily than nationwide ones, while enhanced information flow via technical and institutional mechanisms would disseminate successful results. Finally, there is enormous potential for cooperation. Linking experiences between small firms and community development groups inside and outside the United States offers mutual benefits to all.

Appropriate technology thus provides a framework by which to develop balanced social and environmental relationships within renewable-resource and recycling-based economies worldwide. It offers the possibility of a dynamic and humane world order.

15. Edgar Owens and Robert Shaw: *Development Reconsidered,* D.C. Heath, Lexington, MA, 1972; Arjun Makhijani: *Energy Policy for the Rural Third World,* The International Institute for Environment and Development, Washington, DC, 1976; and reports by the Board of Science and Technology for International Development, Commission on Internal Relations, National Academy of Sciences, National Research Council, Washington, DC.

15

ENERGY CONSERVATION AT THE BUILDING SCALE: AN INNOVATION PROGRAM

Donald Watson

Sections of this chapter are adapted from a report by the author, *Innovation in Solar Design,* prepared under an AIA Research Corporation Subcontract for the U.S. Department of Housing and Urban Development and the National Bureau of Standards, 1975. (Consultants: William Meyer for The Ehrenkrantz Group; Everett M. Barber, Jr.)

The process of innovation is crucial to any proposal for energy-conserving building design. Attempts to introduce new building products and construction processes may fail if they cannot be easily integrated into conventional practice. New concepts or methods of architecture and engineering design may fail if design professionals do not take them up. Even the most agreeable innovations may fail to the extent that they do not take into account established consumer preferences, financing methods, or building codes and standards. More business failures have occurred in building construction than any other part of the commercial sector, many due to lack of foresight or control over barriers that await a new concept on its way to market through the innovation process.

Any energy-conserving proposal or invention must be evaluated in terms of barriers inherent in the institutional structure of the building industry. Similarly, these barriers should be addressed to create a more favorable institutional context for innovation.

Energy-conserving building technology thus presents a classic problem for innovation planning. The more changes required in normal building practice the more difficult one can expect the innovation process to be. Unfortunately, energy conservation presents challenges throughout, in the way buildings are financed, designed, built, and used.

This chapter views the prospects of energy-conserving innovations in building design and construction in light of the institutions that support, and in turn are supported by, the building industry. As will be seen, the design process itself could play the crucial role. The extent to which design professionals become sensitive to the energy impact of decisions implicit in financing and planning parameters, construction methods, and use patterns may ultimately determine whether the design is to be successful in terms of energy and resource conservation. Without addressing these institutional constraints, a "minimum-energy building" design could be just a "back-filling" exercise in an attempt to overcome wasteful energy decisions that are already set in motion.

The intent here is to assess the prospects for change required to achieve energy conservation at the building scale, firstly, in terms of the magnitude of the effort required, and then in terms of the specific proposals that might be made part of a coordinated innovation program, so that the promise of conservation initiatives can be best assured.

How Energy-Conserving Buildings Might be Designed

To determine whether or not the transition to energy-conserving building might be easy or difficult, consider the solutions being proposed by which to reduce the now wasteful consumption of energy in the building industry. The institutional context of building design is established by *land planning practices,* with transportation and zoning envelope constraints, which in themselves may predetermine a design solution; by the available *energy infrastructure,* such as existing power plants and energy delivery systems, which represent an investment already in place; by *construction methods,* not simply those a building designer might wish to specify, but those established and available in the marketplace; and finally *financing mechanisms,* including factors such as the availability of capital, the time-frame of amortization and depreciation, and the ultimate marketability of the building project under either private or public sector terms. These, in effect, are the parameters of building design that are established before an architect is assigned a building commission.

Land planning parameters that affect over-all energy efficiency include existing or available transportation infrastructures and resulting energy costs as a function of building density and travel distances; the possibilities of gaining and maintaining access to ambient sun and wind energy for heating and cooling by design features at the building site; and land preservation options that create an ecological balance between built form and open land for air and water purification, food production, and recreation. In densely built urban areas, with the high cost of land and resulting high-rise building, land use is controlled by zoning limits based somewhat on natural light and air considerations—but only slightly, and for the most part fruitlessly, since the modern skyscraper is air conditioned and artificially lit. Zoning based on exclusive-use, single-ownership patterns has resulted in a predominance of single-use buildings. The separation between places of work, residence, and commerce, in turn, increases travel distances. Multiuse zoning, in contrast, not only would promote urban diversity, but could promise energy efficiencies by reduced travel at the neighborhood scale, and rationalized urban transit options based upon more intensely used transport networks. Multiuse zoning also increases the diversity of energy requirements and thus offers opportunity for load leveling, cogeneration, and cost-sharing of small-scale urban-sector power plants.

Solar heating becomes practical at the scale of low- to medium-density buildings, where existing roof areas are sufficient for solar domestic water-heating and solar-assisted space-heating installations. In new construction, concepts of passive heating and cooling become possible, wherein the building shape itself can be designed for winter heat gain and summer shading, and building groups can form protected intermediary spaces, such as forecourts and atria, based on natural climate control principles.

The energy infrastructure comprises the energy-producing and transport facilities, including power plant, fuel storage, pipelines, roads, and fuel transport vehicles. From this standpoint, the cost for construction of the energy infrastructure and for transport of energy to a building should be considered in evaluating the economics of on-site power generation alternatives, be they windmills or solar collectors, or, as discussed in preceeding chapters, the building itself. Inefficiencies inherent in recovering and burning primary fuels at a power plant and in transmission losses through long distances are often ignored when comparing energy sources in the selection of building energy systems—electric resistance heating being the oustanding example: reputedly near 100% efficient when used at the building furnace, but at the sacrifice of 40% to 50% inefficiencies in producing and transmitting electric power to the building.

The *scale* of energy infrastructure is the crucial issue. While energy systems completely autonomous to a particular building are possible, they are rarely economical. What is reasonable are building groups whose energy systems are shared to suit an energy-efficient power facility, perhaps at the neighborhood or urban-sector scale. The cooperatively owned solar collector

Fig. 1 Free University of Berlin. The in-fill panel system is completely demountable. Shadrach Woods, Architect. Candilis, Josic, Woods (Photos courtesy of Val Woods).

system for an apartment building is a modest example of shared power-producing equipment (Figure 1, Chapter 14). Fuel cell technology and other heat recovery and cogeneration options are more promising developments, wherein the total efficiency of primary energy is increased by matching load to the optimum level of producing and transporting energy in the form of electricity, hot water, or steam, for urban neighborhood sectors.

The problem this poses to the owners and managers of large utility systems is that the investment in the existing plant and infrastructure has already been made. From their standpoint, any effort to decentralize energy plants can be seen as a reduction of their market. This is a matter of a balance between public policy and vested market interest based on economic and social prospects of continued dependence on large-scale energy consumption, a serious issue indeed. But the fact remains that decentralized energy-producing facilities, scaled to the building in the case of passive or active solar heating, or to the urban sector in the case of fuel cells, are more efficient in matching primary energy use to end-use.

The construction process itself involves energy expenditure for building materials and components, to be manufactured, delivered to the construction site, put into place, maintained and repaired over the life of the building, and ultimately to be demolished or reused at the end of the building cycle. The energy thus embodied in building construction can add a significant amount to the net energy expenditure, enough to alter the outcome of any projected energy savings that fails to account for it. However, embodied energy costs are highly variable, depending upon efficiency of energy production at the plant, where current practice could be greatly improved. Manufacturing energy cost also depends upon the particular utility rate structure in effect at the time of production, and this varies depending upon source-energy purchases available to the power plant. Also, energy expenditure for a durable and reusable building product may be justified if it is the best alternative by which to increase its reliability and flexibility of use, thus extending the life of the product.

Remodeling and renovating existing structures has typically been viewed as the more costly alternative to large-scale demolition approaches to urban renewal. Even aside from the air pollution that is caused by demolition—and in the case of asbestos building materials, the serious health hazards that result when these are released back into the air or water—net energy analysis may show that in terms of energy costs, urban restoration is as economical as it is desirable in terms of social rehabilitation and cultural preservation goals.

Thus, from the standpoint of embodied energy cost and the environmental considerations of waste disposal, future buildings and related building products should be designed for the longest life possible. This might take the form of plug-in–type structures, in which the physical skeleton and the costly infrastructure of circulation and service networks are permanent, but generalized enough to facilitate smaller-scale infill and remodeling. These would be based on "loose fit," or perhaps self-help, construction components, not unlike "sites and services" urban development strategies[1] or Shadrach Wood's master plan and structural component system for the Free University of Berlin (*Figure 1*). Because fuel costs are subsidized and pollution costs at the power plant or at the manufacturing plant are not represented in the sales price of the product, real energy costs are not reflected in market costs. If they were, the economic advantage of recycling materials would improve, and new sorts of building products, based on local resources, reclaimed materials, and multiple and flexible use of building components, might be brought onto the market.

This brings us to the "bottom line," the cost of an energy-

1. John Turner and Robert Fichter, eds.: *Freedom to Build,* The MacMillan Company, New York, 1972.

conserving building, which in most instances involves a greater first cost than present-day construction. Current financing mechanisms make many energy-conserving building alternatives unaffordable and unmarketable due to economic disincentives, including lending limits, increased property tax assessment, and, for operating costs, tax write-offs and other budgeting procedures in which accurate energy costs are not specifically identified. As a result, at present, it is more profitable to build cheaply, letting the future purchaser or renter pay the utility bills. This might be helped by marketplace cost adjustments, a better-informed consumer, and subsidies addressed to current fiscal barriers, including lower interest rates for financing energy-conserving building investments, tax credits, and life-cycle cost budgeting.

The point is that present market economics do not reflect the real cost of energy over the life of the building. As fuel becomes more scarce and difficult to recover, its true cost approaches infinity. Its replacement cost includes the conversion of plant to alternate energy sources, whether at the building or at the power station. The social and environmental costs are measured not simply in dollars, but in terms of public health and safety, social and economic stability, and the choice between a beautiful or despoiled environment. These are the terms that should make up the bottom line.

If such changes in building design and construction are to be envisioned, it can be seen that the transition from conventional building practice will not be easy. As summarized in *Figure 2*,

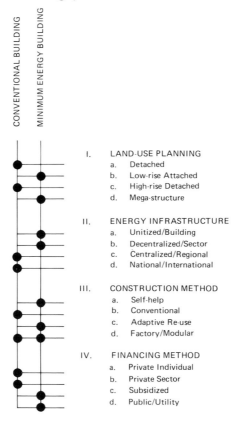

I.   LAND-USE PLANNING
  a.   Detached
  b.   Low-rise Attached
  c.   High-rise Detached
  d.   Mega-structure

II.   ENERGY INFRASTRUCTURE
  a.   Unitized/Building
  b.   Decentralized/Sector
  c.   Centralized/Regional
  d.   National/International

III.   CONSTRUCTION METHOD
  a.   Self-help
  b.   Conventional
  c.   Adaptive Re-use
  d.   Factory/Modular

IV.   FINANCING METHOD
  a.   Private Individual
  b.   Private Sector
  c.   Subsidized
  d.   Public/Utility

Fig. 2 Comparison of conventional buildings and minimum energy building in terms of institutional parameters.

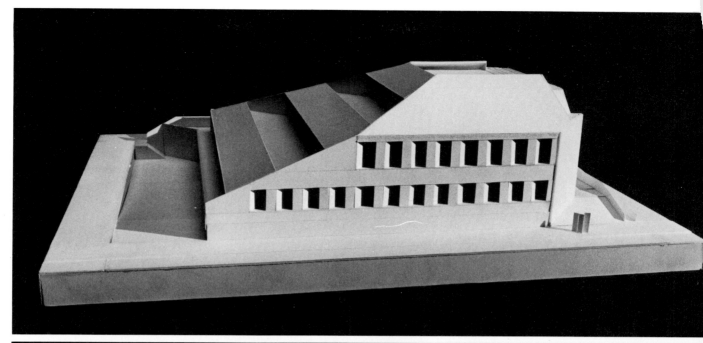

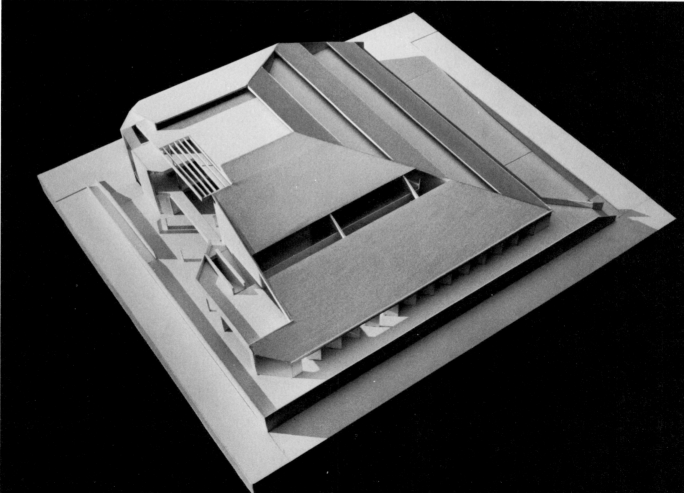

Fig. 3 Proposal for an office building, based on the solar envelope for a site in Los Angeles by architecture student, Alan Victor, under the direction of Richard D. Berry and Ralph L. Knowles. USC, 1977.

Fig. 4 Embodied energy profiles of 1,600 ft² house, typical of those existing on the New Haven site, comparing embodied energy and operating energy (in Btu) for various retrofit options. The symbol ● indicates the point at which net energy savings of each alternate exceeds the existing base case.

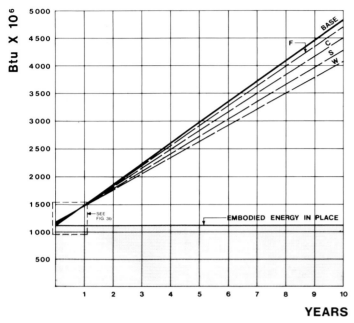

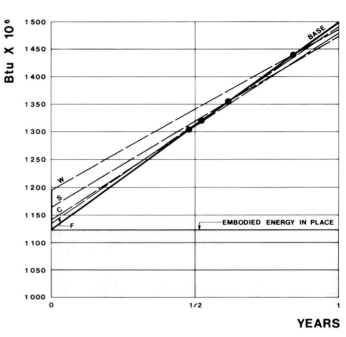

4a Case 1—Retrofit under market conditions: Base—existing house with no retrofit; F = floor insulation, R = 26.54; C = ceiling insulation, R = 37.09; W = wall insulation, R = 26.09; S = storm windows and doors.

4b Case 1—enlarged view of first year (symbols same as 4a).

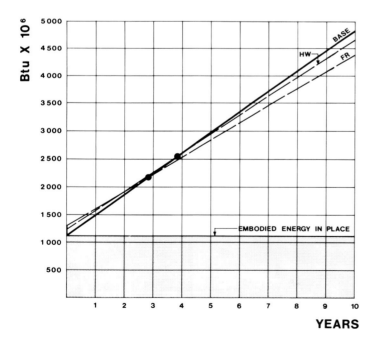

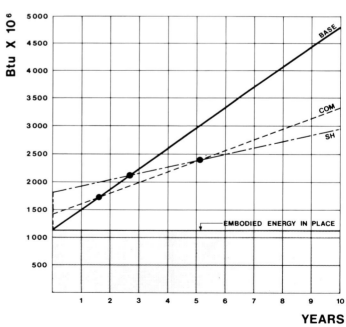

4c Case 2—Retrofit under subsidized or sweat-equity conditions: Base—existing house with no retrofit; FR = furnace replacement and re-ducting; HW = solar hot water.

4d Case 3—Solar heating on all unshaded and properly oriented roofs: Base—existing house with no retrofit; COM = all retrofit measures in cases 1 and 2; SH = solar heating.

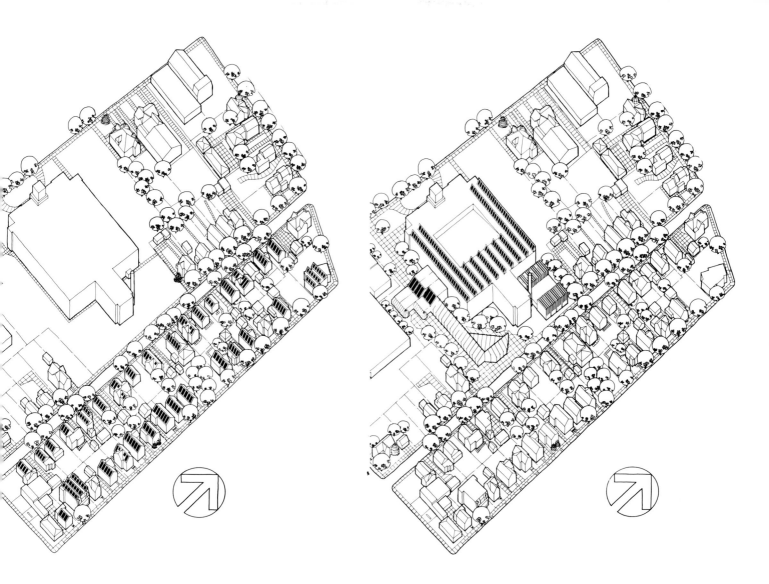

Fig. 5   New Haven Case Study: Solar heating using existing unshaded and properly oriented roofs for solar collectors.

Fig. 6   New Haven Case Study: Solar heating using school roof for collector array; neighborhood-scale fuel cell; new community structures for multiuse of school property.

these proposals of how energy-conserving buildings might be designed—and they are proposals that emerge from the chapters in this book—require innovations in the areas we have been reviewing here as the institutional parameters of the building industry.

It is obviously easier to build new structures or urban clusters for energy efficiency than to remodel existing buildings and neighborhoods. But, the solutions to each emanate from similar design principles and, in fact, may not be so different from approaches already familiar to architects and engineers. In the case of a new urban center, one could combine the transportation node envisioned by Steadman with the solar zoning envelopes of Knowles into an urban structure based upon passive climatic design in which the structure itself provides shading in summer and solar exposure in winter (*Figure 3*). The structure, designed and built for long life and loose fit, should include the permanent circulation system and services, but otherwise could be generalized and open to change and growth by leaving interstitial areas and double- or triple-height spaces to allow succeeding users ample room for fine-tuning.[2] The north side of a multistoried structure could include roof gardens and terraces with optimum solar exposure during the growing season.

While such planning principals may appear utopian the more they depart from existing conventions, they can be applied to existing urban parcels as a guide to renovation. *Figures 4, 5* and 6 show a study by Paul Edmeades of an inner-city development parcel, typical of urban New Haven, with a mixture of commercial, public school, and residential buildings. The net energy investment involved in various renovation alternatives are compared in the accompanying graphs (Figure 4), including options to "winterize" the existing buildings under market economics; to winterize under subsidized and sweat-equity programs; and to "solarize," first as might be justified under short-term payback, and then to maximum solar capacity (Figure 5). Other options that can be compared to these results are to replace individual building furnaces and boilers with a neighborhood sector fuel cell (Figure 6); and finally to demolish existing buildings and rebuild new structures more suited to energy conservation requirements.[3]

The Ladder of Innovation

The view of design assumed above is that it serves a coordinating role in selecting between planning, design, and construction alternatives already available in the marketplace. The designer might play another role as proposer or inventor of building concepts, products, and systems that might be developed and marketed for the building industry. The work of Ezra Ehrenkrantz demonstrates the seminal role that the architect might play, not simply in choosing off-the-shelf building products, but in establishing performance standards for new product systems and concepts and then encouraging their development by innovative market incentives (*Figure 7*). The opportunity in the building industry now offered by energy conservation makes such efforts even more important: energy design relies upon building products and processes not now readily available or affordable in the marketplace. Indeed, many new building components now proposed for energy conservation have been invented and developed by architects and engineers.[4]

The process by which new concepts reach the market is discussed in this section as the *ladder of innovation,* a series of innovation barriers that must be overcome to meet widespread market acceptance. The reason that the building designer can play a key role in energy innovation is because the final proof of a concept, be it a design idea or a building product, depends upon the ease with which it can be integrated into the conventional

2. Donald Watson: "The Process of Activity and the Built Environment" *AIA Journal,* October 1969.
3. Paul Edmeades: "Net Energy Analysis of an Urban Renovation Project," School of Architecture, Yale University, Master of Environmental Design Program, unpublished thesis, 1978.
4. To cite only a few examples: *Beadwall* (Dave Harrison); *Drumwall* (Steve Baer); *High R® Insulating Shade* (Tom Hopper); *Lite-A-Part Luminarie* (Sylvan Shemitz).

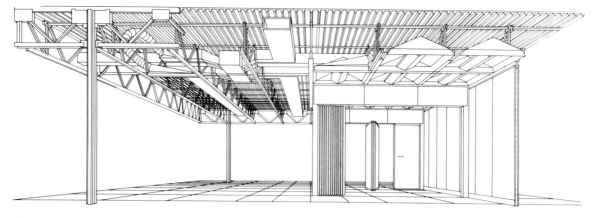

Fig. 7 School Construction Systems Development prototype. The first systems building project in the United States began in California in 1964. Manufacturer/builder firms proposed integrated buildingsystem designs based on specifications that established performance levels, without proscribing the construction materials. (Drawing: The Ehrenkrantz Group)

Fig. 8 The Ladder of Innovation.

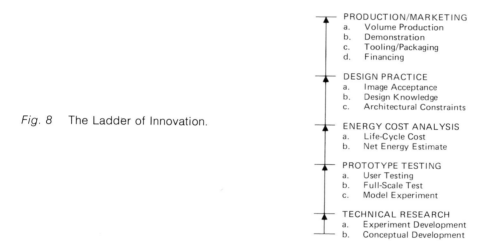

PRODUCTION/MARKETING
a. Volume Production
b. Demonstration
c. Tooling/Packaging
d. Financing

DESIGN PRACTICE
a. Image Acceptance
b. Design Knowledge
c. Architectural Constraints

ENERGY COST ANALYSIS
a. Life-Cycle Cost
b. Net Energy Estimate

PROTOTYPE TESTING
a. User Testing
b. Full-Scale Test
c. Model Experiment

TECHNICAL RESEARCH
a. Experiment Development
b. Conceptual Development

building process. A new concept or product must meet requirements, not only of technical efficiency or potential contribution to energy savings, but of acceptability to designer, builder, code official, and ultimate user.

An energy-conserving concept must pass many different points from its inception as an idea, to the stage where that idea is embodied in a product available to the market or in a design applied to buildings. The process of research and development thus evolves through a series of barriers listed in *Figure 8* as the ladder of innovation. Some concepts can be incorporated into buildings without a dramatic change in building practice, for example, additional insulation in walls. However, most concepts and equipment associated with energy conservation design, and with solar technology in particular, impose constraints on conventional building design and construction. Thus, the development of new concepts presents a series of risks; an idea that may promise significant fuel cost savings at the outset may be destined for too limited application due to building design constraints and resulting marketing limitations.

In the early stages of *Technical Research,* an idea must be realized in a form that can be tested, simply to prove that the concept does work and deserves further development. At such a point, questions of practicality or economy may be held in abeyance because some problems can be resolved only after extended testing and development.

Once it is out of the laboratory, a concept may proceed through various stages of *Prototype Testing,* where it is built to model scale or to full scale. Ultimately, a building design innovation must be tested in "live-in" experiments in order to determine its practicality under occupant-use conditions.

A step farther up the ladder involves calculations of *Energy Cost Analysis,* whereby a concept must promise energy cost savings within a reasonable payback period. This stage is critical for any product that will depend for its economy upon mass market or volume production. For example, to compete with other financial investments that yield a quick return, a product may have to prove it is cost effective in a two- to five-year period. Thus, even with the realization of economies in design, production, and installation, energy-conserving technology that is cost effective in net-energy or long-term life-cycle terms may require some form of subsidized support to compete in a marketplace where survival is determined by low first cost and short-term payback.

Once a concept or product shows that it is potentially cost effective, it may encounter constraints in the area of *Design Practice,* due to established architectural practices, or unfamiliarity with the concept, or lack of consumer acceptance of the resulting building design. In such cases, professional and consumer exposure to demonstration projects will help. When a concept has shown it can meet consumer acceptance standards as well as cost performance estimates, there remain constraints in *Production and Marketing.* However, these the building industry may be able to resolve once there is a demonstrated market that justifies the large financial investment required to establish production capacity, or to otherwise make the concept available. These constraints now typify many solar equipment designs as well as new window insulating devices. Problems of installation, packaging, and servicing are being "debugged," and packaged components are entering the market.

Barriers to Innovation Due to Design Practice Conventions

The process of innovation required to initiate a self-supporting energy conservation technology in the building industry is not now possible with traditional market incentives, because invest-

ENERGY
CONSERVATION
AT THE
BUILDING SCALE:
AN
INNOVATION
PROGRAM

289

ments of longer term than is considered justified in the private sector are required. Combined private and public efforts in a coordinated program of innovation are needed for several reasons unique to present energy-conserving building technology. First, a greater first-cost investment is required in building construction in order to achieve significant operating economies. However, life-cycle cost investments are at a disadvantage in traditional market competition. Witness year-to-year budgeting in state legislatures, the heroic efforts required to finance public school construction by local tax assessments, and the limited access to capital of most first-home buyers. Secondly, current ideas for energy conservation may be only half-formed and risk obsolescence if not subjected to rigorous development and testing, and this further delays its market entry. As a result, accelerated innovation must be supported by the following mechanisms (see *Figure 9*):

- *Research and development* to advance the technical performance of energy-conserving concepts.

- *Experimental prototype construction* to demonstrate the performance and cost advantages of optimized component integration in building designs.

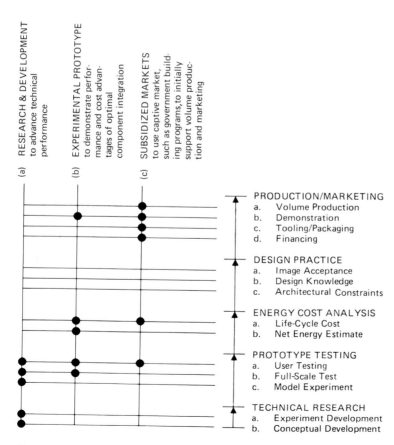

Fig. 9 Traditional innovation mechanisms.

• *Supported or partially guaranteed markets* to initiate the rationalization and industrialization of energy-conserving components, perhaps through initially subsidized volume production and marketing.

However, with the exception of some current solar demonstration projects that test architectural constraints and public acceptance, barriers in the area of *Design Practice* are not specifically addressed by traditional innovation support mechanisms in either the private or the public sector. Design Practice barriers include the *architectural constraints* imposed on energy-conserving concepts, the *design knowledge* required for the proper engineering and use of the resulting technology, and *image acceptance* by the designer and the consumer of the new character and forms of conservation design.

Architectural constraints may seriously limit application of a particular concept if it does not meet the basic architectural and building requirements for a structurally sound and aesthetically pleasing design. Examples could possibly exist in collector designs that require a large roof or extended building envelope, window shading devices whose operational requirements conflict with wind and snow load requirements, or the installation of insulation that cannot be smoothly coordinated within existing building trade processes or codes.

Design knowledge required for proper energy-conserving design may impede widespread acceptance of otherwise promising concepts by resistance from design professionals. Technical calculations are required to predict the performance of energy designs, including factors such as heat storage capacity and time-lag effects, reflective gains or losses, and air stratification and movement. In most instances, such calculations must be done for each specific application and are best done with computer-assisted methods. The calculations would achieve energy economies by assuring the appropriateness of each design decision. Widespread application of energy conservation by design professionals will also require general rules of thumb or quick computational methods that are not now readily available, as well as a willingness on the part of design professionals even to learn about energy-conserving design.

Image acceptance barriers prevail in the public's mind, such as the impact of solar collectors or large solar-oriented window walls on a building exterior or interior, or the incorporation of storage surfaces or volumes into a building structure. Although traditional building forms have steep roofs, and century-old houses incorporated many natural heating and cooling concepts as part of their design, the optimum integration of energy-conserving design ought to develop its own style, appropriate to each climatic and cultural region of the country. But, such a departure from conventional images is frequently mentioned as a potential barrier to innovation which, alas, is not avoided by putting buildings underground.

Proposed Innovative Mechanisms to Overcome Design Practice Barriers

That portion of the ladder of innovation that deserves particular attention for programatic mechanisms is *Design Practice*. The barriers inherent in architectural constraints, design knowledge, and image acceptance are not covered by existing private or public sector innovation support, even though they present the major stumbling blocks to proper integration of energy components with design concepts. The following discussion of programatic mechanisms to relieve design practice barriers suggests strategies that could be made part of a coordinated program for innovation, which could otherwise prove to be the Achilles' heel of conservation initiatives in the building sector.

Overcoming Architectural Constraints Various inhibitors to innovative concepts present themselves as architectural constraints wherein a new energy-saving concept or component might not be adopted because it raises problems of adaptability to traditional architectural or building practices. For example, architectural requirements may negate any advantages of solar collectors which required too great a roof or wall area, thus eliminating design options for south windows, balconies, and patios.[5] However, there is the possibility that, given programatic support, some concepts could overcome architectural constraints by improvements found through project demonstration, field test installation, and monitoring of field performance.

Innovation support mechanisms related to demonstration experiments which test potential architectural constraints include proprietary rights protection, uniform test procedures, and warranty incentives.

Overcoming Design Knowledge Constraints Inhibitors to application of energy-saving concepts that exist in the area of design knowledge are: lack of accurate energy data; the traditional separation between mechanical engineering and architectural design phases; insufficiently researched concepts; a need for new energy-design decision aids; the inaccessibility or unfamiliarity of new computer programs to the traditional on-board designer; the lack of experience with life-cycle cost calculations, and so forth.

Innovation support mechanisms that would help to relieve these constraints include design manuals; accessible computer programs for energy cost estimating on a shared basis, such as through local professional societies; professional training programs; and for the longer term, courses at professional design schools, including ways by which students of architecture and of

5. Donald Watson: *Designing and Building a Solar House*, Garden Way Publishing, 1977, pp. 137—143.

engineering might be exposed to the working concepts of one another and other related professions.

Overcoming Image Acceptance Constraints   Although it may be less important than is pictured, the image of a building that incorporates new design concepts may be considered a liability as a saleable or resaleable product. Whatever the case, it is clear that even a marginal concept that can be easily applied to conventional building styles under the banner of energy saving may have a greater market acceptance, disproportionate to its real energy effectiveness, if compared to more radical building forms. The support mechanisms to overcome such barriers to potentially innovative components and design concepts—outside of their incorporation in demonstration projects themselves, which itself would serve as "image acceptance advertising"—are market research and advocacy programs at the local marketing or financing institutions.

As summarized in *Figure 10,* the program mechanisms discussed above respond to constraints in design practice, the key area for any coordinated policy for innovation in the building sector, particularly because it relies so heavily upon architectural and engineering design. Innovation in energy conservation design should be accelerated simultaneously with building research, new product development, and studies in production and marketing. Unless the specific hurdles to innovation are identified early, and

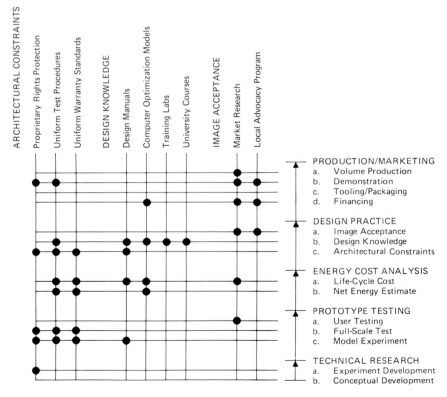

Fig. 10   Proposed innovation mechanisms to improve energy conservation design practice.

ENERGY
CONSERVATION
AT THE
BUILDING SCALE:
AN
INNOVATION
PROGRAM

293

support mechanisms are ready at hand to help potentially useful concepts over those barriers, then any research and development program or demonstration program will discourage innovation by default.

An Innovation Program to Overcome Institutional Barriers

As discussed in the previous section, the design professional is able to identify and help develop a particular concept or building product from the unique vantage point of being the design integrator of performance factors and of engineering and construction requirements, a role which many architects and engineers have, in fact, pursued as inventors or product design consultants. A more important role exists, although perhaps the more difficult one, as coordinator of decisions from land planning and financing to construction, implementation, and post-construction evaluation. From this perspective, the design professional is constrained by the institutional parameters discussed at the beginning of this chapter. But, to the extent that the designer is to be effective, it is these constraints that must be relieved if design innovations are to be possible at the scale implicit in the national need for energy conservation. In short, the innovation effort must address the land-use and financing conventions, energy infrastructure, and construction methods that predetermine the design solution, particularly as to its net energy effectiveness.

The innovation process in the building industry can be analyzed as a series of decisions within these institutional parameters, with the result that changes can then be encouraged by appropriate adjustment of the controlling variables. Each of the chapters of this book have addressed one or several aspects of energy conservation building design, with many clearly argued proposals that need to be implemented. As a summary of these proposals, they are reviewed here under four headings, (1) Finance and Planning Innovations; (2) Technical Innovation; (3) Design Practice Innovations; and (4) Social Innovation.

Finance and Planning Innovations To facilitate rational analysis of energy use, more accurate performance data is required about how buildings actually use energy. As discussed in Chapter 4 by Lawrence Spielvogel, energy use at the building is often not metered separately (say, between space heating, service hot water, or electric lighting), and even then does not measure source energy used at the power plant. While calculation methods of building energy demand are now being refined and computerized, these often do not correlate with actual performance data, which of course is a direct function of climate and use variables that may be off the statistical norm. Studies of the energy embodied in construction, as represented by the pioneering work of Richard Stein and Diane Serber (Chapter 10), are only beginning and depend upon energy flows in the industrial and commercial sector that are very difficult to track at this point in time. Yet, the obvious prerequisite to any analysis of energy in the building sector is to obtain accurate data through *energy cost accounting,* including indirect environmental and social health and safety costs.

Energy conservation nearly always means increasing the capital cost of building construction, an investment that may be quickly paid back and that can be cost-justified from the standpoint of life-cycle costs, as described in Chapter 9 by Harold Marshall and Rosalie Ruegg, but which nonetheless involves increased first costs. In a marketplace where low cost is the first priority, with durability and reliability a poor second, the improved construction required to achieve life-cycle cost savings may simply not be marketable. The life-cycle approach requires that consumers learn to buy for long-term value. Most investments in building are, in fact, based on a 20- to 30-year mortgage period, but the implicit energy costs over the same period are too often ignored. Nevertheless, consumers run into lending limits for their own investments, which in turn makes them the more conservative in approving publicly financed building projects. Witness, as an example, the typical school building scenario: architect designs building; building comes in over budget; taxpayers refuse to approve budget increase; architect lowers cost of construction by eliminating many of the design features, such as insulating glass, that would in effect have been repaid many times over in operating costs over the life of the building. The same merry-go-round occurs in state legislatures with year-to-year budgeting, each time requiring a floor fight to justify construction funding, a process that too often assures that increased energy conservation investment is not made in publicly funded building. As a result, no one is able to act on the fact that the public interest—not to say the public coffers—is best served by investing now and saving later. In the private sector, the same result occurs, but with "liquidity of cash flow" as the criterion that is used to argue against long-term investments in building construction and plant. Existing tax write-offs for all energy and operational expenses also act as disincentives to improved building quality.

The point to be made in the face of all of these examples is that there is no mechanism by which to make long-term planning investments in the building sector, given a "lowest first-cost" market mentality and resulting decisions made at the expense of energy economics. Market corrections are needed that will properly credit the ultimate savings in capital that can be achieved by energy conservation investments; in short, mechanisms to support *a future planning perspective.*

In the last decade, many building innovations have been made economically viable by "turn-key" construction, "fast-track" construction management, "packaged" delivery systems, market aggregation, and other means of more closely integrating the process of building development. Similar *innovative forms of implementation* can be looked to by which to streamline the process of energy innovation with new, and perhaps unprecedented, forms of cooperation between the public and private sector. Proposals have been made by which private utility companies finance and install energy-saving or energy-producing equipment (insulation, solar collectors, or sector fuel cell power plants), charging the consumer a monthly rate that includes a fixed finance rate instead of an escalating fuel-cost rate. Load sharing, cogeneration, and heat recovery opportunities might also be made possible as a result of heretofore untried cooperation efforts.

Technical Innovation Breakthroughs in energy development are greatly to be hoped for, particularly to supply energy for uses for which no simple alternative exists other than our current fossil fuels, such as for pharmaceutical and fertilizer production. What makes energy conservation at the building scale of great promise and urgency, however, is first, the current wastefulness of energy

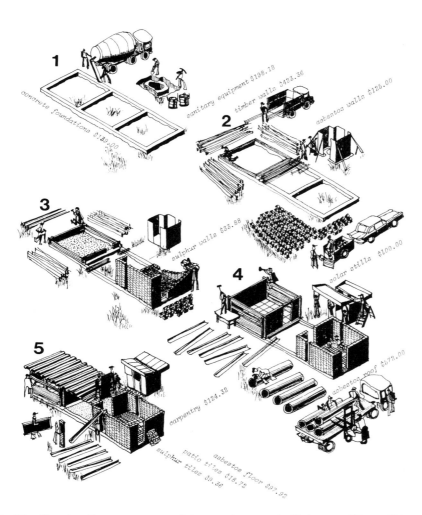

Fig. 11 Construction sequence of low-cost owner-built house. (From Ortega, *The Ecol Operation.*)

ENERGY
CONSERVATION
THROUGH
BUILDING
DESIGN

use in buildings, and secondly, the relatively modest technical solutions that can be implemented to maintain comfort conditions in buildings, including passive and climate-based design, as described by Doug Balcomb and his coauthors in Chapter 5, and by Murray Milne and Baruch Givoni in Chapter 6. The method of determining the appropriate technical solution implicit in the Milne/Givoni method is *energy source matched to use;* in other words, to properly scale the energy technology, be it by building design or by equipment, to the size and nature of the energy requirement. The same holds true for service hot water, where in many situations solar collectors can supply the relatively low temperature requirement more economically than any competing energy source.

A second direction of technical innovation is *better use of existing resources,* including techniques of recycling, renovation, and design of long-life buildings and products. Similarly, increased use of local resources might be encouraged once the energy costs of transportation are reflected in market prices. Examples include the use of locally available adobe in the southwest, of local wood for plywood in the southeast (now made possible by the development of improved glues), and the reclamation of sulphur waste for use as the binding agent for structural blocks for buildings, as proposed by the McGill Low-Cost Housing Group (*Figure 11*).[6] Also included here should be the many "technical fixes" such as fuel economizers; improved use patterns of buildings, including delamping and controlled thermostat setbacks; and other low-cost or no-cost adjustments, as discussed by Fred Dubin in Chapter 11.

In Chapter 14, Eugene Eccli put, under the heading of "appropriate technology," those grass-roots efforts that combine job training and sweat-equity efforts with modestly scaled building technology in community-based projects, thereby placing technical innovation in a framework of improving environmental and social conditions by the direct participation of those most affected.

Design Innovations Specific proposals to stimulate innovations in building design practice have been detailed in the preceding sections of this chapter, in addition to the many concepts discussed above and in previous chapters, especially those of *design matched to local climate* and of *passive design.* An energy-efficient building may not need to look radically different from those we are used to, its energy performance being subject more to construction and use factors that are not visible. The opportunity remains, however, to develop designs that symbolize new energy conservation concepts, just as previous architectural styles were based on the exploration of new industrial materials and structural innovations. But conservation design may be more modest. From a net energy perspective, *adaptive use* and rehabilitation of existing structures—"make-do-and-renew"—should become more important and economically viable than they are now,

6. Alvaro Ortega et al.: *The Ecol Operation,* School of Architecture, McGill University, 1972 (out of print).

where in some instances an existing building is a tax and insurance liability, cheaper to tear down than to maintain.

Previous chapters provide evidence enough that whatever new architectural styles do emerge in response to energy design will depend upon the creative collaboration between architect and mechanical engineer.

Social Innovation To contrast the argument of many proponents of technical innovation that social change is completely dependent upon advances in technology, the point that may need to be stressed is that the technology already exists, as do the required expertise, production capacity, and labor force, to put energy conservation into effect. What is needed are programatic social and economic incentives.

Essential to creating the social milieu for conservation investments is the emphasis proposed in the introduction to this book on *improved environmental quality*. So that while much of the discussion, of necessity, dwells on "energy efficiency," it is the cultural, aesthetic, and ecological benefits that should ultimately motivate social action toward conservation.

Many innovations are dependent upon financial and legal parameters that now inhibit effective local action, whether related to the investment policy of large utilities, which in turn affects local utility rate structures, or to adverse conditions for small business or community participation opportunities. In a very direct sense, the development of decentralized energy sources depends upon *decentralized economic structures*. Examples include the relatively high rate of construction financing borne by the homeowner who wishes to install a solar heating system, compared to the tax subsidies and credits that encourage utilities to increase power production capacity; or the lower rate structures for bulk industrial users compared to other users who, in this sense, subsidize industrial energy consumption. These examples are not given to say that such tax credits or differential utility rates are wrong or immoral—there are enough people arguing these points elsewhere—but to point out that they do have the result of discouraging energy conservation investments. The issue here is equitable access to capital to support appropriately scaled energy production and conservation initiatives.

The phrase that might best summarize the point is that appropriate technology requires a corresponding *appropriate sociology*, if this is what we can call the process of implementing innovative solutions to new energy and environmental quality standards in building design, construction, and use. Just as the environment is the physical model of culture, changes in the way we design the built environment require a corresponding social impetus.

The purpose of reviewing these ideas in this section is not to propose an exhaustive innovation agenda, but to show the scope of concepts that should be considered in a comprehensive initiative for energy conservation at the building scale (*Figure 12*).

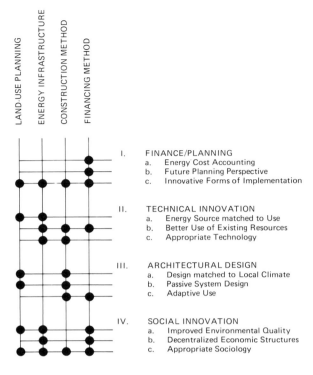

Fig. 12 Energy conservation through building design: summary of innovation concepts.

While the number of factors involved may appear to be discouraging, it need not be so. The point of any innovation program is that a number of small efforts be made simultaneously. Like a group of people lifting a heavy table with their fingers, if mutual effort is expended at the right instant, the task is easy. In this respect, our most limited resource is not energy, but time.

Summary: The Conservation Initiative

We know how to design energy-efficient buildings, as evidenced by the preceding chapters. It is at this moment a matter of implementation.

We can conceive of this as requiring three steps. The first is relatively easy, that of utilizing *technical-fix* measures to reduce energy waste, with little cost or change in currently available building methods. The second is to address the fundamental patterns of energy use in the built environment by *improved design* of building and transport systems and other consumer products. As we have seen in this chapter, improved design alternatives depend upon what changes can be made in institutional barriers in the building industry that act as disincentives to agreed-upon conservation goals. The third step—the most difficult, but an inevitable one if we are to meet our responsibility to ourselves, to the large segment of the world that is without even subsistence-level energy and resources, and to future generations—is a refocusing of our cultural values and social actions on a *conservation ethic.*

ENERGY
CONSERVATION
AT THE
BUILDING SCALE:
AN
INNOVATION
PROGRAM

299

Viewing energy conservation efforts in terms of these steps—the technical, the institutional, and the ethical—helps to integrate technical invention with aesthetically coherent and ethically appropriate designs, as well as to relate cultural and social goals to our capacity for design innovation. Despite the apparent difficulties that await the necessary innovation program, there is a real basis for optimism and motivation in the renewed emphasis on quality. It provides the basis by which to make a distinction between those technologies that are disruptive to the environment and those that can be considered as *integrative technologies:* ones that help place us in balance with the ecological imperatives that ultimately bound our action; ones that help connect us to our natural world and through nature, to ourselves.

The *quality of energy,* rather than quantity, is the measure of efficiency with which a given end-use requirement is produced. A solar collector that supplies heat at 130F for domestic hot water is more efficient for this purpose than the remote power plant. The building constructed according to "bioclimatic" design principles is more efficient than the building that requires purchased energy to overcome the designer's disregard of natural energy flows. The heat pump that utilizes available heat sinks is more efficient than electric resistance heating of buildings.

Matching energy sources and conversion technology as closely as possible to the quality of energy of end-use requirements gives the analytic basis for an energy and building-systems technology that minimizes entropy and maximizes waste-energy reclamation at each point at which that energy is converted from a higher to a lower level.

The *quality of design* in terms of energy and resource conservation is measured, not by conspicuous consumption that is still so much a part of the packaging of consumer products, automobiles, and buildings, but quite the opposite; by the elegance with which the end result achieves artistic integrity by economy of means.

This is not to argue for a simplistic spartan aesthetic, or even one of strict functionalism by which, for example, Shaker furniture attains its beauty and thus speaks for itself. The act of creativity has always been subject to great discipline from inspiration to execution. Energy conservation provides new terms of analysis; there is perhaps the more important impetus, to embody into design emerging cultural aspirations toward the conservation ethic. Instead of using energy and natural resources to serve technology, the quality of design will be measured by the way in which technology is utilized to place us more in balance with our larger ecological context.

The *quality of the environment* and energy conservation are not incompatible, despite arguments to this effect by private interests who would like to see environmental control standards lowered. Each time conventional energy is consumed, there is an impact on the environment in terms of waste and pollution. Energy conservation offers a sane alternative by which to reduce such impact.

To improve the *quality of life* does not require increased energy consumption. Social and economic growth and stability are not threatened by energy conservation. The living standard in other advanced industrial societies, such as the Scandinavian countries, where per-capita energy consumption is as little as one-half that in the United States, attests to the fact that there is not necessarily a correlation between high energy use and a high living standard. In fact, energy conservation saves capital for other necessary social investments and creates jobs as well.

The quality of life, of the environment, of design, and of energy use are thus crucially interdependent. Just as the study of energy requires a crossing of disciplines and of boundaries, it also serves to connect. The solution to problems of energy and resources requires unprecedented cooperation between all segments of society, between private and public sectors, from local to national and international levels.

We can improve our buildings, our cities, and our land by eliminating wasteful use of resources and by adopting qualitative, rather than quantitative, goals in meeting technical and social needs. The proposal that emerges from the discussion in this and previous chapters is thus for a concerted *conservation initiative* towards this end.

Francisco Arumi is associate professor and research director of the School of Architecture, University of Texas at Austin, and director of the school's Numerical Simulation Laboratory. His previous positions include physics research associate, Center for Controlled Thermonuclear Research, University of Texas, and physics research specialist of the Council of Central American Universities. He is a member of Sigma Pi Sigma, Physics Honor Society, and Pi Mu Epsilon, Mathematics Honor Society. He has been awarded several Fulbright-Hays visiting lectureships by the Council for International Exchange of Scholars and is author of over 20 published books and articles, some of which are listed in the references of Chapter 8. Professor Arumi is a member of the editorial board of the journal, *Buildings and Energy,* a board member of the Consortium of Architectural Research Centers and a member of the American Institute of Physics, the International Solar Energy Society, and the American Association for the Advancement of Science.

J. Douglas Balcomb is assistant energy division leader for Solar Programs, Los Alamos Scientific Laboratory. He has authored and coauthored over 30 technical reports on solar heating, some referenced in Chapter 5. He has designed a number of solar buildings and lives in a passive solar house in Sante Fe. Dr. Balcomb is a technical advisor to the Department of Energy Solar Working Group and a consultant to the Solar Energy Research Institute. He is a member of the Board of Directors of the International Solar Energy Society (ISES) and the ISES American Section and chairman of its Passive Systems Division.

Robert Bruegmann is an assistant professor at the University of Illinois, Chicago Circle, Department of Architecture and Art History. He has previously completed work for the Historic American Engineering Record and Historic American Buildings Survey of the National Park Service. Dr. Bruegmann is author of *The Architecture of Benicia, California* (1978).

Jeffrey Cook, who contributed to the historical perspective in Chapter 1, is professor of architecture at the College of Architecture, Arizona State University. He is the author of *Architecture Anthology* (1966 to 1971), *The Architecture of Bruce Goff* (1978), and over 80 articles. He is recipient of the Silver Medal of the Royal Architectural Institute of Canada. The architect of numerous passively heated solar buildings, he serves as a director of the Solar Energy Associations of New Mexico and Arizona and is a member of the Committee on Design of the American Institute of Architects.

Fred S. Dubin is a professional engineer and president of Dubin-Bloome Associates, P.C., New York City. He has served as consultant on energy conservation and management to the U.S. General Services Administration, the Department of Energy, the National Science Foundation, the Department of Housing and Urban Development, the Ford Foundation, the American Institute of Architects, as well as many state agencies. He has lectured at universities throughout the United States and Europe and was named "Engineer Who has Made his Mark" in *Engineering News Record,* 1975. He is an advisor to the National Academy of Engineering, the Building Research Advisory Board, the Federal Energy Administration, the National Society of Professional Engineers, the Scientists Committee for Public Information, and a fellow of the Society of Heating, Refrigerating and Air-Conditioning Engineers and of the American Consulting Engineers Council. Most recently, Mr. Dubin was awarded a master's degree from Pratt Institute School of Architecture.

Eugene Eccli, a physicist by training, is president of Design Alternatives, Inc., Washington, DC, a multi-disciplinary consulting group in appropriate technology and energy conservation. He has served as consultant to the Montana State Department of Community Affairs, the U.S. Agency for International Development, the U.S. Community Services Administration, the U.S. Information Agency, and Total Action Against Poverty, Virginia. In addition to the studies reported in Chapter 14, he is editor and coauthor of *Low-Cost Energy-Efficient Shelter,* technical editor and co-author of *Producing Your Own Power,* and was a founding member of the magazine, *Alternate Sources of Energy.* He has taught and lectured widely on appropriate energy technology and has collaborated on the design of several solar buildings. He is an advisor to the Council of Environmental Alternatives (Consumer Action Now) and to the National Council of Churches. Mr. Eccli is a member of the International Solar Energy Society, a board member of Alternate Sources of Energy, Minnesota, and of the Energy Task Force, New York City.

Baruch Givoni is professor of environmental engineering, Building Research Station, Technion-Israel Institute of Technology, Haifa, Israel, and director of the Desert Research Station, Ben Gurion University, Beersheva, Israel. He also is visiting professor at the School of Architecture and Urban Planning, University of California at Los Angeles. He is author of *Man, Climate and Architecture* (1969 and 1976).

James C. Hedstrom is a member of the staff of the Solar Energy Group, Los Alamos Scientific Laboratory (LASL), and is author of many technical publications on solar heating. He is also responsible for the computer analysis of active solar heating systems at LASL and the validation of the mathematical techniques.

Ralph Knowles is university professor at the University of Southern California, Los Angeles, and author of *Energy and Form: An Ecological Approach to Urban Growth* (1974), as well as numerous research publications. In 1974 he was recipient of the American Institute of Architects' Gold Medal for Research in Architecture. He serves as advisor to the American Institute of Architects Research Corporation and the Association of Collegiate Schools of Architecture.

Harold E. Marshall is chief, Building Economics Section, Center for Building Technology, Institute for Applied Technology, of the National Bureau of Standards. He is recipient of awards from the National Bureau of Standards and a member of Alpha Theta Nu and Omicron Delta Epsilon honor societies. He is author of over a dozen research reports and publications on building economics. Dr. Marshall serves on the advisory board of the American Economic Association.

Robert D. McFarland is a staff member of the Solar Energy Group, Los Alamos Scientific Laboratory (LASL), and a mechanical engineer with a special interest in fluid mechanics and heat transfer. He is responsible for computer modeling and simulation analysis of passive solar buildings at LASL and is author of the PASOLE computer code.

Murray Milne is currently professor of architecture and urban design at the School of Architecture and Urban Planning, University of California at Los Angeles. Before teaching architecture, he was a senior research engineer for North American Aviation, Apollo Division. He is author of *Computer Graphics in Architecture and Design* (1969) and *Residential Water Conservation* (1976), as well as numerous published research papers on computer-aided design and environmental controls for buildings. He has served as advisor to the Design Methods Group and the journal, *Environment and Behavior*. Professor Milne's design for a condominium in Malibu, where he presently lives, received an honors award in the 1977 AIA/Sunset Magazine Western Homes Competition.

Donald Prowler is an architect and member of the faculty, University of Pennsylvania School of Architecture. He is author of *Fuelsavers: A Kit of Solar Ideas for Existing Homes* and has written a number of published research papers on passive solar design. He currently serves as chairman of the Mid-Atlantic Solar Energy Association, as co-director of the Second National Passive Solar Conference, and as a board member of the Energy Task Force of New York City. He is designer of several solar buildings including the passive solar research test-project for the University of Pennsylvania.

Rosalie Ruegg is an economist in the Building Economics Section of the National Bureau of Standards. She is recipient of the Department of Commerce Silver Medal Award and the Special Achievement Award, and is a member of Phi Beta Kappa Honor Society. She has authored more than 20 reports and journal articles on life-cycle cost analysis, solar heating and cooling, fenestration, industrial-waste heat management, and new building technologies. Dr. Ruegg has served on the National Research Council's Committee on Nuclear and Alternative Energy Systems and is a member of the American Economic Association.

Diane Serber is an architect in private practice in New York City and was formerly project manager for New York State ERDA and associate of Richard G. Stein and Partners. She is a 1962 graduate with major honors of the University of Pennsylvania School of Architecture, and a member of Tau Sigma Delta Architecture Honor Society. Ms. Serber is author of numerous research publications and a member of the New York State Energy Office Code Review Committee and has served as chairperson of the New York AIA Energy and Environment Committee, the Manhattan Community Board, and the New York State Environmental Planning Lobby.

Lawrence G. Spielvogel is a professional engineer and president of his own consulting firm in Wyncote, Pennsylvania, which specializes in energy management in buildings. He is a member of the visiting faculty of the University of Pennsylvania Department of Architecture and the Yale School of Architecture. He is recipient of the Distinguished Service Award (1975) and the Award of Merit (1976) of the American Society of Heating, Refrigerating and Air-Conditioning Engineers. He has been a consultant on numerous major energy conservation projects both for the U.S. government and for private companies. Mr. Spielvogel is currently serving on the ASHRAE Research and Technical Committee, the Standard 90 Executive Committee and is chairman of the HVAC System Panel.

John Philip Steadman is lecturer in design, the Open University, United Kingdom. He previously taught at the Cambridge University Department of Architecture and was assistant director at the Martin Centre for Architectural and Urban Studies. Professor Steadman's publications include *The Geometry of Environment*, coauthored with Lionel March (1971); *Energy, Environment and Building* (1975); and *The Evolution of Designs: Biological Analogy in Architecture and the Applied Arts* (1978); and is currently serving as director of Applied Research for Cambridge, Ltd.

Richard G. Stein is an architect, principal of Richard G. Stein and Partners, New York City, and adjunct professor at the Cooper Union School of Architecture. He is a fellow of the American Institute of Architects, past-president of the New York Chapter, AIA, and chairman of the New York State Board of Architecture. He is recipient of numerous design awards and twice recipient of the Brunner Scholarship awarded for advanced research in architecture. He is author of *Architecture and Energy* (1977) and over two dozen journal articles. Mr. Stein serves as advisor to the National Bureau of Standards Task Force on Illumination, the Building Research Advisory Board, and the American Institute of Architects Research Corporation.

Sim Van der Ryn has been a teacher, writer, and practicing architect. He has taught at the University of California, Berkeley, since 1961 and is presently professor of architecture on leave. He is the founder and President of Farallones Institute, a community of scientists, artisans, and designers who are developing energy-conserving alternatives for individuals and communities. In October 1975, Governor Jerry Brown appointed Mr. Van der Ryn as California State Architect. He is responsible for a $200 million

ENERGY
CONSERVATION
AT THE
BUILDING SCALE:
AN
INNOVATION
PROGRAM

305

construction program that is demonstrating the potential of solar and other renewable technologies in projects throughout the state. He also established the nation's first State Office of Appropriate Technology. Mr. Van der Ryn lives in Sacramento and Inverness, California, in a house of his own making. His most recent book, *The Toilet Papers,* is about designs to recycle human wastes and water.

Donald Watson is an architect and visiting professor at Yale School of Architecture, where he serves as chairman of the Master of Environmental Design Program. As principal of his own architectural firm, he has completed over 20 solar projects and is recipient of several design awards, including a 1974 Honor Award from the Connecticut Society of Architects for the Westbrook House, the first solar house in Connecticut. He has served as consultant to the United Nations, the U.S. Department of Energy, and the American Institute of Architects. He was awarded the ACSA-AMAX Research Fellowship in Architecture (1967–1969) and a Rockefeller Foundation Fellowship in Environmental Affairs (1978). Mr. Watson's publications include *Innovation in Solar Design* (1976), *Designing and Building a Solar House* (1977), and numerous research publications, and he was editor of the February 1977 *Journal of Architectural Education* special issue on energy and architecture. He is an advisory board member of the Council of Environmental Alternatives (Consumer Action Now), the Energy Task Force of New York City, the AIA Energy Notebook, and is an AIA liaison member for the ASHRAE Committee of Energy Conservation in Existing Buildings.

John I. Yellott is distinguished visiting professor in architecture, College of Architecture, Arizona State University, and director of the Yellott Solar Energy Laboratory, Phoenix, Arizona. He previously served as professor and department head, Department of Mechanical Engineering, Illinois Institute of Technology. He is a fellow of the American Society of Heating, Refrigerating and Air-Conditioning Engineers, the American Association for the Advancement of Science, and the Royal Society of Arts, London. He is recipient of outstanding service awards from the Chicago and the Illinois Junior Chambers of Commerce, and the American Society of Mechanical Engineers' Gold Medal for Education. His publications include chapters on solar energy utilization in McGraw-Hill's *Encyclopedia of Science* and *Marks' Mechanical Engineers Handbook,* also in the *Encyclopaedia Britannica* and the 1974 ASHRAE *Handbook of Applications,* as well as numerous research articles. He is currently chairman of the ASHRAE Committee on Solar Collector Test Standards and past-chairman of the ASHRAE Committee on Fenestration and Solar Energy Applications. Professor Yellott has served as advisor to the Department of Energy Passive Systems Committee and the Arizona State Solar Energy Research Commission, and as past-director and vice-president of the International Solar Energy Society.

INDEX